THE AMERICAN
POLITICAL NATION
1838-1893

STANFORD STUDIES IN THE NEW POLITICAL HISTORY

Allan Bogue, David W. Brady, Nelson W. Polsby, and
Joel H. Silbey, Editors

The American Political Nation, 1838-1893

JOEL H. SILBEY

STANFORD UNIVERSITY PRESS
Stanford, California

*This is the first book to be published
with support from the fund established
by friends, family, authors, and
colleagues in memory of Leon E. Seltzer,
Director of Stanford University
Press from 1955 to 1983*

*Published with the assistance of the
National Endowment for the Humanities.*

Stanford University Press
Stanford, California
© 1991 by the Board of Trustees of the
Leland Stanford Junior University
Printed in the United States of America

CIP data appear at the end of the book

Original printing 1991
Last figure below indicates date of this printing:
03 02 01 00 99 98 97 96 95 94

Stanford University Press publications are
distributed exclusively by Stanford University Press
within the United States, Canada, and Mexico;
they are distributed exclusively by Cambridge
University Press throughout the rest of the world.

To
Rosemary,
Victoria,
and
David

Preface

THIS IS A BOOK about the world of politics in the party period of American history. In it, I am revisiting some well-trodden historiographic ground. Nineteenth-century American politics has lacked neither excellent description nor penetrating scholarly analysis. Even as political history has lost its dominant place in the study of America's past, political historians have continued to turn out important studies of individual episodes, biographies of a range of political actors, and in-depth analyses of the various eras that followed each other in the century after 1800. These studies have greatly expanded our knowledge. Some of them effectively challenged the conventional scholarly wisdom about specific details, causes, activities, relationships, and effects. Many of them also, I believe, suggest the need for some fundamental rethinking about the way that historians organize and articulate their understanding of the development of American political life since the colonial period.

But despite the good work available on the many parts that, together, make up our political world, both between 1800 and 1900, and more generally as well, that fundamental rethinking has been, at best, episodic. An integrated, descriptive analysis that incorporates recent insights and approaches to the study of past politics and that offers, as well, a needed, somewhat revised organizing scheme from that usually accepted, has not yet appeared—at least in a form that I find satisfactory. This book is my attempt to fill that gap: to elaborate and synthesize a generation's research, including my own, and to present a description and an interpretation of a particular, half-century-long moment in American political life, a moment unlike any other before it or any that has existed since it passed from the scene in the 1890s.

The idea for this study grew out of collaborative work that Lee Benson and I engaged in over the course of some years, generously supported at the outset by the National Science Foundation. We presented the results of our joint efforts in a number of papers and published articles in the late 1970's. I am in Professor Benson's debt for a stimulating association that was an extraordinary experience and an important intellectual benchmark for me. Circumstances dictated that the collaboration be put aside for other things. Nevertheless, whatever is here has been richly informed by our original interaction.

Allan G. Bogue has, once again, contributed beyond any calls of duty or friendship to the development of my ideas about nineteenth-century American politics and about the framing and quality of my argument. I owe a great deal to him. He, Nelson Polsby, and David Brady were splendid intellectual companions while I composed the first draft of the book, and they have remained vigorously supportive and helpful since. Samuel T. McSeveney demonstrated, once again, the unusual quality of his friendship by reading and commenting on what I have written and by being immediately responsive to my questions as well as charitable and helpful about my notions and arguments. Phyllis Field and Richard L. McCormick, at the outset, and Lance Davis, Robert Bates, Stanley Engerman, Marc Kruman, and M. Philip Lucas, as the manuscript progressed, were always ready and willing to wrestle with my ideas. At Cornell, two challenging colleagues, Walter LeFeber and Theodore J. Lowi, have done much over the years to make me think through what I believe about American political history. Almost daily conversations with Glenn Altschuler have been both provoking and very important to me. His sharp and incisive reading improved the manuscript in innumerable ways. Others at Cornell who influenced my thinking include Stuart Blumin, Michael Kammen, R. Laurence Moore, and Mary Beth Norton. I thank each of them.

As always, I cannot say enough positive things about the resources and staff of the Cornell University Library. To single out Alain Seznec, Marie Gast, and Carolyn Spicer for special mention in no way lessens my gratitude to the rest of a fine group of people. The Library of Congress, more anonymously, was also an important source of fugitive and rare nineteenth-century political materials. A great deal of my work with political pamphlets was done there as well as in the magnificent collection of the New York Public Library's American History Room, now lamentably closed as a separate entity. I am grateful to two members of the staff of the latter institution, Jerome Stoker and Leon Weidman, who guided me through its material.

Part of this book was drafted in the congenial atmosphere of the Center for Advanced Study in the Behavioral Sciences in Palo Alto, California. The excellent support of its staff, led by the then director,

Gardner Lindzey, and the associate director, Robert Scott, the stimulation of many colleagues, and the delightful facilities and surroundings are all cherished as having contributed to a most productive time. Similarly, the uncommon place that is the Russel Sage Foundation provided an indispensable setting in which to finish the final draft. Eric Wanner, its president, Peter DeJanosi, its vice president, Vivian Kaufman, my assistant, and the rest of the staff could not have been more splendid in extending their generosity during my year with them.

Cornell University, through the Provost's Office, the College of Arts and Sciences, and the Return Jonathan Meigs Research Fund, provided much of the financial support that allowed me to carry on the project. A National Endowment for the Humanities grant to the Center for Advanced Study in the Behavioral Sciences supported my year there.

I have had the opportunity to present preliminary versions of these ideas before a number of audiences over the past decade, including the Rutgers University History Department, the Indiana Association of Historians, the Abraham Lincoln Association, the Institute of Government Studies at the University of California at Berkeley, and the American History Seminar at Moscow State University. I am grateful to those who invited me and were my hosts on those pleasant occasions, among them, Richard L. McCormick, Morton M. Rosenberg, Nelson Polsby, and Yuri Rygulov.

I very much appreciate the friendship of Linda Polsby, Carolyn Brady, James Fuller, and David Maisel, whose kindness during my stays in California and New York City contributed a great deal to bringing this book to completion. At Cornell, the History Department's support staff, led by Connie Kindig, was always ready to meet my many needs with their usual competence and grace. In the last stages, Muriel Bell and her colleagues at Stanford University Press have been editors without parallel. Finally, *The American Political Nation* would have been impossible without the remarkable work of a generation of new political historians and their colleagues in other disciplines who shared a historical bent. While the use and interpretation of their findings is mine, my indebtedness to these scholars is to be found on every page that follows. Rather than listing them all, I will let the endnotes indicate my deep obligation to them individually and collectively.

The dedication inadequately celebrates a relationship that has always made everything so rich.

J. H. S.

Contents

Illustrations follow page 140

THE AMERICAN
POLITICAL NATION
1838-1893

Political Parties are the natural product of free government. Wherever there is freedom of speech and freedom
of the press, discussions and conflicts will arise; and where
the people rule or elect their rulers, there will be clashing
of opinions in regard to public affairs.

—Nathaniel Sargent, *Public Men and Events*, 1875

The genuine lover of democratic principles . . . regards the
general interest as of paramount importance, and adheres
to his party, not in the sordid expectation of personal
emolument, but as a means of subserving the public good,
[and he] will be ready to sacrifice his individual preferences
whenever such a course is demanded by the higher considerations of the general welfare, and the duty he owes
through his party to the state and country.

—*Albany Atlas*, Oct. 23, 1846

Introduction:
"The Lost Atlantis"

THE CHRONOLOGICAL BOUNDARIES of this study are unconventional but not arbitrary. I argue that a distinct era in the country's political history ended almost one hundred years ago. It had lasted for more than half a century. It was a political world—or better, political nation—markedly set off from what had come before and what would follow. As the United States moved into an era of great internal growth after 1815, and as the American people moved from their republican fears for the survival of a fragile nation to the exuberant optimism of middle-class egalitarian nationalism, their political dynamic substantially shifted.[1] A politics largely rooted in elite-dominated factions gave way, by the late 1830's, to a populist-oriented, institutionally organized political nation dominated by a system of two-party politics "unique in its power and in its depth of social penetration."[2]

The surface components and institutional structure of American politics have remained remarkably stable over two hundred years. Parties nominate, and the people elect Presidents, congressmen, and other officials to staff the same institutions of government. But in specific ways, the forces at play in political life have varied so markedly as to form distinctive political nations—as in the years covered here. Each nation has had a singular political landscape, containing many familiar elements from the previous one, but in a unique mixture. Each has dominated a block of years and thus defined a specific chronological era. In each of them, the cast of mind and specific behavior are distinct; the political resources present—that is, all of the elements constituting the American political nation—come together differently and relate to one another in their own special way.[3]

As an example of what I am suggesting, a two-party system has been part of American politics for most of the country's history under the Constitution. Yet only from 1838 to 1893 did political parties all but totally dominate the political nation. Before 1838, the political nation rested on personal, family, and clan ties and deferential, informal organizational structures. After 1838, the distinguishing elements of that particular nation gave way to something else: regularized, impersonal institutions of political activity, the political parties. Given the changes that occurred on the American scene generally, leaders and led had to learn new ways of acting together, defining their relationships with each other, establishing the boundaries of each other's role, accepting how the system would function, and agreeing on what was acceptable and what was not. In particular, politicians realized that political will and desire were not enough. Effective organization was also necessary. Politics was not inert; it needed to be run, but in new ways.

As a result, the American political leadership built a system that organized unceasing political conflict within the new social and economic milieu of the nineteenth century. Despite the frequently expressed paeans to American individualism, organized, collective, partisanly defined and shaped behavior became the norm in the political realm. The new political nation, rooted in the dominant impulses of the party system, broke sharply with America's political past, although, of course, it rested on that past, drawing sustenance from and being channeled by many aspects of what had gone before.[4]

Much of the story of American politics in these fifty-plus years has been very well told. Some of its structural components have been fruitfully examined as well.[5] The historian of nineteenth-century American politics lacks neither a wide range of useful information nor solid attempts at interpretation. But a great deal remains to be said. Many elements of the political world, to understate the case, have not been charted in any great depth or with sufficient texture. Further, the essential unity of this period is not clearly marked. Allan Bogue's conclusion that "an integrated, systematic view of the political life of the nation in historical perspective has not yet emerged" remains largely true. The political nation itself remains ill-defined and, in some respects, the subject of great disagreement. Much of what I intend to do, therefore, is taxonomic: to sort out, clarify, and organize the elements present, to detect connections, to record what is distinct, to underscore the commonalities, and to examine as systematically as possible the workings of all aspects of the political nation. At the same time, a statement about how those elements came together to define and form a distinct political nation is needed and will be developed here.[6]

Political historians have used a variety of approaches in recent years to understand their subject. Although some of those approaches have been controversial, each has contributed something to our understanding. To place this book in context, I have drawn on all of these different research traditions, quantitative, behavioral, ideological, and organizational. The new political history, with its quantitative and controlled theoretical emphases and its focus on the grass roots, provides a bedrock on which to build a study aimed at illuminating the full range of the political process.[7] But my reliance on traditional political narratives, with their use of nonquantitative evidence and emphasis on ideology and leadership, is also substantial. Newspapers, manuscripts, biographies, and traditional studies of political events supply the details needed to texture the whole. The accumulated wisdom of all these materials allows for a more expansive, synthetic analysis than is usually attempted.

Finally, my study is grounded in a commitment to understand politics as a distinct phenomenon of American life. History certainly is no longer only past politics, and the study of American political history has not thrived recently in the way that it once did. But the case for extensive and ongoing political description and analysis, as one part of what history is, remains plain to me. I agree wholeheartedly with Samuel P. Hays that political historians have to make clear in their work how much the politics they write about is part of larger societal matters. At the same time, while never independent of the socioeconomic structure, political forms, customs, and behavior together form a unique way of shaping and reflecting larger societal forces. They inhabit a terrain of their own. Like J. R. Pole, I believe that "the character of politics makes the difference between success and failure in other fields." The study of politics, in J. Morgan Kousser's words, helps us to understand "how institutions and elites refract society's desires."[8] There is, therefore, reason to describe and characterize the American political nation as it existed in each particular era.

The study is broadly divided into three parts.The first details the background—the nature of the ideas and operating principles and their sources, and the institutions and ways of engaging in politics that emerged out of that in the years up to 1838. The second focuses on the response to the new forces, the development of new political forms, and the actions taken: the organization and the tools of political life, and the popular and legislative voting, the state and national behavior, and the public policy making that characterized this political nation. The third part describes the roots of, and reasons for, the major transition that began in the late nineteenth century and culminated in the massively different American political nations of the twentieth century. Together, the three parts recapture, as fully as possible, what Walter Dean Burnham has called "the lost Atlantis of nineteenth-century politics."[9]

CHAPTER ONE

The Contours of the American Political Nation: The Road to 1838

THE FIFTY-FIVE YEARS from 1838 to 1893 remain fascinating to American historians for their great personalities and vibrant confrontations, as well as for their ordinariness, confusion, and frequent failure to address deep-rooted national problems. Originating in the drama of the Jacksonian era, continuing through the intensity of the rise of sectional conflict, the Civil War, Reconstruction, the Gilded Age, and all that subsequently occurred into the 1890's, it was a crucial time when much happened to several generations of Americans. Traditional periodizing schemes argue for the Jacksonian period and the Civil War years as major nineteenth-century watersheds, with different periods on either side of the 1820's and 1860's. American political life was first democratized, then sectionalized; finally, the nation itself was economically transformed. The Civil War left deep political scars and bitter memories for a century and more thereafter; industrialization and urbanization reshaped the way Americans lived and directly affected the political world explosively and persistently.[1]

While these periods, from the Age of Jackson onward, remain central to historians' understanding of nineteenth-century American politics, other, more recently developed periodizing schemes have come to dominate the study of America's political past. Over the past two decades, a number of scholars have moved away from the focus on great events to trace the underlying patterns structuring political life. These historians have convincingly argued that the many discrete events of the past have had a particular order that can be discerned and measured. Specifically, the critical election—party system interpretation of American political history has become a powerful and widely applied scholarly convention. There have been five party systems since 1788, each characterized by a different pattern of electoral choice, William N. Chambers, Walter Dean Burnham, and their co-authors argued in their seminal 1967 book. The first system stretched between 1788 and 1828, the second lasted into the 1850's, the third existed from then until 1896, and the fourth and fifth divide the twentieth century around the presidential election of 1932. In each party system, voters aligned themselves with one of the major parties, not haphazardly and occasionally, but repeatedly and predictably, regardless of short-term excitements, great personalities and events, or powerful inducements to shift their allegiances. These patterns were never entirely stagnant, however. Each period of electoral continuity was usually bounded by a critical realignment involving a major shift of voter commitments, producing a new set of electoral relationships and, therefore, a new party system.[2]

But though many political scientists and historians accept these organizing schemes, neither does justice to the range and shape of American politics over two hundred years. In particular, given its widespread recent application and interpretive power, the party-system model needs to be supplemented. While critical-election theory effectively captures patterns of popular voting behavior for much of our history and marks some significant changes in national direction, it does not adequately deal with the many other elements in the political order or too readily subsumes them under the electoral-pattern framework. Moreover, popular voting behavior has shifted so markedly since the 1960's that it no longer appears to conform to the reigning party-system model. Certainly, much evidence suggests that no realignment has occurred since the 1930's, that the electoral universe dealigned instead, making it impossible to have another realignment and a new party system. As a consequence of such omissions and anomalies, there has been growing criticism of the paradigm and a search for more encompassing organizing principles.[3]

American Political Eras

A perspective that steps back from the party-system approach and considers the role played by the many other constituents of the political nation besides electoral behavior—the nature of political leadership, the importance of particular political institutions, the strength of government, popular attitudes toward politics, and the like—a perspective that looks at the political era, in sum, seems an appropriate way to organize and synthesize the American experience. In that perspective, the rhythms of American politics form a pattern unlike the one postulated by the party system model. While five party systems have apparently existed in American history since 1789, they are not

TABLE 1.1

American Political Eras

Era	Political characteristics	Type of alignment
1 (1789–1838)	Antiparty, elite-factional	Prealignment
2 (1838–1893)	Partisan-factional	Alignment/Realignment
3 (1893–ca. 1948)	Postpartisan, bureaucratic	Realignment/Dealignment
4 (1948–present)	Nonpartisan-personalist	Postalignment

readily comparable because the presence, role, and weight of the political and other factors present varied a great deal and came together in a different chronological pattern from that suggested by critical realignment theory. There have been, more cogently, four political eras: the first, an antiparty, elite-factional era, existed between 1789 and 1838; the second, a partisan-factional era, lasted from 1838 to 1893; the third, on the scene from 1893, was a postpartisan-bureaucratic period; and the fourth, a nonpartisan-personalist era, probably began around 1948 (Table 1.1).

Such an arrangement takes account of the fact that a different kind of society and different kinds of political institutions, norms, and behavior can be singled out in various periods—that in each of these eras, much agreement emerged about what was at stake, what counted as proper behavior, and what political resources and institutions were important and how they were to be used—which is to say, about what was needed to manage political life, about how to define the political agenda and advance the purposes of politics. A basic cental thrust, a direction in the course of events, was present and discernible each time.

The attitudes, assumptions, and values of the people involved in the public political order directly and indirectly, the leaders and the led, the politically active and others, all shaped the institutions in which the basic social forces present in national life were organized and managed as they became politicized into a distinct form culminating in a distinctive kind of government behavior and policies. Electoral and legislative behavior, the role and actions of elites, the interaction between them and the mass of voters, the choice of workings of political institutions, were all part of a particular web of relationships and interactions. A political-eras perspective of this sort is not incompatible with the critical-realignment perspective. It is only that, in this perspective, the way voters align is just one of the elements, albeit a crucial one, in the pattern, not the sole thing defining it.[4]

Political life originates in the interaction among individuals and groups within local communities and the development of a general viewpoint growing out of each's particular experiences. That viewpoint includes not only an understanding of the role politics plays in dealing with matters of importance, but also specific ideas about ways to meet individual and group needs and goals. A set of commitments follows—to an individual, a cause, or an organization. Finally, there are specific political norms, rituals, and routines within which all politically involved Americans are constrained to operate. Together, these viewpoints, commitments, and norms, along with their institutional embodiment, merge into the distinctive configuration that is the political nation in a given era.

There is a developmental pattern to all of this, a multistage process of growth. Each stage is characterized by particular actions, usually by different members of the political nation. Individual and community perceptions of political needs occur everywhere in the population; in the subsequent moments of focus, definition, and institutionalization, when the system is structured, the initiative is taken by the political leadership. In the stages of acceptance and penetration, when the new ways filter throughout the political nation, both leaders and voters are directly involved. In the last stage, everyone in the system is caught up in the impulses shaping the political nation, impulses that take on a force of their own stretching well beyond the life of the matters that initiated the particular political sequence.[5]

The first watershed in my schema is the election of 1838, or, more precisely, its aftermath. In addition to a new pattern of popular voting allegiances, a cluster of elements, at least in their relative proportions and importance, and their interaction, ultimately came together at that point, I argue, in ways distinctly different from other times. On the other hand, though the subsequent voter realignment of the 1850's significantly altered the social basis of the core electoral confrontation in the United States, it did not fundamentally redefine the structure of the existing political nation, that is, the ways that Americans engaged in politics. The second and third party systems had a unity to them, and together they differed greatly from what had come before and what emerged later.

To put it broadly, what happened in the era between 1838 and 1893 was the replacement of a political nation based on personal, family, and clan ties, and deferential informal structures, with one based on collective behavior and regularized, impersonal institutions. To be sure, the new system drew substance from many aspects of what had gone before. But it was no less a sharp break with America's past ways of political activity for all that. Most critically, the political world now became deeply partisan. The primacy of political parties was the dominant fact of this political era (and of no other). Parties defined the terms of political confrontation and shaped the behavior of most participants in the many levels of political activity.[6]

The Civil War experience takes on a quite different meaning in this perspective from our usual understanding of its impact on American politics. It was unarguably a massive and transforming event in national life. But for all of its extraordinary effects on American society—the end of slavery, the recasting of the role of the South, and the opening up of new racial, economic, and urban-rural fault lines— there were few changes in popular voting coalitions beyond some intensification of the partisan commitments established in the 1850's.[7] In fact, despite both the real and apparent discontinuities of American life, the political elements remained pretty much fixed across the Civil War divide.

Although the political agenda shifted in the 1850's, new parties appeared, and voting coalitions were transformed, the institutions and central defining tenets of American politics, its essential structure, did not deteriorate. Party commitment and party unity were disrupted. The political nation was not. As the nation came apart at the outset of the 1860's, much of the existing political structure continued as before, as did the accumulation of ideas, habits, and instincts underlying the political world. In short, the war did not alter the driving impulses of the political nation, no matter how badly it may have battered, even profoundly reshaped, many of its elements. The party system proved strong enough and malleable enough to control all but a small area of the political nation, to resist attacks on it, and to survive electoral change, war, and for a time, new socioeconomic realities. The second American political era continued to operate after 1865 largely as it had for more than twenty-five years past.[8]

But then, in the 1890's, what had been established in the late 1830's unraveled. A voter realignment began in the off-year state elections in 1893 and widened over the next three elections, in 1894, 1895, and 1896. Voting commitments shifted as they had forty years before. In addition, a series of forces were unleashed that ultimately destroyed the central role that parties had so long played. As in the years around 1838, a new predominant political thrust emerged as the balance among the defining elements shifted significantly into a different configuration, inaugurating another era.[9] The contrast with other eras, earlier and later, could not be sharper. Political parties and partisanship did not significantly affect the political nation before 1838. They exist, but have been in decline, and less and less influential in the years since 1893. In the era in between, they defined the political nation.

A Vigorous Political Heritage

The political nation that emerged at the end of the 1830's was the end product of a two-century-long historical process stretching from the elite-dominated politics of prerevolutionary America to the emergence of a continuous world in need of organization and direction in the Jacksonian years. There were clear marking points along the way. First, an informal constitution had always existed in America—a mixture of political ideas, institutions, and practices reaching back to the colonial period and the country's English heritage. Second, persistent tensions, political debate, and elections, rooted in social, economic, and ethnic differences, were important parts of the landscape before the American Revolution and remained on the scene after independence. Third, in the 1790's, national parties emerged, despite resistance to them, to shape the course of elections and policy making in the larger, postconstitutional political world. And finally, in the expansive years after 1815, new forces and new pressures came onto the scene to add to the existing mix and provoke a search for new directions. It took many years to work out what followed in the political realm and for the emergence of, in Richard L. McCormick's words, "distinctive . . . patterns of party policies, electoral behavior and economic policy that set it [the new era] apart from the eras that came before and after." [10]

Colonial America was vibrant politically. Despite a broad ideological commitment to the social harmonies stressed by classical republicanism, divisive issues appeared early. Each provoked bitter political combat. From the beginning, legislatures and elections were the main arenas of confrontation. The social elite in each colony dominated politics through the legislatures, but they could not ignore the frequent electoral contests that brought them there. Colonists in America had to be appealed to, consulted, and manipulated—in short, involved politically. And there was a great deal to fight about in the policy arena, from economic activities and developing relations with the Indians to the treatment of religious dissenters and alien ethnic groups. By the end of the colonial period, there was a long tradition of political warfare and institution building in response to conflict, albeit alongside an intellectual tradition that decried such conflict. [11]

All of this was, primarily, a local phenomenon. Every colony, and then state, had its own political system and unique political history. But alongside inevitable local differences, there were also great similarities in their experiences, including the growth of the power of the legislatures; a political leadership that, though largely made up of members of the upper classes, was divided into factions constantly at odds over government policies and the spoils of office; the expanding involvement of many white adult males in the election process; and continuous confrontations between local power and central authority. Moreover, this colonial political nation, highly pluralistic and fragmented as it was, shared a fear of factions and parties, and any "overuse of political art" to win votes.[12]

This long-standing antipartyism continued to do much to shape American politics after 1788, with two major modifications. First, a national political framework, defined by the Constitution, appeared. Second, despite the strong, lingering suspicion of the arts of political management, there was a growing need for a more extensive commitment to political action on an organized basis. That commitment did not happen all at once. On the contrary, it came only after some years of confusion and uncertainty. But the direction of the whole became clearer as time passed. American politics was never at rest, moving from the period of intense postconstitutional conflict in the 1790's, through the angry and dangerous divisions of the Jeffersonian era and the highly localistic and always contentious Era of Good Feelings, into a period dominated by the rise of a new national focus to political conflict from the mid-1820's on. The nation's political culture reflected the republican synthesis that deprecated persistent political conflict as dangerous. But so much was at stake, and there was so much play in the rules, that many opportunities arose to shape the political process for desired ends. Americans took up the opportunities offered.[13]

Ronald Formisano has, most directly and comprehensively, articulated the notion that the years 1789–1840 were a period of transition betwen two very different political nations—from the colonial revolutionary one of classical republicanism, with its deferential process, limited democracy, and antiparty ethos, to the new world of egalitarian partisanship, with organized, persistent internal political warfare shaped by powerful national parties. In the transition period, elements of both the old and the new coexisted so uneasily in various combinations that "the period from the 1780s to the 1820s," Formisano argues, "possessed almost a split personality: intensely passionate in partisan conviction but inhibited by powerful antipartyism assumptions about the nature of politics and society."[14]

These contradictory tendencies existed because, from the beginning, there was a sense among Americans that politics was purposive, that it was to secure great ends—local, regional, and national—or was to protect the nation from threats, evils, and enemies, foreign and domestic. George Washington's election to the presidency in 1788 was an orderly affair, in fact a celebration of unanimity. That orderliness was aided by the existing set of rules and ideas and attitudes drawn from England, the colonial experience, and recent events. But it was short-lived. America continued to be torn by wide-ranging economic and social, not to mention regional, differences. The rules of politics, elections, and the shaping of public policy under the new federal framework were not yet clearly established. The Constitution left a great deal vague and contained many awkward passages concerning the specifics of institutions, rules, and practices. The states controlled the electoral process, determining eligibility, timing, and reach. As a result, there was wide variation in the process. Political realities—the search for power in a divided society—quickly intruded.[15]

The Hamiltonian initiatives in the 1790's suggested the potential power of the central government. State governments were active as well. In addition, there was a strong sense that the nation was a fragile experiment in republicanism, that it had much to fear from external enemies and from internal tendencies toward fragmentation. There were fears everywhere, about the power of government, about the threat of chaos, anarchy, and weakness, about the future of liberty. As a result, different perspectives, needs, political demands, and programs covered the landscape and led to persistent battles everywhere, from the national arena to the states.[16] Political leaders realized that they had to use politics to impose a balance between individual freedom and social cohesion. From the Constitution onward, therefore, the quirky American federalist system, with its divided sovereignties and responsibilities, found a need for national political institutions that could organize and integrate the disparate political functions and power centers that existed. Americans were never fully happy with this—resisting combinations that they had been taught threatened liberty and remaining eternally vigilant against manipulative political leaders.[17]

The Halfway System

Beneath the surface of these conflicts and the growing awareness of the centrality of politics, a particular structure, was settling in. From the 1780's onward, a set of rules, regulations, assumptions, and institutions evolved that clearly defined and bounded the American political environment. The reach of government remained fairly limited. By the beginning of the nineteenth century, federal authority was well established, but its powers remained circumscribed. In fact, the federal government contracted substantially in the years after the excitement of the Hamiltonian era. After 1815, the central government was increasingly focused on frontier policing; its role in economic affairs had retreated from Hamiltonian regulative initiatives to become distributive—the Land Office grew into one of the main instruments of national focus and operations. There was a vigorous central bank as of 1815, but it was about to disappear. The executive branch remained small. At first, there were only five federal cabinet departments; the sixth did not appear until 1809. Neither the President nor the officers of the administrative agencies had their time fully taken up by their duties for many years after 1789.[18]

Indicatively, the length of congressional sessions was not very long. After a brief flurry of extended activity at the outset, the average length in the first, or long, session of each Congress ran around five months in the years between 1800 and 1828, compared with about seven or eight after 1838. And Congress considered comparatively few bills: 100–200 in each session in the 1790's, and 500–600 in the 1820's, compared with 1,500 between 1838 and 1854, and over 5,000 in the years 1868–92. State governments were larger and somewhat more energetic, but on the whole government institutions did not loom large on the American political scene.[19]

The backbone of this system was the series of regular elections mandated by the federal and state constitutions. In any given year, in every state, an extraordinary, even staggering, number of elections occurred. In the first part of the nineteenth century, local, state, or federal elections were held somewhere in every month of the year except January and July. Rules defining the eligible electorate initially carried over from the colonial period but were modified after the 1780's. Voting rights were a state responsibility, and each state legislated as it saw fit. Thanks to the wide variation at the state level, only about half the adult white males had the vote in the 1790's. But eligibility steadily widened thereafter, and by the 1830's almost all white adult males could vote.[20]

The actual turnout at the polls illuminates the boundaries of the system. Walter Dean Burnham's estimates show that in the early national period there was a steady increase in the percentage of eligible voters who actually went to the polls in presidential contests, though their numbers never reached significant proportions (see Table 1.2). Interestingly enough, the turnout for state elections was always higher than for President, reflecting what many Americans believed to be the greater importance of politics below the national level.[21]

TABLE 1.2

National Turnout to Vote, Presidential Elections, 1789–1812

Year	Estimated turnout	Year	Estimated turnout
1789	11.5%	1800	31.4%
1792	3.9	1804	25.4
1796	20.4	1808	36.9

SOURCE: Walter Dean Burnham, "Elections as Democratic Institutions, in Kay Schlozman, *Elections in America* (Boston: Allen & Unwin, 1987), 27–60.

Another centerpiece of the emerging postconstitutional American political nation was its political leadership. As in the colonial era, the general population continued to accept the social elites as the natural leaders of the community. Accorded, as before, an uncoerced deference from below, they were generally the men elected to office; they ran politics at every level, their role and place secure. Also as before, these elites tended to divide into highly charged factions and to fight bitterly for the control of offices and policy making. And as in the colonial era, they continued to involve the electorate in their battles, now in increasingly wide-ranging ways. As Gordon Wood has put it, after 1789, America's leadership class had to deal with "a politics that would no longer permit the members of an elite to talk only to each other."[22]

But there was something new in all of this. Often, in the 1790's, the persistent political conflicts at every level took on partisan coloring and labeling as two national parties emerged to battle for the nation's future. It was not that the deep sense of republican fragility or the persistent antipartyism weakened, only that now coordinated efforts to select candidates, manage campaigns, attract voters, and bring legislators under the discipline of a central organization, all later staples of American politics, appeared on the scene. Republicans and Federalists articulated different visions, leading to the growth of party spirit and some institutionalization of party warfare. In places like New York, New Jersey, and North Carolina, the full range of partisan paraphernalia appeared: nominating conventions, partisan newspapers, central coordinating committees, county and local organizations, and frequent mass meetings to mobilize voters. In Congress, party preference began to figure in everything, from voting to living accommodations in Washington, attesting to the continued divisiveness of American political life despite the rhetoric of organic unity and antipartyism.[23]

Nevertheless, there were very great differences in this era from what was to come. There was always an intermittent, ad hoc quality, a casual attitude, toward these partisan forms. Ideological resistance to parties continued. Persistent partisan political alignments and behavior never characterized this period. Consistency in political procedures and behavior was lacking, as were organizational structure and, most of all, commitment. Organizational development was both primitive and erratic. There were caucuses, even conventions, and many of the organizational trappings that would characterize the next political nation. But they were haphazard and intermittent. Party labels might or might not be used, or stick. In the pamphlet warfare that dominated campaigns, political agents hesitated to introduce partisan labels, fearing a backlash against such unacceptable usages. Usually, the people as a whole were appealed to by candidates for office, rather than a specific, identified, like-minded section of them labeled either Republicans or Federalists. When someone called himself a Republican in this atmosphere, he was not usually labeling himself as a party man with a clear policy focus, but merely expressing certain vague but important values about the society and government's role in it.[24]

Similarly, in Congress, few efforts were made to formalize party relationships and to institute mechanisms of party discipline. A Republican congressional caucus did appear in the 1790's, but it met intermittently and was always highly informal, hardly a powerful directing institution. Popular voting remained volatile as well. There was little persistent evidence of party loyalty from election to election. People voted for individuals or for local reasons unrelated to party policies and labels, and whatever party voting did occur was transitory. When the Federalists declined as a major force after 1815, what little sense of party commitment and discipline the Republicans had weakened considerably.[25]

In short, parties still did not belong in America. They were dangerous expedients to be tolerated only briefly and unhappily. Even the builders of the first parties—James Madison and Thomas Jefferson, feared the divisiveness of organized, sectarian political conflict. Madison had raised the alarm in *The Federalist Papers* about the dangers of faction. Jefferson echoed his revulsion and fear. "I never submitted," he wrote to Francis Hopkins in 1789, "the whole system of my opinion to the creed of any party of men whatever, in religion, in philosophy, in politics or in anything else, where I was capable of thinking for myself. Such an addiction is the last degradation of a free and moral agent. If I could not go to heaven but with a party, I would not go there at all." With such words, Jefferson expressed the continuing values held by most politically involved Americans. People knew that they did not want something collective, institutionalized, and permanent intervening between their own individual commitments and the government apparatus. And rightly so, according to Elbridge Gerry, for "the manners and morals of the people . . . are sapped and contaminated by the influence of parties."[26]

All of this added up in a particular way. Although party played an important political role between 1790 and 1815 or so, neither a full-fledged partisan *system* nor a deep partisan *commitment* ever did. As several scholars have argued, this was a prepartisan political culture. The reach of party was rarely wide, its importance episodic at best, and a substantial mind-set against parties continued. Lee Benson's critique of the idea that a real party system was on the scene in these years remains potent: "Until the idea exists that parties are legitimate, that there are necessary divisions within a complex society, that there are continuous, enduring group conflicts that can and should be organized in a sustained partisan political fashion, until then it seems to me hopelessly anachronistic to call the partisan associations anything but factions organized around temporary issues."[27]

The American political nation under such ideological conditions contained many elements, including parties, temporarily, but its dominant impulse was nonpartisan, even antipartisan. The essential character of the era was individualistic in political temperament, volatile in voting and result. Numerous personal, local, and regional political factions vied for dominance across a broad landscape.[28] It was an era in which, as William N. Chambers has concluded, "even at their apogee . . . the parties of Hamilton and Jefferson were still limited in the appeal to voters and in the development of organization, and their lives were comparatively short. In the long sweep of American history, they stood as half-way houses on the road to the fully organized parties of the later Jacksonian era."[29]

"Union and Concert" and the Origins of a New Political Nation

The American political scene began to shift dramatically in the 1820's, fueled by major changes in the nation's geographic reach and socioeconomic pattern. The eighteen states of 1815 became twenty-one by 1820 and thirty-one by 1850, as the United States expanded into the transappalachian West. The population grew from about four million in 1790 to 9.6 million in 1820 and 23.2 million in 1850. More to the point, larger and larger numbers of these people moved away from the coast to inhabit the inland regions of the country. Transportation improved to accommodate this growth and the economic development that followed. Finally, the expansion of commer-

cial agriculture in both the West and the South, the early stages of industrial development, and the further extension and penetration of a
market economy were all transforming America and contributing to
sharp social differentiation in both existing and emerging urban centers, as well as a great deal of turmoil and tension among competing
economic and social groups everywhere.[30]

All of this is a familiar enough story, which had a not-unexpected
political impact. The growing pluralism of interests on the energized
and changing American landscape, interests often in conflict with
each other, stimulated a need for more focused political activity across
a much larger geographic span. In the ten years after 1815, a national
two-party system did not exist. Nearly everyone was a Republican. But
at the local level, political excitement increased in intensity, extent,
and location. New issues and conflicts, fueled by the rapidly changing
socioeconomic conditions, appeared on the political scene. Throughout the period, despite hostility to the idea of permanent organized
divisions, a sense of differences within America, a set of alternate political visions, created deep and persistent political tensions.[31]

Specific events fostered conflict: continued battles at the state level
over the reach of government, the devastating panic and depression
after 1819, the admission of new states, sectional differences between
East and West over development, and between North and South over
the expansion of slavery. Most critically, the reawakening of hostile
battles for control of the national government in the early 1820's provoked powerful political confrontations. Many saw in the national
governmental vigor espoused by John Quincy Adams after he took
over the presidency in 1825 the "revival of Federalist heresies." The
call to resist was clear enough once that perception sank in. Factional
combinations among political leaders, for and against Adams's vision,
quickly developed. At the same time, more and more people got the
vote and became involved in these conflicts as states loosened their
eligibility requirements. All of this suggested that political society
needed definition in new ways. Endemic factional conflict and the
growing popularization of political culture reawakened the necessity
to develop and apply effective institutions of political management. A
larger electorate, amid wide-ranging policy battles, had to be organized and politically directed. But there was a sense that existing political institutions were not up to the task. Without restraining individualism or liberty, some way had to be found to tame pluralism,
aggregate interests, and coordinate demands across the broad national landscape.[32]

The result was a new system, a reconfiguration and development of elements already present. The process was a multistage one: first, the eruption of constant political conflict; then, the coming of wider popular participation in politics; finally, most concretely, the evolution of the tools of political management—party organization. The key element in all this was the sustained perception of a need for party, the development of the organizational apparatus of party, and, then, the spread of proparty ideas and forms throughout the political nation. All took time. Noble Cunningham's study of the circular letters of congressmen to their constituents notes the strong upsurge of interest in politics, especially in the presidential elections of the 1820's. Again, much was at stake. But as one reads accounts of the elections of 1824 and 1828, it is clear that these were still essentially factional battles among different leadership groups. Organizational structures remained largely informal. And they were neither pervasive nor sustained. Most developed spontaneously, existed briefly, and set no immediate precedents. Still, in these years, the temporary, volatile, and fragmented behavior and conflicts moved increasingly into permanent bipolar division with important political consequences.[33]

The seasoned New York politician Martin Van Buren, as much as Andrew Jackson, was the catalyst for the political transformation under way. His role as a national political organizer in the 1820's was crucial.[34] But he built on existing examples. Much of the impulse toward mass politics and collective political organization originated with outsider political movements. Groups like the Antimasons, the Workingman's party, and the (New York) People's party took the lead ahead of the conventional political leadership in their willingness to mobilize the masses and in learning how to do it. In particular, Antimasonry led the way. Originating as a political movement to resist corrupting forces unleashed in society, its leaders adopted the institutions of collective political organization that had existed intermittently, and demonstrated their utility in mobilizing vast numbers of voters. Their example was not lost on many astute political observers.[35]

The Van Burenites—Martin Van Buren and his well-organized New York associates, the Albany Regency—strongly made the case for party, for acting collectively and accepting the direction and discipline of such an institution. As Michael Wallace puts it, "for the individualism so dear to Whig and Republican theory," the New York school "substituted an almost servile worship of organization." They did it by taking a new tack. In the run-up to the presidential election of 1828, as Wallace shows, Van Buren and his followers essentially "drew upon the argument [that] organization advanced democracy," making themselves the logical instruments to mobilize large numbers on behalf of desirable policies. A Van Buren lieutenant, Churchill Cambreleng, set the new tone in a speech in Congress in 1826. Political parties, he argued, were "indispensable to every Administration, . . . essential to the existence of our institutions; and if . . . an evil, [they are ones] we must endure, for the preservation of our civil liberty." But parties "never yet injured any free country. . . . The conflict of parties is a noble conflict—of mind to mind, genius to genius." Van Buren himself, in his autobiography, later pronounced political parties "inseparable from free governments and . . . highly useful to the country." That attitude he forcefully iterated throughout the 1820's.[36]

Some might find, one pamphleteer argued, "novelty" in collective action for political purposes. But such organization was necessary to achieve an "honest expression of public sentiment." Americans had to remember that political conflict was inevitable and preferable to "the calm and quietude of despotism." Collective action was the only way to harness and manage that conflict; this would allow those "periodical and wholesome storms" to "purify the political elements and bring with them increased health and vigor." The ideological shift was striking. The conceptions fueling and shaping what was under way were altogether different from the earlier stress on social harmony and deference. Party leaders accepted pluralism as a persistent fact of life. They believed that America could not escape the contentiousness that flowed from it. Egalitarian commitments also grew stronger, albeit imperfectly and incompletely. As Harry Watson sums up, "The emergence of professional politicians, the noisy proclamations of universal political equality among whites, and the creation of contentious mass political parties were all part of a rejection of the stately and genteel republicanism which dominated affairs in the early national period."[37]

The effects of this vigorously espoused propartyism were felt throughout the nation after 1824. In Indiana, for example, lengthy diatribes against faction and party, which had been "standard fixtures" of political discourse, no longer appeared by the late 1820's. Instead, groups calling themselves "Friends of Andrew Jackson," or, alternatively, his foes, now identified themselves as blocs standing for specific policies. Everywhere they continually raised the new rallying cry that "we must be prepared to act with concert and unanimity, in order that we may act with effect." Discipline and management were acceptable and necessary. "The spirit of party," one participant at a town meeting in Philadelphia argued, "is inseparable from, and within certain limits, essential to Republican institutions; it invigorates the body politic and gives it a healthy habit." On the other hand, "the canting cry of no party is the poisonous deadly charm of the political reptile."[38]

Of course, the commitment still remained incomplete and often ambiguous. In some places, the old ideas retained great power. In Mississippi, legislatures still "relied upon county needs and personal considerations to govern their actions" in the 1820's; there the political leaders "fully implemented the pre-partisan political assumptions of anti-partyism and the virtues of uncontrolled pluralism." Traces of old arguments persisted as well even among the Jacksonians. In the late 1820's, many of them, including Jackson himself, still denounced party and faction and denied that they comprised either. If some of their antipartyism was purely tactical, it nevertheless reflected the continuing strength of the long-standing fears about Van Buren's "New York School of Politics."[39]

Van Buren's opponents were certainly not convinced. They constantly condemned the "engine of party." Daniel Webster reminded his constituents in the early 1830's that in protecting the Constitution, "the appeal . . . is to the People. Not to party, not to partisans; not to professional politicians." He and others particularly denounced any evidence of party organization—conventions, for example—as unacceptable and malignant attacks on republicanism. The Jacksonians in 1828, these opponents claimed, had "forgotten their country" in their efforts to promote party coalitions and labels. They pushed "the dictation of the political managers" with "excessive/partisan/zeal," to the point that "the harmony of social intercourse [had] been impaired, . . . ancient animosities [had] been revived [and] new schisms [had] been created." Efforts to force public opinion into certain channels through collective action introduced "an intolerable tyranny" into public affairs. "The executive officer of the United States should be the President of the people, not of a party."[40]

The result of all of these efforts, the opponents of party concluded, was "the bigotry of party," a "spirit of faction generated by the lust for power," not for the achievement of great purposes. So had all republics ended in the past: "Ambitious, rather than wicked men, created factions; factions introduced distractions, distrust and animosities; liberty became worthless and irksome and was thrown away." Since the American people were "all members of one great family," with the same interests, their "end and object should be the same." For that reason, Americans were surely "too proud to wear the livery of any man." Such hostile attitudes toward "Management" and toward parties "found a ready response in every quarter." Mississippians, as M. Philip Lucas has shown, "employed the terms faction, party, clique and junta interchangeably to conjure up images incompatible with republican government."[41]

Still, in contrast to earlier times, these classical republican fears were constantly and effectively challenged. As more people could vote, as conflict became endemic, many political observers accepted parties as inevitable, useful, and necessary. The election of 1828 reflected the trend that was redefining the political nation. There was a more widespread acceptance and use of the organizing conceptions and institutions developed and perfected by the Albany Regency. State nominating conventions named both Jackson and Adams in 1828, for example. (The older forms still survived as well. Mass meetings and caucuses also nominated presidential candidates in that year.)[42] Beyond that, the rhetoric of conflict was sharper and more partisan than ever. To the Jacksonians, the stakes in the election were clear-cut. This was "a contest for principle, to vindicate the violated rights of the people, to rescue the constitution from the rude grasp of those who regard only its *form*, . . . to sweep away the leeches from the national treasury, and to restore to its regular action the public will." This was not a "personal" controversy between two men. Jackson was "a republican," ever known for "his adherence to his ancient principles and his devotion to his country." The Adams people talked only about personalities, the Jacksonians, in contrast, about the principles that divided the two contending groups.[43]

Interestingly, some National Republican leaders proposed to emulate the organization, unity, and energy of their foes, calling on Adams partisans to "act with concert and unanimity, in order [to] act with effect." But most of the Adams group did not see the election in this way—as a battle for principles or demonstrating the need for party. Principles "are almost unknown in the party distinctions of the day," Adams supporters in Virginia claimed in 1827. What they faced was simply "a conflict between opposing men, . . . competition for power and place." Voters should therefore confer their vote "on *merit*, independent of party." What that meant was clear. Party organization and combinations were not legitimate expressions of people's opinions, democratic yearnings, or distinctive policies. Rather they were, as they had ever been, manipulative, power-hungry, selfish attempts to place certain unfit men into positions of power. Jackson's character, having been "probed and found tainted to the core," filled Americans "with serious apprehensions." The emphasis on character, as against the expression of collectivist principles, clearly belonged in the culture of the first political era.[44]

The 1830's thus began in much confusion. The impulse toward partisanship and organization was growing. But earlier forms were still strong and had to be taken into account. Among the Jacksonians, partisan ways were influential if not yet dominant. There was much uncertainty, about the party names and the role of organization, if not about what was at stake, throughout the period. Two parties might face each other in most state and local situations, but over a very large political landscape, with many political jurisdictions, each with a unique history and pattern, the parties had many different names and, until the mid-1830's, little national focus. Most politically involved Americans still preferred the label "Republican," albeit with some adjective in front of it. In the mid-1830's, "while it was becoming acceptable for groups of men to unite around a set of principles or specific policies, as the Democrats and Whigs did in Mississippi over national issues, Mississippians [still] were not nearly so amenable towards institutions or structures to such unions." In general, by the early years of Jackson's presidency (as Alvin Kass says of New York state), political loyalties had not been built up, nor had traditional habits of action with respect to local personages, leaders, parties, and issues disappeared. As a result, "flux, fluidity and uncertainty in political behavior were the rule."[45]

But the emerging partisan tendency continued to grow through the two Jackson administrations. The continuing policy disagreements stimulated conflict on a more permanent basis. Three "roughly defined states," Harry Watson suggests, characterized the political transformation:

> In the first, the career of Andrew Jackson disrupted the informal politics of the Era of Good Feelings, and simultaneously, county leaders began to face the economic and political implications of the Transportation Revolution. This stage ended in 1829. In the second phase, political organizers drew on prior community values to build plausible linkages between political and economic issues at the local, state and national levels. At the same time, they used long-standing regional, ethnic and class alignments to assemble two rival voting blocs, each with a different perception of the issue. . . .
>
> The process of constructing coalitions and shaping ideologies continued throughout Jackson's first six years in office. . . . The third and final stage began in the state and national elections of 1836, as county voters accepted the

partisan perspectives hammered out by party leaders in the county seat and joined the townsmen in the routines of stable party operation. By 1840, the process was substantially complete.[46]

Changing attitudes and behavior, then, as well as party formation, created the conditions for a new era. Old Hickory's vigorous presidency sharpened the lines of conflict, clearly marked what was at stake, stimulated the building and acceptance of institutions of electoral combat, and focused the whole system in the direction it was to go. As Alfred Balch, a Tennessee politician, wrote to James K. Polk, "Hitherto, there has been . . . too much personal politics. At last we have principles to fight for and I thank God for it." The years between 1828 and 1832 were a period of perception of these new matters; the presidential election of 1832 was one of focus and definition. Earlier, "it had been sufficient to judge candidates on their established reputations; now [candidates for office had to] declare themselves on public questions."[47]

In the race between Jackson and Henry Clay in 1832, while some observers continued to express their horror that the American people were becoming "intoxicated with the insanity of party zeal," others, even National Republicans, accepted and disseminated the message favoring "union and concert" as "necessary to ensure the success of many engaged in a common cause. [They] must act in concert or be overthrown." Political conflict was continuous. As the Ohio State Democratic convention put it in 1832, "This tendency to collision among the people of a free State seems to be the invariable result of social organization." New Hampshire Democrats summed up the case in familiar terms:

Party collisions are incident to all countries and all governments. They spring from propensities inherent in human nature—from conflicting principles and interests, which exist always and everywhere. They arise mostly from a love of power and a disposition to abuse it on the one hand, and a regard for the rights of the people on the other.[48]

The Bank War not only sharpened the lines of conflict; it also suggested that the conflicts that were creating parties were permanent. "Bank or no bank will be the question for years to come," Thomas Hart Benton told the Senate in 1834. The issue was—as in 1791—"ascending to the true fountain of party distinction." And, all around him, the evidence proliferated that things were moving ever stronger toward this new system of public affairs. National politics had not attracted much attention in Mississippi before 1834. "After that . . .

everyone seemed to be caught up in the great national debates under way." Similarly, the Massachusetts legislature, "influenced by Whig-Democratic partisanship, departed from eighteenth-century practice and held many more roll-call votes" after 1834. In Alabama, the "formal organization of the Democratic party" dates from the meeting of a convention in December 1835, which nominated an electoral slate favoring Martin Van Buren for President in 1836.[49]

Other states throughout the nation joined the trend. Linkages between local issues and campaigns and national matters and divisions now went further than they ever had before at the state level. Local leaders sought like-minded allies in other parts of their state in order to win control of its governments; state leaders came together to gain control of the national government. Long-standing local divisions thus began to be linked to the larger national conflicts, and their organizational champions became a means of bringing people together across a broad political terrain.[50]

By the middle 1830's, many American political leaders believed that principled parties were the key to everything. Party appeals had become the centerpiece of the Jacksonians' strategy. More than anything else, Democratic leaders believed, jealousies, indifference, and internal squabbles over candidates had to be prevented. "Union, harmony, self-denial, concession, everything for the cause, nothing for men," was how one Democratic congressman put it as the campaign got under way. There were real differences between the parties, Democrats argued, and the stakes in each upcoming election were clear: the Whigs were determined on "that train of measures introduced by the administration of John Quincy Adams"—the Bank, the federal financing of internal improvements, and a high tariff, all of which would destroy the prosperity and threaten the freedom of the people of the United States. All Democrats were called to battle. "If Van Buren be the rallying point of antibankism, antinullification, what republicans will fail to rally around him? Is his mere name to frighten men from their principles?" The answer was no, and the relationship between principles and candidate was never forgotten.[51]

The election of 1836 continued the surge. It saw wider, if not yet total, acceptance of the new elements shaping the political landscape. The second national Democratic nominating convention met in Baltimore in May 1835. The meeting was orchestrated as a grand rally of the party faithful designed to reaffirm party principles and to pass the leadership mantle from Andrew Jackson to Martin Van Buren. The convention unanimously nominated him, as "the executor of [Jacksonian] principles" whose election would "preserve the power of our party and secure the triumph of his [Jackson's] principles." Second place on the ticket went to Richard M. Johnson of Kentucky, another party stalwart. Those matters out of the way, the convention then issued an elaborate statement of party ideology—a quasi-platform— to publicize and underscore the Democratic stance and Van Buren's place in it. Everything that the Democrats did in the campaign that followed echoed the basic strategy of calling all party members to their duty to back Van Buren in order to preserve what had been gained.[52]

The Whigs, on the other hand, continued to express antiparty sentiments even as they campaigned as an increasingly organized opposition suitably labeled. In 1834, the Mississippi Whig convention viewed with "indignation, shame and regret" the state Democratic acceptance of "that miserable and corrupt system of New York politics . . . by which a man is bound to surrender his principles upon the altar of party." And, in contrast to their adversaries, the Whigs in 1836 were not nearly so well organized. Still in their shake-down phase as a party, with several different power blocs in often uneasy alliance, they had not yet developed any deep sense of party attachment or loyalty. They were particularly deeply divided over who their candidate should be. Whig newspaper editorials were filled with hopes for harmony on a single ticket and an acute consciousness that it could probably not be achieved. A national convention would only underscore these divisions. The Whigs relied instead on the traditional way to bring forward their candidates. Informal legislative caucuses, local meetings, and conventions in different states named Hugh L. White, Daniel Webster, and William Henry Harrison for the presidency.[53]

To further their goals, Whigs ran a campaign, particularly in the strong Democratic areas, deemphasizing party identification and appealing to dissatisfied Democrats to break the shackles of party discipline. At the core of their strategy as it developed, therefore, was a full-scale attack on party organization, discipline, and loyalty as reprehensible and subversive of American institutions. "Party division," the editor of the Cincinnati *Daily Gazette* wrote, "is an unhealthy and unsafe condition of things. Its tendency is to substitute mere party objects and coercive party discipline for the exercise of sound discretion in deciding upon measures." The government under Jackson had been "administered for the party—not for the People." But "the watchword of every American," an Indiana Whig meeting resolved, "should be 'our country,' not 'our Party.'" The Whigs' target was, of course, the "little magician" of American politics, Martin Van Buren, the organizer of party institutions. "The Vice-President, thro' the Kitchen Cabinet has supplanted most of the early friends of the President, and has succeeded in establishing at Washington the discipline of the New York school of politics."[54]

Nevertheless, the change in political temper affected Whigs as well as Democrats in 1836. Both parties campaigned hard. They set up local and state committees, organized fund-raising activities, held local and state conventions, established newspapers, and coordinated their activities through state central committees. Newspaper editorials from the party press, extensive pamphleteering, and campaign biographies set the tone; rallies, barbecues, dinners, stump speeches, and debates followed as part and parcel of the American campaign style. Local addresses to the people, similar to those issued nationally, appeared. Even the presidential candidates themselves toured a bit to attend the rallies and dinners in their behalf. Harrison did the most, going to New York, Pennsylvania, and Virginia at one point or another in the race. The activity did not quite reach the level or intensity of later years, but it was substantial for the time. Certainly it went beyond anything yet known, in keeping with the whole thrust of the campaign. Neither party was more passive than the other. If the Whigs' efforts were imperfect, this reflected more their late development than any lack of will among many of them. Where they had been active for some time, they made use of existing party organizational techniques as well as the Democrats did.[55]

"The Noble Strife of Political Parties"

The partisan tendency became even more pronounced after 1836. In the aftermath of Van Buren's election, some of the hesitant were more ready to shift to the proparty side than they had ever been. Throughout 1837, Henry Clay kept pressing other Whig politicians to adopt the discipline of party organization—not to allow their opportunities to slip because of a failure of unity or a lack of flexibility. "No time has ever occurred within my knowledge," he wrote, "in which it was more evidently the duty of us all to repress individual aspiration or ambition and to dedicate our individual energies to the rescue of the Country." Reminding one colleague that "division is weakness, as union is strength," he told another that the only thing that could keep Democrats in power was "*Our* division," which was "*their* only remaining strength."[56]

As the Van Buren administration wore on, the partisan tempo increased. The economic depression that began in 1837 proved to be "one of those convulsions" that led to advances in political development. It raised major questions about the nature and purpose of government and the future of the country. These were largely answered in partisan, not national, terms. In Prince Edward County, Virginia, for example, "almost overnight following the Panic of 1837, the issues debated from Maine to Mississippi became the focus also of elections in Virginia's Southside; local and national politics were integrated in an unprecedented fashion. [Both the local Whigs and Democrats] basically followed the national party line after 1840. . . . As elsewhere in the South, political debate revolved around national economic issues— banking, tariff, land policy, and the distribution of the surplus."[57]

The panic, Charles Sellers suggests, "served to make party considerations paramount to personalities." Those participating glowed with vigor and activity. "This *is* a crisis to any man's soul," the editor of the *Democratic Review* wrote. "We exult in it. Those who engage in the noble strife of political parties, with worthy motives of enthusiasm and devotion to principles, may rejoice in it with all the stern joy of a patriot in the last battle for all that is nearest and dearest to him." The Whigs spent their time, in Daniel Webster's words, "beseeching the people to relieve the Country from unbearable distress, by a change of rulers."[58]

Each party reacted to the panic differently, and the voters responded to the parties' stance and their own condition. The "economic roller-coaster ride between 1837 and 1843," in the words of Michael Holt,

was clearly the predominant influence shaping American political development in those years. Not only did it spur the two parties for the first time to formulate clear and contrasting economic policies, but it also molded office holders in the respective parties into disciplined phalanxes who supported their rival programs in state and national legislative bodies in order to establish contrasting records to take to the electorate.[59]

Thus, thanks to the growth of new environmental forces and a larger more attentive electorate in the 1820's, the excitement of the Jackson administration defining itself, and the battles over the presidential succession and economic policy in the mid-1830's, a new style and situation, adding up to a new political nation, loomed larger and larger. The push for parties came out of three streams: the need for institutions to handle mass electorates; the need for coalitions, that is, the coming together of pluralist factions in a bitterly divisive political situation in order to win elections; and the need to find a way to enact specific policies, or to avert the serious public danger that would occur if the wrong policies, people, or groups dominated the nation. The first two, stressed by Roy Nichols and Richard P. McCormick in their excellent descriptions of party growth, primarily affected the elites, the managers of elections and political business; the third, stressed by Lee Benson in his study of New York voting, affected the masses themselves and their worldviews. Whatever the sources, something was now clearly at stake.[60]

Intermittence, individualism, and voluntarism in politics moved to persistence, structure and organized professionalism. Not everything had been worked out as yet—the balance between individual freedom and the need for disciplined working together, for one example; how and what institutions would be used, for another. The variance in party development and acceptance in the nation was great. As an Illinoisan wrote in 1834, "it is difficult to catch the hang of parties here, for although there is considerable party feeling there is very little party organization." That was still the case in several states later in the decade. Formisano's cataloguing of the level of party development on a state-by-state, function-by-function basis shows much variation as late as 1840. The Middle Atlantic states led the way in party development; Democrats and Whigs had high visibility and meaning there, in the electorate, among officeholders, and in organizational structure. Some Deep South states were at the other end of the scale, with the rest of the country mostly falling between the two extremes.[61]

The deeply ingrained habits and outlooks of many generations did not pass away readily. But ultimately they did. The critical thing was that the nation's mood seemed clearly to be moving in the same direction: toward a much higher status for party involvement in American political affairs. Sustained partisan-like rhetoric and mentalities were in evidence now as never before. Moreover, and critically, permanent partisan organization and regular partisan response had become part of the political landscape. The central focus of this system was, in Formisano's terms, the creation of the "party in the electorate," with all of the associated paraphernalia of organization, commitment, and style necessary to its operation.[62] Organizational cadres emerged to work in an arena where their particular talents were needed—and accepted. The success of their efforts was marked by voter response, not in intermittent and volatile style, but in regular, recurrent ways. First, as these political activities increased, so did popular participation. As Table 1.3 shows, the turnout for presidential elections grew throughout the 1820's and 1830's, to reach the highest level nationally to that point. Although the turnout for state elections continued to be higher than in national contests, the gap had narrowed significantly.[63]

Once at the polls, people now looked for party labels. What had

TABLE 1.3

National Turnout to Vote, Presidential Elections, 1816–1836

Year	Estimated turnout	Year	Estimated turnout
1816	20.5%	1828	57.1%
1820	9.8	1832	56.7
1824	26.7	1836	56.3

SOURCE: See Table 1.2.

TABLE 1.4

Total Average State Percentage Differences
Between the Two Parties, 1828–1844

Year	Average percentage difference	Year	Average percentage difference
1828	36.7%	1840	10.8%
1832	36.7	1844	8.6
1836	12.2		

SOURCE: Sven Petersen, ed., *A Statistical History of the American Presidential Elections* (New York: Frederick Ungar, 1963).

been a highly personalized vote for President became a two-party competitive situation throughout the country as the parties came into focus and became more relevant to voters everywhere. Andrew Jackson's personal victories in 1828 and 1832 were characterized by lopsided margins in many states. This changed with the election of 1836. As Table 1.4 indicates, the average state margins of victory fell precipitously in 1836 from what they had earlier been, and remained low thereafter.[64]

The year 1838 was a profoundly important marking point in the transition under way. In the state elections in that year, the energy and intensity of two-party politics noticeably increased. The contests established a new plateau in voter turnout and party competitiveness as the Whigs surged forward to national political respectability, including winning the governorship of the vital state of New York for the first time. In that and the eleven other gubernatorial races that year (see Table 1.5) the two major parties (Whig and Democrat) dominated the scene to an extent not seen earlier. In the gubernatorial elections four years before, when the Whigs were first becoming nationally established, only six of the eleven races had had two candidates. The races were closer, too. The average percentage difference between the two parties' popular vote fell from roughly 21 percent in

TABLE 1.5

Gubernatorial Elections, 1834–1838

Year	No. of races	No. of two-candidate races	Average pct. be-tween parties' win-ner and runner-up	Percentage of vote for two major parties
1834	11	6	20.7%	83.8%
1836	13	12	17.2	100
1838	12	12	6.9	100

SOURCE: *Congressional Quarterly's Guide to U.S. Elections* (Washington, D.C., 1975).

1834 to under 7 percent in 1838. Finally, the Whigs and Democrats together increased their share of the vote substantially.

The congressional races showed a similar pattern. In the 1835 Tennessee elections for the 24th Congress, for example, three candidates ran in two of the thirteen districts, and each won a substantial proportion of the popular vote. Three of the other seats were uncontested. And in six of the other eight contests, the winner received better than 60 percent of the vote. Putting it another way, only two of the Tennessee races were competitive two-party ones. The state, of course, had distinguished itself by giving its native son, Andrew Jackson, better than 95 percent of its popular vote each time he had run for President (although congressional and gubernatorial contests had been closer). Tennessee was hardly a state with an effective two-party voting pattern in the mid-1830's. But four years later, in 1839, when Tennesseans voted for Congress, there were no multicandidate races, only one unopposed race, and just four in the noncompetitive (60 percent of the vote and better) category. Eight contests were now within the boundaries of two-party competitiveness.[65] With some deviations and backsliding, that general pattern continued to hold there and in the whole country as well in this period.

Voter turnout increased dramatically in many places as well in 1838, jumping to over 83 percent of the eligible in New York State's gubernatorial contest, a level that was more characteristic of the era about to begin than of the one passing from the scene. Further, and perhaps most significantly of all, in 1838, New York's voters, who till then had behaved with great volatility from election to election, locked into place behind their parties—and stayed there. Thereafter, they were persistent, all but immovable party supporters on every election day for every office contested: President, Congress, governor, state legislature, even local positions. That pattern appeared elsewhere in the country as well, and again for the first time in 1838. William

Shade points out that Prince Edward county, Virginia, "evolved from a county lacking any semblance of party competition in the early 1830s to one system by the late 1830s. The yearly vote for the House of Delegates was less consistent than the presidential or congressional vote but generally correlated with it." The correlation remained high thereafter.[66]

By the late 1830's, the perceptual changes had prompted institutional breakthroughs. The identification of offices as properly partisan (such as the speaker of the national House of Representatives) became more widespread at every level. Local organizational development continued to expand. In 1834, for example, the Whigs of New York City met in general committee to organize and plan their campaign. They appointed various subcommittees to parcel out the necessary campaign tasks: executive, finance, corresponding. This sort of meeting increasingly became the norm there and elsewhere. At the same time, more and more statewide nominating and policy-articulating conventions were held. As a result, a new form, the partisan coordinating committee, spread widely at both the state and the local level.[67]

A four-step pattern of development had come to fruition. In the 1820's, mass participation had expanded, along with a perceived need for electoral organization. In the early 1830's, policies and issues began to shape a dichotomous political environment; between 1834 and 1836, participation, organization, and issues had begun to connect; and in 1838, it all came together. As Formisano has summed up the situation in Massachusetts, "In the second half of the 1830's, Massachusetts politics dramatically polarized into two mass parties whose almost ritualized electoral warfare replaced the creative chaos of the early 1830s. . . . Political factions tied to traditional networks grew into organizations harnessing the discipline of factories and the fervor of revivals."[68]

The key difference by 1838 was that, as noted earlier, what had been absent or intermittent—high interest and commitment and strong party institutions fed by intense partisanship—became permanent, deeply rooted, and powerfully determining of the nature of the political nation. The editor of the national Democratic organ, the *Daily Globe*, put it well when he wrote in 1838, "There never existed so thorough a separation, and so exact a delineation and opposition of the two parties, as at this moment." It was a hot-house political year. The people of the United States were "divided into two great parties; each striving to establish certain principles, completely opposite in their tendencies. To one or another of these parties every man belongs."[69]

Although not yet complete, the transition from prepartisanship and ambiguity to the new partisan political era had been made. Michael Holt's summary of what was happening is apt:

The transition between 1836 and 1840 . . . involved far more than the hardening of voters' partisan identities and mobilization of new voters. It was also marked by the elaboration of party machinery and by the emergence of impressively high levels of internal party cohesion and interparty disagreement. . . . For the first time . . . the parties articulated coherent and contrasting platforms regarding proper governmental policy at the state and national levels.

Most of this occurred at some point in the late 1830's and early 1840's but, as I have suggested, 1838 is a particularly important date in marking the transition. "Not until 1838," Donald Ratcliffe notes for Ohio, "did an almost complete identification take place among state, local, and national politics." [70] Then it did, and not only in Ohio. Rhetoric, belief, and behavior aligned. They were neither different nor separate from one another.

None of this means, to repeat the point, that there were not dissenters and other options and values expressed. It does mean that these elements added up to something like a consensus that dominated debate and actions. This new system involved the emergence of a mass electorate (consisting of adult white males), the creation and acceptance of modern political parties, the development of a professional politician class, and the flowering of egalitarian partisan rhetoric as a staple of political warfare. Acting together, all of these overturned and replaced the earlier worlds of classical republicanism and mixed forms of deference, antipartyism, volatility, inegalitarianism, localism, and factionalism. This formal system and the developing substructure of organized conflict and informal but powerful political institutions, fused together by sets of ideas, values, and expectations, were the elements that emerged in the late 1830's to cement the second American poltical era into its characteristic form. [71]

CHAPTER TWO

"The Country Demands
the Existence of Parties"

IN THE AFTERMATH of the presidential election of 1836, John C. Calhoun complained, in a speech to his South Carolina constituents, that the United States was undergoing the "most remarkable change in [its] political institutions since the adoption of the Constitution." Always a deeply committed antiparty man, Calhoun was outraged by the new partisanship that enabled powerful party leaders to control "the voice of the people." This was neither the first nor the last time Calhoun assailed political parties. Unswerving in his resistance to the growth of partisanship, he unrelentingly railed against party leaders and "the mere trammels of party" throughout his career.[1]

Despite his eloquence, Calhoun was out of step with the political times. The blending together of the elements of partisanship into a powerful force had moved forward at the end of the late 1830's, thanks to the continuing "hurricane of excitement" in American politics and the intensification of "harsh controversies on Capitol Hill" and elsewhere throughout the political nation. Party lines were by now sharply drawn, and partisan activity constant and extensive. Everywhere one turned, as Richard P. McCormick has shown, there was a widespread acceptance of the party role in American politics.[2]

But what was occurring went beyond mere acceptance. The sequence of party development that had peaked in 1838 was now followed by a final stage, in which partisan ideas, commitments, and organization not only spread throughout the Union but, more critically, penetrated the system deeply and completely enough to become the mainstay of the political nation. The ideological case for party became more dominant; it took on a different tone as well, less defensive, more assured and assertive, more celebratory. Spokesmen made a sustained, unambiguous case that rarely wavered. They extolled parties as necessary to the effective operations of the republican experiment. They were "the people's surrogate sentinels guarding the fortress of popular liberty."[3] As the editor of the Whig *American Review* put it in the first volume of that journal:

We regard the presence, activity, and vigilance of great political *parties*, in this country, as alike essential to the permanence of liberty and the best security for the virtual and beneficent dominion of constitutional government. . . . The generous spirit of party, vehement though it be, invigorates and warms, cherishes and sustains, the whole fabric of the state.[4]

For the most part, these two developments—the penetration of party values and the general acceptance of party dominance—occurred in the key period between the presidential election of 1836 and the run-up to the election of 1844. Political leaders set the scene with their powerful challenge to antipartyism and their unremitting advocacy of the necessity for party. From these elite arguments, a spreading ideology of party grew apace through newspapers, in election campaigns, in legislative halls, and in the executive offices of state and national governments.

But there was much more going on than the expression of rhetoric. Building on the arguments made, powerful partisan perspectives grew and, most critically, were adopted as the nation's norm with important behavioral consequences. It was in these years, in Ronald Formisano's words, that party organizations "established an unassailable command of . . . routine political life." Parties and partisan consciousness, for the first time, "achieved full legitimacy," so that, as Harry Watson describes the process in North Carolina in the 1840's, the new system "reached every country and crossroads hamlet and recruited village *salons* into multiple networks of committees, conventions, platforms and caucuses. It stretched out further, beyond the circles of local notables, and enlisted individual citizens who never sought an office, never made a speech, and never chaired a meeting."[5]

The Tempo Increases

In the late 1830's and early 1840's, both Whig and Democratic leaders and their communications networks enthusiastically articulated a vision of an American political nation in which party was all. "The country demands the existence of parties," the New York Whig leader William Henry Seward wrote to John Quincy Adams in 1841. They had always existed in all countries, John Reynolds of Illinois told his fellow congressmen in 1840. "And I have no doubt [they] always will

exist. All history confirms this position." Parties were the "natural consequences of a Republican and Representative Government," another
congressman went on; "their regular formation shows the political
body to be in the healthy action." They might lead to frequent "agita-
tions of the public mind" because party spirit could become violent.
But in its fire, the real issues and matters of political concern would
emerge "brighter, purer and more durable than ever."[6]

There was a clear utilitarian case for parties. They "bring into action the greatest talents, they excite a jealousy and vigilance which en-
sures fidelity in public functionaries: They check attempts at the usur-
pation of power, and thereby preserve the right of the people."
Therefore, "no man ought to desire that we should be free from political parties; no free Government can exist without them." Parties
"are schools of political science, and no principle can be safely incorporated into the fabric of national law until it has been digested, limited, and defined by the earnest discussion of contending parties."
They "diffuse knowledge" and "cultivate the popular mind." "Show
me a man that belongs to no party," Alexander Duncan said in Congress in early 1840, "[and] I will show you a man without principle.
Show me a man who has no party feelings and predilections and I will
show you a fool or a knave. . . . Party is the salt of the nation. It estab-
lishes a watchfulness and wholesome guardianship over the institutions of our country; it checks and restrains the reckless ambition of
those in office and never fails to expose the nonfeasance, misfeasance,
or malfeasance of those in power." As the Albany (N.Y.) *Argus* reminded its readers in 1844, in political parties, "obligations to men are
secondary, and ought always to defer to the greater and broader duty
of the cause." This had to be done with due deference to the rights,
perspectives, and expectations of the individuals present. But the
message was clear enough. "Let us remember," the Whig *American Review* argued in 1846, echoing its Democratic counterpart, "that this
country must be governed by a party—always—forever."[7]

It was also clear that what these proponents meant was a two-party
system. "Parties are incident to popular government," William Seward
told a Whig mass meeting in New York in 1844. "Two parties exist
now, as two have always existed and always will. . . . We can only reach
the administration, and influence its course, through one or the other
of these parties." To organize and support a third party was "to re-
nounce" participation in public affairs. All the other "fragments must
be absorbed by the great bodies"—the Whigs and Democrats. Seward
returned to this theme before a Massachusetts Whig mass meeting in
1848. "There can be in this country only two parties, . . . two parties

only." It was not possible to succeed with third parties because society was already "classified into two great, all pervading national parties or associations." No other course was possible: "the interests, the sentiments and the habits of society forbid" any other course.[8]

Not all politically active Americans agreed. Some continued to denounce the "low atmosphere of party strife" and called on the concerned citizen "who loves his country better than party" to come forward and assert himself. In 1844, the Baltimore *Sun*, complaining that there was too much combativeness in partisan warfare, hoped for the return of a perspective that would "temper [the] violence of partisan confrontation." The antipartyists argued, in familiar terms, that "party discipline should never be applied to measures of legislation" and rallied against the energies devoted to dividing the people "into bitter and inimical factions."[9] But antipartyism was clearly on the defensive, receding from the center of public affairs as it was drowned out by the louder voices of the new spirit. What Senator William Rives of Virginia called "the fatal bondage of party" was replacing the hostility to party activity that had once dominated American political thought, and with it, the political nation as a whole.[10]

Several historians have forcefully argued that antipartyism remained powerful among the Whigs, even at the end of the 1830's, so that their party repeatedly failed to function with the same commitment, enthusiasm and effectiveness as the Democratic side. But that argument does not seem fully persuasive. Some articulate Whigs certainly continued to be hesitant about parties. But there was less and less of that after 1838. For every Whig who lambasted party "intrigue" and spirit, there were many others who practiced the first and spoke in favor of the second.[11]

Whigs were well aware of what party commitment and organization had done for their opponents. The Democrats, a Whig congressman wrote home to his wife at the end of 1839, "are always at their posts and [they] always act together." Among the Whigs, in contrast, several "were out of their seats" when a crucial vote was taken, "and there is no lead—each manages on his own hook." While the Democrats "maintain themselves in all the integrity of the Macedonia phalanx, all governed by one impulse, . . . we, like so many Arabs, have been *careening* upon their flanks, charging upon them with desperation but without system." The Whigs had the numbers; their problem was "the WANT OF CONCERT." The Democrats won through "organization, committee, correspondences, circulation of information, and in a thousand operations keeping in play every mind and every hand." The Whigs must do the same. "If these means are not wielded, and with a giant's arm, we might as well give over the struggle at once." [12]

The time had come, the Whigs of Chester County, Pennsylvania, felt, for them to organize themselves "upon a separate, distinct and permanent basis." They agreed that the people of free societies are "necessarily divided" into political parties. What followed from that was a familiar theme: "Union, harmony, concession, compromise, self-denial, everything for the cause, nothing for men, is the prevailing sentiment, we should say the universal sentiment, among the Whigs." The Whig congressman Solomon Downs and his friends believed "in the necessity of political parties," he declared in 1844. "It is necessary for men holding similar opinions to unite and combine to carry them out." [13]

In the end, as Douglas Jaenicke has written, the Whig party leaders "capitulated to the Democrats' model of a political party." [14] They adopted the trappings of the party—its organizational imperatives and practices, its call for discipline and loyalty, its way of looking at the world. After their defeat at the hands of superior party organization in the election of 1836, they very substantially increased their partisan activity. And they unabashedly sounded like their opponents. The editor of one New England newspaper listed the party members' duties as election day approached in 1839 (the sort of list frequently printed in other newspapers then and later). "Are you ready?" he asked. "Is every town properly, thoroughly organized? How are the committees of vigilance? Are they on the alert? Are the Whig lists completed, that every town knows its strength? . . . Have arrangements been made to secure the attendance of every man at the polls? Carriages and attendants provided for the aged and infirm? And, lastly, have the printed votes been received—the Whig votes—in every town?" [15]

Many prominent Whigs echoed these partisan aspirations. "I go, first," Thurlow Weed wrote in July 1837, "for a national convention. Next, when the convention meets, I go for the strongest man, whoever he may be. My whole heart and soul is for Mr. Clay. . . . But with all my personal and political attachment to him, if, when the time to nominate comes, a stronger candidate is presented, *I am ready to sacrifice him for our cause and the country.*" One congressman reported that his constituents had met in caucus in 1837 looking toward the establishment of a newspaper "to advocate the Whig Cause, without reference to any particular candidate for the presidency." Whenever the party did agree on a candidate, the paper would accept him as the candidate of the party. Until such an event, however, the newspaper

would be "non-committal as to *men*." In short, Whigs had to be prepared, despite their personal preferences, "to sustain any candidate
who [would] best unite the elements that must combine to save the
country."[16]

All of the elements of party consciousness were there: the commitment to bend to the preferences of the collectivity, the willingness to
sacrifice individuals, no matter how eminent, to the larger cause, the
strong sense of discipline from the top down. Whatever hesitancy
some Whigs had about political parties, most played by the new rules
for the sake of specific policy ends. They built parties and organizations, and celebrated what they were doing. Abraham Lincoln, the
Whig leader of Illinois, was unflinching in his dedicated organizational building from the 1830's on, and in his commitment to party
discipline. He and other devoted party men drew a great many of
the Whig rank and file with them. By 1848, some Whigs routinely
sounded the party-first theme: "We must look to our *cause*. We must
give up *men* [so] that the cause may triumph." Those Whigs who continued to profess traditional antipartyism saw that, despite their mis-
givings, party was everywhere on the rise. "You can scarcely form an
idea of the strength of its bonds, and of its irresistible influence over
the mind," one skeptical congressman lamented.[17]

The tone of the American political nation had unmistakably shifted
by the late 1830's. Among most politically active Americans, from the
busiest participant to the occasional voter, the partisan impulse grew
stronger and stronger. Party men were no longer defensive about
what they were doing. What had begun as a means of taming political
tempers was developing, rhetorically at least, into a system for managing all political activity, a system that was seen as correct and proper,
the only way to engage in politics, and therefore one that was ever
more widely accepted—and ultimately celebrated. "Consultation,"
"compromise," "discipline," were the new watchwords. "Principles
rather than persons, measures rather than men," was the new litany
of American political commitment. Harmony and concert, not individual partialities, were the rule; or as the new editor of the Whig *Ohio
State Journal* put it in early 1839, "I go for the Whig party of this State
and of the Union, and for the Whig party alone, WITHOUT REFER-
ENCE TO MEN, and uninfluenced by local personal preferences."[18]

The Spread of Party

There was much more happening here than a shift in rhetoric. In
the late 1830's and early 1840's, Americans engaged in a range of

actions in their every-day politics that identified them as part of a partisan political nation. This could be something as simple as identifying oneself as a Democrat or Whig, rather than a "republican" or a "friend"—or enemy—of the administration, or of Andrew Jackson. Clear demarcation between the parties became the custom and marked an important turning point. The capitalizing of party names became commonplace, indicating the permanence of what was happening. All of this certainly could be seen in those most critical of political arenas, the electoral and the legislative.[19]

The systematizing of party operations—"the mere drudgery of organization"—was a prime indicator of the acceptance of party. Well into the 1830's, the nominating process, at every political level, was unsystematic and irregular. But as the decade progressed, so did the channeling of all phases of political life. At the state level, an array of committees, conventions, and caucuses sprang up and met regularly. Such party vehicles were not confined to only a few places as they had once been. What was said for Alabama, that after 1839 the Whigs "may be considered to have possessed a relatively well-defined party organization," held everywhere. And as organization developed, in every state mass participation in them increased and in less haphazard fashion than formerly. State party conventions became less unorganized mass rallies of "the people" and more well ordered, with regular rules designed to advance the party cause.[20]

Various government bodies were also affected by the spreading partisanism. Everything in Congress, Leverett Saltonstall of Massachusetts wrote home in 1839, went "by party and party combination and intrigue."[21] The public face of that "party combination" became clearer and clearer. In 1842, Mississippi state legislators sat on opposite sides of their chamber, based on their party membership, for the first time. One legislator celebrated the arrangement because it gave the members of each party "a better opportunity for free consultation and concert." The occasional cry against turning something such as the legislative election of a state printer into "mere partisan squabbles" was still heard. But all such issues became imbued with partisan meaning. The election of the Clerk of the federal House of Representatives was an occasion to notice so "thorough [an] organization of party" that "every man marched up to the point," whatever "twinge of conscience" he might have had.[22] (It is not clear that there remained many such twinges.)

The growing partisanship went through three stages in the legislative arena. In the first, there was only occasional party discipline. Policy matters were the occasion for much partisan voting, but purely housekeeping affairs—the election of a printer or a doorkeeper—

often were not. In the second stage, an all-encompassing party discipline extended to those matters as well. Party ratios on legislative committees and partisan chairmen replaced haphazard composition and
leadership based on a range of nonpartisan considerations. In the
third and last stage, automatic, ingrained party discipline was accepted and acted on without comment. By the end, party organization
was the norm. The legislative caucus became the recognized authority
for defining the agenda and choosing leaders for the party as a whole.
Caucuses met regularly at the beginning of a legislative session to select leadership candidates, then they met again in order to define and
articulate party positions or settle party differences or work out problems. As Mills Thornton has well put it, "The decisions of the legislative caucus, like those of the convention, were enforced only by the
feeling which most politicians had of deference to party authority." In
addition, consultations between the legislative caucus and a state governor of the same party became regularized. Governor James Polk
was, in 1839, "the first Governor of Tennessee to function as legislative leader of his party."[23]

How powerfully parties now figured in popular elections is clearly
demonstrated by the presidential election of 1840. Beyond the well-
known excitement of the "log cabin and hard cider" extravaganza, as
William N. Chambers has written, party organization "reached previously unprecedented levels. If the party was not yet a machine,
it could muster a political drill that matched or over-matched the
uniformed militia of the time. To rally the faithful, win recruits,
and mobilize the voters—such was the militia style," brought to perfection at that moment.[24] Newspapers were fiercely partisan and
merchandised their party nominee and his stances far and wide. Both
parties held national conventions that involved a great deal of partisan calculation about leadership, candidates, and electability, as well
as consideration of what the party stood for. The Democrats issued a
national platform, and although the Whigs did not, they campaigned
on the major matter of the day: the Democrats' failed economic policies and indifference to the suffering of the American people in
the face of the depression. Their Democratic opponents understood
how well the Whigs had done. The Whig organization and "systematic
course of electioneering," one editor wrote, "is so perfect that it
has given [them] the character and efficiency of an *organized military
force*."[25]

The election of 1840 was clearly one that was in the hands of the
new-style party managers. It set all sorts of precedents for the future;
and though much of what it introduced had marked earlier state elec-

tions, notably those in New York two years earlier, when the Whigs swept to victory, the important experience of a major national campaign solidified the routine, partisanly driven nature of American politics. These tendencies spread everywhere in the country from then on. As Richard P. McCormick has shown in his careful study of the state-by-state emergence of parties from 1824 to 1840, all but one (South Carolina) demonstrated development in a similar direction— toward coalition, organization, discipline, and acceptance. There was some variation in the breadth and depth of this partisan style, a variation that was largely to disappear as the years passed. New York's precocious partisans of the 1820's had advanced very far by 1840 and continued to advance in the ensuing decades. Their degree of party acceptance, organization, and behavior formed one end of the scale. But Democratic, and then Whig, leaders in Ohio, Pennsylvania, Illinois, and Virginia were not very far behind.[26]

Partisanship penetrated down to the lowest level of American politics. So developed had the rationale for the existence of parties become that one newspaper could claim that "a town or city, as well as a State or Nation, is never better governed than when its officials act under the searching gaze of a hostile political party." There, too, party was "the most watchful and sleepless sentinel." Local elections, like legislative, congressional, gubernatorial, and presidential elections, all came to be "of a partisan character." Locally, as elsewhere, an individual's responsibility was the same. As the editor of the Albany *Argus* put it in the mid-1840's: "the first duty of a Democrat is to vote; the next to vote the regular ticket." Partisan behavior in government activities followed along. All were of a piece.[27]

Though these trends had originated primarily in the Northeast and the Midwest, the partisan phenomenon was not sectional in nature. Southern and Western political development generally followed the same trends in this period. Philip Lucas's study of Mississippi, for instance, illuminates the similarity of the basic process there. Nor was Mississippi alone among the slave states. Despite the region's commitment to such consensual values as the need for African slavery, a two-party system evolved in the Deep South. There was a great deal to contest for—as there was elsewhere. By the late 1830's, both the Whigs and the Democrats had extensive partisan organizational structures and ways of doing business in every Southern state except South Carolina, all linked directly to their national parties. The electorate in every state, as well as each party's representatives in government, responded to and were guided by these organizations as they were elsewhere.[28]

The Acceptance of Party

All of the hoopla of 1840 reflected the deeper truth of the American acceptance of party. The Democratic and Whig organizations were no longer looked on with either hostility or mixed emotions, but were regarded as natural and legitimate. Their functions and purposes were understood and sanctioned. They were seen as instruments to carry out the people's will and the nation's purposes. The editor of the Democratic Albany *Atlas* put it well, in the mid-1840's:

The genuine lover of democratic principles . . . regards the general interest as of paramount importance, and adheres to his party, not in the sordid expectation of personal emolument, but as a means of subserving the public good, [and] will be ready to sacrifice his individual preferences whenever such a course is demanded by the higher consideration of the general welfare, and the duty he owes through his party to the state and country.

And this idea had now spread widely to incorporate individuals everywhere throughout the political nation. The period of definition was over.[29]

There was no receding, or let up, thereafter. By the middle 1840's, the case for party was prominent and routine, the intellectual underpinnings were clear, and the focus of discussion was quite different from the earlier political eras. By the end of the decade, the paeans to party, the acceptance of party norms, and the virtues of partisan behavior were deeply embedded in the culture of the American political nation. As the *Democratic Review* summed up in 1853: "Constitutions are but parchment, and Republics a vain theory. . . . Next to the organization of a government itself, the organization of a party is of paramount importance. . . . The capacity of law-making and [the capacity] of political combinations [are] equally needed for the conduct of so vast a frame of government."[30]

The Whigs continued to be as adept as Democrats in proclaiming these arguments from the mid-1840's on. "Reasonable controversy" being "always useful," it was not only "the right, but the *duty* of every citizen . . . to attach himself to one or the other of the great leading parties of the country." Once there, "organization [was] the thing . . . to insure vigorous and harmonious action without which it [was] vain and futile, even to anticipate success." Nor did they confine themselves to rhetoric. After their success in 1840, and its frustrating aftermath, Whigs continued to expand their commitment to the same organizational and behavioral patterns as their opponents. They had been moving in this direction in the late 1830's and now caught up to the Democrats in partisan maturity. As Michael Wallace sums up, "After the Tyler debacle, the Whig party was a changed party. The antipartyism of the thirties did not vanish, but it was relegated to a purely ceremonial role. . . . Ritual affirmation took second place to tough-minded appreciation of the merits of organization and an acceptance of the tenets of the [Albany] Regency code." It had become clear, Thomas E. Brown continues, that if the Whigs "were to function as a stable element in a two-party system, it was necessary for individuals to subordinate their views to the cause of party unity. Party unity in effect became for the Whigs, as it was for the Democrats, an expression of the highest patriotism."[31]

This sentiment was certainly demonstrated by the way the Whig leaders in the mid- and late 1840's joined their Democratic counterparts in celebrating their partisan commitment. "Without organization, method, discipline, agreement, in short, *without party*," little could be accomplished in politics. "It [was] a very common error among the ignorant to cry out against party, and to disavow partialities"; but "there must be parties—that is, there must be a union of those who will compromise their minor interests to save their major ones—who will sacrifice *some* of their preferences or interests for the sake of other and more important of their wishes and principles." The "existence of parties," was "not therefore an evil to be regretted, but [was] to be regarded as a necessary ingredient of the form of Government itself." A national political system without such "would be destructive to the institutions of the country, and the end of free Government." Party spirit was "the very living principle of our being and our growth. . . . The opponent of party spirit [was] anything but the advocate of freedom."[32]

The reasons for party unity remained as clear as they had been when they were first articulated in the classrooms of the "New York School." By the 1840's, Whig leaders had become convinced that national parties were the only means of bringing order to the country's politics, defining what was at stake, and mobilizing sustained support behind specific policies. Underpinning this was a deeper appreciation and a fuller, more comprehensive acceptance of pluralism by American political leaders. The American scene had always been divisive. Now divisiveness was accepted as normal, and permanent, and not a danger to the Union. Politics was the recognition of difference, the reconciliation of interests, and the avoidance of crisis. "Our only differences are on questions of opinion, as to what men should be chosen and what measure be pursued—who can best represent the whole, and what are the best *modes* of benefitting the whole."[33] The pluralist accepted that no policy was clearly reasonable to everyone—that there was no single right answer, only preferred directions.

Parties based on such pluralist notions helped define social reality. They provided a degree of cohesion and order in a system of great heterogeneity and potential fragmentation. They provided restraints on competing pressures and came to represent different coalitions of clashing interests. Each party was a congeries of allied interests. The highest political virtues were flexibility and sensitivity to other perspectives. Political leaders had to be managerial, patient, responsive. Their followers had to take a similar stance. "Let us never forget," the members of the Indiana State Democratic convention resolved in 1836, "that in our extended confederacy, embracing as it does every variety of climate and staple productions, there is of necessity a great diversity of interests; and concession, compromise, and mutual sacrifices are necessary for the harmony of the same political family." These were the only ways to achieve anything in the sprawling, adversarial political world they inhabited. Politics also taught, however, that whatever the talents utilized and the efforts made, victory was not always won. Losses were to be expected in a pluralist political world— and had to be accepted. They were part of the whole experience of the new American politics. In 1856, one commentator summed up a generation's intellectual and behavioral journey by arguing that "without party spirit there would be almost innumerable diversities of political opinion, feebly entertained, and producing no effect on government."[34]

None of this was easy. There was always tension between individual political sovereignty and the collectivist pressures forcing the creation of political parties. Anyone who reads about the bitter disagreements between Know-Nothings and Republicans, Antimasons, National Republicans, and Clay men, Calhounites and organization regulars, quickly perceives the extraordinary difficulty of getting these groups together, of easing the friction among men of quite different casts of mind: tribal and political, sectarian and coalitionist, antiparty and partisan. The successful party leader, coalitionist to the core, realized what had to be done and calculated what must be sacrificed to achieve greater ends.

This attitude, in turn, strongly shaped attitudes toward political opponents. Richard Latner recounts how Andrew Jackson, when President, reflected an earlier period in American political life, when differences between interests "so violently convulsed the country." Old Hickory believed that only his friends and supporters were virtuous.

His enemies were evil and illegitimate, and had to be smashed. "It was an unnatural state of things, this violent and embittered antagonism—this equally sincere belief which seemed to have taken possession of each, of the 'total depravity' of the other." The shift in such attitudes a decade and more later was quite clear. Whigs "entertain a different view of government" from Democrats, said one of the latter, "and we are willing that they may enjoy their opinion." Such differences arose "from the constitution of our nature." They did "not necessarily imply a want of patriotism in one party more than in another. . . . We should be careful, therefore, neither to arrogate infallibility to ourselves, nor impute unnecessarily, intentional error to our political opponents." To be sure, some ideological anachronisms remained, but generally, as Formisano has written, Whigs and Democrats, while watching each other carefully and with great suspicion, also "assumed that the opposition was there to stay."[35]

By the early 1840's, in sum, Americans had adopted, gotten used to, and internalized a set of arrangements that characterized and defined the political world and the political culture in which they found themselves. What had been clearly established, as the editor of the Albany *Argus* put it in 1848, was the widespread acceptance of the idea that "in a government based upon free discussion and an untrammeled liberty of opinion, parties are unavoidable." Americans having accepted that, the Whig and Democratic parties had become everything in politics: they organized, shaped, articulated, presented, processed, and legitimized. Even when someone challenged something about them, the challenge was usually presented in partisan terms. When, in 1848, several Ohio Whigs objected to holding a state convention, they did so out of a wish to promote party harmony, not because they wanted to shake free of collective discipline.[36] The American political nation had come a long way.

CHAPTER THREE

"Organize! ORGANIZE! ORGANIZE!"

> Go to work, we say, at once, and organize every ward, pre-
> cinct and county. Break these organizations again into
> smaller subdivisions; appoint officers in each; have your
> captains of thousands, your captains of hundreds, and your
> captains of tens, as the Jews did before you.
>
> —*Richmond Whig*, Oct. 3, 1848

THE CELEBRATION OF PARTY continued unalloyed from the early 1840's onward. But more than rhetorical affirmations were now at play on the American political scene. The energies of this political nation lay in mobilizing voters on behalf of specific policies or general visions of national purpose subsumed under a party label. Party leaders devoted much energy, therefore, to building increasingly elaborate organizational structures to manage their affairs and to mobilize voters and legislators and instruct them in their partisan duty. The whole adult white male population was now directly involved in politics, along with others who participated indirectly. Given the numbers involved and the need to operate nationally, how politics functioned had to change. At the same time, organizational development was also particularly stimulated by the chronology of the nation's political events—the rhythms of politics that energized and made relevant the building of nationwide party structures.

The Rhythms of Politics

In the nineteenth century, there was always an extraordinary amount of political activity in the United States. Governments had their regular schedule of legislative sessions and administrative operations. Congress and most state legislatures met annually, for example, usually in winter. But it was the electoral universe that was particularly busy—all but never at rest. Election activity filled most months of most years. The parties were repeatedly nominating, running, or preparing to nominate or run some candidate for one or another of the wide range of elected offices in the United States. Newspapers were filled with notices for city or local party conventions, the "primary" meetings that began the process which culminated at the state convention later in the year. One such notice, in August 1843 in the

Albany (N.Y.) *Argus*, called all Democrats to meet in their respective wards on August 14th; each of these meetings were to select three delegates to the Albany county convention on August 16th, which would in turn pick three delegates to the State Convention to be held on September 25.[1]

In presidential election years, of course, the national convention capped the busy pre-campaign phase of the political cycle. Party meetings were also called after the state and national conventions "to ratify" the nominations made. In 1860, Illinois Republicans met in their local and county conventions in March and April; their state convention met on May 9, followed by the national convention in Chicago on May 16. Ratification meetings throughout the state followed in late May and early June, culminating in a grand ratification meeting in the state capital, in Springfield, on August 8. Then intensive campaigning began.[2]

There were many election days each year in the 1840's and after. Presidential elections were not held on the same day until November 7, 1848. In 1844, the states voted on nine different days, stretching from October 25 to December 1. Most states (fifteen) went to the polls on Monday, November 4; New York, Tennessee, and Louisiana voted the next day, New Jersey over two days, November 5 and 6, and so on. Congressmen were chosen in different states in 1852, on August 2 and 5, September 7 and 13, October 4, 6, 11, and 12. State-level elections occurred from March to November, most clustering either in August or October. In addition to these, the most important contests, county, town, and city elections were held everywhere throughout the year.[3]

Occasionally, major state and national elections were scheduled on the same day, as in Delaware before the Civil War. Usually, however, they occurred on different days, even when they fell in the same year. In Indiana, for example, the voters elected a governor on August 3, 1840, and then returned to the polls to vote for President on November 2. Most of the time, balloting for the major state and national offices occurred in different years, and even in those states where the national and state elections coincided, local elections were usually held at a different time of the year. Voters were at the polls several times in each twelve-month period, year in and year out.[4]

There was no major national election in 1843. In New York state, choosing the members of the lower house of the state legislature was the main electoral activity of the year. Nevertheless, the reports in an Albany newspaper suggest how busy the political world was, even in the absence of major contests. There were ten different summoned meetings, conventions, and mass rallies in Albany county that year, as well as three different election campaigns, each filled with the usual range of activities. The following year saw these activities supplemented by even more conventions and mass rallies in connection with the presidential and gubernatorial races.[5] The fragmented calendar, together with a vigorous political outlook, ensured that Americans were caught up in semipermanent and unstinting partisan warfare somewhere throughout the year every year.

The Organizational Revolution

These political rhythms put enormous pressure on all of those involved in American politics and placed a premium on the development of effective political organizations. To win, parties had to go beyond speeches and frequent cheering. They had "*to organize, to work.*" Each party's strategy began with "*one important word*—ORGANIZATION." "Organize! Organize! Organize!"—that was "the first duty of a party." It was "also the best guaranty of success," the first step "before anything [could] be effected in politics."[6] The Seneca Falls (N.Y.) *Democrat* in 1842, well encapsulated this powerful, and now commonplace, perspective. "ORGANIZE, ORGANIZE," its editor wrote:

Democrats of New York arouse! Commence your country, town and school district organizations. The enemy is in the fields. Be you up and doing. Now is the time for action. Attend your party meetings. Distribute party papers. Look out for the thousand and one plots and lies that will be attempted by the federalists. Your property is at stake—your character is at stake—the future prosperity of your children is at stake. Is this the time to be indolent and inactive?[7]

The rhetoric and the ideology underlying these organizational impulses were martial and collective, not individual and consensual. As the editor of the *New York Globe* put it in 1847, "Parties in our republic, in their contests, may be compared to contending armies; there must be system, discipline, order, regularity, union and concert of action." Other spokesmen played the same theme very hard. "Concert, arrangement, organization, are as necessary to a political party when a great question is to be decided at the ballot box, as to any army when about to enter into a great battle." The reasons were clear. "Arm a hundred thousand men with the most approved weapons of war, and put them in the field without drill or discipline, and what are they? A mere mob. . . . A political party is the same. Party organization is as necessary to the success of principles as truth is to their usefulness and vitality."[8]

Much later, at the very end of the period, spokesmen had refined and developed the military metaphor. But its central impulse remained the same. "No political party," Richard Croker of Tammany Hall, wrote in 1892,

can with reason expect to obtain power, or to maintain itself in power, unless it be efficiently organized. Between the aggressive forces of two similar groups of ideas, one entertained by a knot of theorists, the other enunciated by a well-compacted organization, there is such a difference as exists between a mob and a military battalion. The mob is fickle, bold, and timid by turns, and even in different portions it is at the same time swayed by conflicting emotions. In fact, it is a mere creature of emotion, while the drilled and compacted battalion is animated and supported by purpose and scientific plan. It has leaders, and these leaders are known to every man in the ranks and possess their confidence. It is thus that a single company of infantry is able to quell almost any popular outbreak in a city; and a regiment is completely master of the situation, even if it be outnumbered by the malcontents in the proportion of ten or twenty to one. The value of organization in the case of political parties does not appear so obviously upon the surface; but in point of fact organization is one of the main factors of success, and without it there can be no enduring result. In the immense Republic of the United States, which is really a congress or union of over forty separate republics, each having its interests more or less disassociated from those of the others, and yet acknowledging the bond of a common political interest, the organization of a national party must, to a large extent, be based upon a system of deferential compromise, and be an aggregation.[9]

What this meant in practice was that political leaders spent much effort on minutely detailed organizing and did not rely on spontaneity, as exemplified in the previous style of mass, unfocused rallies of the faithful. As a Virginia Whig wrote, "One of the great follies of our party has been to rely too much upon GENERAL DEMONSTRATIONS—large meetings and big speakers; and to believe that, when that is done, all that is requisite to success has been done." Democrats agreed. "Men of enthusiastic and ardent temperament are apt to forget how essential the mere drudgery of organization is to the success of the cause." That cause was "better subserved by the men who attend to these details, than to the most brilliant orators." Organization remained "the first step, the indispensable step towards success; and after organization [came] systematic effort."[10]

Statements like these underscore the very different style and commitments of this era from earlier times. Coalitionist cooperation, structure, vigorous activity, all were now necessary. Individualism and exuberance alone were not enough. As Thomas Ritchie summed it up, "Be active, friends, and be not too sanguine, lest you become supine." This became both a battle cry before an election and an explanation of the outcome once the contest was over. The only reason that a party ever lost an election was because of its want of "a thorough organization" and the "superior drill and discipline" of its opponents. The opposition, it seemed, was always better organized and earlier in the field. Whigs believed that the Democrats, "like skillful military engineers, have been searching out the vulnerable points in our ramparts, and directing all of the energies of their missiles to those points." Thus, the "absence . . . of organization in a single county or in a single town may be fatal." The party lost in 1840, the national Democratic paper lamented, because "our numbers then were like untrained militia brought against a disciplined army, who made up the want of numbers by regularity, rapidity, and concert of movement."[11]

All of this put enormous pressure on everyone involved in American politics. No one could escape. All Whigs had to "stand to their arms." Everybody had to "consider the election as his own business. Let him act as though the fate of the union depended on him." All Democrats should be willing to "give one day to their country by working actively on behalf of the ticket." The newspapers were filled with detailed information on what the individual's responsibilities were during campaigns and, especially, on election day, when "all have a duty to perform." To work, then, party stalwarts were told, "delay no longer the work of local agitation and local organization" and "consider your duty accomplished when every man in your township has deposited his ballot and not until then."[12]

In their exhortations and calls for organization, political spokesmen made very clear the kind of detailed structure they envisaged. "A perfect system of organization brings every vote to the polls—it deals in facts, not speculations—and is the stuff out of which not dreams are made, but majorities are figured up and great results are accomplished." Therefore, "to be efficient," organization "must be minute." Organize "in the State," the Democratic state convention of Ohio advocated in 1844. "In the counties, in the township and county be polled. . . . Establish Clubs, for an exchange of courtesies and sentiments among ourselves and for the dissemination of information among the people, by means of papers, pamphlets, speeches and by every correct means."[13]

The persistent rhetoric was matched by elaborate and successful efforts to develop an effective system of party organization from top to bottom. The structures built were, once established, the hallmark of this political nation. They were tripartite in location—local, state, and national—and pyramidical in shape. They began at the lowest level of political activity: the school district, town, precinct, or similar small governmental unit. "It is in our townships, neighborhoods and school districts where the labor of the canvass rests. . . . If one or two efficient men will *act* there, all will be well." In New York state in the late 1840's, there were about 11,000 school districts. Each of them "should be thoroughly canvassed and organized; meetings should be held; papers, tracts and other documents circulated. We hope the work will be commenced immediately in town, county and state."[14]

It almost always was. Committees were the key at every level. As A. O. P. Nicholson wrote to James K. Polk in 1840, "The democrats of Columbia [county] met last night and made all the preliminary arrangements for a thorough organization of this county. We have our Central Association formed to meet monthly and our Central Committee of five with power to appoint Committees in every civil district." Some of these civil district organizations consisted of only one or two people in a particular locality; others involved great numbers. The point was always kept in mind that "no town is *well* organized that it is not *perfectly* organized." Such organization was, as one editor put it, "the first and most important object on which all future success depends."[15]

Committees supervised day-to-day campaign activities in their particular location. The district or town committees were supposed to "institute a thorough, detailed neighborhood organization, so as to ascertain every voter and to secure his attendance at the polls. . . . Sound documents and campaign papers were to be extensively circulated. Good speakers should also be provided." From the local committees also came calls for meetings and their arrangement. They were also expected to keep the next highest organizational level, the county committees, informed of all that they were up to. "Let every town, village, parish, precinct, and school district in the county be visited by your scouting parties. See that reports are systematically rendered to your rendezvous, and so passed up to headquarters."[16]

Their direct work began with the voters. The committees compiled lists of them and entered their names into poll books. "Let every school district in the . . . state have its vigilance committee, let the committee canvass every vote, learn the names of the wavering, stimulate the inactive and pour a flood of democratic truths into the fortresses of the doubting." A perfect poll list was "worth more than twenty speeches." To these men, there could be "no perfect organization without such a list."[17]

The committees deluged voters, faithful and waverers alike, with campaign documents and frequent visits during each campaign. "Documents of the right sort must be made to pass around like hot cakes, going into every hole and corner where there is the least possibility of making a convert to our faith." Parties ordered thousands of copies of their convention proceedings, reprints of prominent speeches, resolutions, addresses and pamphlets, quite often published in a foreign language as well as in English. In his run for governor of Tennessee in 1839, James K. Polk paid a printing bill for 8,400 documents, reproducing 21 speeches and pamphlets. The local committees and, where possible, partisanly appointed government officials such as postmasters made sure these materials reached their intended audience. The committees set up partisan reading rooms at a central point, where the party's written messages, in all their variety, were available throughout the campaign.[18]

Organization continued upward from the districts and town to the counties and congressional districts. The county committees supervised the local ones. The accompanying figure reproduces Abraham Lincoln's organizational plan for the Illinois Whigs in 1840, beginning at the county level. Each level's organization and activities, in turn, generally resembled all of the others across a wider canvas. At the top were the state central committees. Located in the state capitals, they worked closely and repeatedly with the committees below them and supervised the whole range of activities in their state, down to supplying detailed plans of organization similar to Lincoln's to every location in their purview. Supplementing these central committees, and created by them, were a number of statewide speaker, finance, and publication committees, each with its specific role to play. The whole structure was what Mills Thornton describes for Alabama, a "partisan power chain which led from the party leaders down through their adherents to the county and beat [minor civil division] levels."[19]

At the national level, congressional and presidential campaign committees were appointed for every individual race. Located in Washington, their goal was to ensure the broadest focus for their party. The Democrats established a national committee in 1848. The Whigs followed suit in 1852, and the Republicans in 1856, each of them supported by small staffs and a number of collateral committees. Coming as late as they did, and in a nation still decentralized in focus, the national committees served less to direct or coordinate matters than to do whatever they could to help the state committees throughout the Union.[20]

The Whig county committee should

1st.   Appoint one person in each county as captain, and take his pledge to perform promptly all the duties assigned him.

Duties of the County Captain

1st.   To procure from the poll-books a separate list for each Precinct of all the names of all those persons who voted the Whig ticket in August.

2nd.   To appoint one person in each Precinct as Precinct Captain, and, by a personal interview with him, procure his pledge, to perform promptly all the duties assigned him.

3rd.   To deliver to each Precinct Captain the list of names as above, belonging to his Precinct, and also a written list of his duties.

Duties of the Precinct Captain

1st.   To divide the list of names delivered him by the county Captain, into Sections of ten who reside most convenient to each other.

2nd.   To appoint one person of each Section as Section Captain, and by a personal interview with him, procure his pledge to perform promptly all the duties assigned him.

3rd.   To deliver to each Section Captain the list of names belonging to his Section and also a written list of his duties.

Duties of the Section Captain

1st.   To see each man of his Section face to face, and procure his pledge that he will for no consideration (impossibilities excepted) stay from the polls on the first Monday in November; and that he will record his vote as early on the day as possible.

2nd.   To add to his Section the name of every person in his vicinity who did not vote with us in August, but who will vote with us in the fall, and take the same pledge of him, as from the others.

3rd.   To *task* himself to procure at least such additional names to his Section.

Abraham Lincoln's Plan of Organization for the Illinois Whig Party, 1840. Source: Roy B. Basler, ed., *The Collected Works of Abraham Lincoln* (New Brunswick, N.J.: Rutgers University Press, 1953), 1: 180–81.

All of this activity relied heavily on the effectiveness of each party's communications network. Party newspapers were the linchpin of the whole system, "the fortresses of party." Each state capital was home to both a Whig (or Republican) and a Democratic sheet: Richmond (Va.) had its *Enquirer* and *Whig*, Springfield its *Illinois State Register* and *Illinois State Journal*. Similar partisan sheets were published in county seats and market towns. Where a party did not have a newspaper, the leaders worked hard to establish one; otherwise they believed themselves to be under a great "disadvantage." At the top of the pyramid were the national organs of each party, in Washington the *Globe*, the *Union*, and the *National Intelligencer* and in New York the *Tribune*. The editor of a party's national newspaper was considered the "natural field marshal of his party." Or, in the words of Jabez Hammond, "Newspapers are to political parties in this country what working tools are to the operative mechanic." Whichever analogy was used, military or industrial, each was accurate.[21]

The editors, at every level, filled their columns with discussions about what was at stake and what had to be done. They provided a wealth of details about candidates, upcoming meetings, and campaign procedures, mixing ideals, policies, tactics, and organization. As the "bridges" between political leaders, party workers, and the voters, they had to "utter the principles which the great mass of [their party united] in advocating." Prosaic and banal at one moment, soaring at another, they never lost sight of their function to rally and direct their cause. They were "barometers of orthodoxy" for the committed; their object was "to harmonize the actions, and promote the efficient organization of the Whig party, as well as to diffuse its principles and arouse its spirit and enthusiasm."[22]

Each editor was fully aware of his responsibilities, that his paper's "true office [was] to impersonate its party and give it a language, harmonious, life-like and truthful," to "spread . . . the principles and build up the strength of the party." The last issue of one Democratic campaign newspaper in 1844 summed up its efforts of the previous months. "If we have succeeded in turning one repentant Whig from the error of his ways, or in preventing a single Democrat from straying to the camp of Henry Clay, we are content with having labored for the good cause." Such editors succeeded, in Michael McGerr's phrase, in making "partisanship seem essential to men's identity."[23]

As party organizations developed, the number of partisan newspapers increased greatly. In Georgia, for example, there was one newspaper for every five white males in 1810, one for every three by 1850, two for every three adult white Georgians by the 1860's.[24] Although the goal of a party newspaper published in every county was never realized, their numbers and geographic reach were indeed impressive. In many campaigns in the 1840's, national and congressional in particular, special campaign newspapers, *The Campaign*, *The Barnburner*, and *The Campaign Democrat*, appeared to supplement the regular dailies and weeklies already on the scene. In the presidential campaign of 1844, for example, at least sixty-three special newspapers were published before the national conventions for Clay, forty-three for Polk, four for the Liberty party candidate, James Birney, and nine for other candidates. Usually issued weekly for the length of the electoral season, they provided a scrapbook of campaign materials for use on the hustings. The first issue of a Democratic national sheet in 1848, for example, contained biographies of the candidates, Lewis Cass and William O. Butler, and the Democratic national platform. Subsequent issues reprinted editorials from various party newspapers, representative speeches, and the whole range of materials that made up the party appeal that year.[25]

The party workers' store of campaign ammunition also included compilations of speeches in book form and political almanacs filled with the record of important events, political statistics, platforms, and other "official" useful material. Local editors and speakers quoted from such works extensively in their efforts to persuade voters to do the right thing on election day. Campaign biographies appeared in the early 1850's as well. In 1852, the Whigs printed almost a million copies of their biography of Winfield Scott; in 1860, the Republicans printed over 100,000 copies of one of Lincoln.[26]

All of this activity took a great amount of money, which was provided at every organizational level by dues, assessments, and gifts. Parties were never hesitant about approaching their well-to-do supporters for financial help or in expecting officeholders to contribute to the party that had put them in their position. The New York Whig Committee assessed a prominent member and occasional candidate, Daniel Ullmann, $250 in 1851. Later in the century, with inflation, larger sums became the norm. Money raised at the state level was sometimes sent to the national committee in presidential election years. Some went to the districts and towns; most was used to finance statewide activities. It was not a one-way process, however. State committees often asked their local and national counterparts for help.[27]

The amounts raised were minute by later standards. In 1852, the Democrats sought to collect $100 from each congressional district for a national party fund; about $20,000 was raised all told. In 1840, New York City's Fifth Ward Whig Committee spent $590 to rent meeting halls, print documents, and hire cabs to bring people to the polls. And when Chauncey Depew ran for the state legislature in 1861, he spent less than $100. As Roy Nichols concludes, "These were days of small things." But the amounts did not seem small to those trying to find the wherewithal, and considerable ingenuity was expended in figuring out what to do. The treasurer of the Massachusetts Whig Central Committee reminded the national committee in 1852 that he had "pledged and paid" it $20,000 and that another $12,000 to $15,000 was needed for state campaign activities. "Our committees have assessed $2,500 upon New Bedford"; the rest was still to be found. "Write to me," he concluded plaintively. "What plan shall we pursue to get this money up immediately, as we must be up and going at once."[28]

The candidates were the centerpiece of all this activity. They could not rely solely on print to get their message to the people. In every contest they took the field, "armed and ready for combat," to follow an exhausting schedule of stump speaking and debates with their opponents. In Polk's grueling race for governor of Tennessee in 1839, he was in the field for months, speaking on most days, usually several times a day. He appeared in thirty-seven counties, giving forty-three scheduled speeches and many impromptu ones. A year later, the Whig candidate for governor of North Carolina covered the state with an average of four public meetings a week in the six weeks before the election. Surrogates for the candidates also campaigned hard. In 1852, the veteran Democrat John A. Dix, who was not a candidate, spoke fourteen times in October alone throughout New York state. When David Turpie ran against Schuyler Colfax for Congress in Indiana in 1862, the two held joint meetings at all of the county seats in their district, as well as in other towns, for six weeks before the election. They met every day except Sunday. At each meeting there were two timekeepers and two moderators, chosen by the two parties. The meetings lasted for three hours, with one candidate making a one-hour opening statement, followed by a one-and-a-half-hour response and a half-hour closing rebuttal. The candidates alternated in leading off and closing.[29]

The speakers appeared before the characteristic venue of this political nation: the mass rally of the party faithful. Part entertainment, part information, all exhortation, these were large, often daylong affairs drawing people from all over a neighborhood, with railroads running special trains to the rally site. They were guided by the simple, and apparently accurate, notion that "the American people like to talk politics." Two to three thousand people would show up for a congressional or gubernatorial rally, not only voters, but their families as well, who "expected to make a full afternoon or evening of it. They . . . expected a featured speech to be partisan, stimulating, informative, entertaining—and long." As someone remembered much later, these "were occasions of great social enjoyment and festivity." [30]

Afterward, the candidates appeared in a series of evening meetings in different wards, towns, or precincts, on a schedule carefully worked out by the party committees. In 1852, an Ohio Democratic newspaper listed the meetings that the party's congressional candidate, Clement Vallandigham, was to hold each night. "It is particularly requested that the democrats of each place where appointments are made will provide a church, school house, or other suitable place for speaking, and make all other necessary arrangements." Food was made available, as were subsidiary speakers. It was considered a particular coup if some prominent speaker appeared alongside the local candidate. (The correspondence of the most prominent midcentury political leaders is filled with requests that they appear at some upcoming meeting to rally the faithful.) Careful attention was paid to the time of meetings as well as their frequency. As one New York newspaper put it in 1858, October was a good month for campaigning since "in that month the evenings are of good length, the people generally have leisure, and [they] will come out and hear." [31]

One rally, in Mississippi in 1844, has been well described by a participant, Reuben Davis:

> For the purpose of massing the people of a county at a given time, great barbecues were had, and after [Jefferson] Davis and [Henry S.] Foote had spoken, local orators would harangue the crowd. These discussions would include the very structure of our government, and all important measures of policy which had been proposed by either party since the foundation of our national existence.
>
> The main speakers were expected to be familiar with the history and facts of every subject alluded to, and to furnish the people with full and clear information. These discussions were, in fact, sort of political school, wherein lectures were delivered for the education of the masses. In this way our people were informed of the principles of government to a wonderful extent, and fitted for the freedom they enjoyed, and taught to watch with jealous scrutiny any infringement of that constitution which they regarded as the stronghold for their liberties.
>
> There were public speeches everywhere. Great barbecues succeeded each other, and were attended by multitudes, who thronged to the appointed places in wagons and carriages, on foot and on horseback; travelling for miles to enjoy these social and political festivals.

In these more sober and prosaic days, it may, perhaps, be difficult for people even to imagine the perfect abandonment of a whole population to the excitements and pleasures of such a carnival. The more rigid moralist may be even scandalized by the spectacle of whole communities given up to wild days of feasting, speech-making, music, dancing, and drinking, with perhaps, rough words now and then, and an honest hand-to-hand fight when debate was angry and blood hot.[32]

This extensive activity had a clear and fully calculated purpose: to stimulate the voter to come out and cast his ballot correctly, to maximize the party's totals and win the victory that was there if only everything was well organized and directed. "Inaction cannot compete with action. Supineness cannot cope with energy and activity." The target, of course, was election day, when the final set of organizational imperatives came into play. It was then that "every Whig Voter" (and Democrat, too) was "required to do his duty." This put particular strain on party workers. The *Springfield Republican* presented a characteristic checklist of the Massachusetts men's election-day duties. Each party unit should make sure "that every voting location had perfect poll lists," assign vigilance committees to "watch the polls," and, with teams of horses and buggies standing ready, keep track of who had voted, so they could send for those who had not. Organizations, in sum, had to "be active" and "get out every voter."[33]

Nor were ordinary party members immune from last-minute activity on behalf of the cause. "Let every democrat who can spare the time, devote at least five days before the election to the cause of POLK and DALLAS. Every man has his influence and can do something." On election day itself, it was crucial that "no democrat suffer business to interfere with the paramount calls of duty and patriotism. Vote first— vote at all events—and then see to it that none of your neighbors or acquaintances are remiss in their duty." Each man should "go to the election-ground early in the day, and remain there to vote yourselves and see that your friends vote!" Remember that "your work is not finished until you have brought every Republican voter in your township to the polls." Furthermore, keep track of who is voting, "and if you find that some are not coming, . . . have a buggy sent after them. . . . See that every Republican vote is polled."[34]

The last issues of party newspapers before polling day were filled with instructions, dire warnings about tricks and corrupt acts, and exhortations. Voting was a much less official act in these years than it became later, from the Progressive period onward. Local governments, working under state legislative authority, established polling sites, to be sure. Originally these had been only in county seats, but in this era they were placed in more and more convenient locations: not only in local schools, but in hotels, churches, prominent buildings, even saloons. The ballots, however, were supplied by the parties. They were usually printed well in advance and distributed by the state party newspaper; it was up to the local editors and party workers to get them to the voters.[35] Since all of this made the simple act of voting cumbersome and open to manipulation, the party newspapers carefully described what to look for and do on election day. Each ballot had to be deposited in a separate box by office in New York state, for example. Voters had to be sure that the spelling of candidates' names was correct on their ballot; otherwise it might not be counted.[36]

An essential component of an organization's responsibilities on election day was to preserve the purity of the polls. The other side was always up to something—usually voting people who were ineligible. False tickets to deceive the unwary, "bully boys" to intimidate voters, and forged ballots were all part of the enemy's arsenal. Therefore, party workers had to watch "every ward, township, borough and district." Each "must have a committee composed of stout, able-bodied and fearless men, whose especial duty it should be to watch the ballot boxes, to defend them from federal pillage." And still the work was not done. When the polling day was over, someone had to be on the scene to watch the counting and send the results to the county committees for unofficial tallying.[37]

The argument for organization never let up from the 1840's onward. Both major parties reacted, accepting the need for structure and for unremitting attention to the most minute details. All of that is clear from the reports and rhetoric in the party newspapers themselves, not only at the beginning of the period, in the 1840's, but afterward as well. "If eternal vigilance is the price of liberty, organization is its best guarantee," Tammany's William Sulzer told an audience in 1893. "Nothing can accomplish more good for the greatest number than the determined effort of men united together under one grand leadership, fighting for principles that represent truth and humanity."[38] The statement is perhaps unsurprising from a Tammany spokesman, but it reflected a larger commitment characteristic of the whole political nation and its parties.

"The Delegates Fresh from the People": Party Conventions Define The New Order

The heart and soul of the mid-nineteenth-century political structure, its "indispensable mode of organization," in a way previously unknown and subsequently forgotten were the numerous regular party conventions held at every level of American politics, from local to national. To the Americans of the time, conventions were "the meetings where the power of the people [was] felt and made manifest."[39] Andrew Jackson referred to convention delegates as being "fresh from the people." Others waxed more lyrical. "Our republican institutions offer nothing so splendid, nothing so well calculated to inspire the American with a firmer belief in the eternity and the justice of democracy, as these voluntary and periodical assemblages of the people. . . . These conventions are the voluntary efforts of the great people to retrace first principles, to restore first principles."[40]

Conventions were certainly a colorful experience to many observers, impossible not to notice. A few had been called early in the nation's history, but their real growth occurred in the late 1830's. "By mid-century [they] had become virtually an American art form." They reinforced the democratic, egalitarian commitments of nineteenth-century Americans and countered the image of closed, restricted, elite-dominated decision making associated with the legislative nominating caucus that had been dominant till then. But, critically, as the political nation took shape, the convention's other purposes also became clear. Most political participants fully recognized their larger, pragmatic usefulness, in fact, their "indispensability," in a pluralist political environment.[41]

Conventions provided a mechanism for sorting out differences about policies within a party, resolving the conflicts among partisans of different candidates, and settling the frequent intense disagreements over priorities. There had to be accord among party members, and it had to be reached with the widest possible participation. At the same time, conventions linked candidates to the voters, articulated what the party stood for, prepared it for the upcoming elections, and stamped legitimacy on what occurred under the party's banner. Conventions were called "to establish political principles, to settle political faith, to adopt a political creed, and to fix on a proper course of policy to be followed on all of the great questions of the time." They were "emphatically the *legislatures*" of the party "for the settlement of all minor differences about men and questions relating to party discipline and government." Each was "the high court" of its party, "the highest tribunal known" in the system.[42]

Arguments favoring the holding of conventions were widespread and powerfully articulated. In the early years of the political nation, such arguments were designed to overcome lingering hostility to political management and direction from above. Some emphasized the pragmatic theme: the convention was "the only legitimate mode by which we can concentrate strength for the coming contest." As the editor of the Raleigh *Standard* put it in 1846, "Without conventions we should expose ourselves to endless and aggravated divisions and finally to disruption and defeat." Much of the time, higher principles were stressed. Delegates were "a band of brothers" united for a "particular and virtuous purpose." Conventions were a "supplement to the constitution," the "voluntary and periodical assemblages of the people." The Whig National Convention in 1848 was "the bond of Whig Union."[43]

In sum, parties needed such meetings to define themselves, sort themselves out, and promote their common elements into a unified whole. As the Whig State Central Executive Committee of New York argued in 1841, in a letter to the "Whig electorate" of the state:

To enable [the party] to rally upon its principles, there must be unity of object and concert of action. These can be secured only by a full, free and dispassionate interchange among its members and the determination vigorously and unitedly to carry out and fully sustain the will of the party. Representatives fresh from the people will be able to communicate and concentrate public opinion, and thus furnish the landmarks and guides for the future action.[44]

So, "however objectionable in theory these extraconstitutional assemblies may be," the *American Review* believed, they had "their conveniences, rather . . . their necessity. They [were] a very important part of the machinery by which alone the preferences of a constituency composed of millions of voters, and scattered over a vast extent of country, [could] be concentrated." Further, they were "congenial with the habits of the people; they [were] approved by experience."[45]

Political leaders did not argue differently about conventions in private. As the Democratic editor Joshua Cunningham wrote to Polk in the late 1830's:

One of the best methods according to my judgement, of arousing the apathy of our friends, strengthening our cause, and insuring a full cooperation of our party, would be the holding of a State Convention a few months previous to the next general election. This would bring together most of the prominent men of our party from all parts of the state, ensure a free interchange of opinions, afford an opportunity for a complete organization of our strength, provide means for the communication of political information, and rouse up and reinvigorate the democratic spirit of the whole state.[46]

As a result of such attitudes, what James Chase calls "a layered pyramid of conventions" developed, "each level composed of delegates chosen by the one immediately beneath it."[47] Those at the lowest levels, in city wards, towns, and school districts, were called at the initiative of a newspaper editor or a prominent local party member, or by delegates from the previous year's meeting, a notice of the call appearing in the local newspaper. All were urged to come. Each citizen had, once again, a duty. "Those who stay away from the caucuses and primary meetings of the party have no right, afterwards, to complain if the proceedings are not to their wish; it is their business to attend, take an active part, express their opinions and wishes, and endeavor to make the action of the party what they think it ought to be." [48]

The county conventions replicated the actions of the "primary" meetings below them, nominating candidates, selecting delegates to the congressional district, legislative district, or state conventions, passing resolutions, and appointing the party's county executive committee to run things after the convention adjourned. There was one difference of some significance. At first, all party members and interested parties were urged to attend county conventions, as they did the local meetings. They, too, were originally mass rallies of the faithful. But over time more disciplined processes took over. Membership was limited, so that every town was represented in the convention in some proportion to others, defined by population, or the previous year's vote totals, or the number of state legislators. Much effort was expended to ensure that all areas were represented. Here the notion of delegates, not ralliers, came to dominate. Delegates were "agents or attorneys in fact, to whose care the business of the people is confided." A more professionally coordinated, businesslike way of operating was settling in in party affairs. [49]

Just below the apex of the system were the state conventions. Each spoke the "voice of men fresh from the people, . . . ripened and sharpened by the animated discussion that had passed in the local conventions." Usually called by the party's state central committee, they made statewide nominations, selected presidential electors, chose delegates to the national convention, and appointed the various party committees needed for the upcoming campaign. They were usually held in state capitals or some centrally located city and were scheduled when convenient for the farming and legal populations, the bulwarks of the mid-nineteenth-century political nation. The time fixed was "such as allows the least busy portion of the summer in most agricultural districts for the holding of the town and district caucuses, and thus gives to the farmers ample time to attend and participate in these popular expressions of preference for delegates and candidates." [50]

At the top of the system were the quadrennial national conventions, "the grand inquest of the nation," which only became regularized in the late 1830's.[51] Like the others, they began as relatively unstructured mass rallies and then developed into well-organized, delegated meetings with clear rules and institutional structures. Meeting in some central or tactically advantageous place, they followed the same pattern as all the other conventions in the system. In the Democratic National Convention of 1852, for example, the delegates formed a Committee on Organization to select permanent officers and report rules; had a Committee on Credentials to determine who was eligible to attend and a Committee on Resolutions to articulate the party's creed and policy preferences. Each committee consisted of one delegate from each state, usually selected by the other members of his state's delegation.[52]

All conventions, at every level, were cloaked with tremendous power. Each was the fountainhead of absolute authority within the party—but always within its representative responsibility. Its purpose was not "invention but . . . promulgation; not to discover but to declare." The conventions provided focus for party members and legitimized what the party did. They did their work well. As one campaign newspaper noted in 1852, "by the efforts of the convention the party has been rallied, reorganized, drilled and disciplined afresh. In the platform are the rules of service, the order of battle, and the plan of the campaign."[53]

Conventions in this political nation functioned as consulting and organizing mechanisms out of which a sense of the party emerged. At the same time, they socialized and disciplined people who had come together from all over the district, state, or nation. Occasionally, disagreements of great intensity caused bolts from state and national conventions by disaffected delegates. But despite such critical episodes, party members never lost their faith in conventions as necessary political mechanisms. Most of the time, that faith was not misplaced; party meetings usually met the expectations and hopes held for them. "Men learn to be tolerant in such a setting. They learn to be just: They learn to be magnanimous. Their ideas are enlarged—their horizons extended—their prejudices scattered to the winds." Men learned there "to yield a little to the general good." Finally, conventions always, at all levels, set the course to be followed by party members until they met again. Each party's state committees carried out "the will of the party, as expressed at the [last] Convention." And, as one participant in the Pennsylvania state convention argued, the decisions of the previous national convention were "binding" on all of them "and unalterable until another National Convention" changed something. Its platform remained "the creed of the party" until revised.[54]

"The Minute Men of Party"

This growing network of conventions, local and state committees, speakers, campaign laborers, and poll watchers demanded the services of enormous numbers of people to make it work. It was by their "labor only" that the party could "ensure success." Certain segments of the system had no difficulty in attracting workers. Conventions were always filled with the deeply committed partisans, legislators, local officeholders, and prominent men of the state or neighborhood. As one newspaper reported, a recent convention was composed of sheriffs, government clerks, road commissioners, canal supervisors, and the like, "the minute men of the party."[55] In addition, the new breed of professional politicians, from Van Buren and Polk on down, were always in attendance, as were the party editors. These men also dominated party committees at all levels because of their willingness to serve and their availability at all seasons of the year. To be sure, those who attended conventions and other mass meetings, as well as those who worked the hustings, were not all leaders, or even aspiring ones. Nor were they all in the pay of some partisanly dominated government agency. Still, structurally and institutionally, party organizations were, more often than not, dominated by the professional leaders who set up and ran the apparatus. In William Gienapp's words, in this era, "professional politicians largely controlled the political system."[56]

When it came to actual campaigning and poll work, there was "drudgery to be done by somebody in all political operations."[57] But such labor was usually hard to come by. To be sure, the plain people campaigned and worked at various volunteer tasks, and some times there were enough government workers to do many tasks, as in the census year 1850. But volunteers were always at a premium. It was energetic individuals who made the difference in most campaigns. In 1854, Louis Lott of Seneca county, New York, wrote to the State Whig Committee asking for several thousand printed Whig ballots; he would pay for them. He also informed the committee that he had called the Whig county convention. Polk's extensive personal activities in Tennessee in the late 1830's and early 1840's, not only when he was running but at other times as well, are exhausting to follow. Polk stimulated everything and did a great deal himself, both from his headquarters in Nashville and as he traveled the state on his law business.

He planned and meticulously laid out the details of organization and what was to be done; he exhorted, arranged, and chaired. He spoke himself when no one else was available.[58]

Without men like Lott and Polk, parties could not have operated. Less statesmen than technicians, they characterized the reality of the organizational revolution, the need for leadership and direction to go along with the commitment to widespread democratic participation in party affairs. If a party did not find enough such people in each campaign, its supporters were "like sheep in the mountains without a shepherd."[59]

"The Common Law of Democracy"

As the organizational revolution took hold in the American political nation, it was accompanied by the articulating and acceptance of a set of rules and understandings, and the internalizing of a number of habits, perceptions, and customs, that all together added up to "the common law of democracy." That law defined what was acceptable and expected behavior within the political parties and what was not; it imposed restraints and set boundaries. It was considered "more potent by far than written laws or paper constitutions." One did not readily contravene these understandings, or break the rules they suggested, or challenge the law's definitions of propriety if one wished to be politically active and effective. There could be no "recreancy to the time honored usages . . . of the Democratic party."[60]

The Barnburner-Hunker controversy in the New York state Democratic party in 1848 illuminates how such commitments came into play. Split by the slavery-extension controversy and the Polk administration's treatment of New York party members, both factions repeatedly argued in public about who had best lived by the party's rules and customs. The editor of the Barnburners' newspaper constantly reiterated a simple, but to its editor compelling, truth—that they had, until then, abided by "the traditional usages of the party, are regular, according to the strictest forms of those usages," and therefore derived their title "by descent from the first organization, of the Democracy." Their opponents, on the other hand, had not, and therefore could have no right to the party name, its organization, its place on the ballot, or the support of Democrats elsewhere. It was the Hunkers, not the Barnburners, who had the "taint of irregularity" about them and who were really "in the attitude of a third party." In light of the way the "regular" nominee, Lewis Cass, and his associates had ignored the proprieties, had not given the Barnburners their due at the national convention and accepted the Hunkers as legitimate, the editor stated, they considered themselves absolved from supporting him.[61]

The components of this passionately articulated common law involved, first, as already suggested, the party selection process: who was empowered to call a convention, and what legitimized its actions and thus made a nomination regular. Such regular nominations were the centerpiece of party affairs. A great deal of effort was expended, therefore, to define just how a convention happened, an effort that grew out of the original spontaneous nature of political activity, and that ended with clear rules establishing the correct ways. Parties called their various conventions by action of the previous year's convention, a call of a party committee, or one from the members of a state legislature. Whichever form was followed, party men took pains to conform to "immemorial usage." Despite a preference for Van Buren in 1844, a Philadelphia Democratic Club announced that its members would support the national convention's nominee so long as that meeting was "chosen and held in such time and manner as may be acceptable to a majority of the party," and so long as the voting therein "may be considered just and proper." Over and over again, party members were reminded that "'Regular Nominations' is one of the oldest and safest rules known to the party." This had to be. "We go for our systems and usages, and no party can ever be sustained without sustaining them."[62]

Such attention to propriety never abated, for once it was established it led directly to the most important element of the common law provoked by the organizational revolution and its penetration of the political world. Americans in all eras have often articulated a notion of individual conscience stronger than any collective impulse and demands. Every free person, some would argue, has the right to behave as he or she deems proper, certainly in politics. That was not true in party affairs as they developed in the 1840's. There were powerful pressures against individual action and toward unanimity or, at least, accepting the majority's decision. Once the convention had selected its candidates and drafted its platform, that was the end of discussion. Party members now had their directive. Douglas Jaenicke writes of the Democrats that "neither differences over policy, conscientious scruples nor personal preferences for the candidates legitimated defection." Whigs expressed much the same attitude. A Virginia delegate said in his state convention in 1839, "I come for the great and holy purpose of promoting union, concert and conciliation." In party affairs, "all bitterness and animosity must be laid aside; conciliation and harmony must be preached."[63]

Going one's own way was neither conducive to political effectiveness nor supportive of the American political nation's greater goals. Whatever right individuals had to their own perspective, it had to be subordinated to the good of the whole. It was no honor to be a heretic or a schismatic—two terms frequently used and condemned in the political discourse of the times. Supporting the decisions of a party convention was "submission to the will of the majority, the only principle, the only rule of conduct, the only usage and system" that could keep parties together and effective. Conventions, when properly constituted, therefore, had to be obeyed. As the editor of the *Ohio State Journal* told his fellow Whigs in 1852:

You have held your primary meetings, selected your delegates, held your City Convention and nominated your ticket, which nominations, after they were made by that Convention, were unanimously confirmed. No one has dared to aver that fraud or improper means were used to produce this result. What, then, is the duty of all Whigs? Clearly to support the ticket.

Any delegate or candidate who did not support the convention's decision was "recreant to good faith and implied honor without which no party or association can exist." Party conventions were not under the law of the land; they were "governed by [a] code of honor," and the integrity and success of a party depended on its "rigid adherence" to that code. Accordingly, any violation of "the faith of a Convention by [delegates or party members] should be regarded as a kind of minor treason."[64]

In American politics, "personal preferences must yield to the will of the Majority—and so long as conventions are recognized, their choice must control." When William Seward received a reduced majority in his re-election as governor of New York in a very good Whig year, even though he was "the regular, fairly and unanimously nominated candidate" of the party, New York's Whig voters were severely chastised. No one who was a Whig had a right not to vote for him "for a mere difference of opinion on some secondary proposition or measure." All party factions had to submit "to a majority *when that majority is fairly and honestly expressed. This is the party ligament which connects and holds them together.*"[65]

The Whig *American Review* summed all this up in 1846: "Anything short of immorality or untrustworthiness should be no bar to our voting for the party candidates. We should sacrifice preferences to principles, favorite candidates to important measures, men to policy, personal, local, or temporary interests to national, general, and permanent interests." It was "better to vote for a questionable man, and an unquestionable principle, than for the best of men if his election would afford a questionable principle opportunity of development." Platforms, too, were the law of the party and were "not submitted as a thing to be weighed and pondered and considered." The party convention had passed it: everyone had to fall into line. That was the core of the message. Party discipline was "indispensable." Everyone should always "vote with the party. . . . Let us remember that this country must be governed by a party—always—forever."[66]

The spirit of self-sacrifice and commitment to the collective had to permeate the mind of every party member. That was the ultimate propriety. Members of a convention had to "sacrifice their private griefs upon the altar of the common good." So did party workers on the hustings and the voters they appealed to. The Whig grandee Hamilton Fish laid it out for his fellows in 1856: "It rarely happens that an individual citizen finds in the persons presented, even by the party to which he belongs, precisely the candidates whom he would have preferred; at best he has to yield something of his individual preferences to the wishes and preferences of others." The "very theory of our popular Government by party," the Republicans insisted, was the "concession of the minority to the majority. Every man must concede something. No man can have everything in the arrangement of public affairs precisely as he would wish." Therefore, as an Alabama Whig told a Massachusetts audience in 1849, "the necessity that gives birth to political parties gives birth to compromise. Persons holding extreme positions must submit to the dominant tone of sentiment; they must be willing to wait their time—to yield a little—to give place today, that they may take their turn tomorrow."[67]

The same proprieties were to be observed in government. Party members had to support those whom they had elected. Each had an "implied covenant with the men [whom] he invests with political power." Officeholders, too, had to behave properly. This meant that when someone was elected to office "upon the acknowledged basis of the party [he belonged to], he must either adhere to that faith, and endeavor to sustain the principles embraced therein" on all policy matters, or otherwise become "an apostate." Whatever disagreements there might be, these were overridden by the commitment to the agreement to work together and support one's friends. Anyone who did not do so, "favors the destruction of the Whig party."[68]

Those making the argument claimed that it convinced the faithful. "Thousands [of Democrats] who despised the nominee . . . still voted the ticket because they imagined it as regular and legitimate." Over and over again, such party loyalty was manifested because "individual ideas have yielded to national principles—sectional jealousies to constitutional devotion, and personal aggrandizement to the general welfare of the party." There were some exceptions, to be sure, a few who neither heard nor heeded the message. Some spokesmen argued for the supremacy of individual conscience, evidence that the anticollectivist and antiparty approaches were not dead. But such voices were now thoroughly drowned out. A new common law had established itself in the political world and dominated the arguments—and the minds and behavior—of those who participated in politics at every level, from voter to officeholder.[69]

Skeptics may suggest that all these pleas for unity indicate the continued presence of a great deal of factionalism and fragmentation in American party politics; that all such discussion was in fact a sign of weakness. That there were always disagreements and troubling splits within the parties is inarguable. But the extraordinary dialogue that went on and the direction it took suggest the deepening impression on the body politic of a set of commitments and attitudes, a consensus about certain matters of politics, that underscores the power of the organizational imperative now dominating the American political nation.

How extensive and well organized were the attempts to build elaborate party organizations at every level? A contemporary, Jabez Hammond, had a sure answer: by 1837, "in every town and county of the state [New York] the democratic party was perfect in its organization and discipline."[70] Some modern historians are not convinced, however, arguing that nineteenth-century party organizations were more haphazard and ad hoc, less permanent, dependent not on the organizational imperatives that involved many people, but on the extraordinary exertions of the prominent few. For Marc Kruman, the state party organizations in the 1840's "were not quite the well-oiled partisan machines that historians have contended they were. Such a notion exaggerates their efficiency and power." Nor were the national organizations highly centralized, efficient, or permanent. Kruman, and others with similar views, admit that things developed into more regularized channels in the next decade, although always with considerable variation from state to state.[71]

Certainly, in reading the correspondence and newspapers of the time, it is easy to see that much was exhortation to do better, not report of accomplishment, that every party depended on the exertions of the few such as Polk, rather than the efforts of the many, that complaints abounded about those who did not "do their duty."[72] Certainly, also, party organizations varied widely from state to state in the 1840's, as they had late in the previous decade. State conventions, for example, did not meet every year in a few states. In noncompetitive local areas, where one party dominated political affairs, organizational structures were often haphazard, and district conventions did not meet regularly. Much has also been made of the organizational decentralization and lack of clear authority patterns within the parties. Their pyramidical structure did not mean power from the top down to each successive component below. In particular, the national parties had little authority over the state parties, even into the 1880's. And though the state parties, in their turn, had better control over local branches, they, too, were often limited in their reach.[73]

But the point, it seems to me, is not to expect perfection, tight structuring, and clear lines of authority, based on some ideal model of party organizations. The goal of comprehensiveness was always sought, and many elements composing an efficient model were present, if not yet what they would be later. More to the point was the trajectory of party development and the organizational similarity across the nation. Organization was decentralized; but it looked and generally acted the same everywhere. Organization was imperfect and incomplete; but its roots, defining elements, and thrust were clear. There was, as well, systematic commitment, a movement in a particular direction, and a shift in values toward collectivities as the means of promoting and achieving political goals. The atmosphere and mechanics of each campaign were the same everywhere from the late 1830's on. Each party's component elements had a symmetrical shape across time and place. The triangular organizations of the various committees, the ways each operated, what each expected to do and accomplish, all had a similar substance and look to them. The elements, reasons, and responsibilities were the same. There were few surprises or unfamiliar processes as one moved from state to state.

Moreover, too much has been made of the fact that organizations were the creatures of the conventions that created them for a specific electoral season, and no longer. It is true, if somewhat colorfully expressed, that "on the day after the election virtually the entire organizational edifice . . . entered into a mad race of dissolution." But the fact that there were so many elections following each other throughout every year gave a practical permanence to party organizations anyway. As the editor of the Albany *Argus* said in 1844, "Organization, like everything else, has undergone great improvements during the past four years. It is now far more systematized [with a] minuteness and a certainty [about it]."[74]

The crucial point is that after the 1830's, the balance had clearly shifted and organization had become the norm, seen as necessary for carrying on American democratic politics in this particular political situation. The direction was clear, the trend line starkly obvious. Assumptions and practices were hardening into a consensus and a routine that accepted that organization counted for more than it ever had before. The similarity of Lincoln's plan of organization in 1840 and one circulated in the same year among New York Democrats is compelling.[75] The development and systematic use of these organizational forms varied in time and reach. But they soon emerged across the whole political spectrum. The initiative had originally been northern, but by the late 1830's and the 1840's, as noted earlier, "in the South [too] both parties exhibited a singular aptitude for organization. . . . Both parties recognized the centrality of organization and worked to build effective organization." Indeed, by then few participants in this political nation could even conceive of a partyless politics. As William Seward put it in 1856, "Every party must stand, not on the individual protestations of its members, but on the tendency of its corporate actions."[76]

CHAPTER FOUR

The Connecting Tissue:
Ideas, Principles, and Policies
in American Politics

FROM THE BEGINNING OF this political era there was a strong commitment to the importance of ideas in American politics. In their unremitting arguments about policy, both Democrats and Whigs effectively framed the agenda of the American political nation and placed it before the voters with a relentless rhetorical vitality.[1] As the editor of the Whig *American Review* summed it up: "Those who have composed the Whig party of this country have professed to unite for the purpose of promoting and maintaining certain great distinctive principles, as being essential to the preservation of our form of government, and the advancement of the real interests and the true prosperity of the nation."[2] Such claims and their articulation of what was at stake was a second means, after organization, of energizing the crucial electoral dimension of this political nation.

"The Embodiment of Principle"

Political leaders on both sides began by justifying the relevance of their efforts. Parties, they said, were not just electoral machines, devoid of principles and purpose. "Remember democrats of New York," a party editor wrote in 1849, "it is not merely the success of your candidates that you strive for; but it is for the triumph of principles." Parties, another wrote, "must address the reason, understanding and conscience of men." When "arrayed on this basis they rise above a mere scramble for men and for place, and assume the dignity which attaches to a struggle for principle." Parties were "but the embodiment of principle" and became "faction—dishonorable in its spirit—when [they ceased] to be guided by principle." Still another put it most dramatically: "We will cheerfully worship at the shrine of principle." Principles "constitute our staff of life—our bond of union" as a party.[3]

Party leaders never tried to hide the specifics of their beliefs. They celebrated, as well, their steadfastness to the policies they advocated. Each's ideological positions and policy commitments took up an enormous amount of space in party publications and an enormous amount of time at speeches and rallies. Parties published at every level of their activities, pamphlets, addresses to the people, speeches, and, most particularly, platforms filled with their ideas and policies. The drafters of the platforms and the dispensers of the message were quite conscious of what they were doing: providing "political charts by which everyone can tell for what he casts his vote."[4] Whether in published materials or in speeches on the hustings, party candidates and workers followed the platform's dictates assiduously, both in campaign seasons and out.

Party spokesmen did not take a different stance in private from their public pronouncements. They repeatedly articulated to each other the strong relationship they saw between principles and governing. As James K. Polk put it to William L. Marcy just before his inauguration in 1845: "The principles and policy which will be observed and maintained during my administration are included in the Resolutions adopted by the National Convention. . . . In the Inaugural Address which I have prepared, . . . these principles are distinctly recognized and reiterated." Polk said the same to himself in his diary. "I will adhere sternly [as President] to my principles," he wrote. Polk's biographer has noted that the Tennessean's major public statement at the beginning of his term, his first annual message to Congress at the end of 1845, "called for a complete consummation of every tendency of Jacksonian policy, a final settlement of all the Jacksonian issues." The "pure and holy principles" of the Democratic party meant something to Polk—either personally or tactically, or probably both.[5]

There is, of course, an epistemological problem, never better stated than by a meeting of National Republicans in New England in 1828. "Professions, we admit, are not the surest test of principles and are to be relied on only in the absence of better proofs."[6] Certainly, political ideas could have been a camouflage for interests, or deceptive, if not meaningless, in this political nation. But even if that was the case, the way they were framed had some "substantive and evocative meaning to the audiences to whom they were directed." Politicians gave form to the political world through their party's rhetoric and sharpened the political consciousness of those whom they addressed. What they said to voters had to characterize the world in meaningful and understandable ways. Certainly, their rhetoric voiced something about what people believed or, at least, expected to hear. Beyond that, many of the specific issues that the political leaders talked about touched very deep chords of belief in American society.[7]

Rhetoric appealed to, and helped organize, both specific interests and fundamental values. What leaders said to voters, if successful, tied them to parties in meaningful ways. This was because, in Samuel P. Hays's formulation, parties served as "a critical element in bridging the gap between the smaller context of daily life within which the attitudes and values of voters are formed and the larger strategies of political leaders in state and national affairs." The many mass political subcultures in the United States, each with its own perspective, values, and ideas, had to be linked together and to the larger patterns of belief and issues on the scene. All politics originates as, and remains in some sense, local. But parties mobilized local battles into larger and larger confrontations, reaching across districts, states, and the nation. Party rhetoric was central to this process. "Through words," Daniel Rodgers concludes, "coalitions are made out of voters who, stripped of their common rallying cries and slogans, would quickly dissolve into jarring fragments."[8]

From the late 1830's, the dialogue between the parties expressed quite robust disagreements. "We want no milk and water platforms," one editor wrote. "Give us something to stand on and vital principles to fight for, and all will be well." Whigs and Democrats were different coalitions with different sweeps to them, and both tried to emphasize that difference and pluck the right strings to appeal to their own interest groups. Each party aggregated America's interest groups in a selective way, not reaching out to everyone but only to a portion of the electorate. Neither party digested every demand, interest, and pressure within society or was all things to all men. Each major party, therefore, had a different center of gravity. "In politics," a writer in one party journal pointed out, "there is a moral chemistry which obtains and vindicates itself as imperatively as natural chemistry does in the laws of the physical universe. We aggregate all bodies which have an affinity to ourselves, and this aggregation will take place whether politicians will it or not." Parties could not build what spokesmen often referred to as "unnatural coalitions." As a result, there were clearly distinctive political mind-sets in America: a Democratic mentality and a Whig, later Republican, mentality.[9]

Not surprisingly, the ideological lines became more sharply drawn as organizational development took hold. To be sure, many of these matters had been debated since the 1820's. But, as with the maturing of parties generally, the Panic of 1837 gave the final push that crystallized the issues and where each party stood on them. The crisis of political economy firmly established, as we have seen, "clear, contrasting and durable party positions." As the party in power nationally, the Democrats were on the defensive during the economic downturn. Quick to take the opening, the Whigs vigorously attacked their opponents for their ideological failures: Democratic policies had destroyed the economy; the Whigs "must substitute for these ruinous measures, the provisions that will restore a sound currency and reward industry and enterprise." [10]

The Whig onslaught began in the state elections of 1837 and 1838 and intensified in the presidential campaign of 1840, which, despite its reputation for excessive and nonideological highjinks, "was not [only] huzzas." The Whig campaign that year "skillfully blended a concern for republican ideals with the economic self interest of the voters. In an effective way, it brought into sharp focus the opposition to Van Buren's administration that had grown over the last three years"—that is, to the Democrats' specific policies and the way they had operated the political economy of the nation. Party rhetoric, organized and artfully presented on the campaign trail, sharpened the focus. That much of the discourse sounded not only reasonable, but fresh, undoubtedly helped. It was, in the late 1830's, an energizing new era in rhetoric, as well as in organization, a time when, as Daniel Howe has nicely put it, "the electorate was not yet jaded." [11]

Consensus and Conflict

There was much common ground between the two major parties (and the minor ones as well) at the onset of this political nation. The family quarrels of the American political parties, no matter how intense and bitter, were not great ideological divides over the nature of their society, although they were often expressed that way. As Robert Wiebe has written, partisan differences were a "struggle over the interior design of the same ideological house." Each party tried to establish its legitimacy by appealing to America's republican tradition and aligning itself with a concern for the continuation of the American experiment as a middle-class-oriented, capitalist-driven society. Whatever the parties' differences over definitions and prescriptions for the future, the American ideological battle celebrated the free man in a free and liberal capitalist country. [12]

But these positive values were always threatened by both external and internal enemies. The successful American experiment menaced foreign powers that preferred alternative political forms and hated American republicanism as a model capable of stirring their own oppressed populations. On the inside, the danger came not just from those who clung tenaciously to old prejudices against freedom and individualism; there were always groups and individuals in the United States whose actions, for whatever reasons, threatened to corrupt the American experiment, weaken it, and, ultimately, destroy it. America, therefore, was—and was seen to be—in a perpetual contest to protect republican liberty from its many enemies. The purpose of politics, and of political institutions, was to defend and promote the essential values and well-being of the people against all enemies, foreign and domestic. Politics was central and necessary for a free people to achieve national purposes.[13]

Such consensual views underlay American political discourse in the middle of the nineteenth century. Yet within that consensus, there was great room for differences. As R. Laurence Moore has written in another context, "Competing groups turned similar values to very different uses." In consequence, even as the parties operated over common terrain, they mapped it differently. Each party drew on consensual elements in American life and, by interpretation, found important distinctions between them, differences to fight over, often quite sharply. As the editor of the *American Review* put it in 1846, the two existing parties were "real, necessary expressions of two contrasted policies, of two great conflicting ideas, which go to the root and extend to the utmost branches of the national life."[14]

There were often severe disagreements within the parties, not just among blocs and factions, but among leaders as well. But though there were moments when factions from the different parties came close to one another, these cross-party likenesses were far outweighed by the broad areas of agreement within each coalition and the sharp differences between Whigs, Republicans, and Democrats. Each party, as Horatio Seymour said of the Democrats in 1852, shared "common political feelings, recollections, hopes and fears." Each party had a distinct color, style, set of ideas, and singular bite, permitting political leaders to frame the debate in black-and-white terms. "Whigs and Democrats presented the electorate with rival images of national purpose," Daniel Walker Howe suggests. To put things very broadly, the Whigs proposed a society that would be economically diverse but culturally uniform; the Democrats preferred the economic uniformity of a society of small farmers and artisans but were more tolerant of cultural and moral diversity."[15]

These differences could be expressed in the most searing terms:

To the extent of the respective relations of the two great parties in this country to the constitution, there is just as broad a line of demarcation between them—a line as insurmountable as if it had been placed there by Nature. This line is an organic, a fundamental, and an ineradicable barrier; and though partisans often prate about the union of both parties upon one common ground of nationality, it never has been, and we fear it never will be, the case. You cannot reconcile to the democracy the foes of the constitution. Half-fanatical, half-British, and entirely committed, through years of agitation and of trial, the element that opposes the constitution will no more surrender its fierce hatred of that bond of our Union than the democratic party will surrender its high resolve never to cease its vigilant and determined hostility to its machinations.[16]

Parties remained, forever, nose to nose. "The difference between the two parties admits of no compromise—it is radical—total—almost immeasurable."[17]

Whigs vs. Democrats

Democrats repeatedly argued that there was a permanent two-party division in the United States, dating back to the Revolutionary period but "not fully developed until after the adoption of the Constitution." In the Constitutional Convention there "appeared distinct and tangible, the germs of the two great parties, into which, since the organization of the present government, the country has been divided." The party lines "originally drawn [in the 1790's] are not obliterated." Although "the 'designation' of *Federalists* (that name having become unpopular) has been abandoned, . . . yet the political principles of the leading men of the party, who give direction to its policy whether called '*National Republicans*' or '*Whigs*' are unchanged." The Whig "is the same party which, under the name of 'Federalist,' was encountered by Jefferson in the early days of the Republic. . . . Scarcely a principle or a practice can be named in which ancient Federalism and modern Whiggery are not entirely parallel."[18]

The battle had been between centralization and liberty "from the commencement of the government to the present day." As a result, there had been two great parties in the country, "a national consolidation party and a state rights republican party—the one leaning to the side of power; the other to that of liberty." This conflict was not only permanent but inevitable. "Notwithstanding the rout of the old Federalists by the election of Mr. Jefferson, . . . the efforts of that party for the restoration of their beloved aristocracy have never for an instant been remitted." It remained today "the intention of the leading Federal Whigs to establish a *strong government*, after the *model* of that of *England*." Obviously, Democrats in the 1830's had once again "to fight . . . the battle of '98—We have to meet the same federal party." [19]

Given the fate of the Federalists, it is not surprising that the Democrats made this linkage—or that the Whigs stoutly denied the connection. Political parties, the Whigs countered, should not live in the past. "We have neither taste nor skill for groping among the moldering relics of dead controversies." The "mere names of parties which have sprung up and passed away before our day are to us nothing." To Americans it should matter "very little whether a man were on the right or wrong side of a question which was put at rest twenty years ago." The war of 1812 had "destroyed both . . . old parties." Therefore, both "the Jacksonian Democratic and the Whig parties were in many respects new parties." Consequently, Americans should "place no stress on these by-gone controversies." To argue otherwise was to deceive the people, for "any attempt to connect the *WHIGS* . . . with the *ADAMS* administration [was] as bad as forgery." [20]

These arguments over what was at stake in the 1830's and 1840's resonated with the specific arguments over economic policy and the nature and future of American society. The United States was blessed with vast resources waiting to be developed. The triumph of liberal capitalism in the quarter century after 1789 guaranteed that they would be developed. But how and under what conditions? No one denied that the government had some role to play. But did it go beyond establishing general rules and then maintaining order? In the economic realm, the Democrats forcefully stressed the free play of natural forces and objected to any actions—especially by the national government—that, in the name of promoting growth and prosperity, served special economic interests. Government guaranteed that the rules would be observed, and that everyone would have an equal opportunity to share in abundance. But regulation, control, and specific bounties were dangerous and unfair, especially at the national level.

Democrats, in the words of the *Democratic Review* in 1855, "understood the voluntary system, and are not coercionists. They desire to drive no man." They preferred "the blessings of a simple, frugal and *constitutional* administration of the Government." Representative Archibald Yell of Arkansas summed it up in a congressional speech in 1838: "I am a foe of those who would waste the public treasure," he said. "I am a foe to all splendid schemes of Government; I go for an economical administration of the affairs of the country; and am determinedly hostile to high tariffs [and] quixotic expeditions to the South Seas." Democrats, it was clear, must "agitate for economy." They had opposed "extravagant and exceptionable appropriations" that brought with them the growth of government.[21]

The Whig position was summed up in a statement in the *Whig Almanac* in 1843. The government's role was not, nor should it be, "purely negative." Rather, the government "should exert a beneficent, paternal, fostering influence upon the Industry and Prosperity of the People." Whigs always "distinguished" themselves "from their opponents, by the attribution of a beneficent and protective power to government." The government could and should be used "to advance the welfare of the people, and not as a system of checks and shackles devised to prevent all other action than such as may be necessary to keep the machinery in motion." As the *American Review* put it in 1852, the "first" Whig principle was "the improvement of the natural resources of the country by the action of government." In Howe's words, Whigs supported "purposeful progress versus drift toward chaos."[22]

A number of historians have suggested that, in the early liberal climate of the 1830's, two distinct socioeconomic thrusts informed these rhetorical positions, an agrarian one and a commercial one. As Sean Wilentz argues:

Democrats and their opponents refined their republican appeals—to fight "purse-proud aristocrats" or "executive usurpers"—in ways that promoted their own political interests and liberal ideals but yoked together, at least on election day, the support of a wide range of voters, across the lines of wealth and occupation. The exact nature of these appeals varied at different times and in different places, stressing economic questions, "social questions," and (at times) political personality. Through the thicket of popular politics, however, a general pattern can be discerned: while both Whigs and Democrats were liberal parties led by different members of new and existing elites, the Whigs tended to draw their popular support chiefly from men who believed they (and the Republic) benefited from the ongoing transformation of American market and class relations. The Democrats tended to appeal to those who did not.

The Democrats, unlike the Whigs, talked about the dangers to "the Republican simplicity of our free institutions" and the "pure, simple, self-denying, economical principles of EQUAL REPUBLICAN government." And, as Howe suggests, they viewed "economic change as a 'zero-sum game,' in which one group's advantage comes at the expense of another, an attitude hardly rooted in notions of expansive capitalist growth and prosperity."[23]

Parties divided in the same way over the role of government in noneconomic policy spheres. If America was to become a better society, was that to be brought about by government action? The Democrats said no. To them, "the only use of government is *to keep off evil. We do not want its assistance in seeking after good* [because] he is as much a slave who is forced to his own good as he who is unwillingly plunged into evil." That theme never changed. Democrats, the editor of a major party newspaper reminded his readers, "oppose the intervention of the State to search into the affairs of citizens and coerce them into habits of virtue." They trusted the people to rule themselves because they were "at least capable of deciding upon what they shall eat and drink, upon what due observance they shall render to religious rites, and of restraining their passions without any new intervention of judges, juries and jailors." Any "great multiplicity of laws," Democrats argued, "disgraces a nation." They understood, "as a central consolidated power, managing and directing the various general interests of society, all government is evil, and the parent of evil. A strong and active democratic *government* in the common sense of the term, is an evil, differing only in degree and mode of operation and not in nature, from a strong despotism."[24]

The Whigs, Democrats charged, desired "to bring all subjects relating to human happiness under the control of legislation—to elevate the State into all governing, all absorbing power." It was a charge to which the Whigs readily pleaded guilty. In their search for societal improvement, "they did not believe in leaving others alone." They enunciated, as one of their major principles, "respect for an organized central government, as a means of securing national progress and unanimity." Behind that, in turn, was a debate about order, harmony, and the way to prosperity. Governments were necessary because of the ever-present danger of disharmony in American society. Lawrence Kohl suggests that Whigs feared that "beneath the harmony and union of the Constitution lurked revolution and anarchy." They saw Democrats as engaging in political activities that were "essentially revolutionary" and anticonstitutional. To Whigs, the Democrats routinely adopted principles "inconsistent with obedience to law and the maintenance of order."[25]

They, on the other hand, were "the party of order and constitutional security, the party whose creed [was] positive and not negative, constructive, not destructive." They had "characteristic regard for law and order" and an "unconquerable repugnance to revolution or anarchy." That underlay everything that followed. As John Ashworth sums up: "Just as the Whigs were eager to employ the power of government to facilitate economic growth they were able to contemplate its use to promote essentially moral causes. The assumptions underlying both types of intervention were similar, if not identical. Both proceeded from a view of society which placed the community before the individual."[26]

Within the confines of the American nation, therefore, there was a real sense, powerfully expressed, of deep political polarization, of a great chasm of values and specific differences dividing Whigs from Democrats into unrelentingly warring armies. As one Democratic editor put it in 1852, the "perpetual and glorious issue between the Democracy and Whiggery" was the power of government versus the power of the masses. "Heaven and hell are not wider apart, or more different in character, than these principles."[27]

The Policy Agendas

Each party moved from espousing general perspectives into the commonplace discourse of interest-group conflict. At one level, there was a series of economic policy differences concerning the nation's credit and financial systems, tariff rates, the disposal of the federal lands, and the responsibility of government to help finance and build roads, canals, and later, railroads. Similarly, there were foreign policy matters that flashed alive in the 1840's. Finally, there was a series of matters reflecting deep social differences within the country, both the longstanding political conflict in America "between the Celtic and Puritan races" and another between competing sectional values and perspectives. All of these issues were "important ones, and . . . involved" in every election.[28]

National economic policy, particularly the credit system, structured party policy debates from the 1830's on. The Democrats became anti-Bank in the Van Buren years and remained so. The American business community had indulged in "over-banking, over-trading and [an] insane spirit of speculation." America had created "privileged banking corporations" as a "self-constituted, dangerous and irresponsible power." Therefore, Andrew Jackson's "victory over the United States Bank [was] scarcely less in importance than his victory at New Orleans." Since Democrats believed that "the natural laws of trade [would] best regulate the currency and the exchanges of our country," there had to be an end to "the fatal connection between Bank and State." Democrats wanted the public's money kept "where it [could] neither be wrongfully used, or stolen." The Independent Treasury Bill, pushed by Van Buren in the late 1830's to shift the government's deposits and, therefore, the control of its income, away from banks was America's "second declaration of Independence."[29]

Similarly, to Democrats, a high tariff was a "system of plundering the laboring classes." As their national platform starkly put it in 1840 and every four years thereafter, "Justice and sound policy forbid the Federal Government to foster one branch of industry to the detriment of any other." Democrats wanted no special favors for anyone in other economic development areas either. They stood in "undeviating . . . opposition to harbor and river improvements, to the construction of lighthouses and to the opening of great public roads." To their mind, "legislation [had] nothing to do with building railroads and canals" or directly aiding economic development in any form.[30]

The Whigs took a totally opposite position on each of these "great primary questions." They wanted a national bank, a protective tariff, and government-financed internal improvements. America needed "a just protection of home industry, . . . a sound currency, [and] liberal appropriations" for rivers and harbors. In Daniel Webster's words, "He who decries the use of credit . . . reviles the history of the whole country." To another Whig, the protective tariff was "the cardinal principle" of the party's "faith." The Whigs found these things necessary, proper, and constitutional. As William Seward put it in 1848, the Democrats were "a party of inaction," with a "creed that the powers of government for beneficent action are very limited." Whig policies, in contrast, were "calculated . . . to cause two spears of grass to grow where only one grew before."[31]

When it came to foreign affairs, it was the Democrats who favored a vigorous government, the Whigs who cautioned against it. The Democrats were always more willing than their opponents to assert American national interests, willing to go to war with Indian tribes, Mexico, even the British, as the occasion demanded. The Whigs articulated a more restrained version of American power and even opposed the Mexican War "as the great political and moral crime of the period, for which the [Polk] administration [was] to be held responsible before God and man." Democrats were expansionists, Whigs were not. Democrats liked to think that they faced down the British lion in Oregon; the Whigs worried about what looked to them like an unnecessary provocation by the Polk administration.[32]

Foreign policy disagreements and many of the differences over economic policy were primarily played out at the national level. At the same time, there was also a set of issues concerning religion, morality, and national values that were primarily debated in the states. In the late 1830's and into the early 1840's, the number of immigrants entering the United States began to increase substantially. More important, the basic nature of that immigration changed from earlier patterns. More Germans and Irish, especially Catholics, were entering the basically Protestant United States. As a result, questions of national definition, of what America should be ethnoreligiously, became a source of political confrontation. In the mid-1840's anti-Irish and anti-Catholic, native-American parties appeared in a few eastern cities. By the early 1850's, there was much more widespread sensitivity to, and talk about, the ethnoreligious impulses in American political life, as well as an increasing national dimension to the debate. As a Democratic congressman pointed out in 1856, "Our religious sentiments are the very strongest feelings of man's nature." [33]

For the parties, the questions of who was entitled to be an American and what the increased numbers of Roman Catholics, especially the Irish, portended for the country's future were as contentious as those of economic development and foreign affairs. Stephen A. Douglas laid out the Democrats' position in an 1852 speech. The party "has ever been just and liberal to all foreigners that come here," he said. It "has made this country a home for the exile, an asylum for the oppressed of all the world. We make no distinctions among our fellow citizens. . . . It is this wise, just, and honest policy that has attached the foreign vote to the democratic party." In contrast, whenever the Whigs came to office there was a "Federal hostility . . . towards foreigners." The Whigs had constantly made efforts to "beget hostilities between the natives and the emigrants invited into [the country] by the constitution and the laws." At the same time, they had "successively attempted to array the prejudices of the religious community against Jefferson and Jackson and Van Buren" because of the Democrats' toleration of Catholic Americans. It was "universally known" that "a large majority of our English population are opposed . . . to the Democratic party." This contingent control led the Whig party and gave it its nativism center. Whigs had waged "a bloody and revengeful war against Irishmen, Germans and Welchmen." [34]

In the Democratic rhetoric, the use of government power in such matters was the central issue. The widely copied "Maine Law" of the early 1850's, restricting alcoholic consumption and clearly aimed at foreigners, was an "attempt . . . 'to lay the iron hand' of a gigantic governmental control upon the conscience and habits of a whole people." When the Republicans came along later in the decade, they proved to be no better than their Whig predecessors, wishing, as they did, to convert a "private habit into a criminal offence." As the Democrats saw it, "the Puritan spirit" manifested by Whigs and Republicans was "too bigoted, too intolerant, too illiberal, too cruel, too selfish, to be trusted with the destiny of the world," not to mention the United States.[35]

Whigs were as conscious as Democrats of the political implications of the immigration issue. William Seward unhappily admitted to one of his correspondents in 1840 that the "proscription of immigrants" was "openly avowed as the policy of the Whig party, [which was simply] unwilling" to be just to the Irish in America. As a result, the Democratic party "receives in every emigrant ship a cargo of recruits, [whereas] the Whig party must attain its recruits by slow endeavor and assiduous teaching. [It] must rely on the newspaper editor, the book publisher, the writer, and the schoolmaster, and not on cargoes of humanity." Until their influence took hold, a long and slow process, Whigs had no choice but to "correct the abuses of party spirit and the fatal tendency of foreign influence." What galled them was the Democrats' immigrant-based political strength in election after election. "Did any man ever hear," one Whig asked in 1844, "of a Romanist who was not a Modern Democrat? . . . Every Catholic on the continent [is] a modern Democrat."[36]

In fact, that strength was the result of some considerable effort. Democrats tried very hard to win the political advantage as immigrants from Germany and Ireland increased in numbers in the 1840's. The National Democratic Republican Committee sent out an address in 1848 calling on "our naturalized fellow-citizens, . . . Frenchmen, Germans, Irish, English," to consider whether they wanted to see the Whigs win: "the party that passed the infamous *alien* law—the party who would never permit you to become citizens of this land of liberty, . . . the party that openly leagues with the proscriptive native Americans to overthrow the democracy who stand by your rights and privileges." The Whig Zachary Taylor was "the favorite candidate of the Native American organizations . . . for President." Therefore, "let Irish citizens think well of this matter, before giving one vote to the party of American Orangemen."[37]

In the face of such assaults, the Whigs usually found themselves on the defensive. As one of their papers complained, the Democrats were unrelenting in their drive "to embitter" recent immigrants against them. But while denouncing such efforts, most Whigs realized that they had no effective counterstrategy to prevent the Democrats from establishing themselves as "the party of religious toleration." A decade later, Know-Nothings and Republicans would be more successful than the Whigs had been in exploiting the ethnoreligious issue for their own purposes. In both cases, however, the important point was the shared sense that in the United States in this period, "the contest of race and religion [was] the bitterest of all."[38]

Questions rooted in the differences between the sections were also part of the rhetorical combat of American politics. They were stimulated originally by a small band of northern antislavery advocates and by some southern political leaders. Within the South, for example, a number of party leaders looked to gain political advantage by fighting constantly over which party better defended the section. "We believe," William R. King wrote, not untypically, to Alabama Democrats in the middle of the bitter presidential campaign of 1840, "that the election of General Harrison would be the triumph of northern Federalism, banking and abolitionism; that it would bring into power a political party whose ascendancy would be fatal to the rights and institutions of the South."[39]

Other southern political leaders, led by John C. Calhoun, always wanted to push sectionalism further to the front. Calhoun and his colleagues argued that the South was "in great danger" from the powerful antislavery advocates in the North. Southerners, therefore, had to "forget all petty animosities, bury recollections of past differences and unite . . . firmly and truly in the defense" of their section's interests. But Calhoun's views were frustrated by the mainstream policy issues that divided people along national, rather than sectional, lines. Both major parties tried to find safe, consensual positions on the differences between the sections and to maintain the integrity of a truly national two-party system. "We are told," one southerner wrote, that "all candidates save Southern born men, must be looked upon with suspicion! We repeat that this is unjust to our democratic friends in the North and West. . . . We, at least, have seen no evidence of recreancy" in their behavior toward the South. There was, most of all, a potential for "political disaster" in such "attempts to form divisions within ourselves, resting on sectional grounds."[40]

Not unexpectedly, in the debate over sectional issues the Democrats were against intervention by the federal government on slavery matters directly, or on its extension into federal territories in the West. The mainstream of the party held to that position into the Civil War. Whatever support for intervention there was came from the Whigs, though they were more divided on this than they usually were in the existing political climate. Many northern Whigs argued that the federal government's power in territorial matters was direct and extensive, and included the right to permit or exclude slavery. Southern Whigs were ambivalent and unsure, preferring to evade the sectional issue by ignoring it or by preventing any territorial expansion at all.

Whig rhetoric, as a result, was more strained, ambiguous, and internally inconsistent than on the other policy issues the parties confronted. With the rise of the Republicans in the 1850's to replace the Whigs and broaden their ideological outlook, the lines of the interventionist debate, of course, became as clearly and as starkly drawn at every political level as those over other matters were.[41]

The national and state platforms of the two parties codified their positions on all these matters. In Stephen A. Douglas's words, "the platform is an embodiment of the principles of the party upon all questions to which it extends, and is in perfect harmony with the whole system of principles which it is our purpose to carry into effect." The Democrats' first resolution, in their first official national platform, in 1840 (a statement they repeated every four years until the Civil War crisis), cogently summed up their perspective. "*Resolved,* That the federal government is one of limited powers [and that it is] dangerous to exercise doubtful constitutional powers." Similar statements appeared in their state platforms, one calling for "a strict adherence . . . to the letter of the Constitution, the Magna Charta of American liberty."[42]

The Whigs, on their side, repeatedly defended the constitutionality of their commitment to strong, purposeful government, calling for "a well-regulated currency" and high tariff rates for the "protection" of American workers. Though often less specific in their national platforms than the Democrats, they were no less adamant in their insistence on the differences between them. In all their state platforms and the rest of their public stances, in code words and directly, Whigs were no less committed to Clay's American System of vigorous government in the domestic realm than the Democrats were to their specific policies.[43]

The Nationalizing of Political Divisions

Despite the local character of much of American politics in the nineteenth century, national issues dominated political debate. When Polk ran for governor of Tennessee in 1839, "less than three of the twenty-eight pages" in his widely distributed address to the voters, "concerned state issues." In the same period, the New York Whig leader Daniel Ullmann noted that "the peculiarity of our country is that the politics of the National Government are of such transcendent importance that they draw to themselves the decision of most state and local questions. . . . We are compelled, therefore, in these our Municipal elections to act under the full pressure of national responsibility."[44]

It was a point that was hammered home repeatedly. "All our elections [both state and local] are in a great degree influenced by national questions, and for many years the respective parties have selected their candidates for State offices with as much reference to their opinions on general politics, as to their views on State policy." Or as New York state's Democratic newspaper put it in 1856, in local and city elections, "the same principles and issues are applicable which divide parties in reference to general politics." Therefore, Democrats should "cherish" their principles "everywhere." When Polk ran for governor again in 1841, he told his closest campaign aide that he was "ready to enter upon the canvass as soon as I receive the official announcement of the [national] Cabinet and the [President's] Inaugural Speech."[45]

Party leaders became adept at using the national rhetorical arsenal at the local level. In North Carolina in the 1830's and 1840's, Thomas Jeffrey reports, the official state platforms of each party "concentrated almost exclusively on national concerns. . . . National issues also frequently dominated the legislative elections. . . . A correspondent of the *Recorder* [a state newspaper] agreed that national politics had been the 'constant, unchanged, and unchangeable text' in legislative elections." In an Ohio party platform in 1844, the first six resolutions were all on the usual range of national matters, from the bank to the tariff. The last four dealt with state and local issues. State legislatures, whether controlled by Whigs or Democrats, routinely passed resolutions on national affairs at the beginning of their sessions. The preoccupation extended so far down the political scale that one Tioga county, New York, Democratic meeting in 1840 passed resolutions on nothing else.[46]

The critically important party press reinforced this emphasis. In villages, small towns, large cities, and state capitals, newspapers predominantly focused on national politics. Samuel Kernall's systematic word count of a Cleveland newspaper's political coverage in the 1840's confirms that far more column inches were devoted to national matters than to state and local issues. There was, in Kernall's words, a "steady diet of national messages" in these publications. It seems clear that, to Americans of this era, local, state, and national public political expression was, in the words of the Massachusetts Whig convention of 1839, "inseparably interwoven."[47]

Or to use another metaphor, the debate over national issues was the glue that bonded all levels of the American political nation in the 1830's and 1840's. The national debates resonated with, and focused, local divisions, gave them texture, and, given the pluralism of the United States, strongly suggested a reassuring level of national unity in political discourse. Parties were not local or sectional and, therefore, parochial in their concerns. As one Democratic group put it, "Democratic principles are alike . . . everywhere. They are the same in New York as in Virginia, in the North as in the South, in the center of the union, as at either or every extreme." A candidate presented himself either "as a Democrat or Whig, and voters usually assumed that his views were consonant with those of the party, at the state and national levels."[48]

Continuity and Conflict

The ideas codified and so forcefully enunciated in the late 1830's and early 1840's remained the common coin of American political expression for a long time thereafter. The strong sense of division between the parties continued to run deep. To be sure, the rise of new matters connected first with slavery and the Civil War, and then with the industrial and urban revolutions, sharpened and broadened an already polarized ideological split. But both the Democrats and their opponents remained true to their commitments through Reconstruction and beyond. The Democrats were as steadfast in 1864 and the 1870's as they were in 1844 against "the accumulation of power by the federal government." Indeed, as late as 1884, the Democratic National Convention was still resolving against destroying "the reserved rights of the States" and enacting "sumptuary laws which vex the citizen and interfere with individual liberty."[49]

Their opponents were similarly constant about the bulk of the old issues dividing the parties. When the Republicans emerged, their dynamic challenge to the expansion of African slavery added a major new ideological dimension to the political nation that profoundly disrupted much of it. In itself, the intense debate over slavery and sectionalism suggests the limits of the ideological consensus possible in the United States and the potency of this cross-cutting issue in the hands of astute political leaders, touching very deeply rooted differences within the society. This Republican adding to, and reshaping of, political discourse profoundly redirected the course of the nation at mid-century.[50]

Still there continued to be much familiar Whiggery in the public stance of the Republican party. From the 1850's on, the Republicans continued to push the boundaries of federal power, if not toward twentieth-century versions of the positive state, along the same lines at least as their Whig predecessors. Their 1884 platform called for a protective tariff and the use of vigorous federal power in controlling interstate commerce, and declared that the American people "constitute a Nation and not a mere confederacy of States." Similarly, the Republicans of the 1870's and 1880's often pushed anti-immigrant, anti-Catholic laws, as their Whig predecessors had done forty years before. Though it had moved well beyond Whiggery in a number of matters, the Republicanism of the post-1854 period, like the Democracy in this political nation, continued to articulate the truths of a stable, some might say static, ideological world. The American political nation's flexible continuity over policy differences was one of its major defining characteristics.[51]

Political parties from the 1830's onward enshrined traditional religious, sectional, and cultural animosities in their rhetoric; reflected the most up-to-date differences over the economic direction of the newly liberated, rapidly developing society; and provided a way for politically involved Americans to understand the world and its problems. Democratic, Whig, and, then, Republican leaders presented these differences as interwoven, not separate. National parties were communities of interests and sentiment that sorted out the political world and defined what was at stake. There was a party of social homogeneity and of government vigor in all things, economic and social. There was another party of social and ethnic pluralism, suspicious of too much government involvement in human affairs. The parties clearly and repeatedly hammered home how "utterly irreconcilable" they were—"as opposite to each other as light and darkness, as knowledge and ignorance."[52]

It was all but impossible for anyone caught up in American political life in this era, even at the most casual level, not to be aware of the sharp differences between the parties. In a later age, Americans came to believe that political parties were only interested in keeping their rhetoric as fuzzy and ambiguous as possible, not in espousing real policy differences. This cynicism, or reality, about modern ideological confrontation has sometimes been read back into the Democratic-Whig-Republican world of the nineteenth century. In the political nation that emerged in the late 1830's, however, the presentation of hard-edged dichotomies, not fuzziness and ambiguity, was the coin of the realm. As a result, partisans at every level could see that if their opponents won, their own vision of America was in serious jeopardy.

CHAPTER FIVE

"There Is No Middle Ground": The Idioms of Political Warfare, 1838-1860

> Let the stout-hearted democracy . . . sound their ancient
> battle cry, and rally their forces to the conflict on the 7th
> day of next November.
> —"To the People of Pennsylvania," 1848

ACCORDING TO BOTH Whigs and Democrats, there was much at stake in American politics in the late 1830's and the 1840's. The clash of contrasting policies and alternative ideological visions that they presented was constant, vigorous, and detailed. At the same time, their presentations had another quality as well: they always added a political calculus to the patterns of belief and strong commitment present. Each party sought electoral advantage as they framed discussion of what was at stake. Every political expression was structured in a particular way; each had a purpose; each was strategic as well as ideological. Party rhetoric, therefore, had two purposes, to bind together and to polarize, to sharpen differences among the voters as a whole and to draw together each party's own tribes. In every election campaign, both parties tried "to stir up the lukewarm and convince the wavering."[1] Neither party, of course, was committed to a truly free market of ideas that would lead to fresh, reflective choices by individual voters. Both Whigs and Democrats designed their rhetoric to align with their understanding of existing voting preferences by the constant reinforcing of old habits and truths.

Historians have noticed, nonetheless, that the two parties "mounted significantly different presidential campaigns." The Whigs "put the candidate first," whereas the Democrats "put party first and treated the candidate as the instrument of party." More was involved here than different attitudes toward the legitimacy of claims of party loyalty over individual conscience. Whig or Democrat, the losing side always tried, when it could, to attack the closely held voting loyalties that had benefited the winner in the hope of opening a wedge for itself among the few less certain voting groups. The Whigs, for example, after each of their shocking defeats in the presidential elections of 1836 and 1844, subsequently followed what the Democrats sneeringly called a "no-party" strategy, declaiming against party loyalty and running apparently nonpartisan candidates for President, in 1840 and 1848. To Democrats, behind this deceptive assault on "party and party spirit" lurked "the most intolerant, malignant and persecuting partisans."[2]

Each party, then, sought a particular and appropriate voice, a unique idiom of expression in its platforms, speeches, and editorials, to articulate its vision, point out the iniquities of the other side, and find, thereby, the key to victory. Whether adopting a no-party stance or not, political leaders on both sides added to their policy pronouncements what Charles Sellers calls "gross polemical images" of their opponents. Not content to appeal to the specific, presumably rational interests of the voters, parties also engaged in sharp invective, extravagant overstatement, heated defamation, polarizing excess, and the most threatening and divisive imagery. Recent political history suggested to them that this strategy paid off at the polls. Convincing voters across a broad and pluralist landscape called for clear themes, presented as simply, as starkly, and as fearfully as possible. These, both parties found and unrelentingly presented in every election campaign.[3]

These strategic considerations existed within behavioral constraints. Leaders of both parties made it clear, as the editor of one Democratic journal said in 1844, that "this contest is to be one of principle, and therefore we must endeavor to furnish facts and arguments and appeals which will not only persuade but convince."[4] They put as much emphasis on the convincing as on the denigrating part of the equation. Still, both were present. Party leaders believed that what they said had to ring true for it to be effective. Not everything went rhetorically. One of the characteristic facts of the political debates in this era was that no matter how extravagant the rhetoric became, it was almost always rooted in the basic ideological views that divided one party from the other. So much of what the parties offered was melodrama that it is sometimes easy to forget how much of it contained substance.

There were moments, to be sure, when one or the other party strayed from its ideological reservation, as when the Democrats supported tariff protection in their state campaign in Pennsylvania in 1844. But such moments were rarer than our political folklore has it. More often, distortions were softer, more efforts to get on the right side of some consensual value, as when the Whigs referred to themselves as "Democratic-Whigs" in several early campaigns. Political argument mobilized voters. It took into account their beliefs, expectations, and existing divisions. As Daniel Walker Howe has written, campaigns and debates in this political nation, "accustomed people to ferocious, issue-oriented, political polarization."[5]

"There Never Was an Election of Greater Importance"

Both Whigs and Democrats tended to follow the same rhetorical route. The scene they described was one of perpetual combat, the future one of impending apocalypse. They transmuted every issue into a struggle in which the very existence of the republic was at stake. In these circumstances, party leaders readily slipped into an idiom of negation, angry denunciation, and negative symbols. In his study of Alabama politics in the antebellum era, Mills Thornton notes how freely the state's political leaders exploited "popular fears through the manipulation of symbolic issues," such as the loss of individual liberty, always pushing their statements toward "extreme formulations," readily hurling "the epithet of traitor" against their opponents. And, as he observes, these extremes of rhetoric were not confined to Alabama or to the slave states alone. They were part of a much wider, national political culture.[6]

Party spokesmen characterized each election everywhere in the country as of unparalleled importance in the history of the nation. In the preface to the first issue of the *Democratic Review* in 1840, the editor announced that the Democratic party was "now in the crisis of a contest the most important, and the most trying in which it has ever been engaged." But that was already a familiar cry. This election, a group of Pennsylvania Whigs said in 1838, was "as infinitely transcending in importance, as any that has been hitherto waged in Pennsylvania." The election of 1840 would "be the mightiest . . . since the civil and political revolution of 1801." It "[rose] immeasurably above the ordinary struggles," was "neither more nor less than a final arbitrament of the great questions." In 1842, the people were not "sufficiently awake to the importance of the crisis." In 1844, the country faced "the most important Presidential canvass ever held in this country." In 1848, "there never was an election . . . of greater importance to the interests of the whole country, the integrity of the Union, and the welfare of the democracy. . . . The destinies of a nation hang trembling upon its events." In sum, Ohio Democrats underlined in 1848, "the crisis has come. It has been forced upon you by the fraud, the conspiracy, and the overthrow of the constitution by the leaders of the federal party."[7]

The reason for evoking an ever-impending apocalypse was clear. American freedom had been in great danger from without since the Revolution. But now it was threatened from within as well. As Thornton points out, there was a deep devotion to individual freedom among Americans, defined as personal autonomy and freedom from external control. Each party therefore employed, another historian has written, "a rhetoric that portrayed itself as a paladin against heinous concentrations of power and privilege represented by the opposition and as a champion of the people and of the republican doctrine of government by the people." Each "played constantly upon the fear" that there were conspiracies "to limit autonomy, and thus reduce the populace to subservience." Americans, one party spokesman argued, would soon have "manacles . . . riveted upon" their wrists unless they had the "firmness, energy and . . . determination to die as free men, rather than live as slaves." Pennsylvania's Simon Cameron linked it all together in 1852. "Upon the success of the democratic party," he warned, ". . . must depend, in the end, the very existence of our liberties."[8]

These strong statements were mostly cant, perhaps, but no less indicative of a mood, a temper, a pervasive political idiom for all that. In any case, such extremes of expression were nothing new. A tradition of political vituperation already existed as the era dawned. "A perilous crisis, in the condition of our beloved country," was already "fearfully impending" in the early 1830's. The point is that with the rise of the competitive two-party system from the late 1830's onward, this kind of expression penetrated widely and permanently among the masses, as well as the leaders, to become the acknowledged norm of an increasingly potent political culture. It may have been, as unfriendly critics of the system argued, that there was an unfortunate "recklessness and fury of party spirit" in which "slight differences of opinion" were "magnified into things of awful import." But such "recklessness and fury" were becoming the common way of focusing and mobilizing mass politics in the United States.[9]

Both parties adopted that norm whether or not they were comfortable with it. The prevailing climate saw to that, whatever personal preferences campaigners might have had. Spokesmen everywhere roused, cheered, cajoled, warned, struggled, mixing every kind of assault that brought out some irritant, some fear, to find the right mix, to structure what was most effective within their belief systems to ensure their party's triumph. The idiom was outsized: everything was always at stake; the enemy was always at the gates. The image of this "holy war" was never more clearly stated than by a Mississippi Whig in

1840. "I by no means consider," he said, "[that the presidential contest is] between rival candidates or rival parties, but between political *salvation* and political *ruin*." [10]

"The Spirit of Federalism Is Again Revived"

While the style was the same, party leaders worked very hard to draw lines between themselves, not to emphasize the perspectives they shared with their opponents. Sometimes, they presented simplified versions of reality, reflecting what one side or another wanted its audience to internalize before confronting specific policy choices. "Democracy dwells on the farm, federalism in the streets," one southern Democratic editor said in 1840. "Democracy triumphs in the country [while] federalism seeks the broad glare and noisy concourse of cities; [it] dwells in streets and market places." That was a signal of a particular type—specifically, that in American politics, as the editor of the *Ohio State Journal* put it in 1856, "there is no middle ground, no halfway house, no neutrality in this contest. The line of division is clear, distinct, radical, and cannot be overlooked or mistaken." Though this was said at a particularly polarizing moment in American politics, readers of earlier or later times would have found nothing at all unusual in it. [11]

The Democrats were quick to announce that the Whigs, with their "latitudinarian construction of the Constitution," were "our national evil genius," spouting a "foul morass of aristocratic heresies" from which had sprung, "naturally, and luxuriantly, protective tariffs, sumptuary laws, limitations upon suffrage, property qualifications for office, alien laws, test acts, monopolies." Whigs had a "fondness . . . for an expensive government" and would follow financial policies designed not to benefit America but "to fill the coffers of the British banker or the Jewish extortionist." There was a "perfect identity," Democrats repeated, between "modern Whiggery" and "ancient Federalism." Federalist commitments continued to be "an essential ingredient" of the Whig party. Democrats made the most of the still potent negative image of the federalists of the War of 1812 era, with their pro-British policies, attacks on American liberties, and threats against the very survival of the Union. The Whigs were "the Hartford Convention Federalists." Through them, therefore, "the spirit of federalism [was] again revived. . . . The principle, the foundation underlying both parties, was the same." [12]

Political parties, the Democrats argued, could never escape their past because history defined what they really were as well as who or what they represented. No matter how hard some of them tried to escape, parties were locked into their political past. In America, the stakes and the combatants were clear. Party names may have changed "but the principles which divide us are essentially the same." The Whigs, like the Federalists before them, had an "anti-republican passion for strong, consolidated government." During the whole of the history of the federal government, the Federalist-Whigs had tried "to increase the power and influence of the general government, and the tendencies of the democratic party were to restrain and abase them." But since a majority of Americans had proved resistant to those ideas and supported democratic-republican principles instead, the Federalists had to change their name "for political effect" and hide their true principles. Could anyone, therefore, believe "that the OLD FEDERALISTS who support Harrison now are any more PATRIOTIC or HONEST than they were when they opposed our Government and the war in 1813? Is it believed that they are LESS MONARCHIST now" than they were then?[13]

Policy was the paramount focus of Democratic rhetoric. The two parties were clearly arrayed. On one side stood "State Rights and strict construction." The Democratic party's "creed" was "equal rights to all, both at the polls and in kneeling before the altars of God." On the other side stood "the multifarious fruits of loose and vague interpretations of the Federal charter." It was "demagoguism against patriotism, Federalism against Democracy, the Bank against the people, [the] combination of a few manufacturers and politicians against the best interests of the country, the 'embodiment' of Whiggery against the charter of our liberty—the Constitution."[14]

[The Federalists] had the mistaken notion that a national debt, a national bank, a high revenue, and high expenditures are essential to a strong and efficient government. These things may be necessary under the British government, where the object is to keep the people in subjection, and where the doctrine is that "the people is a monster that must be muzzled." . . . There, the strength of the Government is sustained by weakening the popular arm and by strengthening the aristocracy. Here, the strength of the government consists of its forbearance and moderation.

The Whigs, in sum, "[admired] a splendid rather than a useful government." Their attempt to impose Tory-Federalist policies was not just an alternative vision of what public legislation and activity should encompass. It was a "systematic policy of public ruin" for the American nation.[15]

To this constitutional and divisive confrontation, the Democrats added a second approach that went to the very heart of their opponent's legitimacy. The Whigs were not a true political party, coherent and united on a single, related line of policy. Instead, they were a diffuse conglomeration of bits and pieces of antidemocratic factions. In order to win, Federalists had been, for many years, "busily collecting into a common focus all the diseased elements of society." The party had "rallied every division and fragment of the old Federal Republican, and National Republican parties, including Antimasons and Abolitionists, [behind] the unchanged deformity of their principles." To their "combined factions of British Whiggery, Abolitionism and Federalism," the Whigs, unsurprisingly, added the nativists. "THE NA-TIVE AMERICANS—ALIAS THE WHIGS" had always "adopted nativism" as part of their "creed whenever and wherever so doing appeared likely to strengthen blue light federalism." With all of these disparate elements, the Whigs were not a principled political party but, rather, a grouping of "factions of every hue, the antipodes of each other," that agreed "upon no ground of principle or in any single course of policy, . . . only in a common hatred of and hostility to" the Democrats.[16]

There was a third matter, as well, closely related to the first two: Whig deception of the American people. Democrats constantly accused their opponents of trickery in their political behavior. The Whig party misrepresented who it really spoke for and for what it stood. "The chameleon does not change its hue more frequently than this party their names. The colors of the rainbow are not more various than the mixture of party measures and principles professed in different sections of the Union." The Whig's concealment of their principles "arises from the fact that the Federalists dare not publicly disclose" them "to the American people." Whereas Democrats "have cherished principles to contest for," and do so openly, the Whigs "enter upon a contest for principle, silent themselves." They wanted the American people to support "their mum candidate" without knowing what he stood for. They were "afraid to speak to the people" because they "[entertained] designs and principles which they [dared] not avow." At the same time, as "a coalition of Nativists, Independents, Nullifiers, Whigs and Slavery propagandists," they were "without any common principle" or any "bond of union" that distinguished responsible political parties from temporary coalitions of poorly combined factions.[17]

There were two contradictory lines of argument in this rhetoric. First, as at once tricksters and Federalists, the Whigs did not deserve support because they had pursued such destructive policy excesses in the past. Second, the Whig party forfeited any support from reasonable men because of its unconstitutional, centralist policy commitments. The Federalist-Whigs only survived when they "contrive to ride somebody else's nag" and pursued their policy of "misrepresentations." They won in 1840 because they did all that they could to "minister to confusion. . . . Reason was silenced in the turmoil." Fortunately for the country, the Whigs would not be successful in the long run. The American people "love honesty above all other things." They would forgive "mistakes and errors in their public servants; but if they find that they have been imposed upon, it is vain to think to maintain their confidence."[18]

All of this the Democrats said extravagantly. In the United States, Whiggery meant one who was "in favor of perpetuating British bondage." The old Federalist party "as it existed at the commencement of the present century, [had] adopted various names and disguises, for the purposes of deceiving the people; but it [was] still the same *old federal party of the black cockade dynasty*!!" It had "again and again changed its name, but its designs [were] the same." Federalist "*principles* have undergone no change although it has assumed as many *names* as its ingenuity could devise." Nothing was "more ridiculous than to see the federal party *assuming* to be friends of popular liberty, after having [for] over fifty years ridiculed and reviled the people." Anyone who voted for it would find himself "steeped in British Whiggery, Abolitionism and Hartford Convention Federalism, up to the eye-lids." In sum, "what else is Whigism than the degenerate offspring of Federalism?"[19]

The current leaders of the Whig party, Henry Clay and Daniel Webster, were "men worthy of the best days of Federalism." Henry Clay embodied "the mean, selfish, grovelling, bargaining, intriguing, betraying, deceiving, cheating, falsifying propensities of the younger Adams." Millard Fillmore, the Whigs' longtime congressional leader and 1848 vice-presidential candidate, was "a strong partisan," staunchly holding on to "the high ultra notions of the old school of federalism." Each of the party's foremost leaders, like their forerunners, had "zealously labored . . . to consolidate all power in the federal head." They sought to manipulate the government "to REWARD VICE and TAX VIRTUE!!"[20]

Their presidential candidate in 1848, General Zachary Taylor, embodied all that was wrong with the Whigs. In that campaign, "dishonesty more bald was never before attempted." They went for men and avowed "no declared principles." They wrote no straightforward national platform; they hid what he really stood for. They could say that

Taylor was "a brave and successful soldier." But behind their deception and Taylor's "jack-boots, gold lace, cocked hat and military
spurs," the Whigs would engage, if elected, in carrying out the
"odious policy which lurks beneath the surface of federalism, . . . all
the odious principles and measures rendering [Federalism] a by-word
and [a] reproach from the days of John Adams to those of Millard
Fillmore, from alien and sedition law times to the era of bankrupt
swindling." If the American people voted for him they would vote
"for a national bank, high protective tariff, an enormous and wasteful
system of internal improvements . . . and the whole catalogue of
Whig measures." Americans, fortunately, would "never become the
serfs and dependents of a pampered Aristocracy." They knew that
"the ballot box belongs to the PEOPLE, and not the BANKS."[21]

When the outbreak of the Mexican War provoked Whig outcries
against the Democratic policies that had led to it, the Democrats were
not surprised. The Whigs' denunciation of the war as "the great political and moral crime" revealed their "ancient manifestations of hate
of country and [their] destitution of patriotism." They unsurprisingly
engaged in a "bitter and vindictive opposition to the country in the
present war." The Whig party, "under all its different colors and
shape, [was] *aiding the cause of the Mexicans.*" It was "the Mexican
party," Webster the "*Prince of traitors.*" Zachary Taylor headed "the
Mexican Whigs . . . in a contest" whose object was "to defeat and destroy the American patriots whom he led to victory in Mexico." What
spectacle could be more disgusting? Electing "the Whig allies of Mexico . . . now clinging to his skirts" was tantamount to attempting "to
reinstate Benedict Arnold and the tories of the revolution in the
affections and confidence of the American people."[22]

When the Republicans emerged in the mid-1850's, they were
greeted by the same Democratic refrain. The American people
understood that the Republicans were the "successors of the Federalists," who entered the race for President in 1856 as the Whigs had
always done, "with a parody of a platform and the caricature of a candidate." Their focus on "extending the bounds of freedom was
merely a feigned one. The real issue was . . . still the old one between
the servile tendencies of the Federal party, concealed under new
names, breaking out in new forms, [and] the progressive principles of
the Democrats." Their first presidential candidate, John C. Frémont,
represented "aristocracy, prescription, sumptuary laws, a meddling
priesthood, and all that [had] so often proved itself at war with the
principles of individualism and the true progress of mankind."[23]

"Every Dishonest Principle and Every Revolutionary Doctrine"

The Whig party was as willing as its enemies to engage in the polarizing, confrontational vituperation that characterized this political era. The Whigs may have been conservative by instinct, as historians have argued, but they lived in a competitive political culture that had a mass electorate to be won and one that had a strong commitment to egalitarianism. Whatever their desires may have been for an ordered society, uncluttered by raucous egalitarianism, reality dictated that they come to terms with the democratic messiness that dominated their political world. They began by calling themselves the "Democratic-Whig Party" in 1839 and continued to style themselves democrats for a time thereafter. In their basic behavior, too, they emulated their opponents. For them, as for the Democrats, the very Union was at stake: with "one universal Whig rush" in 1840, "the Republic [would be] safe.[24]

Whigs were as vehement as Democrats in denouncing their opponents for a whole range of political crimes, mistakes, and unforgivable initiatives. They made a pass at turning back on the Democrats some of the consensual fears unleashed against them. It was the Democrats, not the Whigs, who were the descendants of the old Federalists; it was the Democrats, not the Whigs, who were an unprincipled, deceptive coalition of "incongruous elements"; it was the Democrats, not the Whigs, who deceived the voters and "[skulked] away from all avowals of their real sentiments"; it was the Democrats, not the Whigs, who were "hailed by Britain," because their policies were "peculiarly favorable to British interests."[25]

The Whigs, however, had their own brand of argument about Democratic degeneracy. Martin Van Buren, as President, "repudiated the idea that it was the concern of government to render aid or protection to the business interests of the country." Democrats never understood that "negatives are not principles." They always hid behind the Constitution when they found "themselves disinclined to any noble and beneficent act." Their policies benefited only America's competitors. The Democrats were in fact *"THE BRITISH FREE TRADE PARTY*—the foes of the *AMERICAN* mechanic and farmer." Thus, in voting for Polk in 1844, Americans would "but sign the death warrant of domestic industry and condemn yourselves, your children, and your country." Remember, they reiterated, "James K. POLK is a BRITISH FREE TRADE MAN."[26]

Behind those policies lurked deeper dangers. Where the Democrats found British aristocracy and monarchialism in their opponents, the Whigs found their obverse among the Democrats: a commitment to anarchy and degeneracy in thought and behavior, a lack of restraint that endangered the republic. They took as their central theme that the Democrats loved disorder, that they were out-of-control naysayers in a society that needed order and direction for its full possibilities to be realized, for it to achieve both equality and prosperity. The Loco-Focos (the Whigs' counterlabel to Federalist, after the radical Democrat faction of New York City) were "simply a destructive party." The party of "Locofoco Agrarianism" was "the Veto Party, the advocates of War and Carnage." The Democracy "would destroy credit. It would lower wages. It would disturb the Union. It would excite war. It would depress the condition of the masses." The Democrats' commitment to their "corps of foreign mercenaries," the Irish voters, was further proof of that party's determination to destroy the country. In Lyman Beecher's words, the Democrats included in their ranks "nearly all the minor sects, besides the Sabbath breakers, rum-selling tippling folk, infidels and ruff-scuff generally." [27]

The Democrats, moreover, deceived the people by exciting old prejudices that no longer had any meaning. This was a new era, not a simple continuation of the Federalist-Jefferson period. "The mere names of parties which have sprung up and passed away before our day are to us nothing." Those battles had "long since died away." The battles and "issues of a past century cannot be trumped up to serve as rallying cries for either party." Why, then, were the Democrats doing so? It was because they knew that the "doctrines of modern Loco-Focoism" were not "those of the old Democratic party." Their "stale reiteration of Jeffersonian principles" did not deceive anyone. What was facing America now was "a new Democracy, presenting new issues, new measures of destruction, a new and unexampled spirit of ultra radicalism." [28]

The last was the real point as the Whigs argued it. The country was "indeed in the midst of a revolution," involved in a contest between a conservative party, the guardian of order, and a party "anarchial in its principles and tendencies." Thanks to Democratic policies, the United States was faced with a "scene of revolution and Jacobinism." The rascality and extremism the Democrats had exhibited since the late 1820's did not add up to egalitarian virtue, no matter what they claimed. The country's history demonstrated, the Tennessee Whig William G. Brownlow wrote in 1844, "that every dishonest principle, and every revolutionary doctrine, which have found favor among politicians since the election to the Presidency, of *Andrew Jackson*, has been embraced by the Locofocos, and by them promulgated in the name of *Democracy*. And with them to this day, this name is the passport of thieves and scoundrels to office and power." [29]

Worse still, the Democrats had not only introduced this unprincipled political spirit into American life but institutionalized it as well, in order to accomplish their dangerous revolution. Political parties were fine in the American republic, but they had to behave properly and to remain "secondary to measures and principles." But among Democrats "principles [had] become secondary to party." The Democrats were, in familiar terms, a "union of a number of furious and unscrupulous factions," based "upon no other ground but that of opposition to all and every measure of the Whigs." They were "one of the most unholy coalitions that ever degraded any nation." As a consequence, they behaved very badly. They fought only for the spoils of office and fattened "on the garbage of personal scandal." Democrats mistook "cant for argument, and expedients for principles"; and were "swayed" not by great ideas to which they subscribed, but "by the personal feelings and prejudices of their leaders." [30]

In their efforts to break down the strong commitment of Democrats to their party, the Whigs kept returning to an attack on unthinking partisan loyalty. Americans knew that "'*Measures not Men*' [the Democrats' frequently repeated call to battle] has ever been the cry of the most heartless demagogues." Americans lived in the third era of their history, an "age of brass, the period of corruption, and of mere party rule." They had given up their freedom, "the liberty of each and every citizen," in favor of a "close adherence to party discipline" and "the iron rule of the collective whole." In the Democrats' kind of world, "the physical tyranny endured by the Russian serf is not so degrading as the most abject mental vassal into which men are brought by that doctrine of 'regular nominations and the usages of party.' . . . Individual will, and the liberty of speech and action, were as completely subjugated under this system as they were under the religious system of Ignatius Loyola." Only "a New York Loco Foco would consent to take office chained, hoppled, and ringbolted" as these men were by their putting their organizational commitments first. Members of "a party who [ranged] under their masters like branded sheep, and who, when argued with, merely bid you look at their brand" were "not to be overcome by argument, but solely by numbers." [31]

As the Whigs portrayed the modern Democratic party, then, it was clearly not Jeffersonian. Rather, it consisted of two groups: Van Burenism, which took "the Office and Spoils for its share," and Loco-Focoism, which supplied its doctrines and principles. Whigs, therefore, were battling against "a negative creed and a negative man" when they confronted a Democratic candidate. James K. Polk was typical. Apart from his offensive and dangerous policy commitments when he ran for President in 1844, he was someone with "no standing of his own." He was a "mere manager of party, . . . a partizan of the lowest order, . . . distinguished by [his] absolute subserviency to the demagogues of the country." Compared with his Whig opponent, Henry Clay, Polk's "talents, his public services, his merits of every kind," sank "into absolute contempt." Americans had to vote against such Democrats because their principles were wrong and dangerous, because they deceived everyone about what they stood for, because their candidates were of the stripe they were, and because the way they organized and commanded their adherents to support such untalented men was dangerous to the republic. The Whigs' assault on party, then, was to further party ends. They were very good at doing it.[32]

The Republicans continued this vituperative tradition when they replaced the Whigs in combat with the Democrats. "Keep before the people," one of their campaign newspapers said in 1860, "that the Democratic party is composed of Knaves, plunderers and political mountebanks, that sell themselves to the highest bidder for power, place or self, . . . that it has become the rendezvous of thieves, the home of parasites and blood-suckers, the enemy of God and man, the stereotyped fraud, the sham, the hypocrite, the merciless marauder, and the outlawed renegade and malefactor." The Democrats of the 1860's were no less cowardly and traitorous than those of an earlier day, as willing as ever to bring "disunion, . . . national humiliation, submission to an arrogant and defiant enemy and disgrace to the American flag and name . . . at home and abroad." Compared with the Democrats, the "worst Tory of the Revolution was a patriot and a gentleman."[33]

"A Battle More Important in Its Results Than That of Trafalgar"

The presidential election of 1852 was the fourth in the life of this political nation and the last dominated by the two parties that had emerged in the 1830's to shape the era. The size of Franklin Pierce's victory in the electoral college that year was unusual, as was the effect that the staggering landslide had on the Whigs. Nevertheless, the course of the election illuminates a great deal about the era, particularly since it occurred in the immediate aftermath of an angry sectional crisis that challenged the parties' normal national focus on the country's problems. During the campaign all the familiar themes and approaches that had been well established were present: specific, long-standing issues, sectional, economic, and ethnoreligious; an awareness of the persistent problems the nation confronted; the personal factor, in the candidacies of a military hero against a party hack in the Polk mold, as presidential contenders; and a partisan confrontation of bitterness and rhetorical excess.[34]

The run-up to the election shaped its nature. The Whigs had won a close victory in 1848 by running Taylor as a popular hero and capitalizing on unusually destructive Democratic factionalism that resulted in a third-party effort of great strength. In 1852, they offered another general-hero, Winfield Scott, as their candidate, against a good representative of the Democratic notion of "measures, not men," Franklin Pierce, a relatively undistinguished state party leader (though it did not hurt that he had some military credentials, having served briefly as an army general). Neither party platform contained any surprises. The Whigs supported a protective tariff, advocated federal expenditures for rivers and harbors, and called for respect for the power and authority of the federal government as well as the states. The Democrats repeated their opposition to a protective tariff, a national bank, or any other attempts to expand federal power. Each platform contained clear signals of its continuity with the past, understandable in the language and atmosphere of the time. Each added to these normal polarities attempts to damp down what remained of the sectional issue that had flared since the mid-1840's. Someone returning after having been gone for a decade or more would have had very little trouble orienting himself to the existing political situation as the parties squared off.[35]

The campaign rhetoric was familiar as well. The Democrats trumpeted an election "second in importance to none we have had, . . . a battle more important in its results than that of Trafalgar." The differences between the parties remained wide and deep. They were "at an immeasurable distance" from each other "in all that concerns the true interpretation of the constitution and the proper administration of the government." Three things continued to distinguish the Whig party. Like the Federalists, it always supported America's enemies. The Whig administration of Millard Fillmore had committed "treason—treason as black as Arnold's," in its dealings with Great Britain. Second, Whigs were not straightforward; a readiness "to traffic, trade and intrigue" against the people's interests still characterized them. Finally, as always, they were committed to the welfare of monopolies and special interests, an inegalitarianism that threatened the American republic.[36]

The reasons for the Whigs' anti-Americanism in foreign affairs were familiar and clear. The party inherited "from its federal ancestry unbounded reverence and awe for the majesty of monarchy, and great fear for the prowess of England." That, in turn, illustrated the even larger fact that the Whigs were "in feeling and sentiment the 'lineal descendants' of the old FEDERAL PARTY, of Hartford Convention memory, which was opposed to the war of 1812." Beyond that, still further back, they were "identical in sentiment and sympathy with the Toryism of England and of our own Revolution." All this remained the essential "CHARACTER OF WHIGGERY."[37]

Americans knew that the Whigs were "like the Bourbon Kings." Their presidential candidate, who "learns nothing and forgets nothing," was "an old-fashioned federalist" who held to all [of that party's] worst doctrines" and advocated "the ancient principles of their party, in a form more extravagant even than his predecessors," favoring, as they always had, "a loose interpretation of the Constitution." He "would clothe the national government with dangerous powers; [support] a United States Bank, the distribution of the proceeds of the sales of the public lands, . . . the prosecution of a gigantic system of internal improvements, [and] a high protective tariff." For good measure, Whigs were "hostile to the enlargement and aggrandisement of the republic," for Scott "long ago gave . . . his adhesion to anti-masonry and Native Americanism."[38]

The comment about Scott's nativism signaled the intensification, in this election, of an always lurking issue, which now burst full force on the national scene. While there was "a chasm, wide, deep and impassable" between Democrats and nativists, Whigs had "always found nativism a safe and profitable investment." They had constantly "dabbled" in its "dirty waters." But that was understandable. Their ancestors, "the old federal party," had enacted the alien laws, and the Whigs "[entertained] the principles and feelings of the old federalists." Anti-Irish and anti-Catholic, they "should be marked as enemies to our government and to religion."[39]

And, of course, since the Whigs would do anything to win, even continue to hide what they stood for, the Democrats filled their campaign literature with constant warnings about their opponents' deceptive "expediency." In successive issues of an Ohio campaign newspaper, for instance, the Democratic editor headed different stories "Whig Frauds," "Beware," "Look Out for Lies," "The Last Whig Lie," and "Another Whig Falsehood." In contrast, "the democratic party

[had] never resembled an agglomeration of factions . . . and consequently, it [did] not present the spectacle of a league of factions held
together by mercenary motives and corrupt bargains."[40]

The Democrats believed that the main election issue, therefore,
was the need "for the ascendancy of democratic principles, because
the present glory and prosperity of the country [were] the legitimate
results of the ascendancy of democratic principles in the past." After
four years of Whig rule, the country had to return "to the old democratic doctrine of strict construction of the constitutional powers of
the government." It was almost too late. "While the country has been
quarreling about sectional issues," John Dix argued, "selfish men, and
more selfish associations, have been depredating upon the public
treasure." Pierce, in contrast, was a "politician of the Virgina school,
in favor of the economical administration of the general government,
of a strict construction of the constitution, and . . . a republican of
the Jeffersonian cast." He would "restore the legislation and policy of
the federal government to its pristine purity, and scourge from the
temple of freedom the 'money changers.'"[41]

The Whigs were hardly shrinking violets in their own campaign approach. They attacked the Democrats unmercifully and bitterly, echoing all of their traditional electioneering commandments about deception, about specific policies, and about the iniquities of Democratic
political behavior. Whig spokesmen warned that the Democratic
name had been "ingeniously assumed by the Old Federalists." In presenting their party to the voters, the Whigs charged, "self interest in-
spires it, circumstances govern it, and artifice is its main helper."
When a Democrat spoke to a rally, he did "not talk of the issues of the
day" because, on questions of "*free-trade* or *internal improvements*, the
party [dared] not show itself."[42]

The Whigs remedied that deficiency and emphasized their policy
differences. "We wish to be absolved from the necessity of warfare
with Mr. Franklin Pierce," the *Whig Review* ingenuously suggested,
"being disposed to regard him as secondary to the measures of his
party." The Democrats were "the do-nothing school of politicians,
who abjure all the essential powers of the Constitution, and build
themselves up on abstractions and negations." There was, Whigs reminded the voters, a reason for such advocacy; namely, the "alliance"
between "*the Locofoco party in the United States and England to BREAK
DOWN American Manufactures and thus secure the Market for England.*"
The Whigs had "no sympathy with a party which under the guise of
Democracy would encourage foreign industry at the expense of our
own—which plays double on the slavery question, upon the internal

improvement question, and upon the public land question—and which, in its intercourse with foreign countries, is always prepared to play the bully to the weak and the coward to the strong." [43]

In this campaign, the Whigs distanced themselves from their earlier willingness to encourage ethnoreligious prejudices in the society. Some of their leaders, in fact, reached out to Irish voters and even asserted that Pierce, not Scott, was the anti-Catholic candidate. The Democratic claim that Scott, "the Irishman's friend," was a nativist was a "vile charge." The Irish and the Democrats knew that. That was why the Democrats attacked Scott so savagely. But it did little good. The Irish, in the Whig view, were now determined "to abandon [their] locofoco alliances." After all, one Whig editor asked, could they "support the English candidate for President?" Plainly not, for there had appeared on the political scene all kinds of organizations of "IRISHMEN FOR SCOTT." [44]

Although it did them no good that November, the Whigs' campaign of 1852, like the Democrats', manifested the structural idiomatic qualities that had come to characterize the era. From the late 1830's to the eve of the Civil War, and beyond into the 1890's, it would be difficult to find the issues at stake in American politics more forcefully, colorfully, or starkly stated than they were by the publicists of the contending parties. Political rhetoric in this era (as at other times) existed on several levels. One part of political discourse emphasized what a later generation would call negative campaigning, carried on in very powerful and repetitive terms. The extraordinary bombast and sheer outrageousness of expression the two parties used should not blind anyone, however, to the process under way and the particular linkages being forged. Putting aside the nature of the issues, the possible limited range of choices offered, and the suggestion that not much was really at stake after all, these men, both among themselves in the everyday discourse of politics and during the intense heat of campaigns, always articulated a strong sense of division within the nation and exuded a powerful commitment to specific directions and policies, even as they framed the discussion in ways that they believed would catch the attention of, and involve, the mass of voters.

Robert Wiebe has argued that with the country's growing socioeconomic pluralism and complexity, "even the most skilled party managers . . . knew less about the substance of American politics at midcentury than Hamilton and Jefferson had in the 1790s." It may be true that political leaders of the 1840's and 1850's did not command the scene in an abstract intellectual sense—Franklin Pierce and Thomas Jefferson probably would have had little to say to each other about the grand scheme of things. And it is certainly true that party leaders focused much of their attention on the mechanics of political mobilization. But it is also true that they grasped the essentials of the party battle at the day-to-day level, and the clear distinction between them on the major issues. These men were political, not intellectual, animals who understood the nature and purpose of political discourse quite well. The substantive underpinnings of partisan warfare were always clear to them. The Democratic candidate in 1848, Lewis Cass, was, in the opinion of a Georgia Democrat, "the perfect embodiment of progressive democracy as opposed to what the Whigs call conservatism, which in plain English means putting the people in ward, to save them from their pretended ignorance and folly; and the question is not only between free trade and protection, but also whether we shall govern ourselves or have guardians." [45]

Statements of that kind indicate something of the substantive texture of the era's electoral contests. Why would the people involved repeat such things endlessly to themselves and articulate them so forcefully in public, unless they believed that something was being touched and reacted to, believed that they were addressing basic assumptions, real expectations, and important traditions critical to American voters? Why say things that later generations would consider obfuscations, or misunderstandings, unless those things were clearly understood to have substantive import within the particular context of the time? Americans were concerned for the future of their republic; they did have many enemies. Their interests dictated support for certain policies, but that support had to be, as they saw it, given because particular policies benefited the whole country, not just one or a few parts of it.

Instead of seeing this rhetoric as meaningless bombast, in other words, one can better understand the excesses of presentation as part of the process of mobilizing a large audience, a kind of appeal that had been unnecessary when the electorate had consisted of a limited group of political elites. The vituperative style of the era helped to make clear and burn what was at stake deeply into the consciousness of this vastly larger electorate. Political discourse always had a manipulative quality to it. But more was in it as well. Because political leaders and their supporters believed that the very future of the nation was at risk in their battles, they addressed every weakness, confronted every problem, and exposed every error on the other side. In Kenneth Lynn's formulation, they awakened long-familiar ideological positions, and magnified and reinforced them by touching repeatedly on what people already valued and believed and focusing their anger and desires.[46]

There were two types of issues always present here: specific policy differences and the question of integrity and competence. And there was a specially chosen way to air them, a discourse of confrontation aimed at exposing the stark differences between the parties and rousing the greatest possible interest and commitment in a rapidly changing society—one not that long away from the threats, dangers, and uncertainties of national birth and survival. The result was permanent political mobilization through a very powerful, recurrent type of political rhetoric that implanted the notion of an adversarial society. Parties were not only building an institutional structure and shaping an agenda, but also constructing a framework designed to incorporate the new mass voting public that now characterized American political life.

CHAPTER SIX

"The Moral Power of Any Party":
The Boundaries of Politics
in a Partisan Political Nation

AS THE PARTIES ENGAGED in their vicious give-and-take, they repeatedly touched another level of discourse, one that concerned political proprieties. Certain principles and understandings appeared and reappeared in their discussion that added up to an assertion that in America political behavior, decisions, and choices were all supposed to be structured in particular ways. Engaging in pluralist popular politics with many groups and issues at play, this argument went, demanded certain behavioral constraints on all participants. These constraints included limits on how political *organizations* should behave; how *factions* and *interest groups* within party organizations should behave; and, finally, how *political leaders* should behave.

Contemporary commentators expended a great deal of energy discussing and setting the bounds of behavior. In doing so, they demonstrated great sensitivity to the set of standards they developed, and repeatedly tested individual and party behavior against them. But the behavior tested and found wanting was, not surprisingly, that of their opponents. Once the norms were set, each party constantly accused the other of unfair practices and misbehavior. That the Democrats used "the tricks of desperate gamesters" was a not untypical Whig comment or, with the names changed, Democrat. Nor was the assertion that Republicans were willing to "employ every inducement in the way of misrepresentation, professions of purity, money or patronage" in order to win. Each party labeled the behavior of the other's candidates as at best "indelicate and undignified" and more often, downright "disreputable," a "disgraceful exhibition" that was "perfectly contemptible."[1] Perhaps it was because the parties were new at the outset of the era and the demands of partisanship were becoming so compelling as this political nation grew into maturity, that so much time was taken up with the matter. The point is that some very power-fully expressed norms were revealed again and again in every political debate from the late 1830's onward. They were as much a part of the politics of the era as the development of party organization and the articulation of policy issues.

"Fraud Upon the People"

The nature and depth of each party's commitment to principles was the most powerfully and repeatedly stressed norm. After all, the claim went, "the moral power" of any party was "in its opinions." Party spokesmen repeatedly stressed the need to distinguish parties from selfish factions—at least, to distinguish one's own party. Parties were supposed to be coalitions of like-minded men acting together on be-half of clearly articulated common goals. They were not engaged in politics simply to win office or heighten an individual's status or power. As the editor of the *Democratic Review* put it in 1853, most Democrats were men

who neither hold nor desire office. . . . They associate together by a common impulse for the attainment of a common end; not that they may by acting in concert gain official distinction, or the emoluments incidental to place, but be-cause they agree in certain fundamental principles of public policy, which they desire to impress upon the country.

For the Whig congressman John Minor Botts, it was "not a question of power; it [was] a question of right and of propriety."[2]

Parties displayed their principles and desired policies openly be-cause they had nothing to hide: their members agreed among them-selves on their purposes, goals, and common commitments. Factions, by contrast, had no such commitment, dignity, or elevated purpose. They were, rather, sordid combinations of men, at best temporarily acting together for some mere electoral purpose. "Parties refer to principles, factions to men. The one looks to the advancement of doc-trines, the other to the elevation of demagogues." Parties, over time, came together out of many different groups only when they "*conscien-tiously*" agreed on points of principle. But they must forever be on their guard against succumbing to the pressures that could cause them to degenerate into "a factious conspiracy to violate a public trust." When political armies moved under strong command, subor-dinating any differences to the demands of unity, there was always the strong possibility of too much downplaying of issues, too much cynicism and excessive manipulation. Where agreement was put before everything else, the result was "dishonesty . . . degradation . . . impolicy."[3]

This commitment that "except so far as a party represents opinion, it is a mere faction," put tremendous emphasis on two points: asserting one's own congruence with the defining elements of party and assailing the other group as not meriting the name because of its public behavior. In 1838, Van Buren's enemies in Pennsylvania argued that the Democratic party "had not as the basis of its union a community of principle." Rather, it was founded on "the ruins of the two ancient parties . . . and was [therefore] composed of the most heterogeneous and discordant elements." In Van Burenism, there was "no rallying around great principles—no binding tie of attachment or personal devotion." The only "cement" uniting it was "the power to reward in the leaders—the hope of spoils in his followers." To the Democrats, on the other hand, Whigs were "scarcely entitled" to be called a party since they avowed "no distinctive principles nor distinctive measures." They merely represented "the fragments of an ill-digested combination, united only in an unscrupulous opposition to the party in power." They were always "trying to substitute *men* for principles." proving that they were "a mere Opposition, which is nothing else than mere faction."[4]

There was a particular moment that defined and dramatized this continuing debate about propriety and on which most discussions of party behavior subsequently pivoted. A pattern was set in the first presidential election of this new era, in 1840, when, the Democrats claimed, the Whigs had adopted, "for the first time in the history of the American government and people, those degrading practices . . . which characterize the electioneering system of European countries, where the people are treated by the aristocracy as an ignorant herd, and appeals are made to the passions, senses and prejudices, instead of judgment, reason, patriotism and self-respect." In their recourse to a military hero and "hurrah" campaign, the Whigs had treated "the most serious and important of the political duties of a freeman . . . with a levity as revolting as it was new." The whole experience was a "stupendous fraud"—a "fraud upon the people."[5]

By the word fraud the Democrats did not mean "dishonesty at the ballot boxes" or "individual moral turpitude," but "that the people [were] misled, mystified, excoriated, bewildered, by false issues, false charges, false promises." That year, the Whigs had not drafted a national platform. They had therefore "carried the election without principle." In fact, "deception and double dealing marked the whole canvass." They threw "principles aside as obsolete and unfashionable things" and played a "game of hide-and-seek, by which the principles of [their party were] kept from view." They made "themselves all things to all men." For the Whigs, "no charge [was] too bold or unfounded; no misrepresentation too great, or perversion of the truth too palpable for them to use on all possible occasions." Their candidate appeared before the voters "muzzled and mute." He "sullenly refused to answer" questions about where he stood, preferring "to drown in a wild tumult of popular shouts and hurrahs all that calm and intelligent discussion of the great issues at stake." They had diverted the attention of the people "from PRINCIPLES, by amusing us with playthings." They appealed only to the "coarsest appetites of the coarsest order of the people."[6]

In contrast, while the Whigs had "abused the public mind," the Democrats in 1840 had behaved as a real political party should. In their national and state platforms, speeches, and editorials, they had "openly [declared] their principles, without disguise and without duplicity." They had not exhibited "the predominance of passion and the absence of principle which characterized the Whig party." Martin Van Buren and his followers behaved in a principled and dignified manner. They had built "no Log Cabins," had employed "no silly gew gaws, no Tippecanoe minstrelsy and mummery to attract the sympathies of the ignorant," because "a party based on principle need never resort to popular excitement, to secure popular action; but a party without principles . . . must rely upon clamor and delusion, fuss and falsehood, to attain [its] aims."[7]

The election of 1840, then, became the negative model of what should not be practiced in American politics. When William Henry Harrison won, "humbug" triumphed "over principles." But the parties now had a signpost for defining their behavior. In every election after 1840, the Democrats continued to tar the Whigs with the brush of improper behavior, of deceit and deception. Even when the Whigs adopted a clear, policy-oriented national platform in 1844, and ran a straight-out, identifiable party leader in Henry Clay for President, the Democrats reminded everyone that the Whigs really still relied on "clamor, agitation, vain boasting . . . and almost everything else debasing, to excite the passions, drown the reason, and mislead the minds of honest freemen." Whig policy continued to be "the prostitution of all principles" and the building of "the most unnatural coalitions and foul alliances." They had, finally, "in their unprincipled battle for power . . . courted alliances with every faction that [had] sprung up during the season." Even if "they behaved better," that is more straightforwardly, in 1844, that was unusual and, therefore, deceitful in its own right. They were adopting whatever means they thought necessary to win, rather than accepting the propriety of always presenting themselves and their policies in clear fashion. They remained a "humbugging man-worshipping party."[8]

In the election of 1848, to prove the point, the Whigs reverted to type. In "the great political fraud of our time," Whigs confessed by their actions that their principles could not "bear the scrutiny of the people." Their fraudulent platform contained "no opinion in regard to the Tariff; none in regard to a Bank; none in regard to the acquisition of territory; . . . not a word in regard [to] the [Mexican] war." Their ticket was "the most corrupt fusion of party and no-party elements"; their candidate, Zachary Taylor, was "General Mum," a "political chameleon," nominated with the hope that "the glare of his military achievements" would "seduce" Democrats. The Whigs once again proved that they were "an unalloyed evil . . . a mere sham—a most palpable cheat," lacking "the only justification upon which party organization can stand," a clear articulation of the principles in which they believed.[9]

The Democrats felt that they were touching something important in all of this, that stressing their opponents' negative behavior was effective politics. So did the Whigs. Sensitive to the attack, they tried hard to turn the tables on the Democrats, using the same phrases and approaches. It was the Democrats who were engaged in a "wicked conspiracy to *deceive* and *defraud* the voters," who "steadfastly" kept out of view "the real principles of the party (if they have any)." It was they who were "a combination composed of . . . discordant materials," who practiced "miserable hypocrisy, shuffling and deceit," played a "desperate game of fraud, falsehood and hypocrisy," and used "every means that could be devised to cheat and mislead an honest and confiding people." All of this was done to promote "the mercenary designs" of Democratic leaders.[10]

The Whigs' behavior, in their own view, was quite proper. In 1840, they had engaged in fervid electioneering because "while Faction is the bane, a strong and healthy popular excitement is the very breath of liberty. It purifies the political atmosphere." Perhaps their platform in 1848 was not as specific as the Democrats demanded, but everyone knew that Zachary Taylor was "a Whig—a Whig in principle—a Whig in affinities, . . . a Whig upon the noblest model." He, and other party candidates, were more as well. Political parties had a responsibility to pick the best as their candidates. But the Whigs alone chose "patriots and statesmen," whereas the Democrats picked "demagogues and tricksters." Take Taylor, for example. He "[belonged] to his country." He would rule "uncommitted, unfettered, . . . looking to no resolution of a convention, but [only] to the conditions of the country and to the CONSTITUTION."[11]

These themes continued throughout the 1850's and beyond, even as new issues arose, an electoral realignment occurred, and a new party emerged to replace the Whigs. Spokesmen of all parties asserted that "in politics, as well as in everything else, men should strictly carry out in practice, what they profess in theory; and it is as much a moral crime . . . to practice deceptions, falsehood and fraud, for political effect, to obtain from the people their votes, contrary to their expectations and belief, as it is to use the same means to defraud individuals of their good name or property." Party members said the same things, among themselves, in private. In 1850, the Democrats lost the New York governor's race because their "*hush* policy . . . destroyed" them. They had been "timid" in fear of losing supporters "and so . . . lost the battle." When they disguised their principles, voters were "at a loss to distinguish between the two parties," fell into "confusion," and had no reason to vote Democratic.[12]

When party spokesmen talked about propriety the way they constantly did, said that they were motivated by "an earnest desire to seek truth rather than victory" or that they embraced a "bold assertion" of principle "rather than . . . temporizing expedients," the cynic is likely to be unconvinced and to look instead at the electoral advantages to be gained by such declarations.[13] There always were some. But, at another level, whatever their electoral value, or because they had electoral value, one can see statements being made because they were congruent with what Americans believed to be proper political behavior. Something could not be used for electoral advantage unless it struck responsive chords, plumbed some well of belief held by many people.

The local politicians who shaped this era were extraordinary tacticians. They were quite sensitive to the boundaries of the possible. They realized that they worked within constraints. They could not stress electoral advantage but could condemn such motives in others; they could not argue that party discipline and regularity were based on self-serving ends, unrelated to ideological commitments. Parties acted, therefore, within a sense that "men are only great as they represent and defend principles of truth and goodness, and their personal consequence flows directly from their ability to give expression to those principles. . . . *Men* are always subordinate to *principles*." Thus, "better for a present defeat encountered for the truth's sake, than a hollow and insecure victory at the expense of the compromise of our convictions, at the sacrifice of part of the truth."[14]

"The Notes of Conciliation and Compromise"

Parties had to be unified ideologically, certain of where they stood, and clear in their presentation of themselves. *"Whigs of Ohio*, we must see eye to eye," was a common call to arms. Internal party disputes would only cloud the public message and cause defeat. "We must act together as one man. We must make common cause for the stake is common. We must not only pull, we must pull *all together*." But persistent factionalism and repeated disagreements were givens of America's partisan coalitions. Interests and groups within each party united in the essentials of the party's stance, but often disagreed over exactly where its center of ideological gravity lay, what the party should emphasize at a given moment, and how it should handle new and troubling issues. And, of course, there were always significant differences of opinion over candidates and electoral tactics as well.[15]

How were these matters reconciled? Each area of internal party disagreement, whether it was over policies, priorities, or tactics, could, and often did, become intense and bitter despite each party's core set of agreements and common outlook. "Our strength," one Georgia editor lamented, "is too often wasted in suicidal dissensions, [and] in the indulgence of personal animosities. Ever mindful of the need "to harmonize and unite, since without harmony in a party—or at least a wise forbearance—there [could] be no union, and without union, no possible strength or prosperity," party leaders spent a great deal of time trying to work out rules that would make it possible to hold together for the pursuit of their larger goals.[16] The key was "mutual forbearance and generous self-sacrifice." All party members must agree to work together "at any sacrifice but that of principle," must be flexible enough to compromise, within reason, for the good of all. The party, on its side, must do its best to "sink all questions calculated to produce internal tensions." Partisans were reminded that "everything in the political world is the production of compromise." Therefore, "upon all secondary points," candidates in particular, party members should "harmonize, conciliate, yield."[17]

There was nothing wrong with such flexibility and much to be won. Party members could not be stiff-necked even in the best cause. "Members of the same party sometimes think that upon all questions, whether in religion or politics, there must be a perfect uniformity of sentiment. If there is not a perfect agreement even upon minor points, some are ready, at once, to denounce and anathematize such as differ with them as deserters or heretics." But that was neither intellectually possible nor politically wise. A properly calibrated expediency was both necessary and acceptable in party affairs. "In this world . . . we must have a regard, and a large regard, in all political action, to expediency. No party can get along without it." The best party members were those who realized this and "sacrificed their peculiar tenets for the good of the whole . . . in the proper spirit of compromise."[18]

The "proper spirit of compromise" was a simple and logical behavioral concept, one much encouraged within both major parties. But how far did such expediency go? How much flexibility was acceptable, how much sacrificing of "minor points" permissible, in the name of unity? The answers to those questions were rarely clear in a given situation. Everyone agreed that "there were limits to heresy" in party affairs, a line where dissidents had to rein in their demands. But that was a message most politicians were not willing to convey publicly. For popular consumption, they tended to stand with a purist perspective, to insist that a party was always in danger of losing its soul if it was too flexible.[19]

Purism among party members was a reality that was never far from the surface. To purists, "bargaining was anathema" that led onto dangerous shoals. To them, "adherence to principle" had to prevail over "the love of power and the appetite for patronage." That adherence was paramount, deviations from it destructive. As the Democratic leader Preston King put it, "What has democracy to do with compromise, with conciliation? As well might the lamb think of compromise [or] conciliation with the wolf." Democrats required "stronger food than the notes of conciliation and compromise." Or, as a speaker before the Massachusetts Whig state convention said in 1849, Whigs had "certain principles" to push always. They were not a party that existed "only in compromise, expediency or conservatism."[20]

The complication was, as noted, that even party leaders who favored accommodation often paid homage to purist principles. They clearly found it politic to repeat that "a party triumph [could] only be complete when based upon a perfect platform and secured without dereliction of principle." That, after all, was what protected them from the dreaded charge of being deceptive, or only a faction, not a real party. But sensitivity to those considerations made things more difficult. Political parties still had to function. They had to find the right electoral formula. Whigs, for example, knew that they were not so strong that they could "disregard" selecting a "candidate who *can be elected,"* even if his Whig credentials did not meet everyone's strictest demands.[21]

Consequently, party organs repeatedly stressed the norm of flexibility even when they did not define it with precision. They denounced "fanatics and bigots" who pushed purism too far. "*Ultraism* in politics" was "neither desirable nor expedient." To practice such purism, to be unwilling to be flexible within limits, was to ensure the victory of the other party with its detestable policies. In the circumstances, how could anyone "hesitate in their choice?" As Andrew Johnson said during the heated and destructive campaign of 1860, "Suppose there is a difference in the Democratic party on the subject of squatter sovereignty, popular sovereignty, or whatever you please to call it; is not the difference still greater between the Democratic party and any other party?" To vote Republican or not to vote at all, because of disagreements over tactics or the party's alleged failure to be true to its principles, only ensured the triumph of "federalism, abolitionism and disunion."[22]

The intense concern for commitment, flexibility, and compromise endured throughout the life of the political nation. Parties walked fine lines as they sought to build winning coalitions within the understood norms. But this political thicket often entangled those caught in it, as indicated by the parties' frequent splits from the 1840's on, their persistent factionalism, and their never-ending debates over priorities. Nevertheless, the debate did establish a partisan behavioral norm, if one that never settled firmly in a single place. Expediency may have always been a major element in the makeup of politicians, but their whole debate here was about defining and imposing limits on that tendency, about denying that expediency alone ever figured in anyone's calculations. The boundaries were there, no matter how much they moved, and political leaders and their followers accepted that they were a powerful sanction within American politics. Ideological assertion and antagonism to what was deprecated as "non-committalism" came first. This was followed, in clear second place, but powerful nevertheless, by some necessary movements toward using weapons of electability, if the pure assertion of principles was not enough to win the day. Finally, toleration of each other's priorities and particular hobbies usually won out in conventions and campaigns, whatever the grumbling about going too far, or not far enough.

As a result, despite an often wide range of internal disagreements, parties generally stayed together. Their leadership understood the rules of coalition building. Party conventions remained the key. They were occasions to air differences of opinion and then come together.

Conventions were "expressly designed to harmonize different views and interests and to secure united action." They deliberated, allowed everyone to have his say, then decided. Once they had made their decisions, "it was the duty of every citizen to yield up his personal preference for men to the will of the majority, declared according to the usages of party." As the editor of a New England Whig newspaper put it in 1839 (in a sentiment often repeated thereafter), "We have a preference to be sure—but that preference we shall yield to the decision of the majority" at the upcoming national convention. Once that decision was made by the majority, "the path of duty" for all Whigs was "perfectly apparent." It was "to bow to the will of the majority." That was "the duty of law-abiding people; and no party [could] be a successful one which refuses to render cordial and earnest support to its regular nominations." That was the theory and, in the main, it worked. "Personal preferences [usually were] laid aside" by party members. Most members bowed to the will of the majority, no matter how contentious the debate and no matter how much some tried to stretch, others to contract, the boundaries.[23]

Of course, central to the leaders' ability to hold things together was the essential homogeneity of each party vis-à-vis the other. Neither Democrats, nor Whigs, nor Republicans, were all over the lot ideologically. And the members of each party were conscious, also, of how much they differed from their opponents. Such homogeneity and polarization made the establishment of the needed political boundaries possible. When a weary politician asked plaintively, after too many nominating ballots, where his fellow delegates' "spirit of compromise" was, he could be more than reasonably sure that it would emerge in time. His colleagues would join together with him on behalf of party unity. Whatever the source of such internal constraints, they existed, ran deep, and were usually effective.[24]

"Cold Unmerited Neglect Breeds No Friends"

One of the critical boundaries within the American political nation from the late 1830's onward concerned the role and behavior of the leadership. The whole American political process breathed limits on individual, group, and party actions. This affected those at the top of the system fully as much as it did the rest of those politically involved. They, too, were a product of the situation, assumptions, customs, and norms that defined politics, effectively established boundaries, and ultimately dictated the shape and limits of everyone's behavior. Whatever their wealth or status, they had to act within those boundaries, both to advance their party's interests and to maintain their own positions at the top of the political hierarchy.

That, of course, is not the usual description of America's political elite then, or at other times. The stress more often is on the power of those at the top to do as they please because of their wealth, social position, or simple ability to manipulate the process. In the first instance, it is clear that America's leadership did not come from all of the social classes present in the years after 1838, despite the nation's egalitarian assertions and the disappearance of property-holding qualifications for officeholding. It was a given of partisan rhetoric that delegates to party meetings consisted, in the words of a Whig editor, of "the tillers of the soil—the hardy and independent yeomanry, . . . the merchant, the mechanic, the laborer, the professional." But from President on down to state legislators and local party captains, the upper and middle classes of landowners, lawyers, and business entrepreneurs held a disproportionately large number of the elected and appointed offices and positions of party command.[25]

This was unsurprising at the beginning of the era. Colonial notions of deference to one's betters and thus of accepting their political and social authority had not died out in the postrevolutionary era. In the first third of the nineteenth century, American political leadership continued to remain largely "the preserve of gentlemen." America's national political elite was "primarily of upper-class origin" even as late as Jackson's administration, Sidney Aronson notes. "Most of the mob that assaulted the White House on his inauguration day," he concludes, "stayed only long enough to enjoy the punch."[26]

After Jackson left office, the same sector of the population still held on to much of the available political power. There were some changes over time, to be sure, some loosening of the pattern of elite-dominated leadership, some opening to those below the top rungs, particularly as one moved down the partisan institutional pyramid. More people were needed for leadership positions as parties built their organizations, necessitating a wider and deeper reach into the social structure than at the beginning of the process. But the essential point remained that America's political leadership did not, in this period, extend as far down the social scale as democratic ideology prescribed.[27]

In the state of North Carolina, for example, where only 25 percent of all white families owned slaves, more than 80 percent of the state legislators in 1850 were slave owners. Further, the small group of planters who held more than twenty slaves supplied over a third of the members. A quarter of the others were lawyers, men who were also well up in the social structure. Small farmers and other plain folk were in little evidence. In other southern states, the representation reached further down the social scale, but the essential reality remained. In northern and western states, the pattern was similar. Large landowners, merchants, and lawyers held more offices, and more of the most important ones, than people who were less well endowed economically or less well established socially. Even on the frontier, in Trempealau county, Wisconsin, in 1860, 43 percent of the members of the county board came from the top 10 percent of property owners, 63 percent from the top 20 percent.[28]

Nor were there many differences in this respect between the two main political parties. Studies of Michigan's party leadership in the 1840's, as one example, confirm the pattern, as do those of other places throughout the country, from upstate New York counties, to the frontier West, to the state of Alabama. There were some occupational and locational group differences between the parties. Democrats tended to come more from rural or small market town elites, Whigs from the larger population commercial centers of the states. There were some ethnic and religious differences as well. But the essential pattern of elite predominance varied little and has usually been taken to mean that the positions of power within the American political world were dominated by a secure, relatively independent, even oligarchic social elite.[29]

America's political leadership had another undemocratic, or more accurately, irresponsible, feature. Both popular commentators and historians have suggested that the political leaders who did not share this upper-class orientation were no better, that even many of those drawn from outside the social elite were not motivated by ideas of the public good, but operated only "by a practical, marketplace calculus." The political managers of the parties acted, some scholars contend, in largely cynical, manipulative, unresponsive, and uncontrolled ways to further only their personal and narrow electoral and party goals. The notion of the conniving politician manipulating the electorate and the whole system solely for his own or his clique's benefit is a cherished one in American folklore.[30]

Something of this perspective existed in the late 1830's. As William Freehling has pointed out, John C. Calhoun, in his *Disquisition on Government*, contributed in no small way to the notion of an irresponsible leadership totally dominating matters early in the life of the new political nation. He presented there "a picture of democracy gone to seed," with "spoilsmen feuding over patronage" and "the unscrupulous political boss" fully in control. That was because Calhoun "assumed that the average voter is a greedy and gullible creature," responding primarily "to inflammatory appeals to his passions." Therefore, "demagogues bent on securing patronage need only make full use of 'cunning, falsehood, deception, slander, fraud and gross appeals to the appetites of the lowest and most worthless portions of the community.'" Such leaders were always after the main chance for themselves, and they had both the wit and the means to do as they wished. As the veteran politician John McLean wrote in 1856, some Ohioans would always say that "knowing the manoevers [*sic*] of politicians, I am sure we are to witness again, as we have for years past, that the demagogues are to control the people through the instrumentality of a convention."[31]

There is nothing surprising in these patterns of elite leadership nor in the recurring suspicion that these leaders always had their own way. Nor is it surprising, given America's republican ideological past, that there would be suspicion and fear of the sordid behavior of the political mechanics who had replaced the great statesmen of an earlier epoch. But the question is not the class origins of the leadership or the extent of their and their lackeys' practice of the political arts. It is a matter, rather, of the operating assumptions they worked under and the constraints that curbed their power. High social origins did not mean uncontrolled or unchallenged dominance in all things. Whether drawn from the reigning social elite or the new political class, leaders were always fully entwined in the organs of political decision making, be they smoke-filled rooms, caucuses, or conventions. They were the dynamic element in mobilizing and structuring the electoral process, ran the parties, and dominated the institutional apparatus of politics. Nevertheless, they did not rule alone. The process was complicated by a matrix of power relationships that was far from one-sided, that is, operating only from the top down. Leaders had the ability to push hard in preferred directions. But their behavior was guided by a constant interplay with the voters that was more than ritual. It incorporated an awareness that boundaries always existed and constrained them from doing whatever they pleased.[32]

Certainly, constituents were never hesitant about making clear that they expected to be consulted by party leaders. The Whigs of Columbia county, New York, called a mass meeting of party members in 1851, because, as the call said, "the masses want to be talked to a little." These New Yorkers were not alone in arguing that a party "elicits counsel from all its members, while accepting dictation from none." Such remarks were usually said for effect, but Americans did constantly articulate the notion that "the ancient maxim, *vox populi, vox Dei*, [was] the sheet anchor of [their] political system." It is my point that those sentiments were not merely rhetorical. Giovanni Sartori has suggested, as a general proposition, that while "the power seeking drives of politicians remain constant," there are always "constraints . . . on such drives. Even if the party politician is motivated by crude self-interest, his behavior must depart—if the constraints of the system are operative—from the motivation." The constraints were always operative in this political nation.[33]

The nature of this relationship was demonstrated, once again, in the convention system, which, though never a model of pure democratic sensibilities, operated less oligarchically than John McLean's pessimistic observation suggests. It was here that leaders and led interacted and the realities of the political world showed themselves. The convention was the centerpiece of the whole system as it had emerged in America, intellectually and behaviorally, as well as emotionally. People did not exercise their sovereignty directly in "primary assemblies, . . . mobs [or] aggregate meetings." Rather, "the American mode of self-government" was through representative bodies, which were "but agents, servants, and representatives." They had to operate in a particular way. "When they 'form and regulate' they still form and regulate for the people, and not for themselves. Their acts . . . are but the acts of the people, and their deeds but the deeds of the people." Or, as a Whig newspaper put it, "the binding effect of the acts of delegated bodies depends upon the fidelity with which they reflect the popular will."[34]

That was the vigorously asserted intellectual web in which America's political leaders operated. And they, in turn, responded directly to the notions offered. The internal dynamics of conventions generally included the party leadership's careful attention to democratic proprieties. Although convention activites were thoroughly routinized, policies, arguments, and candidates were rarely simply imposed from above. Leaders did not simply direct. Other political skills were necessary—to negotiate, suggest, shepherd, and nudge. Hendrik Booraem has described how one of the great political bosses of the era, Thurlow Weed, treated his Whig party colleagues:

Like most party leaders [he] did not attempt to dictate to a state convention or to force a set of preselected nominees upon it. Rather, his role was that of a harmonizer, who accepted the material with which the convention presented him and tried to produce a state ticket that would attract a favorable public response and preserve a maximum of party harmony.[35]

Weed "stressed communication and consultation" with those below him in the political hierarchy. To be sure, he was working with local party leaders in such activites, but he was also very conscious that each of them represented a broad constituency. As Mills Thornton says of Alabama's pre–Civil War political leadership, "One may call them 'bosses,' but . . . they were less bosses than conciliators, . . . who kept the party together and its program in accord with the current popular mood." They "listened to the voice of the masses, exerted themselves to placate popular fears, and pandered to social prejudices." They accepted "popular instruction" and knew that "the politician's function was not to guide, but to represent. . . . It was the politician's positive social duty to discover and give voice to the will of his constituency." In short, they claimed "to be the captains of the popular army."[36]

Political leaders rarely tried to transcend the moral constraints imposed on them by the ever-present popular understanding and egalitarian rhetoric and expectations. Although the interactive decision-making process in this political nation was filled with tensions and opportunities to cheat and deceive, it was always a reality that was accepted as well. Elites worked to shape the raw material they had, but they worked in ways subject to review. They therefore shaped platforms as they selected candidates, to represent the party's claims and to reflect the desires of the party's constituent elements. Popular will was a part of politics, to be assessed, understood, and listened to. As Thornton puts it, the leaders knew that "public opinion could be focussed, but it could not be invented."[37]

The process, to be sure, was not one way in the other direction, either. The leaders' initiative and power came into play in shaping the voters' demands into something electorally workable and therefore politically useful. At that point, their experience, shrewdness, negotiating skills, and wisdom, they believed, had to tame the raw material of popular expression into a coherent and attractive package that would ensure electoral success. That essential political function could not be done by anyone else, and it needed to be done for everyone and the party's good. Doing that was the leaders' responsibility and they did it repeatedly and well, despite the tensions and disagreements they confronted.

The elements of elite manipulation and cooptation were not the only ones present on the political scene. Both leaders and led, therefore, contributed to the final outcome of the political decisions taken. The extraordinary number of party meetings, mass assemblages, and conventions were all occasions for the rituals and reality of the two-way interaction that was going on. They were places where the party leaders' "deference to public opinion" largely occurred, where they consulted and listened, knowing that, as a correspondent of James K. Polk wrote, "cold, unmerited neglect breeds no *friends*," and that careful attention to the voice of the people provided great opportunities for the exercise of abundant and effective, if not total, power.[38]

In the years after the late 1830's, then, members of both parties acted constantly within the defining norms of their political nation. Parties reflected much of the egalitarian impulses of the age in the way they carried on their activites, while asserting a "moral power" as they did so. American party politics in this era, Robert Wiebe has suggested, had "two distinct sides requiring very different styles and skills. One turned inward to a circle of associates, the other outward to the voting public. One emphasized bargains and arrangements, the other principles and divisions." As Wiebe points out, these different emphases called for unusually talented individuals to carry out the partisan mission. They also called for a series of understandings that made all activites not only smoother—but possible. "The common law of democracy" in the political nation affected elites and voters alike— elites because of their need to structure the party's appeals without division and to mobilize and direct voters to do the right thing; voters because of their commitments to their party and the consequences they feared would flow if they did not support their party in its campaign activities and at the polls on election day.[39]

CHAPTER SEVEN

The Shrine of Party

FROM THE 1840'S ONWARD, a vibrant, noisy, and thoroughly partisan political world existed in the United States. Everywhere one turned politics had taken hold, with "the implacable forces of party" dominating the scene.[1] As a writer in the *New York Evening Post* said of a campaign rally in Illinois in 1858:

It is astonishing how deep an interest in politics this people take. Over long weary miles of hot and dusty prairie, the procession of eager partisans come—on foot, on horseback, in wagons drawn by horses or mule, men, women, and children . . . settling down at the town where the meeting is, with hardly a chance for sitting, and even less opportunity for eating, waiting in anxious groups for hours at the places of speaking, talking, discussing, litigious, vociferous, while the roar of artillery, the music of bands, the waving of banners, the huzzas of the crowds, as delegation after delegation appears; the cry of peddlers, vending all sorts of wares . . . combine to render the occasion one scene of confusion and commotion.[2]

That commotion was everywhere, certainly since the "hurrah" campaign of 1840. Reports of similar meetings recur repeatedly in the contemporary press and in the letters and memoirs of the many participants. The less public party meetings, the caucuses and conventions held at every level, had their own share of involvement, excitement, and intensity. Part of the fervent interest stemmed from the fact that election campaigns served as a major medium of popular entertainment in American life in the half century after 1840. The exaggerated pageantry on display, the inflated drama of the average political speech, the rituals and theatrics of electoral confrontation, drew people into the political orbit.[3] But there was more to the popular commitment than that.

"Party or Faction is Everything"

Beneath the noise, excitement, and occasional confusion so prevalent in this political nation were some important realities. By the early 1840's, the United States had become a partisan nation organizationally, intellectually, and emotionally. The rituals of politics, its rhetoric, its institutions, and most of all, its commitments, were all partisan. Partisanship was the glue that held the political nation together, provided its understanding of what was at stake, and established the structures, rules, and sanctions through which all else ran. When William Henry Seward, in 1856, referred to "the ancient and proper condition" of politics in America, he made it quite clear what he meant. "The condition is one which tolerates two firm and enduring parties." That was an understanding shared by the overwhelming majority of Americans. Routine descriptions of political candidates noted, without comment, each's "fidelity and stern adherence to the principles" of his party "at all times and under all circumstances." He was someone who appeared before the electorate as, in order, "a sound Democrat [or Whig], a polished scholar and [a] refined gentleman." What that meant was plain: "Whatever may be the personal merits or demerits of a candidate, he cannot act otherwise, if he be chosen, than as an agent of the majority to whom he owes his place. The real question, therefore, in every canvass, is, what are the merits of the party by whom a candidate is preferred."[4]

Political parties were serious and Americans took them seriously. They were "the life-blood of the Republic." Two-party competition existed throughout the country to arouse and organize the people and their leaders. Of course, antipartyism still lived in several nooks and corners of the nation, but it never threatened the ever-widening acceptance of the dictates and imperatives of partisanship. Parties had begun as coalitions of specific interests generalizing about proper perspectives and actions in politics. In a pluralist republic with many different outlooks among its people, they were believed to be inevitable. By the mid-1840's, they had become more. In the deep commitment to them, parties had become communities—the sense of loyalty to them, as to a family, a tribe, a religion, or a nation, overwhelmed all else. Dissent and individualism existed in politics, but the sense of community loyalty came first and was constantly exalted as the proper and normal condition of the American people. As one unfriendly observer put it as early as 1839, "party or faction is everything" in the United States. "The people at elections move as armies do under command." Others agreed. Everywhere, the American people had moved into "the comfortable circle of party regularity."[5]

Why did Americans support the Democratic and Whig (and later the Republican) parties with such vigor and intensity? Part of the reason certainly lay in the fact that people continued to see parties as effective instruments of collective political action. Parties did important things for the nation by providing an interactive, institutional filter through which to affect government policy. Parties were, the Democratic congressman Howell Cobb of Georgia noted in 1848, associations of men "acting in concert with each other, to carry out great fundamental principles in the administration of government." That is why, Seward argued, he adhered "to the Whig party and its candidates, through all changes of time and circumstances." He did so "for the simple reason" that he regarded it "as the party through whose actions wise measures and beneficent legislation must chiefly be secured."[6]

National parties had more cosmic, or systemic, functions as well, promoting participation, legitimizing politics in the United States, guaranteeing the freedoms of the American people, and preserving the nation against internal stresses. A party, Cobb continued, "carries the beautiful theory of our system into practical operation." It was "solely through the contests of party from first to last, that we are indebted for all the independence, rights and privileges we enjoy above other nations. When the present political parties, or parties identical in principle, shall cease to exist in North America, the Republic of the United States will have passed away." In fact, as another observer, Nahum Capen, wrote in 1952, "What thinking and acting are to the individual, party is to society. Party is the great engine of human progress. It is a combination of men of similar views, and kindred sympathies, for moral or political supremacy. It leads to the war of knowledge upon ignorance, the conflict of holiness against sin, the struggles of freedom against tyranny. . . . A world without party would be incapable of progress." Even a man like Charles Sumner of Massachusetts, who for much of his career was at odds with the leadership and direction of his own party, agreed. "Parties are unknown in despotic countries," he said in 1860. "They belong to the machinery of free governments. Through parties, principles are maintained above men. And through parties men in power are held to a just responsibility."[7]

All politically involved Americans, from the leaders who directed things to the mass of party workers and voters who joined with them, saw parties as part of, not remote from, daily experience. Parties organized politics, framed meaningful choices for voters, and kept order in a potentially turbulent and fragmented situation. They mediated and managed a range of social tensions. They enshrined traditional animosities between groups, reflected current differences in society, and provided clear ways of looking at the world. "The democratic political system that developed during the first half of the nineteenth century," Morton Keller observes, "became a vehicle for every aspiration, every passion of a brutally vigorous people. The party system dealt not only with the desires for greater political and economic democracy of the Jacksonian era, but with more specific—and more divisive—issues as well: anti-Catholicism and xenophobia, temperance and prohibition, ultimately with the prime social issue of pre–Civil War America, Negro slavery."[8]

In sum, politics was not a separate sphere, isolated from the socio-economic, even personal concerns of most Americans. It was woven into the fabric of society. Thinking about politics was an indispensable way of thinking about society. "Politics was protection against government; it was an avenue to success; it was a source of identity; it was perhaps especially a way to express feelings and to find satisfaction of anxieties and resentments." And the major institutions of this political world, the parties, were instruments for achieving both sublime and mundane objects. Americans saw in the contests between them "something more elevated than a horse race or a faction fight."[9]

"A Grand Combination of All the Loves, Passions, Interests, and Opinions"

At some point in the evolution of the American party system, people's partisan commitments became deeper, more intense, and more self-contained than they had been originally. They became something that transcended immediate calculations of personal gain. Americans celebrated that "the strongest principle in the nature of man was party feeling." There was an "irresistible bond of union" among party members, believing as they did in "everything for the cause and nothing for men." Once such party commitment developed, the editor of the Whig magazine, the *American Review*, argued in 1847, "pride, emulation, the desire of distinction, the contagious sympathy with numbers, and the disguised form of self-love, the *esprit de corps*, all concur to swell the tide of feeling, until the desire of party success becomes the master passion of the human breast." Once people reached that point, their party commitment became "a life-long ardor, a grand combination of all the loves, passions, interests, and opinions. . . . Hardly ever do men change their manners, their religion, or their politics, when these are implanted in them in early years."[10]

Few observers missed the chance to liken Americans' party loyalty to religious commitment. It was not unusual when a local loyalist was said to hold his politics "next to his religion." At a Democratic convention, no one seemed startled when one delegate made reference to "the Democratic church." These sentiments were not confined to the lesser party members by any means. Michael Wallace notes how Martin Van Buren, in his autobiography, constantly spoke of his party "almost as if it were a church, and he in communion with his Party brethren." Van Buren repeatedly referred to "political baptism," "full communion," "political orthodoxy," "political heresies," and, of course, "apostates." To Franklin Pierce, his biographer suggests, the Democratic party was "his family, his fraternity, his church and his country." Whigs and Republicans echoed those sentiments. One Republican editor recalled that he and his friends had loved the Whig party "as a man loves his Religion. . . . Its principles were what we worshipped politically." According to his biographer, the Illinois congressman Shelby Cullom "believed in the Republican party in the same way that he believed in the fundamental Protestantism which molded his early opinions and shaped his attitudes throughout his life." [11]

Such passionate feelings either originated as religious commitment often does, in some extraordinary transforming experience such as the intense battles of the Jacksonian and immediate post-Jacksonian years to define the nature of America, or, in the case of the next generations, which had not lived through the cauldron of the Bank War and its aftermath or the Panic of 1837, grew out of the experiences of one's youth, in the deeply partisan environment of home and neighborhood. Family and community pressures were quite powerful and, most of the time, unambiguously partisan. In Urbana, Ohio, by the 1860's,

it was natural to be a Republican; it was more than that, it was inevitable that one should be a Republican. . . . The Republican party . . . was a fundamental and self-evident thing, like life, and liberty, and the pursuit of happiness, or like the flag or the federal judiciary. It was elemental like gravity, the sun, the stars, the ocean. . . . It was inconceivable that any self-respecting person should be a Democrat.

When the writer broke the pattern to become a Democrat, the reaction in his home town was severe. "It could hardly have been worse had I announced that I . . . was an atheist." [12]

To be a nonbeliever, that is, a nonpartisan, was as heinous a sin as disloyalty to one's party. Neutrals in politics were "contemptible." It was the "positive duty of every man to become a partisan." There was no choice. There could be no uncommitteds in American politics. "Every man is for or against the present ascendancy" and had an obligation to be counted in the correct column on election day. Appeals to come over to the other side or to join a third party were almost inevitably met with disdain. One did not convert to another church. The mass of Democrats, one said in 1849, "have no fellow-feeling either with Whigs or traitors." It was "impossible to alienate [them] from their party affections." Similarly, Republicans were not "political eunuchs" who supported people regardless of party labels. They were loyal to their own, and only their own.[13]

Ronald Formisano quotes a Massachusetts minister offering, as a tribute to a man at his funeral, that he had always been true to his party. "He never crossed the line." And, on a Mississippian's gravestone, in addition to his name and dates, were the words, HE VOTED FOR HENRY CLAY.[14] Unrelieved, unstinting partisan devotion of this kind characterized a population that took its politics, and especially its parties, more than seriously. To some observers, the intensity of the devotion was frightening and frustrating, but it was a recognized, defining reality, nevertheless. It created an unprecedented static element in American political life, one that dictated that all matters had to begin with the fact of intense party loyalty driving the political world.

The Sectional Variation

The severest threat to this powerful partisan imperative was sectionalism. Some sectional tensions had existed in American life and politics from early in the colonial era but efforts to politicize them were generally unfocused, intermittent, and local. That changed, beginning in 1819, when the anger and fear engendered by slavery's presence in a liberal and increasingly egalitarian society fueled an important challenge to the nation's political stability. The fight over Missouri's admission as a slave state was a prolonged and bitter one, lasting into 1821. But in the aftermath of this first great sectional crisis, the furor abated. Americans in the 1820's and early 1830's were not unaware of slavery; some were troubled by it, and others remained on guard to defend it, but most Americans proved to be indifferent. In these days of party building around conflicts that crossed state and regional, not to mention sectional, lines, slavery and sectional irritations occasionally appeared on the scene as flash points, sometimes erupting, but they were never sustainable for very long.[15]

With the maturing of the partisan political nation in the late 1830's, a number of the southern political leaders continued to push a sectional political perspective, but the leaders of the two political parties successfully resisted their efforts. The two-party system's clear establishment in southern politics had a widespread impact on sectional impulses. To be sure, South Carolina's politics remained outside the partisan system, and southerners were on the whole deeply committed, if sometimes ambivalent, to the preservation of the slave-labor system. But they disagreed over the immediacy of any threats to slavery and about the political strategy to pursue if such threats materialized. Most politically aware southerners resisted the creation of sectional political divisions in place of the reigning national pattern of Whigs versus Democrats.[16]

Although the South's great statesman John C. Calhoun "never accepted institutionalized competition as a political ideal," most politically involved southerners did so from the late 1830's on. Like their colleagues elsewhere, they were caught up in the impulses that brought partisan coherence out of the sharp battles of the early and mid-1830's. They espoused the same issues and their party's correct stance on each. They linked their local and regional concerns to those of their national party. The slavery matter was always present in southern political discourse. But as sectional tensions were aired, the parties absorbed them, tamed them, domesticated them, and, I would argue, largely subordinated them—albeit by evading them. Once in office, southern leaders usually behaved as partisans. The two-party system was a reality to them, and there was much else for southerners to fight about, from tariffs and banks to a variety of social and ethnic issues. As William Cooper has written, "By 1841, party had become ingrained in the American and southern scheme; without a party politicians wandered in the political wilderness." Few southerners chose that lonely road:

Whatever else might be said about the development or lack of development in the society and economy of the antebellum South vis-à-vis the antebellum North, southern politicians definitely kept pace with their northern counterparts. Southerners created modern political vehicles [i.e., parties] that successfully negotiated the treacherous terrain of a political system based on white manhood suffrage and broad voter participation.[17]

In fact, as elsewhere, the partisan commitments of southerners intensified in the early 1840's. "With us," the editor of the *Mobile Register* said in 1842, "the integrity—the unity of the democratic party, is the paramount object . . . and it matters less whether we triumph under the lead of a northern or a southern statesman." This was because "the chances of having the Government managed for the good of the great mass of people, who labor for their bread, are better under

Democratic rule; and we shall accordingly do everything in our power to promote the harmony of the Democratic party." That commitment came before the dedication to individuals, even local heroes. When Calhoun withdrew from the race for Democratic nominee for President in 1844, the *Arkansas Banner* made it clear that he had done the right thing. "While we do not love him less, we love democracy *more*; and for the sake of union, harmony, and concert of action among ourselves, we readily waive all our predilections for him, and would even go against him, if necessary, in favor of the choice of our party. Such, we conceive, should be the feeling of every democrat." These attitudes made life very difficult for sectional agitators. When confronted by the insistent anxieties and demands of the sectionalists, most southerners "were slow to accept the fire eaters' devils." [18]

From 1844 on, however, as the ruling Democrats pursued a policy of territorial expansion, sectional agitation in Congress, among political leaders in states and local communities, and in the electorate reached unprecedented heights, culminating in renewed attempts to brush aside the two national parties as irrelevant in the new situation of sectional confrontation. This time, sectionalism took greater hold than it had ever previously been able to do and severely challenged the political nation's existing values just as they were settling so firmly into public consciousness. In the North, the introduction of the Wilmot Proviso to restrict slavery's expansion and the Free Soil revolt against the established parties in 1848 fueled sectional tensions and provided them with a specific political channel. In the South, the dormant sectional unity movement reawakened and took on new force, drawing the attention and support of many who had previously resisted such appeals. As the editor of the Whig *American Review* wrote in 1850, the issue of slavery extension "tends to confound all other distinctions of party." Nonpartisan meetings were held, and political leaders corresponded, however warily, across party lines, seeking to devise a platform that southerners would support regardless of their normal partisan persuasion. [19]

After much preliminary skirmishing and a great deal of agitation, the presidential election of 1848 provoked a powerful test of party loyalty. Some previously intense partisans did succumb and move away from their traditional moorings. Martin Van Buren's leadership of the Free Soil party was a particularly stunning illustration that traditional party loyalties could be set aside. There he stood, as the presidential candidate of a third party, a coalition of Democrats, Whigs, and antislavery radicals, many of whom he had once bitterly fought over the traditional partisan political issues as well as about earlier attempts to bring a sectional focus to American politics. [20]

But, tellingly, most Democrats and Whigs, leaders, officeholders, and, most of all, their constituents, did not follow Van Buren's example, or that of the southern unifiers who pushed for sectional support for the Louisiana slaveholder and Whig candidate, Zachary Taylor. What is compelling about this first powerful test of the strength of partisan commitments is how well the very values under challenge, the loyalty of most Americans to their national political parties, held up. When the sectional onslaught arose, "such convictions did not vanish overnight." Quite the contrary. Those making a sectional appeal found many of their targets ultimately "yielding to party obligation." Parties buckled somewhat, but then bounced back and resumed control of the political landscape. What allowed them to do so was their continued hold on most Americans, a commitment that proved strong enough, in this first episode, to override all else. It was, as an observer noted, that "all parties hug their prejudices and animosities too closely to be prepared to reconcile or suspend their differences for the common good." The pressure may have been great, but party members were "too firmly knit together to yield" to "insidious efforts" to attract them away from their political homes.[21]

"The Wilmot Proviso was paramount to all Party," a South Carolinian wrote in 1847. A year later, the *New York Evening Post* argued that "the principles of Free Soil are the only ones at issue in the contest for President." But most Americans, in the election of 1848, continued to support their own party with "ardor, zeal, and earnestness." "[We] desire," a southern Whig editor wrote, "above all things, the triumph of our party." Whig official pronouncements made the party's position crystal clear. As one state convention put it, "We have never surrendered and WILL never surrender our common principles as a Whig party." An Ohioan added a commonplace personal note, "I have never been anything but a Whig. I don't know how to be anything else but a Whig." The reasons remained familiar. Sectional concerns changed little about the relevance of parties or their principles to most Americans. "The Whig party is a national party." Whatever its members' disagreements "on some questions of government," there was a "general identity of opinion on the great practical questions." Therefore, they had a "duty," and a commitment, to support any "*known, tried,* and *approved* WHIG as shall be designated by the National Convention." That was as conventional as it was possible to be, and quite unsurprising, given the partisan imperative at play.[22]

Once the Whigs came together in their national convention in Philadelphia and nominated Zachary Taylor and Millard Fillmore, therefore, the matter was settled. Taylor "had been nominated by the Whig convention, holden in conformity with the usage of the party, for years past, and fairly nominated. . . . He [was] the only Whig before the people as a candidate for the Presidency." There was no reason for any Whig to seek "temporary advantage" in an "alliance with new lights or untried theories." The only correct policy was the "straight forward course" of party loyalty. As the Massachusetts state Whig convention put it in its 1848 address to the state's Whig voters, "for your own credit as a Whig State, for the honor of the party to which you belong, for the success of the great cause in which you are engaged, and for the welfare of the country of which you are a constituent part, we call upon you to come forward in your strength, and sustain your principles."[23]

Democrats felt the same way—even those who had great sympathy for the Free Soil position on the territories. One of Van Buren's biographers suggests that his nomination by the Free Soil party was "almost a physical blow" to him, given its fundamental challenge to all that he had previously believed in. He was not alone. John Wentworth, leader of the pro–Wilmot Proviso forces among Illinois Democrats, wrote in 1848, "Let us Barn-Burners strive to lick Taylor first. He must be beaten, and if we have an independent organization in democratic states, he will beat us." And after the election, Wentworth lamented that "in losing sight of the old issues between the two parties at the elections," the defecting Democrats had made a great error.[24]

Democratic newspaper editors and pamphleteers made the same points as their Whig counterparts. It was "true," a northerner noted, that the Democratic presidential candidate, Lewis Cass, did not "advocate the Wilmot Proviso, but he is a democrat. On every cardinal point of the democratic creed, he is known to be right, and we have no wish to introduce other issues in this election." Another wrote: "I have so strong a repugnance to see the Whigs . . . elect General Taylor that I am resolved to give my vote to General Cass." He was "with us on all those issues that have divided parties for years past." That was the point. It was the consensus among partisan Democrats, North and South, that it was "the cardinal duty" of each of them, "always, and under all circumstances, to maintain the doctrines of his political faith above all other considerations." Democrats "adhere to [the] fundamental rule . . . that the great principles and measures of the democratic party are entitled to our first, and last, and only allegiance."[25]

All of this echoed the conventional truth to most Democrats and Whigs. Slavery was merely one issue among many; it did not eliminate other policy and loyalty considerations. Thus, as with any other disagreements among party members, there was room for compromise and certainly toleration of different outlooks in the interest of party unity and success. "You suggest," one Democrat wrote to Gideon Welles in 1849, that "Democrats & Free Soilers should come together and 'agree to disagree.' That is my doctrine. . . . I supported candidates last spring so long as they went with the Democratic party, whether they were Proviso men or not." All of them understood the primary "potency of party ties," which, in the election of 1848, had been tested and had largely succeeded in resisting the sectional challenge.[26]

The religious metaphor continued to play a central role in expressions about partisanship. In 1848, Van Buren was "the Kinderhook Iscariot himself," for succumbing, however regretfully, to the third party's appeal. And a disgusted southern sectionalist lamented, in familiar terms, that the rights of the South were always "sacrificed at the shrine of party."[27] Parties, these people ruefully understood, were primary in the American political world. The original politics of policy commitment and organization had grown into the politics of habit by adding the communal passions that helped define and energize the whole. The dedication of Americans to either one or the other of their party shrines was compelling, intense, powerful, and persistent as the 1850's began.

"A Law of Necessity in the Republic"

"Hardly ever do men change their manners, their religion, or their politics," a Whig editor wrote in 1849. Unsurprisingly, some did. In this political world, there were always a few people of doubtful loyalties or shifting commitments amid the avalanche of partisan devotion. No system, no matter how widespread and penetrating, covered everyone. Party leaders were secure in the knowledge, however, that the uncertain men were more vociferous than numerous. The election of 1848 and its aftermath confirmed their optimism, as did the normal partisan election of 1852. Most Americans remained partisan and loyal. Old issues—and the response to them—remained alive. The mass of Democrats continued to "have no fellow-feeling either with Whigs or traitors." To do anything other than go on politically as before was dismissed, on the whole, as an "absurd notion." It was easy enough, looking back over a decade or more, to be complacent about the stability of the system and the inability of anything, present or on the horizon, to challenge its dominance. "The principles of the Whig party are emblazoned on its banners. . . . Is there a Whig willing to desert them? Is there one unwilling to sustain them?" The answer, most believed, was a clear no.[28]

But in addition to the doubtful few and the occasional temporary disruption of the smooth run of partisan politics, there was a dynamic reality in the American political experience alongside the static one of unswerving party loyalty. Despite the hopes and beliefs of party members, the Democrats and Whigs' initial successful resistance to sectionalism in the 1840's did not end matters. The election of 1848 was one episode, not a conclusion. A renewed and more powerful assault on the two-party system and its values rose in the 1850's to disrupt and reshape the normal partisan course of American politics. Sectionalism re-emerged as an issue and was joined by other issues, especially nativism, to challenge party stability. Whig and Democratic leaders tried very hard once again, as they had in the 1840's, to tug the strings of party loyalty. This time they failed among a significant number of Americans.[29]

How could this be? The behavior of the defectors of the 1850's certainly forcefully challenged the "shrine of party" reality that had hitherto appeared to be so secure. In retrospect, it is easy to argue that the shift was inevitable. As Arthur Holmes wrote in 1859:

Reconstruction of parties seems to have grown into a law of necessity in the Republic. Questions once instinct with life become obsolete. Changing events evolve new interests which give a bias to the popular mind that finds an exponent in existing parties, or failing in this, drives them thence, and calls into being other and more efficient political organizations.[30]

The Democratic and Whig parties were both, after all, only coalitions. When disagreements over policy grew sharp enough, political disruption was inevitable—and so, it turned out, was a fundamental electoral and party realignment. New issues had arisen while some old ones had taken on more immediacy and power than they had had. Other issues, once vibrant and demanding, lost their importance and command of the scene. The existing parties resisted any shifts in their priorities and failed to satisfy the new demands emerging, many of which cut across the usual divisions between them. Sectionalism had, at last, crystallized as an effective, widespread, and sustained political determinant. Two new parties, the Republicans and the Know-Nothings, appeared on the political landscape during the realignment. One survived to become the second major party because its leaders, many drawn from the Whig ranks, were able to pull together, successfully, a set of policies and an appeal that met the expectations of the discontented members of the two existing parties. In doing so, sectionalism became a better organized and more important part of the American political nation than it had ever been.[31]

Still, what happened to the powerful devotion to party as party, that sentiment that had come to transcend policy commitments? To be sure, the transcendent, religious-like faith largely held among the mass of the Democrats even under the challenge of the 1850's. To these Democrats, the long-existing differences between the parties would "never die out." These men lived in an unchanging political world. As a result, only a relatively few left the party. The rest maintained and even reinvigorated their loyalties, loyalties that became even more intense in their subsequent years of great trial.[32]

The Whigs were another story. In the face of a powerful challenge, the party was no more by 1860. Its political failure was stunning and, given the nation's experience, surprising. But it was not because of the Whigs' weaker commitment to the partisan imperative, as has sometimes been suggested. Of course, antipartyism had not totally disappeared, and some Whigs continued to take a negative, or a reluctant, stance toward the role of political parties. But this was a much weaker attitude than the powerful antipartyism of the Revolutionary and postrevolutionary periods. In fact, many of the most politically active Whigs had not only accepted the organizational necessities of the new system but also manifested much the same rocklike and unswerving partisan commitment as their Democratic opponents.[33]

But as William Gienapp points out, the Whigs were psychologically battered by their loss in 1852 and their apparently bleak national prospects. Many of them were ripe for new directions, if members of any party ever were. Nevertheless, at first, when the Kansas-Nebraska controversy renewed the sectional challenge in the mid-1850's, some old-line Whigs resisted the changes that seemed inevitable. "The Whig party, 'tis said, is dead," Hamilton Fish wrote during the difficult year of 1855, "its principles obsolete, its issues gone." But, he added, "Whig principles can never die; they are as eternal as the everlasting hills." There was no justification for abandoning the policies "for which we have contended for twenty years." Whigs "should hold onto their present organization with the tenacity of death." Or, putting it in the terms of even deeper commitments, Fish continued, "I am a Whig. I desire no additional epitaph." Few Whigs, in fact, left their party easily or happily. There was much hesitancy and delay, and on the part of some, no little heartache. "I now see," George Baker wrote to William Seward, "what you saw long ago, how hard it is to break up an old party and organize a new one."[34]

Such cries may only have been the last plaintive outbursts of a few holdouts as obsolete as their party. Since the party was no more, those who wished to remain active in politics had no choice but to move on into new coalitions. Still, their policy commitments and emotive loyalties remained potent enough to affect the new political situation in its early stages. The Republicans adopted most of the old Whig principles. Tensions between former Whigs and former Democrats, each group clinging to its memories and its hostility to the other side, were a constant feature of the early history of the Republican party. And when that party took firm hold on the political scene, the emotional intensity of partisan commitment reestablished itself with great vigor. The Republican faithful, even the former Whigs among them, developed a loyalty to their Grand Old Party and antipathy to Democrats that became mainstays of the political world they inhabited.[35]

In the 1850's, to be sure, two-party competition dramatically weakened in much of the lower South as the Whigs gave way to the surging Democrats there. Sectional commitment and party loyalty intertwined within the Democratic party. But in the upper South, as Daniel Crofts points out, popular voting remained reliably consistent with earlier two-party patterns. Whig voters in North Carolina, Virginia, and Tennessee supported the Whigs' successor parties: the American, Opposition, and Constitutional Union. Furthermore, Crofts argues, the continuation of a competitive two-party system in these states initially frustrated secessionism in the crisis of 1860–61. That was because most of the upper South's electorate unsurprisingly "viewed the crisis through partisan lenses."[36]

The failure of the Whigs, therefore, reflected the institutional and political reality: the party's minority status among the voters, which had been powerfully confirmed in 1852, its further weakening with the defection of some of its key constituent groups, and the strategic need to attract dissident Democrats to an anti-Democratic movement. Unless the Whigs considered alternative frameworks, they were condemned to perpetual electoral weakness. All of these factors played powerful roles in the particular direction the political transformation of the 1850's took, stronger than any widespread failure of the partisan commitment characterizing the system on the part of the members of one party to the partisan dialogue.[37]

The political realignment of the 1850's demonstrated that the passionate commitment to party had limits, that powerful, cross-cutting issues could disrupt partisan loyalties among significant numbers of Americans. At the same time, the issues unleashed in the 1850's and fought out over the next decade went right to the heart of the country's values and meaning. The increase in ideological intensity along sectional lines in the 1850's and 1860's shook the political nation as severely as it had ever been shaken or was likely to be. The result was a civil war, the very antithesis of all that the builders of this political nation wanted to accomplish. Nor was its impact either brief or contained. As the years passed, the aftershocks continued to affect the political world directly and forcefully. But those effects were always rooted in the continuing strength of the earlier dominant partisan forces still powerfully at play.

In many ways, the Civil War was the transforming moment for American society in the nineteenth century. The defeat of the South, the end of slavery, and the persistence thereafter of important, sectionally defined cleavages posed new issues of governance and politics. The war's impact called for fresh ideas at every level. It was a vigorous and contentious era—a time also of important social changes that were particularly seen in the recasting of labor and caste relationships in both North and South. But in some arenas, the war, with all of its immense power, did not alter matters much. In the political nation, although the existing partisan system and its imperatives bent under the pressure, they did not break. Electoral coalitions shifted, and sectional tensions became a norm, but the central reality of partisanly defined and shaped political activities remained. The nation's agenda and institutions continued to reflect the dominance of two-party politics and the intense loyalties that had characterized the system since the 1830's. Neither 1861, nor 1865, nor 1877 was, then, a critical dividing line in terms of the existing values, norms, and behavior of the American political nation.

This was underscored by the fate of sectionalist politics in the years after the Civil War. Two-party competition did not slacken in the northern states until the 1890's. In the South, the Republicans tried for more than a decade to establish themselves as a viable, competitive party, particularly among old Whig voters whom they hoped to ally with the freedmen. Their efforts ultimately failed. In the train of those efforts, however, sectional tensions became incorporated into the partisan imperative. A solid Democratic South became the reality of American politics for almost a century thereafter. Southern Democrats, whatever their internal factionalism, continually expressed partisan commitments with an intensity that echoed the normal political discourse of the mid-nineteenth century, and that would have been quite familiar to the political participants of that era.[38]

There were, in sum, three stages to the sectional challenge to the nationalizing partisan domination of American politics. In the first, sectional tensions were always present and potentially important; but they usually remained inchoate and only able to raise the heat at occasional flash points. In the second stage, sectional differences proved powerful enough to reshape the nation's political conflict in significant ways and lead America into civil war. While partisanship remained potent, an important sectional element appeared in American politics and became a controlling dynamic in it. In the third stage, the two forces, of sectionalism and partisanship, intersected and came together within a structure defined by the partisan imperative, but modified in some of its substance by the other, sectional, force on the scene. Still, parties at the end continued to rule on the American political scene—for a time.

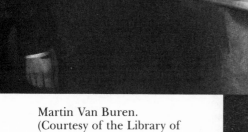

Martin Van Buren.
(Courtesy of the Library of
Congress.)

Abraham Lincoln.
(Courtesy of the Library of Congress.)

James K. Polk.
(Courtesy of the Library
of Congress.)

Thurlow Weed. (From Thurlow Weed
Barnes, *The Life of Thurlow Weed*, 2: *Memoir
of Thurlow Weed* [Cambridge, Mass., 1884].)

The Republican national convention, 1876. (From *Frank Leslie's Illustrated Newspaper*, July 1, 1876.)

Grand national Democratic banner, 1844. (Courtesy of the Cornell
University Libraries.)

Cover of the pamphlet "Report of the Discussion . . . ," 1844. (Courtesy of the Cornell University Libraries.)

Cover of the pamphlet "The Campaign Text Book," 1880. (Courtesy of the Cornell University Libraries.)

Grand demonstration of the democracy. (From *Harper's Weekly*, Oct. 24, 1868.)

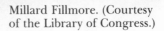

Millard Fillmore. (Courtesy
of the Library of Congress.)

Howell Cobb. (Courtesy of the
Library of Congress.)

Roscoe Conkling. (Courtesy of the
Historian of the United States Senate.)

The County Election, by George Caleb Bingham, 1851–52. (By permission of The Saint Louis Art Museum.)

REGULAR
DEMOCRATIC TICKET.

For President,
WINFIELD S. HANCOCK,
OF PENNSYLVANIA.

For Vice President,
WILLIAM H. ENGLISH,
OF INDIANA.

For Presidential Electors.

AT LARGE.
JOSHUA B. ABBOTT, of Boston.
JONAS H. FRENCH, of Gloucester.

1st District, PHILANDER COBB, of Kingston.
2d " PETER BUTLER, of Quincy.
3d " EDWARD B. RANKIN, of Somerville.
4th " CHARLES LEVI WOODBURY, of Boston.
5th " CHARLES E. HYMES, of Haverhill.
6th " JAMES H. CARLTON, of Newton.
7th " JOHN C. SANBORN, of Lawrence.
8th " LEVERETT SALTONSTALL, of Worcester.
9th " EDWIN CONANT, of Leominster.
10th " NAHUM HARWOOD, of Pittsfield.
11th " SAMUEL W. BOWERMAN, of Pittsfield.

For Governor,
CHARLES P. THOMPSON, of Woburn.

For Lieutenant Governor,
ALPHA E. THOMPSON, of Somerville.

For Secretary of State,
MICHAEL T. DONOHOE, of Newton.

For Treasurer and Receiver-General,
FRANCIS J. PARKER, of Greenfield.

For Auditor,
CHARLES R. FIELD, of Boston.

For Attorney-General,
PATRICK A. COLLINS, of Boston.

For Congress, Fifth District,
SELWIN Z. BOWMAN, of Somerville.

For Senator, First Middlesex District,
DANIEL W. LAWRENCE, of Medford.

For Councillor, Third District,
KNOWLTON S. CHAFFEE, of Cambridge.

For Sheriff,
GODFREY RIDER, of Medford.

For District Attorney, Northern District,
THOMAS T. HILL, of Woburn.

For Commissioner of Insolvency,
JAMES J. McCAFFERTY, of Lowell.

For Commissioner,
JOHN W. McDONALD, Jr., of Marlboro'

For Special Commissioner,
JOHN H. MORRISON, of Lowell.

For Representative, Fifth Middlesex Representative District,
LEWIS B. TRUE, of Everett.
CLEMENT MESERVE, of Hopkinton.
QUINCY A. VINAL, of Somerville.

Ballot for the regular Democratic
ticket, 1880. (Courtesy of the Cornell
University Libraries.)

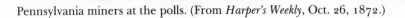

Pennsylvania miners at the polls. (From *Harper's Weekly*, Oct. 26, 1872.)

Marriage of the Free Soil and Liberty parties, 1848. (Courtesy of the Cornell University Libraries.)

John C. Calhoun.
(Courtesy of the Historian
of the United States
Senate.)

Charles Sumner. (Courtesy of
the Historian of the United
States Senate.)

The United States Capitol in the 1850's. (Courtesy of the Historian of the United States Senate.)

CHAPTER EIGHT

"To the Polls": The Structure of Popular Voting Behavior, 1838-1892

Shut up your shops and stores of every description,
Whigs! and go to the Polls. The presence of every man
is necessary.

—*Richmond Whig*, Nov. 7, 1848

VOTERS IN NEW YORK STATE went to the polls on Tuesday, November 6, 1838, to elect a governor, congressmen, and state legislators. In the early morning of that day, Democratic and Whig party workers were already at work at the many voting sites throughout the state, preparing for the busy day that lay ahead. The American political nation relied heavily on parties not only to present the issues at stake and mobilize the electorate, but also to provide much of the administrative capability to make the elections possible. Unfortunately, on that particular Tuesday, there were torrents of rain, and polls became crowded "with loiterers" escaping the downpour. Between the weather and the crowded conditions, only 16,460 votes were cast in New York City, down over 2,000 from the municipal elections of the previous April. "The fact, however, that over 16,000 votes were polled in such a rainy, foggy, muddy, uncomfortable day as yesterday," the editor of the *Journal of Commerce* noted, "proves that our population is thoroughly roused."[1] And so it was, not only that gloomy November day, but on all but a very few of the many election days in mid-nineteenth-century America.

The Americans who went to the polls in all kinds of weather and conditions believed that voting, and all its attendant activities, had great importance and imposed significant responsibilities on them. Casting a ballot at each election, one southern editor argued, was "no unmeaning task," but "the freeman's highest political privilege" and "noblest political duty." Consequently, no American who was entitled to participate had "the right to withhold" his vote.[2] But voting was more than civics. Election campaigns raised the temperature of the country and focused what was at stake. They were serious events in the life of the country, and polling day was the moment toward which all of the efforts and energies of the political nation were directed. It was when all of the arguments made, organizational efforts undertaken, and fissures plumbed came together in an opportunity for popular expression. When the people voted, they demonstrated how well they had absorbed the main elements defining the political nation and understood the significance of the parties' distinctive rhetoric, how much they had internalized the political culture, and what their best calculation was of how to attain their own particular goals in that particular season. Voting was, therefore, at once an indicator of the country's political condition and an indicator of the state of mind of the individual voter.

"The Most Sacred Political Right"

A great many Americans were able to make their minds known this way. The rules defining eligibility to vote were quite generous by 1840—if one was an adult white male citizen. Almost all of that group could legally vote by the time of the Harrison–Van Buren election. Anomalies remained throughout the system, to be sure, but most states had fairly loose legal suffrage requirements, and those that still retained more rigorous standards were beginning to loosen them. Citizenship and some usually undemanding residency obligation were normal, although some state constitutions used the expansive word "inhabitants," extending suffrage to noncitizens. (Twenty-two states permitted aliens, usually those who had declared their intention to become citizens, to vote at one time or another during the nineteenth century.) Further, the existing requirements were rarely enforced rigorously. Those adult white males who wished to vote had little difficulty doing so. In Alabama, Mills Thornton notes, "it was regarded as insulting to challenge another man's right to vote and the action was seldom taken." If challenged, it proved relatively easy in most cases for someone to vote anyway.[3]

There were several good reasons for this attitude toward the right to vote. Although much about suffrage eligibility was still a partisan sore point in the 1840's and 1850's, there seemed to be, by then, broad agreement among Whigs as well as Democrats that white males affected by the actions of the political realm should, if they met minimum requirements, participate in choosing officeholders. Senator James Buchanan spoke for many in the generation that established and first operated this political nation when he declared: "The right of suffrage is the most sacred political right which the citizens of a free government can enjoy."[4]

At the same time, in many places, crucial distinctions that might have limited voting rights proved hard to enforce. The fact that parties scrambled for every advantage in these years also played an important role in expanding suffrage. As Don Doyle remarks about one Illinois town, "In a rapidly growing region, the distinction between residents and transients could hardly be defined with certainty, and the fervid competition between the parties forced both sides to ignore residency requirements." Formally registering voters to determine and list which people were actually eligible was part of the process in some states early on, but there were contentious debates about the need for such requirements in others, and the official registration of voters by state legislation did not become the norm until later in the century.[5]

Whatever limits existed were likely to be set by local party officials hoping to discourage suspected members of the opposition party from voting at a particular polling place. But even the most recent migrants did not have great trouble finding a place to vote in many small towns and villages. A community tended to define all its recognized (white male) members as political participants and entitled to vote, regardless of whether they strictly met the standards mandated in state constitutions. Certainly, election officials, party organizers, and community leaders usually acted in that spirit. They might occasionally raise limiting barriers; they maintained relatively few of them in a universal fashion.[6]

Apart from the rain, that election day in 1838 was little different from the many similar days in other months and other years. As always, there was intense excitement and an exuberant, busy atmosphere. In addition to the voters streaming in and out, and the party workers and election officials who had to be there, large crowds bustled around the polling places: wives, children, and other family members, as well as vendors, entertainers, and simple gawkers. Elections were special events. Amid the continuous electioneering and political arguments, picnics, drinking, and boisterous celebration went on throughout each polling day. As Daniel Walkowitz points out, these activities were not extraneous to the central event. In nineteenth-century America, "voting was more than a political act; it was participation in a social convention."[7]

The actual manner in which the voters cast their ballots reinforced this public ritual. Elections were open events and recognized as such for almost all of the period. A voter usually did not do much to mask his choice when he placed his party-provided printed ballot in the designated box. The party workers from both sides could hardly fail to note the way someone voted, nor were the large group of the faithful or merely curious who were watching likely to miss what each person did. (The political commitments of one's neighbors were usually well known anyway. Few people hid them, and local party workers were diligent in seeking to find out where each man stood.) In addition, as late as the early 1840's, seven states retained the colonial-era practice of *viva voce* voting. The listed voters of Virginia, Kentucky, Illinois, Missouri, Arkansas, Texas, and Oregon simply waited for election officials to call out their names, then declared their choices openly for all to hear. As Paul Goodman notes, an American's political "preference was public information."[8]

Many commentators celebrated such openness. "Secrecy was perceived as fostering nothing but deception" in a society that still vigorously adhered to its small-town and rural values. The Republican senator Lyman Trumbull told Congress, as late as 1867, that he did not want to see anybody "sneaking to the polls and hiding his expression in a secret ballot." It was, after all, "by secret ballots and secret systems of other kinds that liberty has been trodden down everywhere." He preferred "the open, independent voter that goes to the polls and tells how he votes." Others disagreed, and there were a number of attempts to change the system and impose a secret ballot. But for most of the life of this political nation, the advocates of openness had their way as part of the rituals of the political community.[9]

Coming to the Polls

The parties' determined mobilization efforts worked stunningly well. There had been occasional examples of high turnout in the early nineteenth century, usually in hotly contested state races. Now, Americans repeatedly turned out to vote in record numbers at all levels of electoral activity, achieving peaks that have never been equaled since. The fevered 1840 election saw an unprecedented (for a national election) 80.3 percent turnout, and there was not much fall-off thereafter. About 78 percent of those eligible voted in presidential elections between 1840 and 1892, compared with just under 50 percent between 1824 and 1836 (Table 8.1). Turnout in Kentucky's presidential elections, for example, averaged 70 percent between 1840 and 1856, and 73.3 percent between 1876 and 1892. In New York state, 88.6 percent of the eligible voters turned out in presidential elections between 1840 and 1892, compared with 78.3 percent in the state's already partially mobilized condition between 1824 and 1836.[10]

Turnout was comparatively high in congressional, gubernatorial, and local elections as well, particularly when measured against earlier times, although the figures for those offices fell below the presidential totals in the 1838–93 period (which had not been the case earlier).

TABLE 8.1

National Turnout to Vote, Presidential Elections, 1840–1892

Year	Estimated turnout	Year	Estimated turnout
1840	80.3%	1868	80.9%
1844	79.0	1872	72.1
1848	72.8	1876	82.6
1852	69.8	1880	80.6
1856	79.4	1884	78.3
1860	81.8	1888	80.5
1864	76.3	1892	75.9

SOURCES: Walter Dean Burnham, "Voter Participation in Presidential Elections, by State: 1824–1968," in *Historical Statistics of the United States from Colonial Times to 1970* (Washington, D.C.: Government Printing Office, 1975), 2:1071–1072; Burnham, "The Turnout Problem," in A. James Reichley, ed., *Elections American Style* (Washington, D.C.: Brookings Institution, 1987), 97–123; William Gienapp, "'Politics Seems to Enter into Everything,'" in Stephen E. Maizlish and John J. Kusma, eds., *Essays on American Antebellum Politics, 1840–1860* (College Station: Texas A&M Univ. Press, 1982), 18–23; Paul Kleppner, *Who Voted: The Dynamics of Electoral Turnout, 1870–1980* (New York: Praeger, 1982).

TABLE 8.2

New York State Turnout Patterns, 1824–36 and 1838–92

	Mean turnout	
Election	1824–1836	1838–1892
President	78.3%	88.6%
Governor	72.9	82.1
Congress	68.3	80.0

SOURCE: Walter Dean Burnham, "The Appearance and Disappearance of the American Voter," in Burnham, *The Current Crisis in American Politics* (New York: Oxford Univ. Press), 160–61.

Off-year turnout averaged just below 65 percent for the country as a whole. As in presidential elections, turnout for these contests varied about 10 percent between the earlier period and the post-1838 era, as the New York state data indicate (Table 8.2).

There were variations over time in all of these patterns. Turnout regularly remained high in the 1840's, then dipped slightly from these levels in the 1850's, and then rose to higher percentages than ever before. Turnout in gubernatorial, congressional, and presidential elections was 62.8 percent nationally between 1838 and 1844, then dropped to 58.5 percent between 1846 and 1852. It then began to rise again. In 1860, for example, the turnout to vote for President was just below 82 percent of those eligible in the nation as a whole, a normal figure for the era after 1856. This was rooted in the similar pattern existing in most of the states. Putting it another way, between 1836 and 1852 almost 37 percent of the states, with about one-third of the national population, had mean turnouts at the polls of over 65 percent. By 1876, and then until 1892, more than half the states, with two-thirds of the population, reached that figure.

There were differences in this pattern from place to place. In many states, the percentage of those eligible who actually voted far exceeded the national averages. Indiana's turnout for President in 1856–60 reached almost 89 percent of those eligible. In Mississippi, it was 83.9 percent, in New Jersey, over 86 percent in those years. Such patterns also existed below the state level. In Clinton township, Ohio, between 1850 and 1860, voter turnout averaged 94.5 percent. In one county of Illinois, the number going to the polls to vote for President averaged 88.6 percent of those eligible between 1840 and 1852, 78.1 percent for governor, and 73.8 percent for Congress. And all of these figures continued to grow after 1860. In both New York and Indiana, for example, presidential turnout ran better than 90 percent in the years between 1860 and 1892.[11]

Elsewhere, turnout figures were lower but usually significantly greater than they had customarily been before 1838. In the southern states in the pre–Civil War years, voter turnout was relatively congruent with the rest of the country, much higher than it had been in the earlier era but not quite up to the North's totals. In the slave states (excluding South Carolina), turnout for President averaged below the national norm, reaching 70.3 percent between 1840 and 1860. A similar turnout pattern, close to but just below the rest of the country, occurred in elections for statewide offices and congressmen in off-years as well. Between 1838 and 1858, southern turnout in such elections averaged 64.8 percent. As in the North, some states exceeded the regional norm by very large amounts. In Tennessee turnout for President averaged 83.3 percent between 1840 and 1860. In Georgia, turnout averaged 80 percent in state and national elections between 1825 and 1860, with the same chronological deviations as in the nation as a whole: between 1825 and 1837, the number going to the polls averaged 68 percent of those eligible; between 1838 and 1849, the figure reached 84 percent, and between 1851 and 1860, it was 80 percent.[12]

The seven top turnout states in presidential elections between 1840 and 1860 consisted of four northern and three southern states (Table 8.3). Only after 1860, did the southern turnout pattern markedly differ from the rest of the country. Then it sagged far below the North's standard owing to the widespread exclusionary actions taken after the Civil War, initially against former Confederates, and then, more permanently, against the newly enfranchised freedmen. Only when these

TABLE 8.3

Highest State Average Turnout Percentages, Presidential Elections, 1840–1860

State	Average turnout	State	Average turnout
New York	88.95%	Tennessee	83.3%
Indiana	84.3	Ohio	82.8
Mississippi	83.9	Georgia	81.7
New Jersey	83.8		

SOURCES: U.S. Bureau of the Census, *Historical Statistics of the United States, Colonial Times to 1970* (Washington, D.C.: Government Printing Office, 1976); Walter Dean Burnham, "The Turnout Problem," in A. James Reichley, ed., *Elections American Style* (Washington, D.C.: Brookings Institution, 1987), 113–14.

actions occurred (after 1865) did the South significantly deviate from the patterns set by the structural forces defining voter turnout in this political nation.[13]

Americans in the 1840's and later retained the sensitivity to political corruption that had been the hallmark of republican ideology. A number of observers then (and since) believed that corruption occurred at the polls and helped inflate nineteenth-century turnout figures substantially. Every election campaign ended with one side or the other publicly appealing to this belief and insisting that their opponents had permitted ineligible noncitizens and nonresidents to vote, had paid some of them to come to the polls, often more than once, and had miscounted the numbers in their own favor when they could. There were always "frauds at the BALLOT BOXES" to complain about. In 1845, Edward Everett referred to "the indefinite expansibility of the Alien vote" as the key to Democratic success. Foreigners, he claimed, were either naturalized illegally just before election day or else permitted to vote in Democratic areas whether or not they were formally certified citizens.[14]

All of these charges involved alleged practices that added voters to the rolls. The high turnout percentages would therefore be quite suspect. Elements of the charges ring true. Certainly, some multiple voting occurred as "floaters" plied their trade at more than one voting station. In an era of nonexistent or unobserved registration laws, the ability of noncitizens to vote was always a good possibility, as was the participation of nonresidents if there were accommodating election officials and no one to challenge the voter. Instant naturalization occurred. Questionable final vote counts that are out of line with the size of an area's population and previous totals in the same place also exist. At times, "dead men voted in New Orleans, purchased 'floaters' voted in Providence." All of these practices should have inflated the turnout figures.[15]

Such accusations, however, were quickly countered at the time, and a number of historians have expressed their skepticism since about the extent of corrupt electoral acts. William Gienapp suggests that "illegal voting in these decades [1840–60] was neither widespread nor significant." Reuben Davis, a Mississippi congressman, argued in his memoirs that "there was little trickery and no corruption in the politics of those days and a man who had dared to tamper with a ballot-box, or who had been detected in any fraud by the people, would have been torn to pieces without a moment's hesitation." Davis is perhaps too sanguine. But cries of fraud were often considered to be the wailing of losers seeking to explain their defeat and to delegitimize the winners. As Abraham Lincoln told his colleagues in the Illinois legislature in 1840, he "had every reason to believe that all this hue and cry about frauds was entirely groundless, and raised for other than honest purposes." Putting the alleged corrupt practices into context can shift their meaning significantly. At times, for example, people were prevented from voting by nativists and others, often violently. In such cases, the corrupt acts, instead of inflating turnout, may have had the opposite effect.[16]

There is also the question of what constituted citizenship, residence, and eligibility in this era. Many of those who voted, while perhaps technically ineligible, were nevertheless considered to be part of the political universe by their neighbors. As a result, they were often welcomed at the polls and accepted as legitimate voters by many of their contemporaries. Parties worked to maximize their advantage if they could, largely by stretching the limits of what was an ambiguous situation. There were also some strong built-in checks in the system. Party workers were constantly on guard against the depredations of the other side and never hesitant about challenging potential voters on residence and other grounds. As Walter Dean Burnham has written, "Normally, it would seem, the system worked without excessive ballot-box stuffing because in the rural areas of North and West people knew each other and because in the cities the two parties had every incentive to watch each other. Moreover, each organization's cadres had an extremely precise idea of just how many 'troops' the other 'army' had."[17] The extent and success of corrupt practices in such an environment remain problematic, certainly until much later in the century.

Paul Kleppner argues that the high turnout figures were essentially caused by the partisan structure of American politics, which strongly encouraged popular participation. "As party organization became more common and more fully developed, and as higher proportions of the electorate internalized party norms, . . . turnout surged upward and then stabilized at the higher level," that is, from 1840 onward. Party organizations and party appeals did their work well in repeatedly stimulating people to come to the polls everywhere in the country. Yet behind that pattern was a complicated reality, in which "restless migration was a national phenomenon." In the northern states, for example, Robert Doherty suggests, "society was composed of two populations: the stable and the transient." Less than half of an area's population remained there between two census counts, whether it was a large city, small town, or rural crossroad. The other half consisted of new arrivals who, in their turn, usually did not stay rooted in any new community they entered. The nation was characterized by a residentially unstable, highly mobile electorate.[18]

This restless population had a direct impact on the composition of the electorate from one polling day to the next. The very high population turnover at large meant that eligible voters were a different pool of individuals in each place each year. Studies based on the surviving community poll books of the period, in which party officials regularly listed every voter, have fleshed out the picture. The annual population turnover in Washington county, Oregon, in the 1850's, for example, averaged between 24 percent and 35 percent of the adult males. Because of this turnover, the number of new voters in a given election was about 40 percent of the total electorate in Springfield, Illinois, in the 1850's. Moreover, the number who voted in more than one election varied widely and was never an overwhelming proportion of the total electorate. In Clinton township in Shelby county, Ohio, only about 3 percent of the voters went to the polls in every election between 1850 and 1860, about 17 percent voted in more than half of the elections, and 47 percent of the voters went to the polls only once. The figures for Springfield, Illinois, were lower for persistent voters and higher for one-time participants. In Washington county, Oregon, again, only 30 percent of the voters voted in three successive congressional elections in the late 1850's. Kenneth Winkle found in Ohio that, "instead of a cohesive band of faithful voters constantly turning out from year to year, poll books reveal that the great majority of the township's voters were only short-term participants during the 1850s." The active American electorate "was a constantly shifting collection of [such] short-term participants."[19]

There was a social class influence on this pattern of voter turnout. Winkle finds that in both Ohio and Springfield, Illinois, persistent voters were "wealthier" and "more occupationally skilled" than were the members of the other, less participatory categories. At the other end of the spectrum, the bottom 20 percent of the eligible electorate in terms of property holding did not vote with the same regularity as those at the top of the social pyramid. In Prince Edward county, Virginia, nonvoters were more likely than voters to be non-slaveholders in the community. Daniel Calhoun also finds that those least likely to participate in this era in San Francisco and Pittsburgh were from the unskilled-worker, lower end of the scale. "Much of the economic division in politics was between participation and nonparticipation," he argues, "not just between one party choice and another."[20]

"Clearly," Winkle concludes, "political engagement was associated with economic standing." On the other hand, the relationship between social class and turnout was less pertinent in this era than at other times in our history. In the late twentieth century, the association of higher turnout with high wealth and educational status is clear-cut and one of the dominant aspects of American political behavior. In contrast, in the nineteenth century, Paul Kleppner suggests, "there were not the glaring differences in social group participation rates that now mark the electoral universe." Despite the variations that existed, many people, regardless of class, came to the polls in a given election. "Rich and poor, learned and uneducated, participated at reasonably similar levels to produce an almost fully mobilized electorate."[21]

A residentially volatile pattern of electoral participation characterized the American political scene. There was an ever-changing mix of voters in each successive election season, some moving into a place, some moving out, most voting at some point, some voting occasionally, some never casting a ballot at all. As a result of this pattern of residential volatility, Kleppner defines three categories of voters between 1840 and 1892: core, marginal, and nonparticipating. Core voters (those who voted in at least two successive elections for President) constituted just over 50 percent of the national electorate before 1860; marginal voters (those who voted once in a sequence but not the next time) were about 25 percent of the electorate; and nonvoters were also about 25 percent of the voting population. After 1860, the number of core voters nationally increased to over 62 percent; the marginals dropped to around 15 percent, and the nonvoters fell to about 20 percent of the total electorate.[22]

Yet despite the great residential volatility characteristic of most voters, and the marginal participation of some of them in political activities, the end result when the votes were counted was a remarkably stable pattern. Most American political communities, from frontier Oregon, to growing Jacksonville or Springfield, Illinois, to long-established villages in upstate New York, or Alabama rural hamlets, could be counted on to vote in great numbers in regular fashion. At the same time, most of them could also be labeled as being either Democratic or Whig, or, later, Republican, and be counted on to behave consistently in terms of that partisan label, despite the tumult and turmoil of the large population movements occurring in every community.

"Habit, Sentiment, and . . . Inheritance"

Between 1840 and 1892, the two major parties regularly received better than 95 percent of all of the votes cast nationally for President. There was third-party activity in most presidential elections, as well as in some local and statewide ones, most of the time after 1840. Occasionally, in the disruptive period between 1848 and 1860, and at the end of the era in 1892, they received more than 10 percent of the national popular vote. But the proportion of the vote cast for minor parties over the whole era was much less than that. In off-year elections, there were similar patterns of vote stability as communities repeatedly voted for the same parties as they did in presidential election years. The important point is that national stability was not based on counterbalancing voter volatility in thousands of local communities. Rather, most places tended to support one party or the other with great consistency from one election to the next. As Thornton suggests for antebellum Alabama, the beats, the basic political units in the state, "rarely deviated from their usual voting patterns."[23]

A well-defined political system, then, organized a volatile social pattern. As Samuel P. Hays has written, the massive residential transiency characterizing nineteenth-century America took place "within rather stable and continuous physical and institutional structures which give definition to a community and to human relationships." In each election, the vigorous and repetitive electioneering rallies of the political parties, culminating in the exciting sociability of election day itself, had a substantive impact, both on the communities in which they took place and on the American political process itself. "The role of political parties," Don Doyle argues, "as mechanisms for integrating newcomers, as well as for bridging class and ethnic divisions and recruiting and training local leaders, provided important antidotes to the mobility and fragmentation of new communities."[24]

A memoir published late in the nineteenth century accurately commented that "anyone can see, by examining the votes of 1828, how little the strength of parties has changed since. The truth is, that politics, like religion, descend from father to son, with little variation." That descent occurred, one might add, even as fathers and sons wandered from community to community, apparently carrying their party commitments with them. The extensive research on popular voting behavior over the past scholarly generation paints a clear picture of a very stable, highly competitive, and strongly partisan political order (especially in comparison with the era before 1838). Each major party had a "standing army" of loyal supporters after 1838 who turned out regularly to support their partisan community. The consistent level of party support in various geographic entities was significantly interrupted only by the electoral realignment of the 1850's, but it then settled back into its former rocklike stability for more than thirty years thereafter.[25]

After 1840, the correlations of the national vote distribution were very high between succeeding elections, and over more extended time frames as well. Between 1840 and 1852, the mean correlation of the presidential vote in each successive election pair (1840/1844, 1844/ 1848, 1848/1852) across the country averaged .82. The vote in the presidential election of 1852 correlated with the presidential vote eight years before at .80. The 1852 contest even correlated with the disruptive three-party race of 1848 at .78. For the period 1840–60 as a whole, the mean correlation figure was .73. The same stability characterized the period after the Civil War as well. Inter-election correlations of successive pairs of elections between 1868 and 1892 had a mean of .81. National-level correlations for all of the elections across the whole era from 1840 through 1892 averaged .75.[26]

This voter commitment was also apparent in the state-level returns both for President and for the other offices contested. In New York state, statewide elections between 1838 and 1854 correlated at a very high level, usually around .8, sometimes reaching well over .9. After a short period of voter volatility during the electoral realignment associated with the political uproar of the middle 1850's, stability returned at a .85 level between 1860 and 1892. The same stable pattern appeared in most other states. In New Jersey, presidential-level correlations were always well over .90 until the realignment of the mid-1850's. The same pattern was true in Georgia and North Carolina, as was the pattern of high correlations between different offices filled. In North Carolina, for example, the Democrats' vote for President in 1840 correlated with both the 1842 gubernatorial vote and the 1844 presidential vote at .97. Similarly strong relationships existed between different offices and elections in different years throughout the 1840's and 1850's.[27]

The commonly used party ballot form, with its list of all of the party's candidates together on a single sheet, contributed to the major party commitment characterizing the votes cast for the other offices as well. In New Jersey, legislative races in 1844 correlated with the vote for governor at .99 and for President at .97. In Mississippi, the same strong relationship existed. The Democratic vote for governor in 1845 correlated with the vote for Congress in that year at .97, with the presidential vote at .94, and with the state legislative races at .84. So far as the distribution of voters between the parties was concerned, each succeeding election, regardless of the office contested or when it occurred, looked remarkably like the one before. But the relationship went beyond the particular ballot form. Party leaders argued that each office being contested was equal to the others and was part of the same partisan conflict. The returns suggest that local and state races were as "inseparably interwoven" as the party leaders claimed they were.[28]

Even with the powerful disruption of the 1850's, Thomas P. Alexander argues that between 1840 and 1860, about 90 percent of the voters for a party in one election supported the same party in a subsequent contest. Paul Kleppner reports the same figure in the period from 1860 to 1892, and suggests that only about 5 percent of the electorate switched parties between elections in those years. Apparently, "habit, sentiment, and . . . inheritance" held sway in the American electorate. As a result, politicians were able to predict outcomes with great accuracy. Horatio Seymour pointed out during one campaign, in a not untypical comment, that "the October elections will show the drift." They usually did. Political leaders like Seymour "were dealing," Alexander concludes, "with largely intractable masses of voters, who were not likely to accept a conscious change of party."[29]

This extraordinary voter stability produced closely competitive elections. Between 1840 and 1860, the same party won successive presidential elections only once (the Democrats in 1852 and 1856). Contemporary observers believed that the Democracy dominated the first decade and a half of this political nation. "It is claimed by the Locofocos," the Whig *Ohio State Journal* reported in 1852, "and sometimes admitted by Whigs, that the Locofocos have a majority of the people of the United States, and that in order to carry an election for President, the Whigs must gain votes from the other side." In 1852, the Democrats did have a majority, but the national pattern over the whole period was closer than the remark suggests. Democrats won 54 percent of the seats in Congress and the pool of presidential electors between 1834 and 1853. But they won only two of four presidential elections, and the total popular vote actually favored the Whigs, 48.3 percent to 48.1 percent.[30]

The general pattern of competitiveness was based on high levels of party competition everywhere in the country. Alexander has noted that "a close, nationwide rivalry between Democrats and Whigs formed the basic configuration of presidential politics, not only in total popular vote but also within most of the states and even within a number of counties. Neither party could muster as much as a two-to-one majority in almost three-fourths of the nation's counties in 1840, or even 60 percent in considerably more than one half." Paul Kleppner shows that between the early 1830's and the early 1850's "neither party was dominant in any region. . . . The relatively close balance between the two parties at the national level . . . resulted from geographically widespread competition." Further, in the early period, most voters (over 55 percent) lived in very competitive areas, fewer than 4 percent in noncompetitive situations.[31]

Finally, this strong competitiveness existed not only in presidential elections, but in most gubernatorial and congressional contests as well. In Pennsylvania, in four straight elections between 1844 and 1851, the winning candidate for governor never received as much as 51 percent of the popular vote. In Ohio, the Democrats won five of eight governors' races between 1838 and 1851, averaging just over 50 percent of the vote to the Whigs' 47.3 percent. In Tennessee, the Democrats also won five of eight elections for governor, with an average of 50.8 percent of the statewide vote to their opponents' 49.2 percent.

One can examine this pattern more comprehensively by looking at the voting behavior of the largest states in the Union. (Among them were four slave states and five free; three of them were in the Northeast, two lay in the Old Northwest, one was in the Upper South, two in the Border South and one in the Deep South. Together, they controlled over 60 percent of the national electoral vote in the 1840's.). In all of these states together, the Democrats averaged 48 percent of the vote in gubernatorial races between 1838 and 1853, the Whigs 48.4 percent. Indices of competitiveness further underline the close character of the contest between the parties throughout the nation. Measuring the closeness (or one-sidedness) of the parties' electoral competition over a set of contests indicates that six of these crucial large states can be labeled intensely competitive, meaning that each major party received strong enough support in them over the period to win

TABLE 8.4

Indices of Party Competitions, Governors' Races, Largest States, 1838–1853

State		Mean percentage of popular vote	Index of competition
Georgia	D	50.5%	
	W	49.5	.99
Indiana	D	50.9	
	W	47.7	.97
Kentucky	D	46.3	
	W	53.0	.93
Massachusetts	D	36.7	
	W	49.6	.85
New York	D	46.7	
	W	48.7	.98
North Carolina	D	50.4	
	W	43.6	.93
Ohio	D	49.6	
	W	46.1	.96
Pennsylvania	D	51.3	
	W	47.7	.96
Tennessee	D	49.9	
	W	50.1	.998

SOURCE: *Congressional Quarterly's Guide to U.S. Elections* (Washington, D.C.: 1975).

any given election in the set. Neither party dominated election outcomes in such states. Two of these states were moderately competitive; that is, one party was usually in the lead, but the other remained
within striking distance and occasionally won a statewide victory. Only
one state, Massachusetts, lay on the border between dominant one-
party and safe one-party, that is, one party always won out there and
by secure margins. The overall level of competitiveness in these states
was .95, right at the intensely competitive point (Table 8.4).[32]

In voting for members of Congress, there was less competitiveness
in results across the country. In most states, there was a range of competitive seats, a number that were consistently dominated by one
party, and a few that were unopposed walkovers. Examples of each
type appeared regardless of section. In Illinois, for example, between
1838 and 1853, in all the races run, twelve fell within the competitive
band, twenty-four were in the dominant one-party range, and nine
were uncontested. In his study of congressional elections over two
centuries, David Brady found that in the years before the electoral realignment of the mid-1850's, more than one-half of all congressional
districts were highly competitive electorally, with the vote margins between the parties resting at 5 percent or less of the total cast. The
number of such competitive seats fell after the mid-1850's, largely be-

cause of the shift in voting in the South. Nevertheless, they consistently outnumbered the number of safe seats. This situation changed markedly only in the elections of 1894, when, for the first time since the pre-partisan era, the number of safe seats outnumbered those that were competitive. (The number of safe seats in Congress, of course, has grown throughout the twentieth century to approach 100 percent.)[33]

The stable, competitive pattern established after 1838 was interrupted by a powerful electoral realignment that occurred between 1854 and 1860. In that six-year period, correlations between successive elections fell from their former high levels as, in contrast to their usual glacial movement, each party's vote totals and distribution swung wildly from one election to the next, especially in the northern states. In the state and congressional elections of 1854, for example, the Democrats lost 76 House seats (70 of them in the North), and seven governorships (six in the North). In New York state, the Democrats lost the governorship, eighteen of the twenty-one congressional seats they held, and control of the state legislature. Their share of New York's popular vote fell seventeen percentage points, from over 50 percent in the governorship race two years before to only 33 percent of the total state vote. It was a stunning reverse, repeated, if not quite so decisively, in most other northern states.[34]

This was not a temporary setback for the Democrats. The elections of 1854 were the first stage of a process that realigned some American voters into new party homes. High levels of volatility continued for the rest of the decade as the realignment continued to affect successive elections. Still, when the eruption ended in the 1860's, as noted earlier, most voters had stayed put. To be sure, a new party emerged out of the old Whigs, some dissident Democrats, and members of third parties, along with a number of new voters. Robert Fogel argues that almost 90 percent of Abraham Lincoln's vote in 1860 came from constituencies that had voted Whig and Free Soil in 1852. This realignment was, as noted, a significant event in the American electoral universe. But whatever its great importance, after the realignment ended, the same pattern of two-party polarization continued in that voting universe as before. The Republicans replaced the Whigs and added a critical (but small) number of non-Whigs to their ranks. The Democratic share of the national two-party vote leveled off at a slightly lower figure than the party had previously enjoyed. From 1864 to 1892, their presidential vote fell to 47.3 percent from 48.1 percent in the years before 1854.[35]

Republicans seemed to dominate the new national landscape after 1860 as the Democrats had seemed to years before. But overall, at the presidential and congressional level, a new, stable majority did not emerge. Rather, American elections came to be characterized by the closest national competition that the country has ever known. Democrats repeatedly lost the presidency from 1860 on, but between 1876 and 1892, the popular vote margins between the parties were extraordinarily narrow. The contest to control Congress was also very close. Paul Kleppner and Walter Dean Burnham have compared this tight electoral situation with earlier and later moments in American political history. In the era before 1838 and in the subsequent one after 1894, the competitive patterns differ substantially from that existing between 1838 and 1893. In fact, in both periods, American electoral behavior was essentially noncompetitive.[36]

There were important regional adjustments as a result of the realignment of the 1850's that also affected the general pattern of the popular vote. After 1860, there was much more of a sectional cast to party support than had existed before, (although not as much as there would be later, after the political shifts of the 1890's). Southern politics after the Civil War lacked most of the basic two-party competitiveness that characterized most of the rest of the country. Many northern urban centers were also uncompetitive. The proportion of Americans living in highly electorally competitive areas in the postwar decades dropped to 44 percent of the total (from 55 percent earlier). The number of competitive congressional districts fell to 40 percent of the total from more than 50 percent. A system of national two-party competitiveness before the realignment and the war had been replaced by a system that seemed to be similar but that was based on less competition within states and regions than had earlier been the case.[37] Nevertheless, when the smoke cleared after these shifts, the essential structure of the American political nation remained as before. In the older states, the power of partisan commitment in the electorate, if anything, increased from the 1860's onward. The one deviation, Paul Kleppner suggests, was in the newly admitted states of the plains and mountain West. There, partisan bonding was much less potent than elsewhere, voters being "demonstrably more susceptible to the operation of short-term forces." There was also five times as much split-ticket voting there as in the northeastern states.[38]

Although variations in voting behavior always existed, they were within well-marked boundaries of the American political nation. As Americans wandered, apparently restlessly, across the nation's geographic expanse, they were repeatedly drawn into the political system in a particular way. They cast ballots repeatedly, wherever they happened to be, and their behavior at the polls suggested their internalization of party cues, approaches, and arguments. Their long-standing commitment led, in turn, to a persistent partisan stability in the nineteenth-century American electoral universe. Political parties structured the popular vote in thousands of communities across the nation in ways unknown before 1838. They created a sustained, highly mobilized, deeply polarized, and closely competitive electoral order. Whatever the numbers of migrants moving through, whatever the socioeconomic dimensions of mobility and voter turnout, party labels carried the day in the American political nation. The partisan "obstinacy" of the voters gave elections in America a character they had never had before. And, elections would never be the same again as, in the years after 1893, the party-shaped phenomena of high mobilization, intense polarization, and sustained commitment sagged and then disappeared.[39]

CHAPTER NINE

"To the Polls":
The Voter Decides

Let every true citizen . . . vote early, deliberately, and
intelligently.
    —New York *Courier and Enquirer*, Nov. 3, 1857

AMERICAN VOTERS FROM 1838 into the 1890's were
stable partisans in most elections. As each of them distilled the
reality of a busy political world, and sought guides to the best
way to provide their own security and happiness, the political parties
successfully responded, mobilized them into their ranks, and usually
kept them there thereafter. The parties were able to do so because
they effectively articulated perspectives that reinforced powerful, divisive elements present in American life and demonstrated their relevance as Democrats, Whigs, or Republicans to the political concerns
of the electorate. Voters took sides in the electoral wars in nineteenth-
century America for a wide variety of individual and group reasons,
in reaction to the political stances taken by others, either hostile or
friendly to themselves, as well as in response to the way the parties
expressed their general orientation toward government power, or,
most often, the way each party's rhetoric and behavior defined the
kind of society it wished to establish in America.

Contemporary explanations of why people became Whigs or
Democrats were plentiful. Horace Greeley, editor of the Whig party's
flagship newspaper, the New York *Tribune*, was always convinced, in
print, that if elections were fought strictly on the grounds of economic
self-interest, the Whig party would do very well. But he saw Whig success thwarted time and time again by the electorate's stubborn tendency to vote on other grounds—religious, cultural, local, and personal—for heroes and for demagogues, and because of misunder-
standing, delusion, deception, or orneriness. Greeley recognized the
power of these tendencies even as he deprecated them. "Everything
depends," he wrote in 1852, "on the fixing of the public attention on
Principles rather than Names—on the living questions of to-day
rather than the blind, traditional prejudices engendered by the

struggles of yesterday." He marveled, and despaired, at the ability of party leaders to appeal to those baser sentiments repeatedly and successfully. But what he never admitted, publicly, was that the voters' "blind, traditional prejudices" reflected an American reality that all politicians had to come to terms with for electoral success.[1]

The impressive partisan loyalty that American voters exhibited from the late 1830's onward originated in their membership in particular socioeconomic and ethnoreligious groups. Each of these groups had some kind of political agenda, sometimes formal and articulated, sometimes not. Americans lived in a world of many antagonisms and disagreements that readily became politicized. "The members of every community," the editor of the Raleigh *Register* wrote in 1849, "have among themselves jealousies and heart burnings"—petty antagonisms and great problems that became politicized and divided the population into warring factions.[2] "Out of a network of primary-group relationships," one historian has argued, "family, racial, religious, nationality, class, and residential—individuals develop a set of values, beliefs and interests that they often seek to advance or protect in the political arena." As they passed through a succession of communities across the country, voters carried their memories, commitments, and hostilities with them, knitting them into a fabric that shaped their political behavior over the course of the whole era, regardless of changes in the larger contexts of politics and national development.[3]

The Potential for Pluralist Conflict

In the first instance, many of the divisions shaping popular voting behavior after 1838 stemmed from differences among the powerful leaders of a particular area. The battles at the top of the political world from the colonial period onward, over petty personal rivalries or to gain some economic and social advantage, produced enduring antagonisms that drew more and more voters into one camp or the other as the electorate expanded. When the national parties emerged in the 1830's, these preparty divisions helped define party choice. "Market relationships mattered," in party selection, William Shade argues, in one formulation, but the original partisan commitment of a place "most often rested with a more important set of communal and family ties that dictated who would be a Democrat or a Whig." These preexisting, but still potent, alignments drew people across the boundaries of their local angers into the state and national political realms as good party members.[4]

But American popular voting behavior also rested on a rich social and economic subsoil that stimulated new conflicts and divisions while reinforcing existing ones. The fault lines in nineteenth-century American society were many:

Some were social, separating farmers and villagers, laborers and shop-keepers; others were cultural, marking foreigners, native Americans, Protestants and Catholics. Some lines of cleavage followed gradients of class, occupational status and religious involvement; others had a geographic basis, distinguishing voters by their places of birth and county of settlement.[5]

America had always been a pluralist nation, home to many different and often antagonistic ethnoreligious groups, a range of often-politicized socioeconomic inequities, and conflicting economic interests. These differences had stimulated repeated political confrontation and continued to divide Americans from each other in the new political era. As Ronald Formisano characterizes the Massachusetts electorate at the beginning of this political nation, "Networks of influence, old and new, underlay partisan loyalties. So did cultural and religious divisions, some of which reached back several generations, while others had arisen only recently in the rapidly changing world of the early nineteenth century." The parties touched these group antagonisms repeatedly and directly. The parties' rhetoric, their expressions of the contest for the soul of America—for liberty, prosperity, the good republic—provided larger meaning and political direction for most groups. In Prince Edward county, Virginia, Shade concludes, "Certain groups whose local differences are fairly easily defined took sides on national issues that did not always personally affect them but symbolized an orientation toward government and society they found congenial."[6]

Sharp conflicts between different economic interests and needs and tensions over specific economic policies repeatedly penetrated the political world and fueled mass electoral choice. In particular, the surging capitalist revolution after 1815, with its disruptive transformation of social and market relationships and its differential benefits and costs, resulted in, as Richard L. McCormick sums up, "a basic cleavage between people who welcomed the spread of commerce and called upon the government to promote it and those who clung to earlier forms of work and community life and remained suspicious of public support for economic development." While many people eagerly pressed for government-promoted canal building and railroad development and thus became Whigs, urban artisans and rural small producers, among others, clung to old republican, often anticapitalist, egalitarian values and gravitated into the Democratic party.[7]

In addition to disagreements about the general shape of America's economic future, major conflicts quickly developed over such specific economic matters as banking policy, the government funding of internal development, public land distribution, and the level of marginal tariff rates, policy areas that had great significance in an increasingly competitive society. There was nothing like the challenge from cheap English goods entering the country, or the inadequacies of transportation or credit facilities in many areas, or the level of pay received and hours worked, to stimulate agitated group responses that entered the political world in partisan form.[8]

In the South, Harry Watson argues, economic issues in the 1830's strongly influenced the partisan commitments of the region's elites. Some yeomen farmers fiercely resisted expensive economic development promoted by town dwellers and many large slave owners. Like urban artisans, rural marginals, and some immigrant groups who fought to preserve a precapitalist, republican society from the forces of economic modernization, they joined the Democratic party, with its policies of limited government involvement in the promotion of economic development. Those in favor of extensive, rapid, government-supported economic development found themselves more at home among the Whigs. In North Carolina, for example, "people in towns were obviously attracted to the commercial aspects of Whig policy, while those nearby were appalled by it." To the voters of the 1830's and 1840's, in short, the Democrats were the party of economic limits, the Whigs the party of economic expansiveness; the Democrats stood for limited government intervention, the Whigs for generous government involvement in economic affairs.[9]

A "Good Deal of Sectarian Bitterness"

Although there were frequent expressions of these contrasting views toward economic development, and a major economic catastrophe, such as the Panic of 1837, proved the potency of economic issues at the polls, economically rooted behavior was neither the only nor even usually the most influential element dividing the electorate between Whigs and Democrats. Ethnoreligious antagonisms were very strong in the "troubled waters" of mid-nineteenth-century America. America's uneasy cultural diversity promoted political conflict that the parties came to personify, articulate, and organize. A "good deal of sectarian bitterness" was expressed at the polls, and each party could count on an amalgam of religiously and ethnically defined tribal loyalties to sustain it in election after election.[10]

Ethnoreligious distinctions existed in a bewildering array across the country. There was much more to party choice than a simple division between immigrants and natives, or Protestants and Catholics. Irish Catholics and Irish Protestants differed politically, as did the many distinct groups of Germans who had come to America since colonial days. Doctrinal disputes within religions also politicized voters into different party homes. Crusading religious leaders, evangelical preachers, and an occasional Catholic bishop inflamed certain moral questions that provoked both political support and hostility. Generally, in Paul Kleppner's description, "pietist" religious groupings were pitted against those of another persuasion: a "Yankee moralist subculture" faced a "white southern subculture" in many places as each sought to define and shape an area's focus.[11]

The settlement of colonial America by people of different ethnic and religious backgrounds had significantly affected American political patterns from the first. Groups that had been intensely hostile to one another in Europe remained so in the new world. Their antagonisms helped structure early party divisions in the 1790's, and continued into the era of partisan dominance from the late 1830's onward. These hostilities were continually reinforced by the arrival of new immigrants and the attempts of political leaders to seek electoral advantage by exploiting communal hatreds. People did not have short memories about these antagonisms. And if any ever felt like forgiving and forgetting, there was always a great deal on the scene to remind them of what was at stake.[12]

Examples abound of such political confrontation and its electoral consequences. In Northampton county, Pennsylvania, as the new partisan era began, politics "reflected a long-term rivalry between two ethnoreligious minorities and the dominant German Lutheran and Reformed groups," the former becoming Democrats, the latter Whigs. In one county of Illinois in the 1840's, northern Presbyterians voted 94 percent Whig, and northern Methodists 88 percent Whig, while southern-born Baptists were 75 percent Democratic. In New York state, the 1844 presidential contest between Henry Clay and James K. Polk saw a confrontation at the polls among different nationality groups, various Protestant denominations, and Irish Catholics. In Massachusetts, "while some Universalists might be found who voted Whig, or later Liberty party, most Universalist enclaves voted decisively Democratic." Finally, across New England as a whole, Paul Goodman demonstrates, Congregationalists were Whigs, Baptists and

Methodists tended to be Democrats. "From the coast of Maine through the fertile prairies of the Midwest," Kleppner sums up, "Whiggery drew disproportionate support among Yankee Presbyterian and Congregational voters. Both at its mass base and in its leadership, the Whig party was unmistakably a Yankee-Presbyterian-Congregational party."[13]

In the South, the same sort of ethnoreligious forces were at work. In Mississippi in 1844, a Whig paper claimed, "19 in 20 of the freshly naturalized" citizens of the state voted Democratic, while "the Scotch and English of Natchez [were] mostly Whigs." Watson finds "a residual culture conflict between Scots and non-Scots" in North Carolina. But, "unlike the situation in the states of the North," Marc Kruman argues, politics in the Old North State "did not reflect ethnocultural conflict in the society. . . . This is not to say that religion and ethnicity played no role in shaping voting patterns. Indeed, it appears that members of several religious groups had definite party preferences." But religion and ethnicity were not the driving electoral impulses of the day in the South, as they were elsewhere. Still, they could be potent. When southerners met westerners in the borderlands of the Ohio Valley, where two different settlement patterns converged, for example, the cultural antagonisms stimulated by their contact powerfully influenced voting behavior.[14]

These ethnoreligious confrontations distributed voters between the parties in quite different ways. There was a Democratic sociopolitical grouping and a Whig, and later, a Republican one. Democrats tended to be strongest among ethnoreligious outsiders, particularly the Catholics and Scots-Irish but also including a range of others, from Dutch Calvinists and Old School Presbyterians to New England Baptists, Methodists, and Universalists. The Democratic community lay in the urban Catholic wards of large cities and the towns settled by non-pietist Protestants, by the Dutch, and by southerners moving into the Middle West. In the South, where the Democrats were particularly strong in areas of limited economic development, they drew support from some of these same religious and nationality groups. "What these disparate groups shared," Daniel Walker Howe suggests, "was a grim determination to survive in the face of pressures to assimilate" from their neighbors. As a result, the Democratic party championed social heterogeneity. They resisted the attempts of society's privileged to impose their cultural norms on everyone else. "History shows us that the contest of race and religion is the bitterest of all, that it has ever been attended with the most frightful, terrible results," the editor of the *Democratic Review* wrote in 1855. "Government [therefore] ought not to undertake to make, or unmake, religious creeds, for any man."[15]

The Whigs, in contrast, were predominantly drawn from Presbyterians and Congregationalists in New England, representatives of the host culture of that section, who carried its values with them across the country, through upper New York state into the Great Lakes West, defending their heritage against the threats from the despised religions and nationalities of Europe who were flooding the land and fundamentally changing its character. Wherever Ulster Protestants settled, many of them were likely to become Whigs, despite their Irishness, if they found their long-standing conflict with the Catholic Irish invigorated by the presence of the latter. Southern commercial boom areas were also Whig, as were settlements of German Protestants. The Republicans a decade and more later absorbed most of the northern Whigs and attracted some formerly Democratic Protestant groups as well.[16]

The results of this were clear enough. For most social groups, party membership was "a means of expressing and defending subcultural values," an act of group solidarity. Whigs, and later Republicans, opposed cultural heterogeneity and argued that the state should reflect and even impose specific ethnoreligious values on the entire country, as it did in shaping and driving the economy. Whigs, Kleppner writes, "aggressively sought moral integration of the community through enforced conformity to Anglo-Protestant norms." Their party newspapers "labored perseveringly . . . to array Native against Adopted citizens." Democrats, in contrast, were "bound together" by their "resistance to such encroachments" and their "acceptance of cultural pluralism." In sum, "conflicts between political subcultures committed to these contending value systems structure partisan controversy." Whig and Democratic identification became a part of the culture of groups. Partisan loyalty made what was at stake in the political world understandable, real, and personal to each voter.[17]

"Windowdressing for More Latent Economic Discontents"

The political potency of these ethnoreligious divisions was underscored by their impact on class divisions in American electoral politics. Throughout the period covered here, another kind of social cleavage was emerging on the rising urban-industrial frontier, and in various rural neighborhoods as well. Different socioeconomic groups harshly expressed class resentments and opposing social and political perspectives often enough in both North and South. Thornton argues for the potency of such class divisions in antebellum Alabama politics, rooted in the fears of the wealthiest slave owners to the frequent challenges to their position. James Oakes suggests the same kind of class reaction in the South more generally. In the North, Formisano argues that ethnoreligious distinctions in Massachusetts (and elsewhere) in the 1820's, 1830's, and later frequently reflected a conflict between respectable and nonrespectable elements in society—for a form of class polarization, in other words.[18]

Despite the tensions such produced, however, the electoral response of the members of these different social orders was always more complex and multifaceted than any simple reading of their class association suggests. Though Americans did exhibit much measurable ethnoreligious clustering when they voted, they demonstrated a relatively low level of independent class consciousness at the polls. The fact is, an electorate characterized by measurable class-based voting did not exist in the United States in this era. Political parties largely cut across social classes in their popular support. Voters at every economic level cast ballots for both the Democrats and the Whigs.

There were certainly class tensions in this society, and they had their impact on individual and group perspectives. Urban workers showed considerable class consciousness when confronting their rapidly changing economic condition. In the workplace, as David Montgomery points out, they "engaged in economic conflicts with their employees as fierce as any known to the industrial world," but when they entered the polling booth, as they did regularly, they "consistently failed to exhibit a class consciousness." In the presidential election of 1844, "at the close of a decade and a half of hotly contested strikes and severe economic hardship, climaxed by the bitter depression of 1837–1843, workingmen . . . divided their votes along ethnic lines." This was not surprising. Susan Hirsch refers to "the bitterness between natives and foreigners, Protestants and Catholics," among urban workers that "caused each group to withdraw into itself outside the workplace."[19]

Were these ethnocultural animosities really surrogates for hidden, class-based animosities? Were they deliberately created and manipulated by the powerful for their own parochial purposes? There is little evidence to support such a view. Political leaders and social elites exploited the existing ethnoreligious fears and cleavages all right, but they did not create them or give them their strength. It may be that social-class distinctions were ambiguous or only half-sensed, or that economic confrontation was more often expressed in the workplace than at the polls, or that nativism and class were constantly intertwined in people's minds as they thought about politics and made electoral choices. Whatever the reason for absence of clear-cut, class-rooted behavior, to Michael Feldberg, ethnocultural elements "cannot be dismissed as windowdressing for more latent economic discontents. . . . They had a vitality and life of their own independent of their economic component."[20] They were the political norm. As Michael Kazin suggests, "Workers did not check their dreams, ideas, prejudices, and personal relationships at the factory gate; and the meaning of their history cannot be grasped by assuming that the workplace took priority, as a generator of attitudes, over the neighborhood, family, ethnic group, or institutions of popular culture."[21]

In any case, on the many election days, at most polling stations, economic and class-rooted interests, though present, were more often than not overridden by the greater immediate power of ethnoreligious conflict among Americans, particularly outside the south. As Formisano argues, "Popular class consciousness and interest group politics . . . remained relatively stunted and sidetracked in this political world." The voters' antipathy to one another often was able to overcome whatever economic interests they shared. For Virginia voters, William Shade sums up, "occupation mattered, religion mattered, and ethnicity was crucial." If economic class conflict took political form, therefore, it was through the prism of other elements. Stuart Blumin points out, in his study of a Hudson River community, that "native [Kingstonians] perceived the [social and economic] changes occurring around them primarily in ethnic terms."[22]

"Different Things in Different Places"

In this political world, then, tradition, economic condition, and ethnoreligious values intermingled to shape voting behavior. Of course, the power of these influences on individual voters significantly varied in different contexts and environments. There was not necessarily an automatic tight fit between a group's social or economic situation, its worldview, and its political choice. Each overarching influence on voting behavior interacted with a rich variety of other factors to temper and alter the force of any one element. Voters could and often did respond to the particular situation of the moment. Michael Holt's analysis of voting behavior in the presidential election of 1840, amid the economic panic that began in 1837, makes a compelling case for the importance of depression-connected economic issues in mobilizing and affecting voters after 1837, and locating many of them within one or other of the two parties. In 1840, voters surged to the polls, most to vote Whig against what they saw as the totally inadequate response of the Democratic administration, trapped by its own anti-government ideology, to the nation's economic suffering.[23]

That surge to Whiggery fell back, however, in succeeding elections. In contrast to Holt's findings for 1840, Lee Benson's analysis of New York state voter behavior in the presidential contest four years later suggests that when the depression abated, political attachments based on ethnoreligious tensions reasserted themselves as the most important source of voter choice. In areas like the South, where social diversity and ethnoreligious tensions were less in evidence, economic interest group divisions more often predominated in electoral decisions. People in similar economic endeavors worked together against threats to the well-being of their industry or area.[24]

But there was more than a chronological or demographic variant to the influence of different forces on popular voting behavior. People from the same economic or ethnocultural groups voted differently from place to place, even in the same election, as the particular context demanded. These in-group differences were often subtle and multifaceted. But they were there and important. Such contextual impulses could produce some otherwise puzzling results: lopsided majorities for one party or the other in a particular locality, while the voters in other places, with similar socioeconomic characteristics, went in another direction.[25]

Environmental matters counted in affecting voter response to the political choices available when they settled in a region and reacted to the particular configuration and sensitivity of the groups living within a community. Paul Kleppner delineates a number of variations found from the 1850's on: border-state whites, for example, who voted in roughly the same pattern as their northern counterparts when they lived in areas with few blacks, but became very Democratic, regardless of their particular social character, when they found many blacks living among them. Some German Lutherans defected from their strong Democratic moorings in areas where the Democrats' identification as the party of Catholicism was particularly marked. There were many other such variations throughout the life of this political nation.[26]

The apparent power of these contextual variables, coupled with the rapid turnover of voters in communities all across America, has suggested to some historians that very localized environmental forces, not large-scale, divisive ethnocultural or economic tensions, were the primary shapers of American voting behavior. Paula Baker finds, from her study of one New York county late in the life of this political nation, that "men's relationships with others in the community, rather than membership in social groups, shaped partisan choices." Thus, despite their nationally oriented appeals and policies, "parties meant different things to voters in different places." There were variations here as well. "At the very top of the political order, among the visible partisans," Donald DeBats writes, "and at the very bottom among the isolated farm laborers, we find something approaching pure types— individuals responding to system-wide forces and concerns on the one hand and responses which border on indifference on the other. In the political middle, we have the vast majority of voters caught up in one or another of the political neighborhoods, which provided, in their most benign form, a framework for interpreting a broader political world."[27]

In this view, neighborhoods, with their small, permanent, and highly politicized populations, were the stable entity in the voting universe. Most of the voters passing through linked themselves to the neighborhood when they went to the polls. This is a stunning denial of the power of system-wide antagonisms to have much, if any, impact on voters, except, as Holt suggests, when some unusual or critical problem, such as an economic panic, occurred. But though the idea of neighborhood imprinting has some interpretive utility, it seems to me to go too far. People brought their political baggage into a neighborhood—that is, their already deeply imprinted attitudes and loyalties. These commitments could be as much the determining factor in how they acted in their new world, depending on the stimulation and direction they found there, as the power of neighborhood influences. Whatever the proportions involved, both the macrosocietal issues dividing Americans from one another and contextual elements entered into voters' decisions. Within the pattern of economic and ethnoreligious conflict, many reactions were possible and were manifested at the polls in this political nation.

Mobilizing Antagonisms

The variations in the response of voters to the different stimuli meant that a great deal of party effort went into alerting people to what was at stake and shaping their responses. Since no one expected that all voters would automatically see their best interests without strong encouragement, party leaders worked assiduously to stimulate and reinforce what might otherwise have remained inert. As Thornton suggests for Alabama, "No single element was more important in achieving electoral success than wise and agile leadership":

The critical variable in determining a beat's political loyalty was not its location, and consequent economic structure, but the continuity and effectiveness of the political leadership exerted within it. Over the years the residents of the beats adopted one or the other party and stayed with it, largely because of the activities of the beat partisans, who zealously reinforced the ideological inertia of the mass of voters by countering any arguments which might have had the strength, unanswered, to have weaned away a number of adherents.[28]

In short, the activities of the parties in shaping and stimulating, in articulating and mobilizing, were critical to the American political process in this era. Here is where it all came together: the elaborate partisan organizations, the sustained vigor and repetitive power of their arguments, all were framed to catch and hold people's attention and direct them into specific channels of involvement. Political leaders became adept at using the raw material of socioeconomic differences to forge sustained party loyalties. In Milwaukee, Kathleen Conzen argues, German leaders did "an excellent job convincing the rank and file that salvation lay only within the regular Democracy."[29]

Different political strategies followed from the electorate's predispositions. Both parties had national appeal; both had national constituencies. Both structured their behavior accordingly. Democrats, one party spokesman said, "aggregate all bodies which have an affinity to ourselves." Neither they nor their opponents could build "unnatural coalitions" of voters. One strategy was to stress the parochialism of the other party. To John Sherman, speaking in Congress in 1870, "the strength of the Republican party" lay "in the masses of the country people, the farmers, the mechanics, the laborers of the country. The strength of the Democratic party for years . . . has been in the pest houses of the cities where vice breeds." This notion of a set of traditional American values threatened by outside, destructive elements was a Whig-Republican commonplace in the electoral arena into the 1890's. In Jacksonville, Illinois, "a predominantly Republican town," the Irish "suffered special abuse for their rigid loyalty to the Democratic party—'voting cattle,' the Republicans disdainfully called them." There was a reciprocal response from the Democrats. "IRISH VOTERS!" the Nashville *Union* reminded them in 1848, "your enemies are the Whigs of the United States. They insult you on all occasions." And four years later, Illinois's leading Democratic newspaper suggested that the Whig presidential candidate stood "where ever he has stood—at heart a nativist."[30] Such oft-repeated comments were part of a strategy that played down party members' differences and emphasized the things uniting them, while stressing the principles and perspectives (both ethnoreligious and attitudes toward government) that divided them from their opponents.

Electoral Realignment

By the 1840's, as we have seen, the race for the presidency in the United States had become, in Richard P. McCormick's words, "a kind of mass folk festival, incorporating as well the enthusiasms of religious revivalism and the passions of a bloodless internal war." Once the various antagonisms within the society had become politicized and partisan, their tenacity was marked. Whatever the origins of popular voting behavior, over time it hardened into an enduring partisan consistency. Not everyone's party ties were as tightly held as the majority's. There was always some variation in intensity and commitment. But voters, as we have seen, rarely shifted their loyalties in this political nation. Most would as soon have changed their religion as their politics, maintaining that "life-long ardor" for one party or the other that the *American Review* so perceptively noted in 1849.[31] The connection between religion and politics seemed apt to the commentator then, and remains so. The sources of individual voting behavior solidified the party loyalties that were the hallmark of this system.

Only once, as we have noted, in the electoral realignment of the 1850's were individual and group party loyalties shaken enough to have significant political consequences. This realignment, certainly in its initial stages, underscored the importance of ethnoreligious factors to many northerners. Economic strains constantly weaved through and influenced voter choice during the uproar of the decade. But "more than any other factor," William Gienapp argues, "the rise of ethnocultural issues destroyed the second party system." That was because the ethnoreligious tensions that emerged then crossed the existing pattern of party choice and stimulated intense unrest among the formerly settled electorate. New threats emerged to add to age-old conflicts. The flood of Irish-Catholic immigrants into eastern cities, in particular, crystallized matters and provoked a widespread electoral response.[32]

A powerful backlash against the immigrants began the process of electoral realignment because it was intense enough to destroy the loyalties of some Protestant Democrats, as well as those who, while not formal or committed church members, proved to be quite anti-Catholic in their outlook. Robert Fogel points out that hard times among urban native white workers had been a constant for most of the 1840's and early 1850's. From 1854 onward, what he calls "the political revolt of Northern native workers" had nativist, class, and economic interest group components, all intertwined and most often expressed in nativist terms—that is, against a major menace threatening America. Michael Holt suggests that "to apprehensive and often bigoted Protestant Americans, the tide of Catholic aliens inundating their communities seemed to spawn slums, violations of the Sabbath, public drunkenness, pauperism and crime." This perception had immense political consequences. As one congressman put it in 1856, "I go against the Catholic *in toto*." [33]

The growing anti-Catholicism sought a sterner home than the Whigs apparently provided. In the presidential election of 1852, both major parties had courted the foreign vote. But the Whig party's highly unusual bid for Catholic votes backfired, antagonizing many traditional Whig voters, particularly among Presbyterians and Methodists, who subsequently threw their support to the new anti-Catholic, Know-Nothing party. In this, the first stage of the realignment, some voting blocs changed their partisan commitments—not briefly, but lastingly. At the same time, large groups of new voters were mobilized, most of them into Know-Nothing and then into Republican ranks. [34]

Much of what happened also flowed from a hostile North-South confrontation. Despite the parties' success in "nationalizing" the political agenda, the old antagonism between northerners and southerners reawakened and became highly politicized in the 1840's. Slavery extensionism and aggressive southernism touched some northerners deeply. First expressed in the North through the Liberty and Free Soil parties in the 1840's, by the middle of the next decade, the antagonism grew strong enough to upset party loyalties in both sections. Southerners reacted fiercely to repeated antislavery challenges to their way of life, and a sectional cultural divide opened up to become part of America's popular voting universe in ways unknown before. [35]

In the end, some northern ethnoreligious groups bolted from the Democrats, and many southerners bolted from the Whigs, some to become Democrats. Thereafter, sectional and cultural issues were routinely played on by all the parties in their efforts to mobilize voter support. If Republican leaders did not rely exclusively on ethnoreligious antagonisms, they certainly made heavy use of them in building their party in the late 1850's. At times, the Republicans proved to be aggressive cultural interventionists, strongly anti-Catholic, and willing to use government power to shape America economically and culturally. One midwestern Democrat defined a Republican as "a Whig of Know-Nothing and Maine Law proclivities." As William Gienapp writes, in the presidential election of 1860, "Republicans catered to anti-Catholic feeling. . . . The correspondence of the Republican National Committee reveals a very heavy demand for one-time Know Nothings to address Republican meetings." Republican congressmen and other party leaders underscored the "kindly feeling existing between the Democratic party and the Catholic Church."[36]

At the end of half a decade of party disruption, the Republicans were able to blend a Whig cultural and economic worldview and the antislavery extensionism of Free Soilers with the nativism of the Know-Nothings. Kleppner suggests that the Republicans became much more a "Yankee" party than the Whigs had ever been by expanding the Whigs' base into areas of once Democratic Yankee outsiders. By Dale Baum's calculation, the election of 1864 in Massachusetts saw Congregationalists increasing their anti-Democratic commitment, to vote more than four to one Republican. The Baptists, Universalists, and Methodists were a little less one-sided, but still very Republican; Episcopalians were split down the middle; and Roman Catholics were divided two to one in favor of the Democrats, apparently along nationality lines.[37]

Once all the electoral shifts had occurred, voter loyalties remained largely intact for the remaining years of this political nation. In the 1870's and 1880's, ethnoreligious tensions remained very potent in American electoral politics. In most elections, the parties worked effectively to keep the particular tensions that defined them in front of the voters. The Democrats remained attuned to the ethnoreligious and sectional cultural outsiders who made up their community. They continued to advocate limited government involvement in economic and social matters. The Republicans into the 1890's built their appeals around nationalism, anti-Catholicism, and vigorous government interventionism to shape the country's economy and social values. "Differences in religious outlooks," Kleppner argues,

underlay contending definitions of what was, or was not, sin; and religiously rooted differences in conceptions of the nature of man and of the world produced incompatible views of the relations of society and politics. . . . Each party represented, not a single denomination, but a loosely structured set of denominations sharing a collective central tendency. As Republican to evangelical pietists symbolized right behavior and a socially transforming morality, Democracy meant to ritualists right belief and a defense of laissez faire hedonism.

Republicans added to this arsenal the potent anti-southernism that grew out of the Civil War and that reminded everyone of the nature and meaning of American nationality.[38]

In any particular situation, then, a range of socioeconomic elements worked on American voters from the late 1830's into the 1890's. Politics was communal, not individual—it did not isolate voters from their groups; it reinforced their place in them. Tensions within a community, the way particular elites behaved, differences over economic development, deeply rooted ethnoreligious tensions, all affected the way groups of voters came to choose their parties.[39] Party labels clarified what was at stake. Voters reacted to widespread partisan activities that combined appeals to their hopes, needs, and fears. They acted to advance group aims, respond to threats, and protect, or improve, their situation in society. They sorted themselves out, in the first place, in line with lessons learned in their home communities. The great issues of the day were filtered through the prism of local outlooks. Parties constantly made connections between local perspectives and community anxieties and successfully linked them to national issues.

Something else lay behind voters' choices as well. The electors were not an inert mass blindly reacting to party cues without thinking. Political leaders could only work effectively when they successfully struck responsive chords in their hearers. The latter were definers as well. As a Democratic pamphlet put it in 1840, "The period has long passed since the masses of mankind were willing to follow self-constituted leaders without inquiring into causes and reasons." Because of the way they regularly participated in politics, voters became socialized into paying close attention; they expected to be instructed, absorbed what was at stake, and reacted. "Midwesterners," Richard Jensen notes, "turned out by the tens of thousands to march in parades, shout themselves hoarse at rallies, picnic at barbecues, and listen to long-winded speeches on hot summer afternoons":

They followed political developments, recognized politicians, and understood the issues. They sat through hours of speeches without a break, not only to display their support of favorite candidates but also to soak up the details and minute points of the tariff, the money question, educational policies, prohibi-

tion laws, and the myriad of minor issues that erupted from time to time. . . .
Routinely the newspapers published lengthy texts of major speeches, and
there is no evidence that the subscribers hurried by them to the sports pages.

As Albert Parker suggests, "the nineteenth century voter was closer in
terms of participation and information to the traditional active-citizen
model than is the twentieth century elector."[40]

Some voters reacted automatically to partisan stimuli; some penetrated further, to match their specific needs in a specific situation to
what each party offered. "Under ordinary circumstances, men are
holden together in parties," a Cincinnati editor wrote in 1852, echoing a familiar theme, "by the force of association and organization;
and when there is no issue before them that appeals to their moral
sense, mere habit is sufficient to control their acts and to supply the
place of opinions." But overall, there was a deep sense, often expressed
and often demonstrated, that political, policy, and electoral relationships were understood in more than automatic ways. As James K.
Paulding wrote in 1834, "Rely upon it, The People are no fools—they
can distinguish between their friends and their Enemies, and 'tell a
hawk from a handsaw' quite as well as the gentlemen who are pleased
to consider them equally destitute of eyes and understanding."[41]

What ultimately gave shape and direction to the whole were the actions of the leaders of the political parties, working assiduously on the
voters in ways that awakened and stimulated their individual and
group predispositions. They made what could have been inert intensely alive and persistently influential. As a result of their efforts,
parties and ethnoreligious values melded together in the minds of the
electorate, as did parties and distinct economic policies. As everywhere else in this political nation, therefore, parties drove everything
by taking the raw materials of existing socioeconomic divisions and
shaping them into permanent political warfare that was repeatedly
expressed at the polls on election day.

CHAPTER TEN

The Party State: Partisan Government in a Partisan Political Nation

THE ESSENTIAL POWER OF the American political parties was most prominently displayed, after the 1830's, when they repeatedly rallied the electorate on behalf of different political visions. The Democratic, Whig, and Republican parties were indispensable vehicles for mobilizing and ensuring popular participation in elections and for the expression of the interests and tensions of the pluralist society they inhabited. Party activities did not end on election day, however. The American political nation from 1838 onward involved more than its fervid electoral dimension. There was always a purpose behind each party's activities that went beyond victory at the polls. Advocacy and the struggle to control the government were preliminary to the parties' efforts to put everything together, to decide what to do and then to act on behalf of desired ends, to follow through and govern.

But could American political parties do so effectively? And, if they could, what did that mean specifically? The raw materials for governing—the formal institutions of the constitutional order—were at hand. Presidents, governors, congressmen, state legislators, administrative agents, and the judiciary all had specific duties to carry out. But there was a potential problem, first, in converting intense electoral excitement and polarizing campaign pronouncements into expected results once in office. Almost a century after this political nation ended, an editorialist in the *New York Times* cogently suggested that "individuals (and parties) have attitudes, but governments need policies." Unfortunately, the *Times* writer continued, problems usually arise out "of turning a campaign into a government."[1]

Nevertheless, despite the difficulties, throughout the nation's history, party leaders have usually been able to shift from campaigning to governing once an election has been decided. That was certainly true in the American political nation after 1838. As the parties effectively structured and shaped the electoral universe, so they also subsequently applied their skills effectively in order to make use of the available public authority. Democrats, Whigs, and Republicans had, as we have seen, policies to enact and carry out, as well as attitudes to express. As in the electoral arena, therefore, they became the primary influences in structuring and utilizing government power in order to accomplish their specific goals.

The Reach of the State

A familiar framework provides insight into the nature of nineteenth-century governing authority in the United States. Historians have asserted that American government after the 1830's had limited vigor and reach. One scholar refers to "the mammoth nineteenth century disjunction between the wildly expanding participation in elections on the one hand, and the drastically shrinking responsibilities of the central government on the other." Despite Whig, and later Republican, desires to use the state for "beneficent and protective ends," most Americans' experiences throughout the era after 1838 suggested that government power was limited, usually quite diffused, and only rarely a critical factor in their lives.[2]

This had not always been true. In the colonial and early national periods, the state had largely set the tone and direction of America's mixed economy that combined both private and public enterprise. There was an understood government responsibility to license, guide, shape, and regulate the economy in a wide variety of ways, despite its essentially private nature. Until early in the nineteenth century, therefore, a significant relationship between public power and private interests existed, with the government usually taking the lead and engaging in both promotional and regulative activities on behalf of some assumed common good.[3]

From the 1820's onward, however, the balance clearly shifted away from public responsibilities. The government continued to promote and protect the general welfare. But increasingly, less and less direct supervisory activity was deemed appropriate. In the economic sphere, the old idea of commonwealth, which gave government primary regulative responsibility to define and act to carry out the common good, weakened significantly. Private enterprise was given its head as state constraints on economic activity decreased. Whatever power government had was increasingly bounded by a clear, well-understood set of limits. Americans now followed an "individualistic, enterprising, in-

strumentalist, middle-class philosophy," which stressed "private initiative and individual acquisitiveness" in economic affairs.[4]

The same limits on government authority existed outside the economic sphere after the late 1830's. "In effect," Ray Gunn concludes,
"a new political order predicated on expanded suffrage, equal political rights, government inaction, and subordination of public to private authority had appeared by midcentury." That order continued to
reign into the 1890's. National power may have grown sharply during
such episodes as the Civil War and Reconstruction, but the growth
tended to be short-lived and "did not lead to an accumulation of state
authority and power." It appeared, Loren Beth remarks, that "the
more democratic the political structure was, the less power the people
were willing to entrust to it."[5]

Still, a residue of public authority always remained. Obvious areas,
such as providing for the national defense and protecting the social
order from internal threats to its stability were still seen as acceptable
arenas for the exercise of national authority. Neither was an onerous
burden. Even the highly skeptical Democrats believed there were a
few additional purposes for the exercise of political power, though
some preferred to express that belief in negative rhetoric. For the citizen, the Massachusetts Democrat Robert Rantoul said at the outset of
the era, "the whole object of government is negative. It is to remove
and keep out of his way all obstacles to [his] natural freedom of
action."[6]

In the economic realm, Rantoul would not have denied the federal
government's responsibility (and the states') for maintaining a legal
climate in which economic enterprise could grow and thrive. Governments properly removed obstacles to private initiative, created and
maintained capital markets, and secured the stability of the economic
order. It was also, many felt, the government's responsibility to help
finance and build the nation's infrastructure, the roads, canals, and
railroads that the private enterprise economy needed to exploit resources and bring them to market. Finally, the expansive public do-
main, a major national government responsibility, remained to be distributed through sales, auctions, and grants. As a result, after 1815,
the public treasury "became the major source of venture capital" for
many efforts to promote economic enterprise.[7]

This commitment never ran smooth. There were always sharp disagreements about the nature and extent of government aid for internal improvements, as there were about the disposal of the public
lands, the appropriate price to be charged, and whether or not there
should be limits on the amount an individual or a company could ac-

quire. Economic dislocations caused policy changes and restrictions as well. The Panic of 1837 significantly curtailed the state funding of internal improvements, for example, and as land sales fell during the depression, the national government had less money to provide for economic development schemes generally. These disagreements and contingencies were persistent. But as a practical matter, even the small government–oriented Democrats supported some official efforts to promote economic development through the build-up of the nation's infrastructure.[8]

The efforts to energize the economy were the work of both legislatures and the judiciary. As Williard Hurst and Harry Scheiber, among others, have shown, the American judicial system in the nineteenth century was fully entwined with problems of the economy as it handled questions of economic growth, public regulation and the relationship between private enterprise and the state. State and federal tribunals overwhelmingly decided matters before them in one direction: they fostered the promotion of unfettered economic development. State courts, in particular, according to Scheiber, "not only through the mechanism of private contract but also through bold juridical innovation . . . introduced new doctrines that often displaced vested property interests in order to expedite technological change and economic development." In the pattern of its decisions, the judiciary "made significant 'intangible' contributions to capital formation." But at the same time, the courts downplayed, in many cases in this era, their previously well-developed, regulative functions.[9]

Congress and the state legislatures were not far behind the judiciary in fostering internal development. At every level, they briskly went forward on a pragmatic case-by-case basis. In Congress, matters like the tariff, Indian removal and control, the disposal of public lands, the easing of credit restrictions, and the subsidizing of roads, canals, and, most particularly, railroads took center stage from the 1830's onward. Although never a massive exercise of national power, such congressional legislation freed resources for development and provided much of the transportation infrastructure needed for rapid and sustained economic growth. At the same time, the operative policy under which all worked clearly was that, while governments made resources available, it was up to others to put them to use. "Subsidization without regulation" made it possible for a continental national market to develop and to do so fairly rapidly.[10]

In the decades after 1815, as Hurst and Scheiber have demonstrated, state governments also contributed strongly to economic development through laws that permitted the maximum mobilization of community resources and removed existing barriers to such growth. These efforts included legislation defining contracts, permitting the raising of money, limiting the liability of investors and managers, and establishing land boundaries, right of way, and resource-utilization rights. In Hurst's terms, these laws were designed to minimize "the limiting force of circumstances" on economic activity and to open up the system to exploitation. Law was to be used "wherever it looked as if it would be useful" to expand the economic health of the nation.[11]

Governments also tried their hand at noneconomic policy making during the years of this political nation. The national efforts were not very well developed beyond the always present commitments to distribute veterans' benefits in land, cash, and, later, services. State governments, on the other hand, did engage in a range of judicial and legislative activities in the social realm. Although by later standards there was a limited conception of government's responsibility for individual welfare, the states did accept responsibility for education, health, and public safety. That commitment led to the establishment of public schools, mental institutions, poorhouses, and schools for the deaf, run either by the states or their counties. Public expenditures for such purposes were never large by later standards. Georgia, for example, spent about 4 percent of its annual budget on education in the 1850's. Nevertheless, the efforts, if not prepossessing, provide evidence of sustained government attention that remained vigorous in nineteenth-century terms.[12]

Some state governments moved further into the social realm by trying to define and impose standards on the appropriate behavior of their inhabitants. These efforts, including temperance laws and occasional limits on the rights of religious authorities, appeared frequently enough to constitute additional evidence of a state role in shaping the American social arena. Since many of these initiatives were stimulated by anxieties about the "alien threat"—in particular, the increase in the number of Roman Catholics entering the United States—they tended to wax and wane with immigration patterns, but after midcentury, they were never far from the surface of American politics. None of these social actions matched, in their extent, what went on in the economic realm, but they were numerous enough to constitute, and be seen by the people of the time as, an important phase of government activity.[13]

The post-1838 legislative and judicial branches were busy within their understood boundaries of action, reflecting the American conception of the reach of government power. Their activities, however, were rarely systematic or planned, and the few sustained efforts to regulate things were feeble at best. Neither the nation nor the states developed much of a supervising bureaucracy. Hurst derides the federal government's "default of attention" to the unsystematic and wasteful distribution of public lands. The same phrase could be applied to other sectors of public policy. "Forever giving things away, governments were laggard in regulating the economic activities they subsidized." That was intentional and constant. As William R. Brock has written, "Americans were slow to realize that a law did not enforce itself."[14]

The Size and Shape of Government

The existing structure of government in the United States reflected the realities of how Americans defined power and its uses. The essentially distributive activities of governments did not require an elaborate administrative structure. As a result, all elements of government, federal, state, and local, remained small. The federal government, in particular, was unprepossessing, as Leonard White's pioneering studies of the federal administrative structure in this era made clear. The United States employed some 20,000 people at the beginning of the era, 14,000 of whom worked in the post office. Only 1,000 federal employees were based in Washington. The annual national budget was $24,000,000 in 1840. About half of it went for the army and navy, and about 10 percent to pay interest on the public debt. Neither the President nor other major members of the federal government had, or needed, much support staff beyond a few clerks, messengers, doorkeepers, and State Department translators. Morton Keller's characterization effectively catches the atmosphere: "Before the Civil War, Washington was a slovenly, indolent, half-finished city, . . . the physical embodiment of the American distaste for centralized government."[15] A national administrative state never existed in this political nation.

The federal government did grow in this age of economic and geographic expansion, to be sure. The New York customshouse and the post office thrived, for example. So did the federal land office. As the amount of public land increased through purchase, annexation, and conquest, the General Land Office in fact became one of the busiest and most important of the national administrative agencies. Originally created in 1812, it expanded greatly after the mid-1830's, employing surveyors, receivers, clerks, and other officials; the result was a relatively complex administrative apparatus of ten "thoroughly organized" divisions under a commissioner.[16]

The Civil War saw a fivefold increase in the number of civilian employees on the federal payroll, from 40,000 in 1860 to 200,000 by 1865. And in the decade after the war, the federal government engaged in an unprecedented level of social service and administrative activities in the South on behalf of the freedmen. But this effort did not last long or involve very large numbers of employees, and the totals then settled back. When a Reconstruction-era governor assumed office in Florida in 1868, for example, he found just over 160 federal employees working there, including about 100 postmasters and 50 customs employees. The rest were judges, public land officers, internal revenue collectors, a marshal, and a registrar of bankruptcies. Traditional restraints against government power, including the impact of the Democrats' sweeping congressional victories in the elections of 1874, ultimately brought a halt to even the limited expansion that had been occurring. By 1881, the national government had just 100,000 people on its payroll, more than half of whom were in the post office department.[17]

Expenditures also increased during the Civil War and Reconstruction years. From $63,000,000 in 1860, the federal budget reached $1.25 billion in 1865. Though there was also some contraction here, the annual federal budget still increased tenfold, to just over $260,000,000, between 1840 and 1881. But that increase did not signify any systematic increase in the responsibilities of the state. Much of it went to pay for the greatly expanded but traditional veterans' benefits after the Civil War and to reduce the federal debt, swollen by the exigencies of the war. Pension payments made up 21 percent of the federal budget in 1880 and 34 percent ten years later. The Republican leader Roscoe Conkling reiterated a familiar perspective in the mid-1870's. "Statesmanship may do much," he said. "But all it can do is to clear the way of impediments and dangers, and leave every class and every individual free and safe in the exertions and pursuit of life."[18]

To add to the fragility of the whole governing enterprise, federal policy makers did not stay in office very long. Eight of the eleven Presidents elected from 1840 through 1892 served only one (or part of one) term; four died in office. Nor did many cabinet officers remain in place for extended periods, although some, such as Daniel Webster and John J. Crittenden, moved back and forth between cabinet offices and Congress or state government. Overall, in neither size, direction, continuity, nor accumulation of expertise and experience was there much raw material for vigorous activity at the executive departments' end of Pennsylvania Avenue. Keller's description of the

1860's is apt for the whole era: "From the war years there emerged not a Bismarckian state, but rather . . . a system of government dominated by localism and *laissez faire*." [19]

The states had more authority than the central government in this era of "dual federalism," but their executive departments were little better developed than those at Washington. As in the federal realm, state management activities were of limited scope. Many governors were able to marshal electoral (as against governing) power effectively, but most of them, like the President, had very few administrative powers under their constitutions, and they professed no ambitions to enlarge them. In pre–Civil War Alabama, the governorship was "little more than a salaried honor." The incumbent presented annual messages to the state legislature and could veto bills, subject to legislative override by a simple majority. In Kentucky, the governor was primarily the "executor of the will of the legislature." The way the powers of the office were defined, there were "few opportunities for leadership." The chief executives of some states had no veto power at all. Legislatures, not governors, in North Carolina and elsewhere selected most of the executive departments' officeholders.[20]

Beyond the governors, power and influence at the executive level varied from state to state. Some, New York for one, had more extensive administrative structures than others. From the late 1830's on, administrative authority in Albany grew. The offices of State comptroller and secretary of state acquired more and more extensive supervisory, and even regulative, functions. The state's transportation commitments, as well as its policies of lending money to private enterprise and engaging in some limited social welfare activities, all had an impact on the size and function of its administrative agencies. There was, also, the beginning of some state efforts to regulate transportation rates.[21]

The New York experience before the Civil War looked large in comparative terms. But there and elsewhere, the sum of such activities was quite limited. State canal and railroad commissions existed, but their size was small. William Nelson remarks that state bureaucracies were so underdeveloped in this period, even in areas they took responsibility for and funded, that most regulative activities came about "solely through *post hoc* legislative investigations," not by the orders of specialized agencies. Certainly, many of the states' mental and health institutions were understaffed, with the result that there was little supervision and coordination. Oversight, clearly, was not the American way.[22]

During the Civil War, many governors exhibited a new energy and reach as they raised and supplied troops to fight the war and found the finances to do so. The vigor of a man like Governor Richard Yates of Illinois, as one example, substantially furthered the northern war effort, especially in its early stages. But such activities were unusual, not sustained for very long, and much criticized as a power grab by political opponents. The Civil War experience hardly laid the foundation for future growth. It was an abnormal diversion from American reality that was quickly corrected when the emergency ended. Thereafter, state budgets declined, along with the numbers staffing whatever administrative apparatus had been established. By the 1870's, state governments had resumed their limited role; in fact, they had "entered into a period of atrophy."[23]

The fullest exercise of governmental authority in this era was found in the legislative branch. State legislatures were usually the busiest part of the governing apparatus. Most met either annually or biannually. Their budget responsibilities alone meant regular attention to the shape and reach of government. As noted, they also paid much attention to questions of economic development and social behavior. Congress, too, had a persistent vigor throughout this era. In their biannual long session, the House and the Senate met at the beginning of December and usually sat until early summer. With one exception, no congressional session lasted past mid-August until 1887–88. But if the time consumed remained remarkably stable over the whole era, the amount of legislation dealt with did not. Before 1838, congressmen considered about 475 bills annually. In the next three decades, the figure almost tripled, to an average of just over 1,400 a session. After the Civil War, the numbers soared, first above 5,000 a session, and then to 20,000 annually by the early 1890's.[24]

This increased workload, however, did not reflect a major shift in existing conceptions of the scope of public responsibility. Margaret Susan Thompson points out, for example, that more and more of Congress's legislative attention in the decades after the Civil War was devoted to the increased number of private bills that members introduced, in particular, individual claims for revolutionary, War of 1812, etc., pensions—matters that in a later era would be attended to by administrative agencies. Like Congress, the state legislatures dealt largely with specific individual claims, and not matters of more general import. In Pennsylvania, about 90 percent of legislative bills in the decade before the Civil War involved private matters.[25]

Even if the national and state legislatures had wanted to exercise more power, they had certain critical weaknesses that limited their ability to do so. As in the case of the executive branch, most legislative bodies in this era did not have the kind of stable membership that would have given them the experience and expertise the job required. Congressional and state legislative careers tended to be relatively short, certainly compared with later times. In the 1840's and 1850's, for example, the average congressman served under two terms. By the 1870's, the figure had increased only slightly, to over two terms. Thompson has calculated that only 139 of the 477 members of the House of Representatives who sat during Ulysses Grant's second administration, starting in 1873, served three or more consecutive terms. The usual pattern of congressional service was for members to serve briefly and then leave Washington, some voluntarily, for other pursuits, others turned out of office in the highly competitive electoral arena. Some managed to return, often to leave again.[26]

Each Congress thus contained a great many new members when it assembled for its first meeting. In the House of Representatives of the Twenty-sixth Congress, which met in December 1839, for example, eight of the nineteen members from Ohio were freshmen; eight others had first been elected the term before. In 1845, there were nine freshmen in the twenty-one man Ohio delegation of the Twenty-ninth Congress, and six members who had first been elected the term before. When the Thirty-first Congress met, at the end of the decade, only one of Ohio's members had been in office ten years. It was not until the very end of the era that congressional careers began to lengthen and give the body a certain stability in its membership. And it was not until 1900 that the proportion of freshmen congressmen at each session fell below 30 percent.[27]

State legislative membership also turned over regularly. In North Carolina, between 1836 and 1850, more than 60 percent of the legislators stayed in Raleigh for only one term, and 25 percent served only two. This turnover rate continued to the end of the era. About 80 percent of the members of each newly elected New York legislature in the 1840's and 1850's were freshmen. The annual sessions "were essentially convocations of strangers." As late as the 1880's, fewer than 4 percent of the legislators in Illinois, Iowa, and Wisconsin remained in office for as many as three terms. Most of the time, these legislative bodies consisted largely of new members. The same was true of Nebraska, where between 80 percent and 90 percent of the state legislators in any session were newcomers.[28]

Additionally, neither Congress nor the state legislatures developed the kind of internal institutions they needed to facilitate and regulate their business or provide understandable, repetitive, impersonal means of handling large amounts of legislation or increased responsibilities. Committee operations became more complex as time went on, but the committee structure remained underdeveloped, still badly in need of professional expertise and a critical mass of experienced members. A few important committees could command the legislative floor, but a great deal of each legislature's bill-drafting activities occurred in informal and unspecialized, often wide-open and unpredictable, committees of the whole. The patterns of floor leadership were similarly unpredictable. The Speaker of the federal House of Representatives had significant agenda-setting power. But until the Civil War, all but one Speaker in this era served only a single two-year term. Although incumbents were more likely to be reelected in the ensuing years, the gains in stability were only relative. All told, there were nineteen Speakers in the twenty-seven Congresses between 1839 and 1893. High turnover in the leadership and institutional under-development hampered the conduct of legislative activity and, like the rapid and constant turnover of membership, significantly lessened the possibilities of expanded legislative growth and power.[29]

"A Testimonial of My Political Consistency"

Instability in the legislative arena underscores the fragmented and diffused pattern of government activity throughout this era, as well as its limited scope. Americans agreed on the release of energy and stringent limits on government power. The country's available resources were up for grabs. This was a world of group rivalries, of private interests jostling for support from the state and federal governments, of scrambles involving local, regional, and partisan disagreements over plans, routes, needs, and rights. Pluralism created enormous cross-pressures on the state, but Americans would not tolerate any allocating of resources by bureaucratically determined priorities, so that policy making was, in Richard L. McCormick's words, "little more than the accumulation of isolated, individual choices."[30]

Still, these battles never completely lacked coordination or coherence. While the Whigs were always the more development-minded party, the competitive scramble for resources often crossed partisan lines, certainly at the local level, where community boosterism frequently reigned. The clamor for the funding of a road, a canal, or a railroad put a premium on bargaining and log-rolling between legislators, regardless of their partisan commitments, ideologies, and loyalties. Yet, not unexpectedly, there was also a great deal of partisan jockeying over government policies. The partisan imperative permeated the government realm as thoroughly as it did all other parts of this political nation.

Political parties established boundaries and limits in the government sphere, albeit not as conclusively as they did in the other political arenas. Politicians, not planners or professional administrators, were in charge of what went on in the halls of government. When in office, the parties tried to fulfill their campaign promises, and usually succeeded when they had the legislative votes to do so. At the same time, every attempt to engage in some government action was quickly, powerfully, and often bitterly, contested along party lines. As a result, parties were everywhere entwined in what little government machinery there was.

First, parties staffed the government at all levels. Partisan patronage was pervasive and accepted as appropriate. Each party's loyal followers made up the pool from which government workers were drawn, from the most menial doorkeeper or messenger to the very top of the pyramid, from postmasters, land office workers, Indian agents, and customshouse clerks to department heads and cabinet secretaries. As James K. Polk wrote in his diary at the outset of his Administration, "I resolved . . . to appoint no man who was not an original Democrat and a strict constructionist." On being appointed to the Board of Governors of the Union Pacific Railroad in the 1860's, George Ashmun, a longtime Massachusetts Whig politican, remarked: "I never solicited this place, and it has been given to me rather as a testimonial of my political consistency than on account of any other values there is in it, and it is on this account that I am desirous of retaining it." He recognized that board members were "part of the loaves and fishes of patronage." While political patronage could be a two-edged sword, aggravating internal party divisions and creating bitterness and disappointment, in general it "continually revitalized the party's commitment to provide the community with capable men and sound government."[31]

Beyond appointments, party was the paramount force in the shaping of public policy in both Congress and the state legislatures, the main terrain of nineteenth-century American government. From the organizing of the chamber to the whole range of roll call voting behavior, partisanship, more than any other factor, affected the way legislators acted. "The call for yeas and nays," John Quincy Adams complained in the early 1830's, "is the bugle-horn of party, and never fails to rally the pack." It continued to do so thereafter, as well, throughout the political era.[32]

Congress no sooner convened than congressmen met in party caucuses to decide on candidates for legislative offices and committee rosters, as well as to shape their party's stance on what was to come before them. (In the latter instance, they usually referred to the platforms on which they had run). Although the caucuses did not have power to discipline members, and there was always some maverick behavior on the floor, they did serve an important reminding and reinforcing function for party members. Most went along with their leaders' decisions. As a southern Democrat put it in the 1850's, "There is no better party man living than I am. . . . I go to caucuses and abide by caucuses."[33]

Similar partisan institutions existed in the states. At Raleigh, when the North Carolina legislature met before the Civil War, to offer one example of the larger pattern, members met in separate party caucuses to choose candidates for the various legislative offices. After the caucuses reached their decisions, the subsequent party lineup behind each's candidates "was virtually unanimous. . . . No matter how divided a party might be in caucus, it rallied around the majority's choice." There were also frequent opportunities for the ritualistic reaffirmation of party loyalty. North Carolina's legislative party leaders offered resolutions about national affairs: the independent treasury, tariff and land policies, the veto power of the President, the annexation of Texas, the Mexican War. These invariably generated a high degree of party rhetoric and voting and a clear definition of the partisan nature of legislative life. None of this was atypical. From Massachusetts, to Illinois, to Mississippi and Alabama, the atmosphere was such that party "drillmasters were usually able to keep the pilot light of partisan passion burning."[34]

There was, of course, good reason for such behavior. In addition to their own marked party devotion, reinforced by contacts with others of like mind in some capital city, legislators were never out of touch with party members back home. Supporters frequently wrote and sometimes visited. Governors and Presidents tried to keep tabs (and pressure) on legislators as well, reminding them of their duty and what the party had the right to expect. Moreover, both congressmen and state legislators sat in formal session for only a relatively brief time; they spent most of their careers back home, among their constituents and the whole local party apparatus. No one there hesitated to remind them of party outlooks and expectations. Finally, the partisan press, as we have seen, kept everyone in touch with each other and never let officeholders forget their partisan obligations. Congressmen regularly received, as part of their perquisites, local party newspapers. All of this had an effect. As Ballard Campbell sums up, legislators in this era could not become "political recluses."[35]

Policy making within legislative chambers in this environment was essentially and always partisan. Congressional voting behavior, after the late 1830's, "squared consistently with rhetorical positions taken by party representatives in pamphlets, editorials, and on the hustings." Even when American politics was sectionally disrupted in the 1840's and then, more profoundly, in the realignment of the 1850's, traditional partisan norms remained strong in Congress. The programmatic differences between Whigs and Democrats, as well as their nonprogrammatic partisan loyalties, continued to play a major role on Capitol Hill for some time even as new patterns emerged. Once the realignment ended, the partisan shaping of legislative behavior, in its new Republican versus Democratic form, continued to be powerful into the 1890's.[36]

A number of students of state legislative behavior have suggested that party lines did not hold on policy matters on that level with the same force they did on ritualistic matters of partisan affirmation. William Bowers argues, for example, that in the Pennsylvania legislature at the outset of this era, "party was always a leading factor in voting but never consistently important except for national issues and officer elections." Studies of Alabama, Georgia, Massachusetts, and New Jersey support this view. Yet there is persuasive evidence in the roll-call voting record that if partisanship was not always decisive in every substantive area, it did not end with office voting or the rhetorical assertion of national party values. The same "hard line partisanship" found in Congress manifested itself when the state legislatures acted on the agenda set out by each party's national and state platforms.[37]

Herbert Ershkowitz and William Shade, who have studied legislative voting in six widely scattered states, argue that from the early 1830's to the early 1840's, a robust partisan imperative shaped not only economic policy, but policy in such other realms as education, black rights, and social reform. They found no evidence to suggest that these legislatures were dominated "by self-serving politicians," quick to change positions for electoral reasons. In fact, "one could generally differentiate a Democrat from a Whig" in the voting in these six legislatures, and "while a perfect correlation between party loyalty and voting behavior did not exist, . . . by 1840 from 80 to 100 percent of the Democrats and Whigs adhered to the dominant [policy] view of their own party and voted that way."[38]

Studies of individual states suggest that the same pattern continued past the early 1840's. In the North Carolina legislature in the 1840's and 1850's, "the vast majority of men of either party would be found voting for their party's position on state banking, internal improvements, individual liability of corporate stockholders, an insane asylum, or the appointment of state superintendent of the common schools." Even when some of the state's Democrats showed a willingness, in the 1850's, to consider more extended government intervention to promote economic development, "bitter partisan wrangling" erupted over how to finance such commitments. A close study of the behavior of the Mississippi legislature from the mid-1830's to the mid-1840's reveals the same partisan norms on policy matters as occurred on roll-call votes on partisan rituals. Party was the underlying force shaping almost all substantive matters.[39]

There were important exceptions, to be sure. Local, regional, and sectional pressures not unexpectedly intruded. Certain distributive schemes sorely divided party members along local and constituency lines from time to time. There was always great party tension over internal improvements, for example. Intraparty debates on canal, road, and harbor bills were sometimes as bitter as any heard between the parties. The subject repeatedly raised conflicts between quite specific, often emergency- and constituency-driven needs for government aid and deeply held partisan ideals. Voting on such issues, therefore, usually exhibited less partisan structuring than on other issues.[40]

If, in less partisanly competitive states the pressures for party unity were relatively relaxed, in the closely competitive states, from New York and Ohio to North Carolina, Tennessee, and Indiana, partisanship was the norm. Theirs was the more typical experience. On the whole, as this era unfolded, the dominant tendency was for the forces of partisanship to overwhelm counterforces and primarily shape legislative behavior. To the men sitting in most legislative chambers, parties "bridged the related but separate world of community and statehouse." So legislators really did not much need more formal institutional structures, experts, specialized committees, and the like to guide them. As Donald DeBats suggests, "A system in which party provides the overwhelming guide to the behavior and action of individual legislators does not require high levels of membership experience, committee structures, or experienced Speakers." Legislators were linked by their common experiences and understandings as Democrats, Whigs, and Republicans. They knew where they stood on all but a few pieces of legislation.[41]

Presidents and governors were vigorous members of their party communities as well, in terms of both patronage and programs. They understood what was at stake, what had to be done, and what they believed. In a working draft of his first inaugural address, Abraham Lincoln marked the reality well. "The more modern custom of electing a Chief Magistrate upon a previously selected platform of principles supersedes, in a great measure, the necessity of repeating those principles in an inaugural address. Upon the plainest grounds of good faith one so elected is not at liberty to shift his *position*." Throughout the era, other Presidents echoed Lincoln's thoughts. As a result, Presidents (and many governors, too) either tried to push their party's platform through or sought, in their use of the veto power and their influence as party leader, to block any deviations from it, as Polk and Franklin Pierce did over what they considered to be extravagant and expensive congressional internal improvement bills during their administrations.[42]

State and federal courts, from the lowest to the Supreme Court, manifested many of these same partisan impulses. By the 1840's, "a disciplined, party-directed selection process" existed for judges. Parties "imposed . . . coherence" on judicial selection by bringing forward candidates to be nominated by partisan Presidents and governors and confirmed by partisan congressmen and state legislators. Most Supreme Court justices, including Roger Taney, Levi Woodbury, and Salmon P. Chase, had had long political careers before coming to the court, as did almost every judge on the lowest state court. Some of them left the court to return to party pursuits. More to the point, their decisions were infused with the kinds of partisan ideas and rhetoric found in any normal political meeting. Most of their behavior was predictable. Appointments were political, partisan outlooks certainly shaped the decisions made, and the American people saw courts as part of the partisan system that all of them lived under. Partisan court packing was occasionally denounced but was fully expected and always practiced.[43]

Chinks in the partisan structuring of the governmental world appeared from time to time. Some were deep and persistent, but the overall pattern was clear. The decisions made in each local party meeting at the beginning of an electoral season worked their way up through the system, ultimately to affect not only the perceptions of potential voters, but also those of the President, governors, congressmen, and state legislators. Those perceptions, in turn, led to predictable, partisanly driven behavior throughout the government. Even during a national crisis like the Civil War, when fresh thinking and new directions in government activity and power seemed called for, partisan politics continued as usual. Despite forceful efforts to instill nonpartisanship in the face of an unprecedented national war emergency, there was little bipartisan consensus beyond the most general goals. In the North, the Democrats vigorously opposed Republican policy initiatives that seemed at war with their traditional perspectives. Their persistent oppositionist behavior, in Washington and in the states, underscored, once more, how much partisan confrontation shaped all of the branches, and all of the activities, of the American government. Similar difficulties confronted the Confederacy, whose rulers unsurprisingly remained influenced by much of their partisan political heritage.[44]

Glimmerings of a New Era

This commanding partisan government system was increasingly challenged as the years of this political era passed by the emergence of nonpartisan interests seeking to penetrate law-making and administrative institutions. These interests increased in number while the scramble for government aid intensified. In economic affairs, for example, lobbyists for different enterprises were bent on getting what they wanted no matter which party was in power. They, and their employers, had specific, imperative needs that they wished addressed. Their experience led them to believe that they would be best served by predictable, rational government activity, a system of policy making not subject to the frequent, disruptive electoral turnovers so commonplace in American political life. Not surprisingly, given their crucial role in the economy's expansion, transportation companies, first canals, then railroads, led the way in these nonpartisan efforts.

During the 1850's, the Illinois-Central Railroad penetrated the political apparatus in Illinois, dispensing favors to politicians on all sides. It brought people to political rallies and employed leading politicians, regardless of party, to help the line, some as lobbyists, some as lawyers. "The railroad needed the friendship of public men," one historian argues, "and openly courted it with judicious distribution of their legal business, printing contracts, and other patronage, not to mention free annual passes."[45] The Illinois-Central's activities suggested an ideal that other transportation companies reached for in order to advance their interests in state legislatures and in Congress.

As the transportation revolution grew into an industrial revolution, larger and larger interests began to seek more and more favors from the government. Increasingly national in scope, active in both Democratic and Republican localities, such interests felt stymied by a system dominated by party politics, one that was parochial and unwilling, in their view, to respond to their needs. They made no attempt to disguise their growing impatience with, and then great hostility toward, the traditional way of doing government business, with its messiness and ineffectualness. These new national interests wanted ordered and rational, not piecemeal, vague, generally distributive, responses to their needs.[46]

Although their plans would not fully mature for some time to come, there was a growing perception among these interests, and some others as well, that the partisan government system, organized as it was, did not have the will or the capacity to deal effectively with the new economic and social realities. Congressmen themselves realized during the Civil War that they could not cope with many of the new demands made on them, and some began to turn to outside lobbyists for advice and guidance about pending legislation. Things grew worse after the war, when Congress's legislative workload expanded rapidly. As Thompson points out, this "prodigious" increase in responsibility occurred "without a commensurate increase in institutional capacity to respond." As a result, "lobbyists of various kinds became integral parts of the allocative machinery; they called attention to individual claimants, backed competing seekers of jobs, gathered and communicated data, handled paperwork—in short, aided both officials and clienteles in the conduct and routines of Congressional Government."[47]

Lobbyists were reaching out, or being appealed to, to help set priorities, amid a welter of pressures. "At a time," Thompson continues, "when active and effective representation was more essential than ever before, lobbying formed a bridge between particularized publics and Washington." Lobbyists "offered services that were valuable to both clients and officials" of a federal legislature increasingly beset by "clogged agendas, cumbersome committees, obsolete procedures, and amateurism." Without them, given established attitudes, procedures, and traditions, little was likely to be done, whatever the need.[48]

It is in the new efforts to manage the economy that the theme of political corruption reappears, particularly charges of the bribing of public officials in order to receive some government largesse. The felt need to wrest favors and services from unwilling or inexperienced government officers fueled a system of payoffs that could then be used to support the massive electoral machines as well as line the pockets of individuals. The mildness of William Marcy's "to the victors belong the spoils of office" was succeeded, therefore, by the much larger reach, first, of men like Roscoe Conkling and Commodore Vanderbilt, and then of urban political leaders like Boss Tweed. Many historians suggest that graft got out of hand. In 1898, the shocked English observer Beatrice Webb saw the United States being run by a "subterranean government" made up of corrupt officials, lobbyists, and robber barons indifferent to the general welfare. In this version of the story, corrupt politicians and robber barons worked hand in glove, milking the treasury, and dispensing and receiving favors and payoffs; officeholders demanded payments for the most ordinary acts of administration and legislation; and conflicts of interest abounded. "As government became more involved in the economy, the range of corrupt activities became larger."[49]

Others argue that though corruption may have increased, there were always complexities in the situation. Some politicians had always been paid off. The main point, to these scholars, was the pressure of rapid and confused growth against the inertia of government. National demands for action were echoed at the local level as the concentration of large populations in cities put unprecedented pressure on services. Yet, as Morton Keller puts it, "the polity had neither the theoretical nor the organizational means to handle the growth effectively. Bribery and kickbacks [along with lobbying] were a form of accommodation, a way of getting things done." Furthermore, some analysts contend that the degree of corruption has been exaggerated. W. R. Brock suggests that, "lobbies with money to spend might offer cash bribes, but this was much rarer than is sometimes imagined; the cost could be exorbitant and the risk of exposure high."[50]

In any event, although corruption existed, political figures still had independent sources of power, rooted in the dominant party organizations and the intense loyalties of the electorate. Independent party leaders were rarely the puppets of the new economic elites. They served other masters. No one knew that better than those trying to change the American political nation. The governmental process, with its notably partisan roots, could not be counted on consistently, even as late as the 1880's. As long as officeholders were beholden to party leaders and the partisan communities that nurtured them, as long as politicians considered policies with wary eyes on the ballot box and with minds shaped by traditional partisan attitudes, there was an uncertain prospect for the laws, changes, and decisions the industrial elites demanded.[51]

Lobbying and corruption were indications that the existing formal authority system was not functioning well, that things seemed to be getting too complicated and too big in the 1860's and 1870's. Compromises, informal efforts, and some weak attempts to increase regulative coherence did not go very far. And yet, with all of its limits and incompleteness, American government was scarcely moribund. The partisan imperative, coupled with antistatist attitudes of varying intensity, led to a weak, decentralized system that was still able to do many things in the public sphere. The American government proved to be "a generous patron." But it did not rule. It was neither well integrated nor nicely balanced, able to react coherently. It worked best at creating a sprawl, not managing it.[52]

But this ambiguity was inevitable. In the United States in the nineteenth century, government was limited, intermittent, and fragmented, the product of a politically divided republic, whose circumscribed official behavior, until late in the era, most believed appropriate. The United States had no "habit of governance"; its governing scene remained prestatist throughout this half century. As a result, America retained "a popular culture increasingly dedicated to the proposition that government power of almost any sort was suspect." That was the way most of those who participated in it—at the top and the bottom alike—wanted things and expected them to be.[53]

"Talk Not of Regularity and Party Associations": Challengers in the American Political Nation, 1838-1893

THE COMMONPLACE CORE OF American political life after 1838 was its partisanship. The ideology and organization of party shaped and dominated the behavior of those who participated in politics, from legislators, other officeholders, and campaign activists, to the thousands of voters who turned out each election day, usually to vote a straight ticket. Yet, despite the strength of the partisan imperative, there were regular challenges to its central tenets: persistent constituencies of discontent; people ever impatient with, or continually frustrated by, the national parties and the partisan norms they imposed throughout the system. Dissent from a society's central political truths exists in any nation. What is interesting and instructive to a political analysis is the particular form such challenges take ideologically and organizationally, and the potency they achieve at different times in different places.

In the American political era after 1838, as we have seen, these challenges were twice disruptive and realigning: in the 1850's and again in the 1890's, in the first case because one major party replaced another, in the second, because there was a fundamental shift in the competitive nexus of the electoral system itself, a shift that ultimately had extraordinary consequences for the political nation as it entered the twentieth century.[1] Most of the time, however, nonconformist political movements played little role electorally or in policy making in a culture textured by the partisan imperative. The usually successful drive to impose discipline, once the major parties had made their policy and electoral decisions, and the intense popular loyalty to parties undercut the potential for significant accomplishment by those advocating alternative policies, certainly in terms of offices won and legislation achieved, no matter how fervently they pushed or how right they believed themselves to be. Nevertheless, repeated political failure rarely stopped these challengers. They were, as a result, always an integral part of the political nation in this era. Moreover, in pushing a perspective and a behavior at odds with the majority of those involved in American politics they also mirrored a great deal of their political nation as well.

The Outsider Presence

The reasons for the dissenters' nonconformity varied; some of it was originally factional, some of it was ideological, much of it focused on the need for specific policies. From the beginning of this era, each major party always had its share of "schismatics," members who pushed different priorities from the majority, who preferred different candidates, and who quite often threatened to bolt if they did not get what they wanted. A losing candidate for some nomination and his followers, intensely angry at the slight and convinced that he and his ideas should have been preferred, sometimes challenged the party. Defectors from a ticket or dissenters from a particular policy were not uncommon, as Lewis Cass, Grover Cleveland, James G. Blaine, and Ulysses S. Grant all learned. Beyond this, there were party members who strongly espoused their independence from partisan moorings. Although nominally a Whig, John Quincy Adams, whom Daniel Walker Howe labels a "nonpartisan politician," was always uncomfortable among partisan zealots and powerfully resisted party norms. The party loyalty of men like Adams never seemed to run very deep and was often tempered by their belief that larger necessities overrode the demands of the partisan imperative.[2]

Important as these challengers were at critical moments, most of them, even the always difficult Adams, considered themselves Democrats, Whigs, or Republicans and seldom strayed for very long. They could be a headache to party leaders, but they could also be counted on to behave properly, if not at a particular convention, or during a critical legislative debate, or on a specific election day, certainly over time and generally. Their schismatic behavior roiled the political waters but did not rechannel the mainstream of two-party politics. The New York Barnburners' defection from the Democratic party to the Free Soilers, for example, was disastrous for the party in the presidential election of 1848. But most of the defectors returned to their political homes in time for the state elections in 1849 or the presidential election of 1852, many of them never to leave again.[3]

Others in the political nation, however, questioned more than internal party decisions. They were true challengers, in the persistence and direction of their stance, to the predominating standards of the partisan system. Their ranks included those who were dissatisfied with the national consensus in the 1840's and 1850's: John C. Calhoun and other southern rights advocates, as well as abolitionists and Free Soilers in the northern states, all of whom exhibited either anguish or defensiveness over the presence of slavery in American life. Another type, including the post–Civil War Liberal Republicans and Mugwumps, began as a party faction but broke away in the end in their protest to the way politics was carried on in the country.[4]

There were, in addition, those whose stringent critique of American life led them to advocate remedies ignored by the main parties. Taking notions of equality and perfection to a degree usually absent from mainstream politics, they sought to raise the status of women or make Americans behave better by drinking less and eating better; others tried to define who should be an American and under what conditions. Some of these challenges were single-issue movements, mounted by people determined to achieve one goal above all others, rather than pushing an array of policies as the major parties did. Others came together behind a whole package of reforms they believed to be critical to America's future.[5]

Predictably enough, the periods of severe national economic stress and social unrest, in the late 1830's, and again from the 1860's into the 1890's, gave rise to some of the most intense challenges to the political nation. These particular reformers believed that America was deteriorating, even disintegrating, while the two major parties ignored the immense threat to national survival. Their anger, typically class- and/ or economically based, led them to advocate such things as currency reform, radical land distribution, price regulation, and the eight-hour workday as means of meliorating the socioeconomic disasters confronting the nation.[6]

Each of these challenges had its own distinctive frame of reference. Nevertheless, they manifested a common style of understanding, discourse, and behavior, whatever their particular fear, social evil, or remedy happened to be. In the first place, all these challengers were unsparing in their public condemnation of the existing conditions in America. In speeches, pamphlets, and party platforms, in great anger, they documented all that had gone wrong with their society. They powerfully spelled out not only vast degenerative transformations they believed themselves to be trapped in, whether social, economic, or ideological, but also the specific failures, injustices, and uncorrected evils that abounded on the landscape, summoning to that enterprise the rhetoric of class dislocation, republican fragility, and egalitarian striving. Something was fundamentally wrong in the United States, they said, and they wanted to correct it.[7]

Most critically, their discontent led them to censure the American political system and express an unconcealed disdain for its practices. In every case, the challengers believed that party leaders ignored the nation's real problems or played down their importance. Those leaders clearly wanted nothing to do with issues and perspectives they considered beyond the normal run of political discourse and behavior, with the result that the dissenters gravitated toward outsider political activity. Whatever their specific beliefs were, or the specific courses of action they propounded, these people believed that success in correcting societal iniquities began with an unyielding and often bitter critique of existing politics. Ronald Walters refers to abolitionist political activity, as one example, as a "gesture of protest against the imperfection of American political life."[8]

At the margins of the political culture, these people, agitators, challengers, and nonplayers, fought to establish what they hoped and believed was a different political ethic from the one guiding their society. Fired by some ignored idea, needed reform, or fear about what was happening to the United States, their strident assertiveness matched the vigorous rhetoric of the leaders of the major parties. The outsider political temperament contained features unique to the dominant strains of this political era. These people were not institutional loyalists in the political realm, certainly not at all costs. They refused to subordinate themselves to any collectivity, as demanded by the prevailing ideology of partisan commitment. Conventional two-partyism was not for them. Neither major party adequately supported their priorities, nor ever would, given the parties' compromising nature and coalitionist role in this period. The challengers insisted on the priority of individual conscience over any duty to collective political discipline. They put principle or policy first, then held to it with an inflexible commitment. They particularly distrusted the demands for compromise and forced agreement. To them, this meant accepting a delay in their policy goals, something they would not brook. Independent political action was thus the only alternative.[9]

A Perspective on Society: The Failure of the American Political Nation

What had gone wrong in American politics? These critics believed that everything that had been so magnificently designed to set the nation on the right path had become corrupted by the late 1830's. The

American people had lost their way politically. The institutions established by the Founders had degenerated; their purposes had been distorted, lost, or forgotten. Everywhere, a pervasive corruption of political life had replaced once enlightened aims. "The corruption of government and the impoverishment of the masses," the Union Labor party claimed, not untypically, "result from neglect of the self-evident truths proclaimed by the founders of this republic, that all men are created equal and endowed with inalienable rights." Something had to be done. The American Republic, therefore, "must be put upon a new tack."[10]

Each outsider movement had its own candidate for the person or group that had caused the nation's descent into corruption. But whoever the malefactor was, he and his friends wanted to weaken the system. As the Liberty party's platform of 1844 put it:

We are fully persuaded that it is indispensably necessary to the salvation of the union of the States, to the preservation of the liberties of the people and to the permanent restoration of prosperity in every department of business, that the National Government be rescued from the grasp of the slave power; that the spirit and practice of slaveholding be expelled from our National Legislature, and that the administration of the Government be conducted henceforth in conformity with the principles of the Constitution, and for the benefit of the whole population.[11]

If America was to recapture the commitment it had once had, there was only one means of doing so. The active operations of outsider political movements were the only way that Americans had "to remedy existing evils, and prevent the disastrous consequences otherwise resulting therefrom." All these challengers knew where they wished to go, or, more accurately, where they wished to return. Each group began by ringing in the Declaration of Independence and the federal Constitution, which together embodied the wishes and intentions of "the founders of the American republic." The Liberty party in 1844 was "not a new party, or a third party, but . . . the party of 1776, reviving the principles of that memorable era, and striving to carry them into practical application." Similarly, its younger brother, the Prohibition Reform party of 1876, was "organized in the name of the people to revive, enforce and perpetuate in the Government the doctrines of the Declaration of Independence."[12]

The greatest failures in American political life, its greatest corruption, were the two major parties who dominated the nation with an unnatural and unhealthy "tyranny." Parties had once been the strong advocates of consistent principles, but by the late 1830's, they were "permeated by moral decay." "After generations of experience," the Iowa Greenback party resolved in 1877, "we are forced to believe that nothing further can be hoped for through the old political parties." To another critic, hope was not the right word: "Party divisions are the danger of our day; and parties now [are] no more for principles, but for the spoils. . . . Such is the sin and shame of the times." Democrats and Whigs were both "held together only by the strong 'cohesive power of public plunder.'"[13]

Throughout the era, the outsider political movements never let up in their condemnation of the way the major parties framed their appeals, the issues they ignored, their subservience to malevolent interests, and their indifference to real problems. As the platform writers of the Independent (Greenback) party put it in 1876, their party had been "called into existence by the necessities of the people whose industries are prostrated, whose labor is deprived of its just reward by a ruinous policy which the Republican and Democratic parties refuse to change, and in view of the failure of these parties to furnish relief to the depressed industries of the country, thereby disappointing just hopes and expectations of the suffering people." In their place, therefore, abolitionists, prohibitionists, greenbackers, and the rest were fighting "this good cause" to right the political ship—"the cause of IN-TEGRITY against CORRUPTION—the cause of the PEOPLE against the OFFICE-HOLDERS—the cause of the true Democracy against the false." They called on the voters to come with them and turn against the old parties that had "deceived you more than once."[14]

The two major political parties were corrupt in three interrelated ways. First, their leadership was unresponsive to their constituents, unprincipled in their advocacy, and manipulative in their behavior in national affairs. The Albany Regency, Missouri's Boonslick group, the Richmond Junto, Alabama's Broad River Group, the Concord Regency in New Hampshire, and other leadership "cabals" subordinated all political principles to the one aim of being elected to public office. They had no concern for the people's will or the nation's general welfare. They selected their candidates, for example, "with regard only to their political strength and party popularity, regardless of [their] mental capacity, moral integrity, and all the higher and better qualities of man." Americans had become "weary of the vileness and villainy of demagogues." Therefore, "unless party leaders [began to] care more for what is right and less for what is expedient," they had to be abandoned by the American people.[15]

Second, the Democrats, Whigs, and Republicans were not even true political parties. Forsaking consistency, which was the hallmark of real parties, they were no more than motley collections of unlike groups yoked together for electoral advantage alone. As institutions, following their leaders, they practiced a "sacrifice of principle in order to win votes away from the opposition," and this kind of "abandonment of substantial truth" compromised any political party's integrity. A party had to be based not only on the soundness of its principles, but also on its commitment to them. In the United States, there had been

> too much of compromise and concession of principle, . . . too much postponement of agitation of topics of dissension, . . . too much sacrifice of "the truth, and the whole truth, and nothing but the truth" to petty motives of seeming expediency; too much trimming of sails to shifting breezes of temporary popularity; too little confidence in . . . principles and in the eventual rectitude of the popular judgement.[16]

American political parties, the challengers argued, muffled issues. When they disagreed, they fought over trifles. There was, as a consequence, little difference between them ideologically. Their perspective that "one idea, however just, or a single principle, however sound, constitutes a basis too narrow upon which to build and maintain a great Political Party" was an example of their desire to downplay coherence in the name of coalitionism, the preferred means of ensuring their most important goal—electoral triumph. Since the existing parties were "hopelessly unwilling to adopt an adequate policy on this question," challengers were forced to abandon them.[17]

Third, the two major political parties emphasized discipline as the sine qua non of effective politics. Outsiders repeatedly warned against automatic party loyalty and argued that "adherence to party has its limits." As one editor put it, "Talk not of regularity and party associations when you are canvassing the claims of civil freedom." Someone could be "what is termed a seceder from party organization, without in the slightest degree compromising his political opinions," he insisted. . . . Associations are of modern origin, but TRUTH is as old as creation." Or as John Van Buren said in 1848, in his one brief secession from party loyalty, "he thought it quite as important to be right as regular."[18]

The abolitionist leader William Lloyd Garrison, as always, was pungent in his summary of the case against the major parties. In terms redolent of the various themes stressed by the challenger groups in this political society, he described the Democratic party in 1856 as

beyond all question, the most corrupt, the most shameless, the most abandoned, and the most desperate party in existence. From the beginning, "the natural ally of slavery," it has continued to wax worse and worse, till now it is thoroughly Satanic in spirit and purpose; the embodiment of border-ruffianism; its rank-and-file made up largely of the ignorant, the besotted, the mobocratic, the intensely depraved, the utterly lawless, the horribly profane, the fearfully misguided—and governed by the vilest demagogues, the most dangerous conspirators, and the most bloody-minded tyrants; avowing sentiments more derogatory to human nature, more hostile to human liberty, more insulting to Heaven than have been promulgated by all the tories of Europe for a thousand years; laughing to scorn the "self-evident truths" of the Declaration of Independence, and impudently branding them as self-evident lies; perfidious to all its pledges, prostrating every barrier of freedom, trampling in the dust the Constitution it has sworn to maintain, and making it a crime worthy of imprisonment and death for freemen to defend their lives and property against the murderous assaults of roving bandits and merciless cut-throats. Language is inadequate to describe the transcendent wickedness of the Democratic party, in its present position and under its present guidance.[19]

These dissenters were purifiers of the political process. Their condemnation of a "hopelessly and shamelessly corrupt" political system echoed familiar themes. The two major parties had failed. "For more than a quarter of a century," the People's party platform of 1892 charged, Democrats and Republicans had battled "for power and plunder, while grievous wrongs [had] been inflicted upon the suffering people." Both had allowed "the existing dreadful conditions to develop without serious effort to prevent or restrain them." As a result, it was too late for redemption—"a choice between the two impious major parties was no choice at all." They had to be abandoned. All "patriots and good citizens" had to "sever all connections with both" of them.[20]

The Power of Political Norms

The members of outsider political movements believed and repeatedly argued that their political stance differed from the norms of their society. It did to a great degree. Some challengers were never reconciled to what had happened in their political nation since 1838. They certainly articulated, often stridently, a romantic resistance to complexity, political pluralism, and institutionalization in party affairs. As a result, not every dissenter was an enthusiastic participant in the structure of election competition that now dominated American politics. Many preferred the role of political guerrilla. They consciously chose to remain aloof and outside, largely engaged in agitating, fulminating, denouncing, and pressuring. Individual criticism could often be effective, as a number of newspaper editors claimed for themselves, and as John Quincy Adams, for one, had demonstrated on the floor of the House of Representatives. Mills Thornton's description of some Alabamians before the Civil War seems generally applicable: "The negotiation and compromise almost necessarily incidental to the enactment of legislation [appeared to them to be] *per se* corrupt." That attitude infused all that the dissenters claimed they were trying to do.[21]

The indictment of the major parties by these groups strongly resembled the antiparty expressions so pervasive in the United States in an earlier era.[22] Certainly, a good deal of that antipartyism revived after 1838 among some of the challengers and seemed to be greatly invigorated in their critical, denunciatory passion. As we have seen, the same fears of corruption, especially illegal and conspiratorial manipulation against the general good, permeated their rhetoric. But an important distinction existed. Earlier political commentators had considered all parties factious, divisive, and corrupt. They argued that parties did not belong in the American system if it was to survive. Although this absolutist sentiment was expressed by some of the political challengers in the post-1838 political nation, particularly Liberal Republicans and Mugwumps after the Civil War, most of them, grudgingly, and with a great deal of disagreement and heartburning among themselves, accepted the dominant impulses of the day. They shifted from an unadulterated antipartyism to a focus on the misbehavior of particular parties, a tacit admission that parties were important, perhaps even indispensable, in the United States.[23]

The challengers wanted parties to make a crisp, precise ideological commitment to specific policies. They called, therefore, for a different kind of political party from the ones now harming America, a party that behaved responsibly. They reminded voters that parties "have something more to do than to indicate a man; they have to do justice to their cause." Always remember, one outsider had once written, in words that re-echoed repeatedly throughout the era, that "the moral power of any party is its opinions. Except so far as a party represents opinion, it is a mere faction." From that came their determination, in Michael Holt's characterization, to "clean up politics, [and to] cast aside corrupt wireworks and party hacks." But this clean-up would have a partisan structuring to it.[24]

The argument for replacing the corrupt major parties with new ones was clear. "What shall be done in the case in which both political parties err? . . . Surely there is a very simple remedy, [which] consists in deserting a party, rending asunder all its ties, and planting ourselves upon those just and true principles upon which all republics must be based. A new party is formed, the republic is saved and the blind and corrupt leaders with the timid and senseless few who remain with them are plunged together into the political ditch." A third party, "far from corrupting those who endorsed it," would be able "by its adherence to lofty principles and disregard for boodle and swag" to bring "probity back to politics." The candidates it chose would be "fresh from the people, unused to party service, and strangers to political corruption." Such efforts were not only necessary; they would win out. Everywhere, dissidents saw evidence of their success. "The shackles of party seem to have fallen off. Party no longer holds men captive. . . . The dictation of demagogues and ambitious leaders has lost its influence. Men of all parties think for themselves."[25]

These arguments were quite revealing of the challengers' perspective. Despite their persistent outsider questioning stance and self-image, the way they finally participated in politics suggests their adherence to many of the central political norms of their era. They believed that, with qualitative changes, the political system could become responsive to the needs of the American people. Some challengers did not organize political parties. Most of them did, moving from agitation to organization, borrowing from the norms of their political nation, while claiming to depart from them. As one historian has written about the United Labor party of the mid-1880's, its members sought to "yoke an emergent class identity to main-stream politics."[26]

Third-partyism became the dominant organizational form for the expression of the challengers' protests. They established political parties and contested elections right through this era, from the Liberty and Free Soilers of the 1840's, to the Prohibitionists, Equal Rights, Anti-Monopoly, Greenback, and economic reform parties of the 1870's and 1880's, culminating in the People's party mobilizing the force of agrarian protest at the very end of the period in the early 1890's. At least one third party ran in every presidential election in the era, except in the Civil War–period contests of 1864 and 1868. Often several minor parties were on the ballot in the same campaign.

From time to time, some third parties ran candidates in congressional, state, and local elections as well, if never with the regularity of the major parties.[27]

Since election regulation was so informal, there were comparatively few bureaucratic constraints on their receiving votes. Third-party voting was widespread, whatever its total, indicating the outsiders' ability to cast their ballots as they wished—with some notable exceptions toward the end of the era. The very small Liberty party national vote in the elections of 1840 and 1844 was cast in nine, and then twelve, of the thirteen northern states. The Prohibitionists received some popular votes in thirty-three of the thirty-eight states in the presidential election of 1884. Eight years before, the Greenbackers' 76,000 votes were cast in seventeen of the thirty-seven states. Below the state level, Free Soilers cast votes in more than 90 percent of the northern counties in 1848. For much of the period, then, the dissidents' energy, organization, and determination, together with easy access to the voters, won them places on the ballot, if not success at the polls.[28]

In each case, they emulated their enemies. They organized and campaigned as the major political parties did, nominated candidates, drafted platforms, held national conventions, and defined strategies to mobilize voters behind their policies. Somewhat more sporadically, they called state, district, and local conventions. They staged campaign rallies and organized to get out the vote. They issued pamphlets and published party newspapers. In the aftermath of the Free Soilers' national convention in 1848, for example, the party called ratification and organization meetings as well as state conventions, ran candidates for governor in ten of the fourteen northern states where elections were held that year, and put up fifty-nine candidates for Congress. Unlike the major parties, the third parties varied enormously in their organizational and campaign efforts. Generally speaking, the Free Soilers and Populists were the most organizationally and electorally dynamic. But the efforts were made by all of them.[29]

Whatever their individual differences, the leaders and members of third parties demonstrated that they "did not belong to a sect in search of converts but consciously chose to adopt the organizational format and strategic approach of a political party pursuing electoral victory." As the Indiana Prohibition party's platform of 1884 said, "So long as legislatures are made and courts created by political parties, unorganized public opinion, upon any political question, is of but little value." Third parties therefore "tailored their style to the expectations of voters in the political culture . . . and did not hesitate to imitate their adversaries in techniques of attracting voters." If their

efforts were considerably smaller than those of their major adversaries, their actions constituted the sincerest form of flattery—mimick-
ing those they sought to replace.[30]

On the whole, those who advocated third-party action shared with
their adversaries a strong commitment to the political process, a desire to compete electorally, and a belief that they would achieve their
policy goals there. As Alan Kraut has written, "Even the most skeptical Liberty [party] men did not find politics to be irreparably corrupt, just in urgent need of reform." Most of them "agreed upon the
legitimacy of the American political party system. . . . They did not
share the more general anti-institutionalism of many non-political abolitionists." Their proparty perspective was as strongly expressed as
the antiparty viewpoint before it. And though there was constant recognition of the dangers inherent in party politics, the thrust of the
criticism focused on the particular, not on the general.[31]

Yet moving from agitation to organization caused many of these
critics to agonize over the problem of maintaining the purity of their
policy and behavioral stance while, at the same time, seeking votes.
The Prohibitionists, and others like them, believed that engaging in
electoral politics, no matter how guardedly, might well corrupt even
the most high-minded participants among them. They were not certain they could compete for office without losing their souls. Third-
party activists, therefore, tended to spend an enormous amount of
time worrying about how they could appeal to voters and still maintain their purity.[32]

Politics consisted of rights and wrongs, not compromises, negotiation, and dilution. This led the challengers into contortions and confusion from time to time. When they moved from unorganized protest into electoral politics, they remained ambivalent about building
complex organizational structures that might empower political
"bosses." But they built them nonetheless. Further, they strained to
articulate their positions differently from the major parties, replacing
what they thought were too general and vague, negotiated proposals
with highly specific statements of purpose. The Liberty party platform of 1844, for example, contained forty-four resolutions. Prohibitionists, Kleppner points out, argued that they were establishing a
"temporary" political party. Their leaders had no wish, they said,
"to build a pragmatic, subgroup-integrating partisan vehicle, which
would remain permanently on the scene." What they actually did,
Kleppner concludes, was create "an antiparty party."[33]

So the challengers in this political nation mixed elements of the
dominant political institutions of their era with emphases that dif-

fered markedly from them. They potently articulated dissent, but also stood as a testament to the strength and penetration of the party system as it had emerged in the United States by the late 1830's. The levels of purity and pragmatism among them varied, to be sure. Even the most stringent challengers sometimes used antiparty rhetoric for tactical, not ideological, reasons. Above all, however, they were always under the greatest ideological and behavioral stress, for they never resolved the questions of how to engage in politics, seek allies, and campaign for votes without also sacrificing their principles.[34]

The Capabilities of Third Parties

Could third parties, given both their members' own ambivalence and the external constraints posed by the partisan imperative, flourish in this political nation? The size and persistence of this congeries of political protest varied. Most histories of these movements demonstrate that they "rose and declined quickly." They did indeed. Some third parties emerged, contested an election or two, and then faded away forever. Sometimes, they needed a sharp stimulus, a catalyzing event, to move them directly into the electoral arena. But a few, the Prohibitionists most notably, were tenacious, running candidates in election after election over a very long period. Some were precursors of significant changes to come; others fought for ideas never seriously taken up and long forgotten.[35]

Third parties differed over strategy as well as policies. Some saw themselves as an independent balance of power between the main parties, able to exercise great influence in a closely competitive political environment. Others were willing to coalesce temporarily with one of the major parties at a strategic moment to gain an office for one of their members. In the late 1840's and early 1850's, the Free Soilers played this game effectively, working both sides of the fence to elect several of their own members to the House and Senate. Protesting labor and farmer groups followed the same strategy late in the era. As Sheldon Stromquist has written about urban workers in the 1880's and later, in terms that have more general application, "The particular vessel of class politics was not predetermined." Still other third parties held to the belief that at some point they would become strong enough to replace one or other of the major parties and constantly spoke of imminent breakthroughs. And finally, there were the resolutely purist-minded, people who stressed their determination to articulate their ideas and keep them alive, regardless of their electoral prospects. Winning was not as critical as their beliefs.[36]

Party regulars, unsurprisingly, felt that third parties did not belong and moved to counter the threat they posed. Loyalists were quick to challenge and condemn everything about the minor parties, no matter how much they adopted the major thrust of American politics. They argued that the third-party men rode insignificant hobby horses when they exaggerated the importance of a particular issue, rejected a particular candidate, or refused to accept a necessary compromise. They warned that "as a rule, men who are not true to a party will not be true to the public in an official capacity." They chided the challengers for their amateurish, obscure sectarianism and quaint, noisy ways. Regulars also condemned the dissenters for playing games that only demonstrated their political impotence in advancing their ideas and goals. As Paula Baker suggests, regular "party politicians often spoke of reformers . . . in terms that questioned [their] masculinity. . . . Reformers were seen as politically impotent, . . . the 'third sex' of American politics."[37]

Such condemnations were to be expected, but the major party critics raised a more compelling point as well, about the appropriateness and therefore the long-range effectiveness, of the challengers' approach in this political nation. "In our country," the Whig congressman George Hilliard told a party convention in 1849, "in which there is so large an infusion of the popular element, it seems to me there never can be more than two parties. These represent two principles in humanity. They are the party of progress and the party of repose." Politics was a battle between opposites. "There may be factions divided upon minor issues, mere sectional disputes, or what we call ismmatic differences," William Seward went on. "But in no country . . . can there be more or less than two antagonistic camps." The constant "mutual action and reaction" between the two helped "maintain a healthful and successful progress." Accordingly, third parties might appear, but they could not last. Their stability was "not consistent with the nature of man." Since "all the real issues involved in a popular election will ever be faithfully enough represented by the *two* great parties of the country," third parties were nothing but "a monstrous abortion." Whatever differences might arise, locally, sectionally, or otherwise, "there [could] be but two great parties in the Union."[38]

The widespread acceptance of these criticisms was confirmed by the election returns. Although third parties enjoyed flashes of popular support at the polls, particularly at moments of intense economic or social disarray, their national totals were rarely impressive and never enough for victory. Over the years 1840–92, the third-party popular vote for President averaged well under 5 percent nationally, except

TABLE 11.1

Third-Party Popular Vote for President, 1840–1892

Year	Percentage of vote	Year	Percentage of vote
1840	0.3%	1872	0.3%
1844	2.3	1876	1.1
1848	10.7	1880	3.5
1852	4.9	1884	3.2
1856	21.5	1888	3.5
1860	30.7	1892	10.9

SOURCE: *Congressional Quarterly's Guide to U.S. Elections* (Washington, D.C., 1975).
NOTE: No third parties ran in 1864 and 1868.

when it reflected an aspect of an electoral realignment as in 1856, 1860, and 1892. Even in those disruptive elections, the average third-party presidential vote remained under 20 percent, with any significant totals largely centered in a few states. More typical were their minuscule figures in most of the contests (see Table 11.1). In addition, most of them received what support they had within each state in limited geographic areas, no matter how national they tried to be in their reach for votes.[39]

Third parties did better in many of the congressional, state, and local races they contested, mobilizing, at different moments, a small but decisive electoral group behind them. The nativist American party elected Lewis Levin to Congress from Philadelphia three times between 1844 and 1848. Free Soilers won eight seats in the House of Representatives in 1848 on their own, and at least four more in coalition with one of the major parties. Greenbackers won fourteen House seats in 1878, and candidates of the People's party about a dozen in 1892. Henry George's campaign for mayor of New York in 1886 remains a classic instance of the strength a third party could demonstrate in a local election. Nominated by the Union Labor party, he ran second behind the successful Democratic candidate, with 31 percent of the vote. At times, then, there was an explosive surge of support to the third parties. (In 1878, the Greenback vote went over one million in congressional and state races, compared with just 76,000 in the presidential election two years before.)[40]

Despite such surges, occasional triumphs, or close-run defeats, third parties never converted their strong showings into more permanent support. Henry George, for example, received only 6.7 percent of the popular vote in the race for New York's Secretary of State the year after he and his party did so well in the mayoral contest. Third parties rarely captured as much as one-third of the electorate outside of a very particular local situation. John Dix, the Free Soil candidate for governor of New York, received only something over 26 percent of the vote in 1848. In Massachusetts, in the same year, the Free Soilers received 29 percent of the gubernatorial vote. Until the very end of the era, and then very occasionally with the Populists, that was as much as could ever be expected in this political climate.[41]

On the other hand, the small third-party vote occasionally was as significant as some of the leaders hoped it would be all of the time. The nature of major party competition throughout the era gave the minor parties some influence despite their small vote. The Liberty and Free Soil parties had a clear impact on two successive presidential elections, in 1844 and 1848. Similarly, in the very close elections in the Northeast after 1874, the votes drawn off by the Prohibitionists affected the outcome of some important state races. They drew as much as 10 percent of the vote in some counties of New York and, at the least, injected a high degree of volatility into the electoral contest throughout the state. Since the Prohibitionists drew their support disproportionately from normally Republican constituencies, they helped the Democrats to do better than they would have otherwise done. Greenbackers also briefly surged forward in the late 1870's to help make the difference in a number of races, this time drawing support in a more balanced fashion, sometimes from largely Democratic groups, sometimes from Republicans, occasionally from some of both, thereby throwing everyone off balance. As Peter Argersinger points out, the Greenbackers constantly held the balance of power electorally in the nonsouthern states in those years. Their "insurgent raids on the major parties' electoral core . . . could be fatal in the highly competitive environment of Gilded Age politics." Finally, even when Henry George's statewide vote fell so drastically to less than 7 percent in 1887, the electoral difference between the two major parties in that contest was only 0.63 percent.[42]

Still, the third parties never did as well as they wanted or expected to do. Whatever the reality of the problems they called attention to, whatever the tensions and anxieties they represented, as Paul Kleppner notes, "The size of this disaffected group should not be exaggerated; everywhere, as the levels of minor party voting indicated, it was relatively small. . . . There was no 'closet' majority waiting to be drawn to the polls by a party or candidate who offered the nineteenth century version of 'a choice not an echo.'" Further, the challengers' victories were never unalloyed. Many of those that they pointed to with such joy and hope were not quite what they seemed. Most of the Free

Soil and Greenback congressional victories, for instance, were won only because they coalesced with one or another of the major parties, not because they had sufficient attractiveness on their own. That indicated problems for them, no matter how influential they were for a moment. The pull of the old parties would prove to be a much stronger impulse on the legislators elected with third-party support than many of the challengers cared to see.[43]

The challengers' great weakness was that there was no single, underlying constituency of discontent to tap on the American scene. Different outsider parties drew from different groups of voters who did not readily come together in more expansive coalitions. Part of the challengers' support was tactical, when members of one of the major parties temporarily voted with them to overcome the normal majority of the other main party, as in the alliance between the People's party and western Democrats in the early 1890's. Part of it reflected communal values, as was often the case also with the two major parties. Certain ethnoreligious groups disproportionately supported particular third parties. Kleppner notes, for example, that not only the Prohibitionists, but also the Greenbackers at certain moments drew their power from pietist religious groups, tied together as aggrieved communities in a pluralist world and determined to purge society of its imperfections. They wanted nothing to do with other, less pure groups that might be attracted to their party. Part of the challenger support drew on the ideological orientation or specific economic interests of narrowly based socioeconomic classes. The surge of class-related unrest in the 1870's and 1880's was most clearly manifested in third-party voting in municipal elections. Thomas P. Alexander also sees some influence of powerful economic interests at play in the Free Soil vote in 1848.[44]

The sources of support for each third party varied a great deal. Their policies differed. They were inflexible and purist about the particular things they wanted to accomplish, and there was therefore little basis for agreement among them to begin with. To make matters worse for themselves, they seemed to go out of the way sometimes to turn off other outsiders despite their common unhappiness. Richard L. McCormick suggests that "almost none of the discontented groups seemed to want an alliance with others, or to know how to interest a larger public in [their] causes." At the same time, when a third party (the Free Soilers and Populists being the major cases in point) joined forces with another party, major or minor, the different groups in the alliance battled constantly. The People's party was, Peter Argersinger reminds us, more "an uneasy coalition of former opponents temporarily united through dissatisfaction, distress, hope, and hard politics than a unified and cohesive political party." The result was a struggle between people who came from "different political traditions." The same could be said of the early Republicans as they tried to move from minor party to major status in the 1850's.[45]

Internal feuding was endemic to all third parties, not only the Populists. They all proved to be quite as combative within their own councils as they were toward their many enemies. Most were rent constantly by disagreement over tactics, as well as by corrosive disputes of all kinds, what Lee Benson describes as "intense sectarian quarrels, personal jealousies and petty feuds." Though the major parties also had their share of internal dissension, they usually had stronger resources with which to promote ultimate unity. More important, the repetitious disagreements among different groups, temporarily together, or with distinctive notions of what was critical, or different levels of purity, or plain old factional disagreements, all limited the influence and power of the third parties.[46]

Difficulties of this sort convinced many of the challengers that they had not shaken loose of the political nation enough to be able to accomplish what they wanted to do. With the single major, and critically important, exception of the realigning period of the 1850's, the outsiders, even when well organized, could neither replace the old parties nor build themselves into a strong and influential party of protest (as the Populists tried to do in 1892). The Republicans aside, the challengers could not overcome the pull of the central imperatives of the political system they inhabited. They were trying to change the dynamics of voter choice as the necessary prelude to the more far-reaching changes they wanted to accomplish in the political nation. In this era, history was against them.

The result was, in a fairly common scholarly judgment, that the challengers "lived out a politically futile existence." Two great national coalitions confronted each other in every election, offered arguments, clarified perspectives, and shaped choices. They were responded to enthusiastically, widely, and relentlessly, even by some of those who sought to reshape the political landscape. One of Salmon P. Chase's Free Soil colleagues remarked in 1848 that "the truth is . . . we have not forgotten our old party feelings—and until we do, until we realize where we are, and what we have to accomplish, we shall not have the influence that we might or should exert."[47] Of course, many of those who opposed the extension of slavery did forget much of their "old party feeling" in the 1850's in ways that shook the nation.

But, to repeat, this was the great exception in the political outsider experience in the era. When the realigning episode ended, two great coalitions still confronted each other, remained hostile to outsiders, and shared the loyalties of most politically active Americans, preventing any further inroads on the system.

All that said, could the outsider experience be evaluated differently? Were there any areas of promise or payoffs for those who challenged so vigorously? The political outsiders certainly had a great deal of focused energy. And while their failure to overcome the pull of the two main parties on most people told against them and prevented most of them from achieving their goals, several scholars have suggested that they accomplished more than they knew. They were, in fact, more successful as pressure groups influencing policy positions than as competitive political parties. At several points, their presence did indicate that there were some serious strains in the existing system. Even as they were defeated by the partisan imperative in specific elections, they sowed seeds that had an indirect and long-range influence on American politics, pushing policies that were often later adopted. In some cases, Kleppner argues, the third parties' vernacular of particulars crept into the mainstream political language and became rhetorical vehicles that expanded political discourse more generally.[48]

Beyond that, the outsider parties provided opportunities for some people to shake off some of their commitment to the partisan imperative. By doing so, they made the unthinkable possible: that it was appropriate to think and act independently in American politics. As Leon Fink points out, labor third parties, as an example, helped to draw people out of the shell of being Republicans or Democrats by establishing a full range of political and nonpolitical organizational activities, from reading rooms and rallies to a variety of social events—in sum, to socialize people into their ways. In such activities, and in the positive response to them, the outsiders established "a subculture of political opposition" in many communities that not only challenged but ultimately changed the electoral universe and, over a longer period, defeated the Democratic-Republican hegemony over American politics. These developments took time, however, and had to overcome a great deal of political inertia. In the political culture between 1838 and 1893, persistent gadflyism and hope for future change remained the lot of those who challenged the dominant system.[49]

"When the Honor of the Country and the Vitality of Their Government Are at Stake": The System Ages, 1865-1893

> The majority of the people are so wedded to the traditions and customs of the past, and they worship with such partisan and idolatrous devotion at the shrine of party name, creed and leaders, that, like the Hindoo, they would rather be crushed beneath the wheels of the juggernaut of their fathers than to ride in the chariot of civilization that they are capable of constructing by the intelligent use of their ballots.
>
> —J. H. Randall, "The Political Catechism and Greenback Songbook," 1880

MANY OF THE UBIQUITOUS critics of the partisan political nation realized quickly enough how glacially things changed in American politics. Not only did the partisan system survive the traumatic events of the middle of the century, the sectional crisis, the electoral realignment, and the Civil War, but political parties reached new levels of power in the 1860's and 1870's, when the voters' commitment to them became even more deeply ingrained than it had been before the war.[1] Of course, changes had occurred in the political nation, including the replacement of one of the two major parties. But most people were still caught in their party's hold. "I love its memories and revere its past," Congressman Samuel S. Cox said of the Democratic party in 1872. Few of his contemporaries would have been surprised by such sentiments, or disagreed with them. "In a free government like ours," another congressman, Roscoe Conkling, told a Republican meeting in 1874, "parties are the best and safest means of molding the judgment of the majority into laws and giving tone to public action." They "are the inevitable outgrowth of free discussion, and their existence and activity is the sign and cause, as well as consequence, of vigor and health in the political system." Cox and Conkling summed up the prevailing intellectual and behavioral complex of an American political nation that stretched over both sides of the Civil War divide.[2]

"All You Will Need for the Uses of Today"

The reasons for this continued dedication were crystal clear to contemporaries. It was not the power of highly centralized party bureaucracies that anchored the partisan dominance, but rather the overwhelming sense of community that Democrats and Republicans alike shared, an internalized sense of history, tradition, and common values. These went back a long way. The parties still contended, as the voters saw it, along a long-standing ideological divide. Their battle, as it was being waged after the Civil War, was still shaped by the country's ancient issues—issues that never died. As one Democratic leader put it in an 1874 speech, "Go back to the original fountains of Democratic-Republican opinions in regard to government; go back to the primitive sources of thought in our own country. You may find there all that you will need for the uses of today." Similarly, a Republican senator argued in 1887 that "the principles governing the two great parties of this country are substantially today what they were when parties were brought into existence during the administration of George Washington."[3]

In the 1860's and 1870's, party communities reinforced their commitment to the ideas and values that had first shaped their warfare many years before. The duty of the party convention, in its nominations and platform writing, was not "to create a creed, but to apply a known principle to present public affairs." In their campaigns, both major parties reiterated their concern for their ancient conflicts, reaching deep into the history of the country to find guidelines for questions of economic policy, the size and shape of the government, and the nature of the nation. It would always be so, they believed. "That man is a Democrat . . . who seeks hereafter to limit and to localize the powers of government. That man is no Democrat . . . who desires to centralize and enlarge those powers." All else was irrelevant. "Temporary questions such as slavery [and] Knownothingism," one Democrat argued, "may distract attention from the main issue and even change party names. But when disposed of, the fundamental rivalry between local and central power is bound to return."[4]

New issues were readily fit into the existing ideological complex. In the 1860's, the Democrats, faced with their greatest challenge, stemming from the pressures of war and its aftermath, and the Republican determination to expand the powers of government far beyond anything seen since the days of Alexander Hamilton, were quick to recall the past. Americans were "living under a government as centralized

and absolute" as that against which the oppressed revolutionary generation rose up, they warned. Like the Whigs before them, the Republicans were "the 'much government men' who believed that government can create and bestow positive blessings upon its citizens."
They too believed "that the Government should be kind of [a] pulpit
from which laws are promulgated to make men good." In contrast,
Democrats stood on the "historic ground of an ancient party whose
traditions are as old as the nation itself." Unlike their opponents, they
"believed that men should be governed as little as is consistent with
the safety of the community and the individual." Democrats remained
rooted in their ancient commitment "that the ruling authority be not
too far removed from the people."[5]

The Republicans not only expressed their determination to shape
an energetic government and their conviction that Democratic policy
was severely wanting, but also reinforced the constant paeans to the
Whig–Free Soil tradition by adding an element to the situation in the
1860's that intensified party confrontation. It was an element rooted
in the traumatic experience of civil war. Morton Keller suggests that
"powerful mechanisms of mass psychology—of grief, anger, guilt—
were unleashed by the war's climacteric." The Republicans took full
advantage of the opportunity offered, blaming the Democrats for
their prewar support of the South and slavery, and then their ambivalence about fighting the war. As a Republican congressman from Tennessee put it in 1874, "The democratic party, in the influence that
party exerted in bringing on the war, have sins to answer for which
that party in its life could not expiate." To Charles F. Adams, Jr., the
Democrats were "Copperheads and curs—their ideas . . . low and
Irish." Until the party "repents of its sins . . . the Government of the
United States cannot be safe in its control."[6]

The Democrats tried very hard to find a way to respond. As
Thomas Ewing lamented in 1879, since the war the Republicans had
made "the passions of the strife . . . mere party capital." They "hug
the war, and fondle the war, as a loving mother does her first-born
babe." Republicans, their claims to national salvation notwithstanding,
were "full of party passion and party ambition." Their "flaunting before the too eager gaze of the people the red flag of war, the studied
attempts to rehabilitate the dismantled issues of 1860, . . . are but the
common and shallow devices of demagogues to retain place and di-
vert public attention from their astounding frauds, party sins and ul-
terior objects." To Democrats, wartime events did not define the real
lines of battle. The confrontation between them and their opponents

was actually between the country's permanent goals of "union, progress and prosperity" and the demagoguery of "sectional strife, [and] religious intolerance."[7]

Nothing had really changed on the American political landscape. Survivors of the party battles of the prewar years found the political ground a decade and more later quite familiar. It is true that events in the South after the Civil War added new complexities to the political nation. The voter shifts of the 1850's had already strengthened the Democratic party there and cast many Whigs into limbo or retirement. Wartime politics had been tumultuous in the Confederacy, if never fully or effectively organized. The Fifteenth Amendment added a significant number of black voters to the southern electorate. In reaction, the campaign by southern whites to restore a politics uncontaminated, in their view, by Republican-fostered black participation, hardened postwar loyalties to the Democratic party. Nevertheless, in the 1870's and 1880's, there continued to be a varying amount of vigorous two-party competition in many southern states, with high turnout at the polls and intense loyalty manifested to one's political tribe.[8]

The way these complications were confronted, acted out, and brought under control was also quite familiar. In the South, as elsewhere, the forms, institutions, assumptions, perspectives, and habits developed and manifested in the previous thirty years remained as pervasive in American politics as they had ever been. People's "eyes" remained "focused on a past full of familiar friends and enemies," sharpened by memories of the war and the subsequent evocation of a powerful nationalism. Throughout the nation, the deeply rooted, passionate, and unending litany of past enmities burned the political markings of the era deeply into public consciousness. As new voters entered the electorate, immigrants, blacks, and in a number of western states, women, they quickly became caught up in the existing rhetoric and rationale. In such an atmosphere, one's party loyalty continued to define reality, and each election in turn took on an intense meaning for those involved in it. In 1880, Roscoe Conkling told his Republican brethren that the upcoming presidential election was "to be the Austerlitz of American politics. It will decide for many years whether the country shall be Republican or Cossack."[9]

"Blind Devotion to Party"

From the 1860's to the 1890's, when the voters went to the polls, in the American equivalent of Austerlitz, they echoed their leaders' rhetorical rendering of the party battle by their continued extraordinary involvement in political activities and phenomenal loyalty to the parties. Opportunities to display their commitment were as frequent as ever. "We work through one campaign, take a bath and start in on the next," one Iowa politician noted. Despite the constant activity and the many election days, turnout remained at the same impressive levels it had been reaching since the 1840's, averaging just under 80 percent of eligible voters in presidential elections between 1868 and 1892. And some states continued to exceeded the average dramatically. Indiana's mean turnout for President was 93 percent through 1892, New Jersey's was 89 percent. What prevented the national totals from being even more impressive was the substantial postwar fall-off in several southern states.[10]

At the same time, the distribution of the popular vote between the two major parties at the national level remained remarkably close, particularly in the years after 1874. Although the Republicans controlled the presidency for twenty of the twenty-eight years between 1868 and 1896, the margin between the two major parties narrowed in the postwar years, with an average differential of just 1.4 percent in the five presidential contests between 1876 and 1892, compared with 4.9 percent between 1840 and 1852. The Democrats now averaged 48.5 percent of the national vote to the Republicans' 47.1 percent. The Democrats received more votes than their opponents in two presidential races (1876 and 1888) that they lost in the Electoral College, and came within 2,000 votes of the Republicans in a third (1880), out of a total of the almost nine million cast that year. Many congressional races were just as close.[11]

Parties continued to draw support from the same social groups as earlier, some of them going back to the days of party formation in the 1820's and 1830's, others dating their commitment from the realignment of the 1850's. But in contrast to the years before the realignment, each party now depended on a stable one-sided margin in different regions of the country, with close competition between them limited to the belt of populous states stretching from Connecticut to Indiana (excepting only Pennsylvania). Upper New England and the West were safely Republican most of the time. Throughout the South, the Democrats, although sharply contested, won strong electoral majorities from the mid-1870's onward. But whatever the internal composition of each party's voting support, or its regional strengths and weaknesses, so close were the margins in national elections and so stable were the electorate's party preferences at this point, that an occasional surge of voters to one party was a remarkable event. After the Democrats swept the congressional elections of 1874, all that the Republican leader, James A. Garfield, could think was that "the people [had] gone crazy."[12]

This behavioral pattern existed in only slightly less formidable form below the national level. Turnout was high in off-year and state elections, with each party's vote continuing to be highly predictable in election after election. The nation's voters remained "stark mad about party," without regard to offices contested or issues raised. As Samuel T. McSeveney underlines, the American electorate "strongly identified with one or another party: straight ticket voting was the order of the day; voters customarily took the trouble to work their way down ballots to cast votes for candidates high and low." Tradition and continuity remained the key to voter behavior.[13]

The reasons for this were as long-standing as the behavior exhibited. Democrats and Republicans supported their parties as they always had because each was a home to, and articulated, individual group norms and demands, both general and specific. Whatever new issues and problems came on the political scene, ethnoreligious conflicts continued to plague the society and continued to define much of party conflict. Paul Kleppner's description of parties as "political churches," with all of the elements that the analogy suggests, of an intense loyalty, constantly reinforced by emotive memories, and the way current problems were presented and understood, is wholly appropriate.[14]

The voters' relatively unshakable faith in their parties reinforced a commitment to a traditional and unadventurous political strategy on the part of Democratic and Republican leaders. Unlikely to win many votes from the opposition because of the intensity of party loyalty, each party "refreshed memories" in its campaigning, in Richard Jensen's telling phrase, seeking first to reinforce the support of their own loyalists, bring them to the polls, and discourage some of the opponent's voters (by suggesting the Democrats' wartime treason, as one example), and, second, to gain some small advantage in the handful of closely competitive states. As Conkling said in 1874, "We do not need proselytes, but we do need the entire Republican vote, and this means work and attention in every school district in the State."[15]

All of this largely repeated what had been the political nation's pattern for a generation or more. In 1872, the Democrats, having lost three presidential races in a row and the control of Congress with them, did try to break the deadlock in a different way. They ran a "borrowed candidate and platform," joining the Liberal Republican movement in supporting the old Whig warhorse Horace Greeley for

President. They departed from their own norms, focusing on ways "to save the country rather than to sustain a party," holding "in abeyance past *political* differences," and making the "sacrifice of party pride" they thought necessary. But their efforts did not get far at all. Republicans successfully assailed the "hybrid conglomeration" that resulted, "made up of crotchets, distempers and . . . disappointed men." The Democratic share of the national vote fell to its lowest point in this period.[16]

The Republicans' convincing victory underscored the crucial role that parties continued to play in organizing American politics. As the longtime Whig and Republican activist Columbus Delano reminded the Democrats, their 1872 "effort to break down party organization [was] a blow at the foundation of our political system." The Democrats would never receive, by such efforts, the support of the American people, who "desire frank, open-handed dealing" in politics. In contrast, the Republicans had "no disguises" and had won as a result. At the end of the era, then, as throughout its course, political parties dominated. They shaped everything that went on, and gave life, depth, and intensity to the system. The American people were partisan, loyal, and regular. Martin Van Buren's dream remained intact fifty years after he had helped shape the original lineaments of this particular political nation.[17]

"Organize, Organize"

The closeness of the popular vote in the post–Civil War period put a premium on the party's organizational apparatus. Parties needed both "discipline and energy" to bring out their vote on each election day and to ensure that their supporters acted correctly once there. Each party continued to build up its vote-mobilizing and policy-determining institutions. Those structures were more fully developed and more finely tuned in the 1870's and 1880's than they had been, but they stood on a familiar foundation. Each party's local supporters, meeting "in their primary, voluntary, associations," began the process. Further caucuses and conventions met constantly and continued to proliferate and involve the members of the party community. Party conventions, at every level, Alan Peskin suggests, "were surprisingly responsive to grass-roots party sentiment. . . . The delegates were the end product of a chain of township, district and state meetings which provided for substantial public participation even in the absence of the party in a primary election." In 1880, New York's parties required 72 primary elections and 111 convention nominations to make up their ticket. Large numbers of delegates continued to attend every local and state convention. There were, for example, 18,000 attendees at the Republican National Convention in 1880.[18]

In the campaigns themselves, the usual poll lists and the rest of the organizational paraphernalia regularly appeared. Pennsylvania Republicans compiled lists of over 800,000 voters, each carefully classified by reliability and commitment. When Samuel J. Tilden ran for governor of New York in 1874, he had a book listing the names of one or two Democrats in each school district, 50,000 in all, with whom he kept in touch. For each election during the 1870's and 1880's, Indiana's Republicans organized a system of party "district men" charged with reporting on the attitudes and likely behavior of every voter; in 1884, there were 10,000 Republican district men in the state. Church members were mobilized through highly partisan ministers. Presidential candidate James A. Garfield called on his fellow Disciples of Christ in 1880 to support one of their own. They largely did so. In addition, get-out-the-vote clubs were formed, with or without official party sanction, as they had been since 1840.[19]

The many party newspapers continued to shape the elements of political conflict into their final form. "Nowhere else could a loyal partisan, whether county chairman, precinct captain, or average voter, find the arguments, the slogans and cliches, the boasts and excuses, the facts of national, state and local political doings that fed his curiosity, whetted his enthusiasm, and satisfied his need to understand the course of events." As before, the parties compiled handbooks to be used by local committees and speakers, containing platforms, letters, speeches, and statistics. The Democratic Congressional Committee in 1882 sent a circular letter to party editors asking them to run "liberal extracts" from the speeches they would be sent. That would be "of the greatest service in crystallizing and educating the party." Alongside all this, newspapers filled their pages with the familiar litany of responsibilities, duties, and calls to action. "Serve upon rallying committees, . . . employ carriages for the aged and infirm and detectives for the vicious." Everyone should "go to the polls early and stay late."[20]

Most of all, the demands for unity and organizational loyalty were repeatedly heard. "It is now the imperative duty of all good men," Fernando Wood said in the aftermath of his party's national convention in 1876, "to combine in one common effort to secure the ascendancy of the Democratic Party. . . . There must be no faltering, no difference of opinion, no indulgence of preferences or prejudices, for our country is above individuals or personalities." Roscoe Conkling was not to be outdone: "Let our motto be," he said in 1878, "'in essentials, unity, in nonessentials, liberty; in all things, charity.'" The Ohio Democratic state convention in 1879 "commanded that all prejudices should be laid aside; that all bickering should cease; that all animosities should be soothed; that all local preferences should be forgotten; that the voice of discontent should be silenced." The "common law of political parties," as expressed for thirty and more years, continued to be central to everyone's actions and behavior.[21]

The most prominent new element of this period—the growing number of urban political machines—reinforced the system's norms. Urban political bosses, from New York to Chicago to San Francisco, campaigned in the most traditional ways amidst a fundamentally new social environment of urban growth, overcrowding, and government inadequacy, and won persistent support from very loyal voters. The machines' outlook was local and parochial, their approach tribal. As Herbert Gutman has written, "The ethnic political 'boss' created a new dependence that exploited well-understood class feelings and resentments but blunted class consciousness." He dealt and negotiated with hostile outside groups on behalf of his voting bloc, weaving his way through an organizational maze to provide specific, tangible benefits for his clan.[22]

But the machines also broke with tradition in some significant ways, particularly in the area of governance. Their policy interests, for example, lay in the expansion of certain kinds of government responsibilities to meet local needs. In rousing their tribes to political battle, urban bosses called for specific social welfare benefits to ease the shock of urban life on immigrants and downtrodden workers. "Part skilled professional, part tribal chieftain, the boss flourished in that transitional time when a complex industrial society outstripped the instruments of governance." In much of what political bosses did, then, they expanded the boundaries of the political nation somewhat. But in everything they did, in the way they pursued their political mission, they reinforced the nation's basic, partisanly driven nature.[23]

At the center of all of this partisan normality and persistence, even beyond the large cities, continued to be the parties' leadership. Party bosses came into even greater prominence as the political organizations they ran matured. But their leaders, the Platts, the Quays, the Camerons, were still, above all, party men, the people who at every level, from rural precinct to urban ward, organized and directed every element of political activity. They spent their lives in politics, understood its traditions, customs, and laws. They knew how to mobilize and organize the masses, which issues to stress (the traditional ones), which strategies won elections (organization, unity, and harmony). Their forebears had built the system. Now, as the heirs of Martin Van Buren and Thurlow Weed, they were determined to maintain it. They were the very epitome of tradition. Maintaining the status quo seemed to them both natural and desirable. They looked at the political nation and were content with what they saw.[24]

There were always weaknesses and gaps in all these activities. Political organization was never as efficient or as tightly woven as the ideal demanded. Still, the party structures extended everywhere. The commitment to party and its organizational imperatives, if anything, intensified in the war years and the following decades. Congress, state legislatures, and the rest of the nation's governmental institutions continued to reflect the partisan imperative in their organization, membership, activities, and behavior on the issues before them, as much as did internal party operations among activists and the mass of voters. Party discipline remained strong, the dominant definer of legislative life, as one central example. At both state and national levels, roll-call voting remained unsurprisingly partisan, prompting one disgruntled member of Congress to complain that "the blind devotion to party sways the national legislators entirely to the service of party purpose." But, of course, that was an acceptable standard for anyone involved in American politics. As Senator Richard Yates of Illinois reminded his colleagues in 1867, they were bound by the decisions of the party organizations, in this case, each's congressional caucus. Not to be so bound by its decisions, and not to submit to its direction, would be to introduce "a new rule into the well-known history of American politics."[25]

"The Tyranny of Party Must Be Broken"

Of course, nothing in American politics was ever static; nothing ever remained the same. Beneath the surface manifestations of the familiar and habitual, new stirrings, originating outside the political structure, were building toward a critical mass in the 1870's and 1880's that would first challenge, and then fundamentally and permanently reshape, the conventions of American politics and bring this political nation to an unexpected end in the 1890's. A certain restlessness, of course, had always been present. The many challengers, from Greenbackers to Prohibitionists, from agrarian protesters to unsettled urban workers, had unremittingly pressed their demands since the war. But there was now a significant increase in that restlessness and in its direction. The traditional challengers were joined by a major new addition, made up of those who wanted to do a great deal more within the political system than achieve a specific policy by changing the way Americans voted on election day.[26]

The source of this formidable assault was the new industrialism that came to dominate the American landscape after 1865. The activities of industrial leaders, and their demands, never let up from the Civil War years onward, reaching a powerful crescendo in the 1880's and early 1890's. As noted in Chapter Ten, in the last half of the nineteenth century the transformation of the national economy and the American social scene was dramatic and pervasive. In quest of unrestrained growth, efficiency, and greater profits, industrial leaders stimulated a reorganization of the economy that transformed the patterns of manufacturing, merchandising, distributing, and marketing. Similarly, the directly related growth of large population centers, where the full range of economic activities was housed, and the continuing pattern of massive immigration produced unparalleled shifts in the ways that Americans lived and organized themselves.[27]

The organizational revolution profoundly affected society. Although its full force was not felt until the twentieth century, the nation's tempo had clearly been quickening, its way of life fundamentally changing. Everywhere from the 1860's onward, there was social and economic transformation, and the strong suggestion of much more to come. The story is a familiar one. But what had been only glimmerings of change in the 1850's and 1860's had become quite different. By the 1880's, the new industrialism was everywhere prominent. And as before, when it was first getting under way, the blossoming of this industrial/urban revolution in the decades after the Civil War, with its restructuring, consequent dislocations and disorder, soon brought to the center of affairs something equally profound: insistent questions about the adequacy of the existing political system and its institutions, either to serve the needs of the new socioeconomic order now coming into dominance or to defend the interests of those adversely affected by it. The transforming debate was mounted by two groups. On the one side were the many leaders of the new industrialism who were certain that they needed help from the political system and no less certain that they were not getting what they needed from one that had originated in another age and had been built to meet different purposes. On the other were those who argued that political changes were needed to maintain and protect various social and economic balances within the society.[28]

The role of government in American life had continued to increase since the 1840's, if somewhat haphazardly. Beyond its earlier general and unfocused commitment to distribute resources and promote economic growth, the federal government, as we have seen, had taken on added responsibilities during the Civil War and for the freedmen in the South afterwards. So had some of the states, specifically in their commitment to care for the health, safety, and welfare of their citizens, both veterans and others, through legislation and some administrative actions as well. Similarly, a more regulative economic policy had emerged at both the state and the federal level in the 1860's.[29]

But none of this added up to all that much as yet. What was more and more at issue, beginning in the 1870's and 1880's, at least among the avant garde of the new industrial elite, was a growing interest in a larger and more sustained government involvement in shaping the economy, a willingness to have the government move in radically new directions. The new economic elites began to develop an argument that was to crystallize in the 1890's, against "the haphazard style of the nineteenth century."[30] They wanted a commitment to rationalize the economy in more orderly and careful ways than the usual American practice of competitive individualism had ever found necessary before, even during the Civil War. Particularly in the aftermath of the Panic of 1873 and the chaotic labor unrest of 1877, these industrialists sought to enlist the national government in a drive to overcome regressive localism, control debilitating competition, and establish stable markets and financial operations. Vicious competition between different interests caused disquieting problems, too much faltering, and, often, as they saw in the early 1870's, economic disaster. In addition, a range of earlier political actions, or nonactions, now adversely affected the establishment of a national economic system. Local and state government differences over economic policies or the regulation of railroads caused difficulties for those seeking to create large-scale systems. Without a clear and direct commitment to modify these things, the industrial leaders believed that their and the nation's future would be more problematic than it should be.[31]

A great many things needed to be corrected in their view. But traditional politics was a barrier to what needed to be done. There existed in the United States a fatally weak, cumbersome, and defective government, and an indifferent political apparatus, unable any longer, thanks to its basic political habits, to respond to a set of new pressures and meet a set of critical needs. The limits and hurdles of national policy making frustrated any attempt to rationalize the economic system. The leaders of the new industrialism found that there was often militant resistance to much of what they wanted to do from within the political structure, both from the party leaders and from those who sought to use politics in new ways to protect themselves from the growing industrial behemoth. It was an uninformed and destructive resistance, in the industrialists' view, but it was a potent one. Americans were caught in a situation, Morton Keller argues, where "the tension between established views of governance and the demands of a changing society" shaped a new political debate.[32]

In particular, the dominant role played by political parties was called into question with a fervor not seen since the emergence of this political nation. The critics understood how central parties were in the political system, how much they shaped all that went on. That was not the point in dispute. It was how the parties operated that drew the critics' fire. In essence, they argued that, despite their claims to stand for different things, Democrats and Republicans acted in the same, and increasingly irrelevant, ways. Trapped in the past, they both had an agenda in which the nation's economic interests were short-changed in the name of local interests or obsolete abstractions. Local political resistance to national economic currents had to be overcome. Parties refused to challenge such local interests even when they harmed the economy's development. In short, parties sloganeered instead of engaging in a realistic confrontation of current problems.[33]

The parties' exuberant electoral pageantry and constant focus on the reinforcing issues of their traditional attitudes, their nostalgic reaffirmation of the relevance of past battles set in the Jeffersonian-Jacksonian golden ages, no longer made any sense to the new industrial critics. The economy's demands were cross-sectional and national in scope; parties, in contrast, responded almost exclusively to the particularistic, noneconomic stimuli and pressures on them that they found so congenial. Their organizational and policy-making focus was ethnocultural and/or regionally and locally specific. As Kleppner notes, "By the late 1870s modernizing corporate elites demanded more of a political system than inducements to growth and negative safeguards against restriction. They sought the capacity to intervene actively to consolidate and rationalize the corporate system. The prevailing party cleavage, by structuring outputs along other lines, was an impediment" to their plans. Parties, organized as they were, with the perspectives they had, were unable to "integrate intersectional and cross-ethnic class demands."[34]

The way the two parties established their agendas made no sense in this new age. The need to forge consensus among their own factions too often eliminated any consideration of important new ideas or resulted in weak compromises. In practicing the art of the possible, in putting electoral success first, they sacrificed correct policy. To these critics, party leaders calculated their interests, in James McGregor Burns's words, "almost with the accuracy of an apothecary's scale." This did not endear them to many of the new corporate elites. America was a pluralist nation with too many different groups, traditional and new, each able to assert its demands for a share of the country's resources. The demands had to be controlled, some of them emphasized, others discarded. Choices between long-cherished ideas and new forces had to be made. But the party policy making was weak, inconsistent, and at times, chaotic.[35]

The closely competitive electoral situation made the parties even more cautious, especially in pushing new initiatives. The effect, as the critics saw it, was a loss of policy-making energy and whatever innovativeness the Democrats and Republicans may have had. Party warfare, once so vibrant, had become a "narrow front" of contention, automatic commitment, and unreflecting habit. The parties were immobile and recalcitrant, opportunistic and therefore corrupt, amid destructive change. Nor could they correct their flaws. Their leaders had come up through the traditional local and ethnoreligiously driven system. Their impulse was always to maintain the old ways, not change them. In short, parties no longer functioned as they once had, and as they were supposed to do. As Morton Keller has written, "Late nineteenth-century American governance was not so much stagnant as it was held in suspension between old and new social values." Every group on the scene "felt the effects of industrialization and its social consequences. But . . . traditional values and established modes of governance checked the forces of change."[36]

The new economic elites, to be sure, were themselves divided over such specific policies as tariffs and banking, and on how much government regulation they wanted. But they were convinced that American politics, as practiced, was ineffective and obsolete. The new economic system was too complex and their own political fate too precarious to be left in the hands of the masses and their party managers. A new political economy was necessary. Despite their own divisions, a great many of the new industrial elites were thus agreed on the need for a fundamental alteration of the political nation, on the necessity of shifting the political system away from its local roots and partisan emphasis.[37]

There was among these elites a "search for order" in both the economic and the political realm. Those who wished to change the way the political system worked had a good sense of what the purpose of government and politics should be. They wanted a new political dimension added to the nation. They wanted institutions that could be counted on to react to the nation's new forces in new and useful ways and provide what was needed in timely fashion, even if it was not electorally attractive. They wanted cooperation with the political nation, in a relationship they dominated, to promote their interests. For them, "goals such as the strong executive, apolitical administration, and non-partisanship held out the promise of a more efficient businesslike policy."[38]

This assault on traditional politics, then, was something more than the mere questioning of partisan errors and party misdirection. The new elites were willing to leave in politics only the ceremonial and symbolic aspects of election rituals and celebrations. On the serious side of things, they demanded policy making unaffected by the constraints of the existing political nation.[39] Determined to establish a nonpartisan foothold at the center of political affairs, industrial elites funded national economic interest groups. Such organizations as the Railway Managers' Association, the National Association of Manufacturers, and the Iron and Steel Institute spent prodigious sums on propaganda and lobbying; they financed everything from newspapers to direct election activity itself. Their assault on traditional politics was a powerful one that grew more insistent as the years passed.[40]

Despite the industrialists' widespread efforts, financial power, and skillful propaganda against the partisan imperative, they did not get their way at once. Their efforts did, however, revive and reinvigorate the dormant antipartyism within the political nation. That disgust with political parties was still heard and always near at hand. Though a marginal force throughout the era, some Americans remained resolutely antipathetic to political parties of any stripe. To them, "the constant, watchful, deadly enemy of Republican Government from the beginning [had] been party spirit." In the last decades of the nineteenth century, the country remained "under the despotism of party. . . . The illegitimate and irresponsible power of the caucus, the convention and the committee [had] entirely supplanted the popular will in the selection of all public functionaries and in the control of public business." But it was now time, one congressman suggested in 1878, that "party prejudice and party zeal gave place to a higher and nobler impulse and a purer and holier sentiment." It was necessary that "the tyranny of party . . . be broken."[41]

With some allowance for changes in context, these perspectives resonated in familiar ways. The rising tide of political corruption after the Civil War—from the urban-based Tweed ring and the excesses of

Grantism to the various railroad, financial, Indian agency, and other malevolent schemes that filled the pockets of many officeholders— fed this antipartyism. Critics charged that elections were rigged, government activities warped, leaders disgraced, the whole system debased. Each defect stemmed from the dominance of the parties, their powerful organizations, and the blind, unthinking devotion of the masses. The hallmark of good citizenship and reasoned politics was independence from parties. But there was little of it on the scene. The longtime reformer Carl Schurz summed up what had clearly gone wrong. "Woe to the republic," he wrote, "whose citizens think of party and nothing but party when the honor of the Country and the vitality of their Government are at stake." [42]

What was under way was a more intense debate about political parties amid the constant and powerful reaffirmation ceremonies held on their behalf than had occurred in some time. The traditional reformers sought a way to bring back a pure political process, untainted by the unremitting pressure for collective discipline over individual conscience, sordid motives, bossism, and flag waving and appeals to the past, rather than rational analysis of current policy options. What gave these antiparty warriors renewed prominence in the 1870's and early 1880's was their unacknowledged alliance and interaction with the economic elites. Despite the qualms that many of the traditional antiparty types had about the new economy, they found themselves linked with the new economic elites against the dominant political strains around them. While not deliberately or conspiratorially intertwined, both groups sought the same ends. That combined assault gave the ideas of the outsiders more strength than they had had for a very long time. [43]

The whole issue of reforming the electoral process to make it nonpartisan, as it re-emerged in the 1870's, clearly had as one of its many purposes the goal of finding a lever to weaken the perceived control by party leaders over the loyalties of the electorate. But whatever means were found, what was clear was that the parties' independence of social and economic forces had to be overcome. As one Republican put it, "There is a little too much discipline and a little too much machinery in our politics at the present time." The attempt to break what was perceived as illegitimate party power by changing the existing electoral laws and passing new ones on the nominating process and party prerogatives had only limited success at first. But the efforts were intensifying and unremitting. [44]

Some loyal party politicians proved willing to listen to this critique and to consider the needs of the new economic elites. The "Half-Breed" Republicans, for example, sought to accommodate the corporate elites. Led by such national leaders as James G. Blaine of Maine, Chauncey Depew of New York, and Matthew Quay of Pennsylvania, they believed that the traditional political parties had a role to play in meeting the needs of, and representing, the business community. They strongly believed in retaining party authority in political affairs. But they also considered that simply to rehearse the traditional virtues of organization and the old ways was a dead end. "No party can rest merely upon its past," one suggested. Rather, "it must prove itself able to grapple boldly and effectively with the present." These ideas spread to the Democrats as well. The party's principles, one wrote, were eternal; "but to properly apply those principles to the situation of the hour is a duty changing with the time. To say that we will now only apply those principles as our fathers applied them in their day would be as idle as for a man to say he would only wear the clothes he wore as a child." Regardless of political affiliation, these men were looking for a halfway house between parties rooted in the ethno-religious milieu and values that had long dominated the nation, and the needs of economic interest groups whose financial resources they coveted.[45]

Something was clearly happening in the American political nation in the 1880's. The pressing corporate elites and the vocal independents had established a beachhead for their political perspective. The centrality of political parties in the American political nation was contested ground in some circles, in a way that it had not been since the beginning of the political nation. The debate emphasized party sins and revealed their weaknesses and inadequacies in the face of change. It said little about their organizing and democratizing virtues. Parties were occasionally troubled by local defections and some organizational difficulties. Shrewd observers noticed signs of change in the way some voters behaved in key places and in the way many acted in several new western states. Agrarian protest in the South and West and persistent third-partyism affected some previously loyal Democratic and Republican constituencies. As a result, parties looked more threadbare and frazzled than they had for forty years.[46]

All the same, the essential elements of the system held firm. Amid the cries of stagnation, disgust, and resistance, and despite a few signs of slippage, most of those involved in American politics were not ready to look for alternative ways of doing things. To them, the system worked well enough. Although a few party leaders proved to be cautiously willing to shift their emphases, they remained the minor stream in the partisan era. Even as the attacks on the system intensified, a great many politically involved Americans continued to defend and celebrate it and its main institutions as vigorously and consistently as ever. The response of most of those inside the dominant partisan system was decidedly unfriendly and largely unresponsive to the criticisms offered. They retained their confidence in their own ways regardless of all of the challenges offered. To them, parties remained, in Grover Cleveland's words, "the necessary outgrowth" of America's freedom, institutions and continuing divisions.[47]

Tradition thus remained powerful amid unprecedented challenge, with the result that a sometimes turbulent equilibrium reigned. Parties might have changed for the worse, as their critics charged, but they retained their sway. Party leaders maintained a more independent power against all comers—third parties, reformers, agrarian and urban protesters, and new economic elites alike—than any of those groups desired, and despite the vigor of the challengers and the forces demanding change. They successfully resisted suggestions, no matter how strongly made, that they shift into the new world of economic policy making and electoral reform. As the nation entered the decade of the 1890's, there still were only a few signs that the parties' power and reach had declined.[48]

Breakdown and the End of an Era

What continued to anchor the partisan system, and allowed it to retain its power, was that all of the debate and insistence on the need for change had little discernible impact where American politics ultimately still rested—in the hands of the voters. Different elites contended over fundamentally different political and governing styles, but the party leaders had the advantage of a steadfast popular support in election after election. Some historians argue that by the late 1880's, the assault on the parties, coupled with their own competitive frustrations and their inability to come to terms with the powerful industrial elites, had had an effect on politics, despite the resistance to the new ideas. There were signs of strain at various points. The prolonged electoral stalemate bothered even the most committed party loyalists. Contemporary participants sometimes noticed "a slackening of enthusiasm" in the political world, moments when "the brass band, the red light, and the mass meeting seemed suddenly to have lost their power." The Half-Breeds grew more important in Republican party councils as the older generation of partisan stalwarts passed from the scene. As a result, there were stirrings amid all the tradition, calls for change, frustration, and criticism.[49]

The presidential election of 1888, in this view, "reflected, for the last time, the stabilizing influence of party loyalty and army-style campaigns" within the American political nation. Four years later, the new conditions made their power felt, bringing a significant change in political style. Parties were forced to campaign less among their partisans and more among those outside their usual community of support. They were, therefore, less partisan and more willing, it seemed, to come to terms with members of third parties and independent voters. In a closely competitive political system, their leaders pointed out, no one should be discounted automatically. Every voter was important. And as Richard Jensen argues, "By tailoring their appeal to independents and waverers at the expense of their dependent supporters" in 1892, "they contributed further to the erosion of partisan loyalties."[50]

But even with the shifts in campaign emphasis, most voters' loyalty to their parties remained as firm as ever. The move toward a shift in the political nation may have been gathering steam, but among some political and economic elites it remained a tendency of limited scope, and nothing more. There were no signs as the political nation entered the 1890's that its time was passing, that fundamental changes were about to begin. Certainly, the parties had little reason to suspect the sort of explosion in the voting universe that would crack the system wide open, allowing its critics to come into positions of power and carry through on their plans to weaken the parties' hold over the core aspects of this political nation. When it came, the initial overturn was quick and sharp. As the off-year congressional and state elections of 1838 had signaled the advent of a new political nation, so the off-year contests of 1893 and 1894 signaled its end. In a system so thoroughly rooted in electoral competition, a transforming overturn at the polls had an impact far beyond who won or lost on a specific election day.[51]

Ironically, the shattering contests came amid a Democratic revival that seemed to be ending the twenty-year electoral stalemate by giving that party, and its traditional ways, firm control of national politics for the first time since the 1850's. The Democrats had not only surged forward in the congressional elections of 1890, but held most of their gains two years later, when they got their largest lead in the popular vote in a presidential election since before the Civil War—and this despite the almost 9 percent amassed by the agrarian-rooted People's party. Democrats broke through significantly in the largest, most competitive states, taking the whole belt from Connecticut westward to Indiana. As a result of their state legislative gains, they won control of the Senate in 1893 for the first time in a generation. Had the Democrats been able to hold onto what they had gained in 1890–92, they would have been in a position to dominate national politics in a way that no one had been able to do for thirty years past.[52]

The Democrats' potential breakthrough was rooted in the traditional elements of the political nation. The pool of loyal Democratic voters was increasing, particularly in the large urban centers, at a rate fast enough to offset both Republican gains elsewhere and their own losses to third parties. Further, the Republicans had been wrestling with defections from their most pietist wing, many of whom were being seduced by the Prohibitionists and other third parties. Pietist Republicans grew increasingly agitated by their party leaders' hesitant response to the renewed Catholic threat of the 1880's, allegedly because they thought they could get votes from that despised group. In the best of times, the Republicans had only evenly competed with the Democrats since 1874. Now, the small losses they suffered threatened to have a profound and disastrous impact on their competitiveness.[53]

In the event, a Democratic breakthrough never happened. It was thwarted by a severe shock to the economic and social system, which began in 1893. In 1857 and 1873, in the midst of earlier economic upheavals, there had been some voter rebellion at the polls and important shifts in the relative strength between the parties; in 1893, inaction in the face of massive economic disruption brought something more like revolution than rebellion. The Democratic Cleveland administration's inability, or unwillingness, to find, within its traditional political understandings, a way out of the disaster became the fulcrum on which a voter realignment turned. The state and local elections in 1893 not only reversed the Democratic tide that had been running, but also began a process of massive electoral transformation. The state and congressional elections of 1894 extended and confirmed what had happened.[54]

Much about these elections echoed the familiar. The campaigns themselves were largely conducted within traditional boundaries of partisan discourse and exhibited the usual all-encompassing vigor of the party organizations. Turnout remained high, straight party ticket voting the norm. But the extent of the Democrats' losses in the 1894 congressional elections was staggering. In the House of Representatives, they lost 113 of their 218 seats, the greatest shift of the nineteenth century. (The average swing in the number of congressional seats between successive elections had been only 25 between 1874 and

1892; and even in the realignment of the 1850's, the average shift had been only 45 seats.) Democrats also suffered severe losses in the state elections in the eastern half of the nation. Their disaster continued in 1896, when the Bryan campaign, combining the Democrats and the People's party, split the party. The depression's ongoing impact finished the job. Although the Democrats improved their congressional performance slightly from their nadir in 1894, their share of the presidential vote fell almost eight percentage points from their combined vote with the People's party in 1892.[55]

Republican leaders shrewdly ran their campaigns in these elections in ways that were aimed less at mobilizing their own partisans than at attracting converts, independents, and the previously uninvolved to them on the issues connected with the depression. As McSeveney says, "The major political struggle of 1894 pitted a Republican campaign based on economic issues arising out of the depression against a Democratic campaign based on cultural issues that had defined politics before the depression." The third parties benefited little from this. In this powerful two-party system, voters either dropped out or voted for the other major party. The Republicans won more than 50 percent of the presidential vote in 1896, a rare achievement in this political nation, and the first time a party had garnered a majority since 1876. The Democrats' share of the vote shrank among their normal groups, such as the urban Irish. And the Republicans won in places that had never before been theirs. One New Jersey newspaper reported that two counties there had "at last stopped voting for Andrew Jackson."[56]

The voting shift between 1893 and 1896 was not temporary. Despite Democratic gains in the South, its most obvious result was Republican electoral dominance on the national scene. Except for moments when the GOP split apart, it became the normal majority party in the nation for a generation and more thereafter, until another depression, a powerful voter reaction, and the New Deal ended the Republicans' rule. That dominance, in itself, was a critical fact affecting the nature of government and the shape of the system. But something even more profound occurred in the aftermath of 1893–94. The destabilization of the electoral system turned into a more fundamental systemic disintegration. The elections in those years not only ended America's "third electoral system," but also unleashed forces that led to the basic reorganization of American politics.[57]

Not all that the elections of 1893–96 meant or portended was immediately apparent, of course, even to those most directly involved. But in the train of the destabilizing elections of the 1890's came a full-scale assault on parties and legislative efforts, ultimately successful, to weaken the powerful partisanship that had made the system what it was. Parties found themselves less able to resist the reformist onslaught than they had once been. As a result, the equilibrium between them and their challengers was upset. Political party dominance was never again as it had been once the partisan nation began to unravel. The marking point, as at the beginning of this political nation, was what happened on a particular election day. Otherwise, the boundary markings were somewhat different from each other. In the elections of 1838, all of the elements of a new political era clicked into place after a forty-year period of transition. In contrast, the elections between 1893 and 1896 were moments when only the first significant block fell away from the existing structure. Others remained in place and potent.

There was no sudden upheaval or coup d'état. What was significant was that the American polity after 1893 entered another period of transition to fundamentally different political forms. With both moments, 1838 and 1893, things were no longer the same as they had been before in ways that went to the basic nature of the political nation. In each election, the nation's political centers of gravity, their means of definition and action, shifted. What began to occur in 1838, I have suggested, was a tipping over from prepartisan and ambiguous conditions into the new partisan political era. In 1893–94, the reverse process began: a tipping over from a partisan political era into a new era of mixed qualities, confusion, and ambiguity. In both cases, the political terrain may have looked much as it had the year, or decade, before. After the 1890's, Democrats would continue to battle Republicans over a range of issues and cleavages that were familiar. But the look was deceptive: the continuing party battle was locked into a quite different context than the one that had dominated for the past half-century. What had happened was fundamental. The American political nation was not yet a postpartisan one. That lay in the future, a half-century later. After 1893, however, it was certainly a postpartisan-dominant one.

CHAPTER THIRTEEN

Epilogue:
After the Fall

THE CONTRAST BETWEEN THE basic impulses defining different American political nations has been clear-cut. Each era in the country's history has had a distinct political life of its own. Seeking to find ways to govern a sprawling landscape containing multiple attitudes, demands, and values, all of them aggressively championed, America's political leaders have drawn on whatever resources were available and seemed appropriate in their particular environment to develop specific means of focusing conflict, presenting alternatives, and organizing the full range of political activities. Like all the others, the American political nation from the late 1830's into the 1890's had its own distinct mix of perceptions, realities, intellectual constructs, and tribal impulses, all interacting with the structures built to contain, manage, and integrate them.

The search for societal order and political responsiveness in the 1830's led to the creation of national political parties, which, their advocates believed, melded together America's diversity, provided an effective and durable means of fostering political involvement and cooperation, and kept often quite contentious conflict in reasonable bounds.[1] There were many political communities in the United States in the nineteenth century. Some of them were locally rooted; others were state, sectional, or national in their origins, meaning, and operation. The localist impulses originally shaped popular voting choice and promoted a close interaction between party structure and individual citizens. People at the local level could participate in politics directly and repeatedly, while keeping those politics within a framework of meaning clear to themselves and their neighbors. The national elements focused all of these and linked people and localities across much larger dimensions of attitudes and actions by providing symbols and meaning for abstract notions. All of the components, from local to national, gave meaning and texture to the whole experience.

It was this local, state, sectional, and national mix, part real and part symbolic (but no less real for that), encased within the containers of national parties, that gave American politics its specific texture and persistent meaning from 1838 on. One could always find intimations of other perspectives to be sure: the stubborn persistence of antipartyism amid a partisan culture, for one example; the powerful countervailing force of the disruptive sectional divisions, for another. But after the late 1830's, these existed within the larger partisan order and had to confront and deal with the power of the parties. The presence of contrary elements should not deflect anyone from appreciating the central truth of this era: that from the late 1830's into the 1890's the American political nation reflected the impulses of a unique, partisan era.

"To Banish All Forms of Traditionalism"

After 1893, the contours of a new political nation appeared on the scene. The new era opened with an extended period of transition, during which many of the institutions, values, and approaches of the past continued to be important. Nationally, the Democrats vigorously contested the new Republican electoral hegemony in their traditional manner, maintaining familiar ways of defining themselves, resolving their divisions, choosing their candidates, and running their campaigns. They now had to contend with primary elections as a major new form of nominating candidates. But in most places, the influence of party leaders remained largely as it had been, as did their approach to government staffing, responsibilities, and policy making. Though there was an increased vigor in third-party movements, and a number of critical changes in the major parties' campaign styles and electoral activities, on the surface, "the system of 1896" seemed to be at first merely an important electoral realignment, not a major systemic shift.[2]

But what followed was not a limited transformation at all. Not only elections, but the whole apparatus of politics—the role of parties, the nature and reach of government, and indeed the nation's political style in general—began to shift fundmentally, albeit slowly, into new channels. The vigor of American electoral politics, rooted in the passionate confrontations between two well-developed and dominant parties, was sapped by what was ultimately an antiparty, and then a nonparty, way of carrying on political activities. As other forces built up on the scene and affected the political order, the impulses for creative policy making started to move away from the hustings and smoke-filled rooms to, over the course of the next generation, board rooms,

committee chambers, civil service offices, and, eventually, faculty sem-
inars in schools of public affairs and independent policy institutes. At
the same time, as the new era took hold, the power of federal and
state governments grew dramatically, first regulating both the electoral arena and the economy, and then undertaking to ameliorate the
nation's social conditions.[3]

The electoral changes of the 1890's were the keys that unlocked the
door. The secure Republican northern bastion upset the previous
competitive partisan balance. The now permanently Democratic
South also contributed to the change. With the loss of electoral competitiveness in many parts of the country, the fires of political confrontation cooled; ultimately, its organizing elements became flabby
as the losing parties in one-sided electoral situations lost workers,
heart, and vigor. Electoral changes only began the process, however.
At the same time, as a major part of the nation's transformation, an
alternative vision of political propriety developed and then took firm
hold. The ambivalence it manifested toward the political world became, over the years, a disdain toward it, stimulated by what was seen
as excessive political expediency and a sordid partisan manipulation
of democratic politics. Coupled with the rise of new, very powerful
external forces that were reshaping the society, it was able to impose
its view of propriety on the American system.[4]

The reality that undergirded all of this, in James McGregor Burns's
words, was the clear "wasting away of parties" in the American political nation throughout the twentieth century. Again, the decline went
on for a long time, and not always in a clear direction. But the trend
line was inexorable. From the 1830's to the 1890's, political matters
had all settled in one position—that of partisan organization, definition, and dominance. From the 1890's on, everything in the nation's
politics moved in another direction—away from the partisan imperative. Ultimately, Americans went from a strong commitment to one
party or the other, and occasional vituperative dissatisfaction with one
of them, to vituperative dissatisfaction with all parties. Echoing an
earlier theme, many came to believe that politics "was too important
to be left to politicians."[5]

Early in the new era, the Progressives sought, as Richard Jensen
has succinctly summarized, "to banish all forms of traditionalism—
boss control, corrupt practices, big business intervention in politics,
'ignorant' voting and excessive power in the hands of hack politicians." To them, political reform, especially the concerted attack on
the parties was prerequisite to all they wished to accomplish. They re-
defined politics as a detached search for objective and therefore cor-

rect policies, a search unrelated to the passions, rituals, self-interest, and deception connected with political parties. In the first decade and a half of the twentieth century, the Progressives and their allies took a series of legislative actions that attacked and finally severed the links between parties and voters. They energized the efforts under way since the 1880's to reform election laws, especially to institute voter registration and government-controlled official ballots. Their successful passage of a great deal of such legislation had a major impact on the political system. Nonpartisan electoral reforms weakened the partisan imperative, by challenging, first, the parties' control of nominations and the election process, and then the party-dominated, unrestrained wheeling and dealing over policy priorities.[6]

Meanwhile, in the economic realm, there was a steady increase in the number and activities of nonpartisan interest groups, each of which continued to look for a way to shape specific government policies without the mediation of political parties. The various well-organized pressure groups representing some industry or economic activity, or those it affected, were everywhere on the scene in unprecedented numbers, organizing and lobbying on behalf of specific legislation. Progressives promoted the growth of government power and a shift from distributive policies into regulative channels that demanded technical expertise and well-developed budgeting and financial skills, rather than the more generalist negotiating talents of party leaders. In addition, as time passed, government took over responsibility for matters the parties had traditionally controlled—social welfare, for example. The civil service continued to expand, challenging and ultimately weakening the patronage resources that had been so important to party operations.[7]

All of this indicated the success of what Daniel T. Rodgers describes as "the explosion of scores of aggressive, politically active pressure groups into the space left by the recession of traditional political loyalties." This nonpartisan occupation had significant long-range effects on the political nation. The emerging organizational society of technicians, bureaucrats, and impersonal decision makers had no faith in or commitment to mass politics, especially as expressed through the parties. As their numbers and reach increased, their outlook became more widespread. The Progressives' political agenda was nonpartisan in direction, brilliantly publicized, and vigorously pushed against the resisting party leaders. Reynolds and McCormick suggest that "energized by skillful leaders, the movement against party machines . . . became a popular rather than merely an elite phenomenon." Some of the old-style political leaders joined the movement to reform political practices in the hope that they would be able to control such efforts or shape them to their own ends. They were successful to some limited extent, and only for a time. But the whole process was not one in which parties and their traditional elements would survive in the same form or with the same reach as they once enjoyed.[8]

These changes worked their way through the political nation slowly. From the first, the reform challenge meant that parties had competition at the center of the political world for the first time since the 1830's. But for decades, well into the 1940's, in fact, there were different balances between the old forces and the new. In some areas, parties retained vestiges of influence and a capacity to shape events, as evidenced by the electoral vigor of the urban political machines and the success of their policy initiatives. For a time, during the New Deal years, there were indications that parties could still have a strong kick, reminiscent of an earlier day. The electoral realignment of the 1930's not only restored the Democrats to power with a new policy agenda behind Franklin D. Roosevelt, but also partially reinvigorated voter loyalties, fired by the Depression and the Rooseveltian response to it. Democrats and Republicans posed strong policy alternatives to one another. They behaved differently in office. These differences took deep hold and shaped much about electoral politics and something about policy as well for a generation thereafter. The 1890's had ended one era. What existed from the 1890's into the late forties and early fifties was a new and distinct political era of mixed forms where, amid party decay in government affairs, policy making, and the structure of electoral involvement, partisanship still anchored much voter choice as it had in the past and continued to influence other parts of the political order as well.[9]

"At Best Interlopers, at Worst, Rapacious Enemies"

The revival of partisanship, powerful as it was for some years after 1933, was only a deviation from the long-range pattern of party collapse. A new political era dawned in the decade after 1948. The decline of political parties resumed at an even faster pace as the New Deal began to fade from popular memory while other, extraparty elements became even more firmly entrenched on the landscape. Party control of the electoral process continued to weaken. Shifts in the way political information was presented, from partisan to nonpartisan sources, had been under way throughout the twentieth century.

Party newspapers, with their relentless and unambiguous message, gave way to a different journalistic style serving a broader clientele. Cheap, sensationalist, nonpartisan and often politically cynical newspapers came into their own at the turn of the century. Partisan guides were less readily available, and that was to make a difference in the long run.[10]

This transformation accelerated greatly, aided first by radio's growing political importance in the 1930's and then, even more so, by television's role from the 1950's on. Both sharply broke with a partisan presentation of reality. Parties had once been able to argue that all political legitimacy lay with them. Independent newspapers and broadcasting stations challenged that in both direct and indirect ways. Television especially, to the parties' detriment, emphasized imagery and personality over substance. Skillful "media" candidates were more and more able to ignore or downplay the specific marking points distinguishing parties.[11]

In the post–World War II period, also, the size, reach, and influence of the federal government became the central fact of the political nation. With this growth of state power, an interest-group pattern replaced partisan priority setting and influence. Well-entrenched, nonpartisan economic interest groups began to forge permanent links with the legislative and administrative branches. Their belief that parties were a barrier to their best interests was succeeded by the growing irrelevance of parties to their activities at any level. In Congress and the rest of the expanding government apparatus, there continued to be a core of party-shaped behavior. But it declined precipitously over the course of the twentieth century. Party-line legislative voting behind relatively consistent, party-defined policy positions dwindled in linear fashion as the years passed. Building legislative coalitions became very difficult amid all the pushing and pulling of the contending interest groups. Certainly, appeals to party membership and loyalty were no longer universally effective. In their place, there was an "increasing fractionalization" on the floor of Congress, a process repeated elsewhere in the government as well.[12]

At the same time, rising to a crescendo in the 1960's, there was a renewed assault on the legitimacy of parties, echoing a theme once dominant and now take up again with virulence and power. All of their earlier deficiencies, from corruption, elite manipulation, and the denial of democracy to their failure to present contrasting policy positions and to confront the nation's real difficulties, were widely rehearsed. Media commentators transformed the assault into repetitive reality, especially given the examples of such unpleasant episodes as the disorderly Democratic National Convention of 1968. The unrelenting negative commentary took a toll. This intellectual offensive against parties, coupled with the new techniques in mass communications, built on Progressive changes in the game to impel the creation of a new, nonparty political nation.[13]

All of the antiparty tendencies at play became quite clear by the end of the 1950's and determinative in the next decade. Since the 1930's, the expansion of nonpartisan interest groups had continually accelerated, reaching well beyond their original economic base among the new industrial forces to encompass any segment of the society that sought government action. By the 1960's, every policy impulse had found an organization with which to enter the legislative and administrative arenas, largely as if parties did not exist. Many different groups, with many different agendas, articulated issues, mobilized voters, financed campaigns, and organized legislative and administrative support for their own, limited goals. The result was a cacophony of voices, continuous discordant battling, and, often, policy fragmentation. It was all but impossible to piece together coalitions out of these single-interest groups and bring them behind a party.[14]

Despite some residual effectiveness from their New Deal–era revival, parties played a limited role in the 1960's. They had, by then, lost much of their force as coordinators and shapers of political activity, and as the main conduits for articulating and organizing popular demands. A *New York Times* reporter was to claim that John F. Kennedy, at the outset of the 1960's, was "the last great representative of the politics of loyalty, human intermediation, compromise and tradition." With him, the parties' last bastion—the electoral arena—gave way. Certainly, as the 1960's passed, the ways in which mass politics was organized, its rituals displayed, its supporters mobilized, shifted profoundly. Party-dominated mass meetings, conventions, and campaign rallies continued to be held, but they were increasingly irrelevant to the country's political business. Thus, while national party conventions still nominated candidates, they exerted less and less influence over the actual process of choosing who the party would put forward. Delegates had lost their power to bargain, review, and reflect. In Richard Jensen's apt summing up, more and more candidates for office "selected themselves" by mobilizing the nonpartisan resources on the political scene. Television played a key role in this, as did the nominating primaries, which increased in number in the 1960's and afterward. This reality affected the campaigns for office as well. Party labels became less salient as candidates ran as individuals, emphasizing their personal qualities rather than their adherence to party norms.[15]

All of this was of a piece. Where supporting one's party had reflected national political realities in the nineteenth century, parties and partisanship now seemed simply an irrelevant side-show. Scholars increasingly argued that there was a separation between elections and policy making. The latter was little affected by, nor did it always reflect, voter or party choice. In the 1970's and 1980's, the reputation of political parties continued to plummet, irreversibly, it seemed. In Austin Ranney's words, parties were "at best interlopers between the sovereign people and their elected officials and, at worst, rapacious enemies of honest and responsible government." Few people seemed to disagree or care. All this was a very far cry from the celebration of parties and their role that had once so forcefully filled the American scene.[16]

Martin Van Buren's Time and Our Own

The impact of the century-long decline of parties on the way the American voter engaged in politics was enormous and emblematic of the whole thrust of the post-1893 political nation. The most telling characteristic was the lack of individual involvement in the electoral system, a dropping out that began earlier in the century. The American voter in 1990 no longer behaved as his or her ancestors did in 1890. The size of the electorate expanded during the twentieth century as various legal and social constraints on participation fell away. But even as that occurred, popular interest in politics waned. It could be reinvigorated from time to time, as in the New Deal years, but, once again, the trend line is clear: it was downward—toward nonparticipation. More starkly than anything, the steep drop in voter turnout shows how far the political parties had fallen in less than a century.[17]

The southern states led the way. Their voting behavior at the beginning of the twentieth century at first deviated sharply from the rest of the nation. But then the rest of the nation followed along. The pattern was steady, beginning with a nationwide turnout rate of almost 80 percent of eligible voters in the presidential election of 1896, and 69 percent in the congressional elections of 1894, and arriving at just over 50 percent in presidential elections and around 33 percent in congressional off-year elections by the 1980's—both insignificant

TABLE 13.1

National Turnout to Vote, Presidential Elections, 1828–1988

Election period	Mean percentage	Election period	Mean percentage
1828–1836	56.7%	1944–1960	59.6%
1888–1896	78.7	1964–1988	57.2
1900–1924	60.6	1840–1892	77.9
1928–1940	59.4	1900–1988	59.2

SOURCE: Walter Dean Burnham, "The Turnout Problem," in A. James Reichley, ed., *Elections American Style* (Washington, D.C.: Brookings Institution, 1987), 113–14.

echoes of the nineteenth-century political nation and more consonant with the figures in the prepartisan nation before 1838 (Table 13.1). By the 1980's, in fact, there was a sizable "party of nonvoters"—people who were eligible to vote but usually did not do so. Moreover, the willingness to turn out was now distinctly related to education and socioeconomic status, unlike the pre-1893 pattern. Disparities between rich (high) and poor (low) involvement in the political system—even in the simple act of voting—were greater than they were in the heyday of political parties. Clearly, one of the central defining elements of the political order before 1893, attendance at the polls on election day by Americans across the social spectrum, no longer characterized the political nation.[18]

Added to popular disinvolvement was popular partisan dealignment. When they did come to the polls, voters demonstrated that they were increasingly unstuck from party moorings and caught up, instead, in what Burnham refers to as a "volcanic instability." The public was no longer much influenced by the reinforcing, collectivist, clanlike ethnoreligious loyalties that had so dominated the period after 1838. People's perspective on political matters shifted toward highly individual and/or group economic determinants that cut across community loyalties. The all but automatic identification with parties became a minor key in voter behavior. Although economic or social issues could reawaken party identification for a while, they became less and less influential as time passed. The once great dividing issues like race that had set parties off from one another no longer did so with any consistency. Whatever auras suggesting their differences the parties gave off, whatever distinct ideological and policy stances they fostered, they could no longer draw voters to them in the old routine way. Shifting issues and perceptions had overwhelmed them. The electorate, in Everett Ladd's terms, less and less considered "voting for 'my party' a sociological or psychological imperative."[19]

As a result, by the late 1890's, in addition to the party of nonvoters,

TABLE 13.2

Party Identification, 1940–1988

Americans identifying themselves as:	1940	1988
Democrats	42%	36%
Republicans	38	30
Independents	20	33

SOURCE: *Congressional Quarterly Weekly Report*, various issues, 1988.

TABLE 13.3

Average Percentage Difference Between Voter Turnout in Presidential and Adjacent Congressional Elections, 1838–58, 1874–94, and 1974–86

Period	Average percentage difference
1838–1858	12.3%
1874–1894	8.9
1974–1986	16.0

SOURCE: Walter Dean Burnham, "The Turnout Problem," in A. James Reichley, ed., *Elections American Style* (Washington, D.C.: Brookings Institution, 1987), 113–14.

there was, as well, a growing party of voters independent of all party ties. The party label continued to affect the behavior of many voters, particularly in nonpresidential elections, but fewer and fewer Americans were willing to identify themselves as committed to a given party (Table 13.2).

The fall-off in the numbers of the most intense and committed voters affected turnout in another important way. Much as voter participation in the highly visible, dramatic, and extremely personalized presidential elections dropped, the fall-off was far more severe in off-year elections for Congress. As a result, the gap between the size of the electorate in the two types of elections widened (Table 13.3).

Paul Kleppner has traced individual voter behavior from one presidential election to the succeeding off-year congressional elections over the period from 1840 to 1978. He has computed from that the number of core, marginal, and nonvoters present in the American electorate over the past century. The shift downward in the number of core voters, and upward in the number of nonvoters has been striking. In the late nineteenth century, in the years between 1876 and 1890, core voters outside of the southern states averaged 68 percent of the total, marginal voters 16 percent, and nonvoters 16 percent of the electorate. A century later, between 1960 and 1978, the figures were 48 percent core and 17 percent marginal, while nonvoters had more than doubled their share of the voting pool to 35 percent.[20]

All of this has had a substantial impact on the political system. Each election, at every level of political activity, becomes a new throw of the dice, the electorate behaving unpredictably each time in its support of either party. Observers with memories going back to the New Deal and war years have been struck by the change. "The politics of the 1930s and 1940s resembled a nineteenth century battlefield," Anthony King observed in 1978, "with two opposing armies arrayed against each other in more or less close formation; politics today is an altogether messier affair, with large numbers of small detachments engaged over a vast territory, and with individuals and groups frequently changing sides."[21]

So large have the swings in the vote from election to election been in our times that large voter movements in the presidential elections, in particular, have become the norm. Thus, 1960 saw a narrow Democratic victory, 1964 a Democratic landslide, 1968 a narrow Republican victory, 1972 a Republican landslide, 1976 a narrow Democratic victory, 1980 a Republican landslide, and 1984 an even greater Republican landslide, but with few gains by the Republicans elsewhere. The election of 1988 was the Republicans' third presidential win in a row, but it again showed immense Democratic power at the congressional level. As Burnham notes, "At some time between 1960 and 1964, the voting coalitions in presidential and congressional elections became disassociated from one another to a degree unprecedented in the history of American electoral politics." Congressional incumbents have become, in fact, all but invincible, holding on to their safe seats regardless of the national parties' fortunes in their own districts and elsewhere. (In the congressional elections of 1988, more than 98 percent of those who sought re-election won.) No such wild swings from election to election, no such separation of results between different offices, no such unpredictability, marked the earlier political era. In 1844 or 1888, there was a clear relationship in popular voting behavior between national, state, and local elections. Split-ticket voting hardly existed until late in the era; it certainly never became as pervasive as it is today.[22]

As the American voter continues to make different choices at different office levels, regardless of party labels, there has developed, in this volatile political nation, not one, but three separate electorates, or four, if one includes the large bloc of perpetual nonvoters. Some voters remain traditionally party oriented (although with much less commitment than in the nineteenth century); others respond primarily to candidates, not to parties or specific programs. A third group is made up of single-issue activists, those who respond to *the one* transcendent policy matter that is central to them above all else.[23]

Given this volatility and the absence of strong, widespread partisan influences across the voting universe, electoral strategy has had to shift. Candidates, already themselves free from many party constraints, no longer run for office primarily by mobilizing the party faithful, if they try to do so at all. There are not enough of them to make the effort worthwhile. Most go after the "weakly attached voters." Campaign advertising almost never identifies a candidate with a party, emphasizing instead, his or her personal attributes. Asking who or what a person is has become the centerpiece of political campaigns rather than examining a party's policy stance or calling on deeply rooted partisan loyalties. In those offices where incumbents seem to be all but immune from ouster, campaigning has turned more and more to emphasizing the opponent's personal deficiencies. More and more often, this has descended into what some call "mindless cannibalism." Amid all of this chaos and without effective political parties as alternative anchors of voter choice, electoral realignments, with their strong swing of some voters to one party or the other, no longer seem possible. As a result, electoral dealignment has replaced realignment as the most prevalent form of change.[24]

"Anarchy Tempered by Distrust"

By the early 1990's almost a century after the end of the partisan political nation, there could be no uncertainty about the nation's distance from its political past. A highly individualistic, volatile, and antiorganizational politics has displaced the highly coalitional, pragmatic yet quite ideological, collective politics of the period before the 1890's. One observer notes that the presidential election of 1988 affirmed that "party ties count for less today than at any time since a mature party system took shape in the 1830s." Once parties drove substantially everything. Reactions to other pressures were sporadic and unusual. Now the power of the elements at play in the equation are reversed. Parties can still be influential, but only rarely and intermittently; nonpartisan factors have become the central impulses of a new American political nation. Two commentators recently characterized the political party as having become "a Hertz car we all rent around election time," which has no permanent usefulness or value otherwise.[25]

The weakness of the parties at first stimulated few tears for their passing. The socialization of Americans against parties and partisanship, and the concomitant growth of cynicism and hostility toward politicians was unrelenting by the 1980's. "It's sickening," the *New Republic* quoted a primary voter in 1984, that politicians "never do what they promise anyway." The point is that much in contemporary American political culture came to emphasize individual expression, something that has encouraged quarrelsome disagreements, coupled with a constant wariness about subordinating oneself to collective discipline as a means of working out these disagreements. The reputation of Walter Mondale, the Democratic presidential candidate in 1984, as "the consummate partisan," Sidney Blumenthal wrote in that campaign, "is interpreted by many in the institution-wary younger generation as a sign that he represents something compromised."[26]

The last comment underscores the growth of purism in politics, an extension and exaggeration of the Progressive impulse. It began with an aversion to the give-and-take of politics, the pragmatic assessment of what is politically possible, in contrast to what is right. The rejection of the notion that politics involves compromise—that many answers may be legitimate in a pluralist society; that politics can be messy, vulgar, and shallow, and still be useful—has come to dominate the center of the American political outlook. As one observer suggested about Western politics in general, "Compromise itself has been reduced to a synonym for capitulation, and the business of conciliating social interests—once thought to be the very art of government—has come to be seen as an exercise in appeasement." Old politics stressed collective action and the need, therefore, for collective discipline. New politics stresses individual expression and self-imposed and self-defined standards of behavior, and a loathing, frequently, for externally imposed constraints.[27]

Given all of that, Americans have come to live in what Burnham calls the "hyperpluralism of an exploding universe of intense, particularized and unconstrained interests." The nineteenth-century political nation reflected a culture that sought to bring people into the system and tame them and their desires through disciplined collectivities. America's powerful individualism, it was felt, needed such domestication. Now, toward the end of the twentieth century, the political process places a premium on the pursuit of individual objectives, one's own special interests, rather than party-defined ones. Members of Congress, an old party wheelhorse and House chairman pointed out in late 1989, "are independent contractors. They have more narrowed views about whether or not compromise is fair, and now they can get bites on the television news if they raise enough cain." This development has its costs. There is in it "a paralysis of contradictory claims and entitlements," a system "registering and proclaiming so many demands," without the mechanisms of management and priority setting, "that the ultimate effect is endless litigation, process without outcome." A century after the heyday of the partisan imperative, "the smooth flow of party supremacy has given way to the abrasive anarchy of granulated politics."[28]

Yet in the 1990's, just as political parties have seemingly lost all importance, just as the issues argued and the methods used to win through have seemingly ceased to be clearly and primarily identified with them, a new language of criticism has emerged in some quarters. This time, it expresses a proparty impulse. With the decline of parties, the political nation has "lost an instrument for harnessing together its diverse and centrifugally inclined parts." There has been a dramatic decline in the ability of the government to make policy, or, more accurately, to find the mechanisms to build up coalitions to accomplish policy-making ends. Morris Fiorina asserts that "through a complex mixture of accident and intention we have constructed for ourselves a system that articulates interests superbly but aggregates them poorly." In consequence, "there is [a] proliferation of the people who have to be consulted. For purposes of individual expression this may be admirable, but for collective legislation it leaves something to be desired." The process includes too many elements that encourage fragmentation rather than coherence, too many people who follow narrow perspectives. Or, putting it somewhat more pithily, the American political scene has become "anarchy tempered by distrust."[29]

The proparty critique has been powerfully articulated by a number of scholars and journalists. To them, the decline of parties suggests more than a change in the ways things are organized. In their view, the end of much role for, not to say the dominance of, political parties on the American landscape poses a significant risk to the nation as a whole. As Walter Dean Burnham has put it, "From very early on in our history as a nation, it has regularly happened that whenever party is absent or heavily eroded, the result has been paralysis, deadlock and [a] 'governability crisis.' Without the countervailing weight of partisan bonds and channels of political action, the centrifugal constitutional scheme itself becomes a literally unworkable instrument of government."[30]

The eventual outcome of these few steps toward political counterrevolution are unclear, but the outlook does not seem particularly promising. There are few signs that party effectiveness, let alone dominance, is returning. Quite the opposite, in fact. America's postpartisan era has become as strong, and as well entrenched, as the partisan era once was. Despite the weaknesses of the new system, there is no evidence of any widespread shift away from norms that now dominate all parts of the political landscape. The case for parties no longer has a large natural constituency, responsive to the argument's merits and eager for a partisan rebuilding effort. Americans have been long habituated to another way, testimony to the chasm between one political nation and another, each defined by its unique qualities. Whatever continuities have existed over the course of American political history, and there have been many, its chronologically bounded discontinuities remain central and critical to understanding that history. The contrasting qualities discussed here, defining two political nations a century apart, sharply underscore that fact.

Notes

Notes

The following abbreviations are used in these Notes:

AR   *American Review: A Whig Journal*
AHR   *American Historical Review*
CG   *Congressional Globe*
CR   *Congressional Record*
DR   *Democratic Review*
JAH   *Journal of American History*
JER   *Journal of the Early Republic*
JIH   *Journal of Interdisciplinary History*

Introduction

1. Richard L. McCormick, "The Party Period and Public Policy," *JAH*, 66 (Sept. 1979): 279–98.

2. Morton Keller, "Powers and Rights: Two Centuries of American Constitutionalism," *JAH*, 74 (Dec. 1987): 679.

3. There was, of course, a world outside the political arena that had many political dimensions. Social and family experiences and gender and caste relations had political dynamics of their own. Some of these impinged on the formal public political arena but were never totally part of it, certainly not in a sustained way. A number of them will be touched on below. See Joan W. Scott, "Gender: A Useful Category of Historical Analysis," *AHR*, 91 (Dec. 1986): 1053–1075; Paula Baker, "The Domestication of Politics: Women and American Political Society, 1780–1920," *AHR*, 89 (June 1984): 620–47; and Mary P. Ryan, *Women in Public: Between Banners and Ballots, 1825–1880* (Baltimore: Johns Hopkins Univ. Press, 1990).

4. The setting of chronological boundaries in history is both difficult and contentious. And historical eras neither begin nor end abruptly or completely. Nevertheless, there are very clear differences from one to the next. See Joel H. Silbey, "Beyond Realignment and Realignment Theory: American Political Eras, 1789–1989," in Byron E. Shafer, ed., *The End of Realignment?* (Madison: Univ. of Wisconsin Press, 1991), 3–23.

5. Joel H. Silbey, *The Partisan Imperative: The Dynamics of American Politics Before the Civil War* (New York: Oxford Univ. Press, 1985).

6. Allan G. Bogue et al., "The New Political History," *American Behavioral Scientist*, 21 (Nov.–Dec. 1977): 213. Among the many excellent studies that I have found useful are Ronald P. Formisano, *The Transformation of Political Culture: Massachusetts Parties, 1790s–1840s* (New York: Oxford Univ. Press, 1983); and Richard L. McCormick, *From Realignment to Reform: Political Change in New York State, 1893–1910* (Ithaca, N.Y.: Cornell Univ. Press, 1981). Both are very perceptive studies of single states that chronologically frame the particular era I am discussing here. William Shade's essay "Political Pluralism and Party Development: The Creation of a Modern Party System, 1815–1852," in Paul Kleppner et al., *The Evolution of American Electoral Systems* (Westport, Conn.: Greenwood Press, 1981), 77–111, is a seedbed of many stimulating ideas about the early years of the party period. In addition, J. Mills Thornton, *Politics and Power in a Slave Society, Alabama, 1800–1860* (Baton Rouge: Louisiana State Univ. Press, 1978), and Marc Kruman, *Parties and Politics in North Carolina, 1836–1865* (Baton Rouge: Louisiana State Univ. Press, 1983), are well-executed in-depth studies of political life during the era. Paul Kleppner, *The Third Electoral System, 1853–1892: Parties, Voters and Political Cultures* (Chapel Hill: Univ. of North Carolina Press, 1979), is a mine of information and ideas. In a class by itself is Morton Keller, *Affairs of State: Public Life in Late Nineteenth Century America* (Cambridge, Mass.: Harvard Univ. Press, 1977).

7. The best introduction to the work of the new political historians is Allan G. Bogue, *Clio and the Bitch Goddess: Quantification in American Political History* (Beverly Hills, Calif.: Sage, 1983). His most recent appreciation of that work is Bogue, "The Quest for Numeracy: Data and Methods in American Political History," *JIH*, 21 (Summer 1990): 89–116.

8. As Samuel P. Hays has written, "society drives politics," and "the study of politics cannot afford to stray too far from the study of society." "Politics and Society: Society and Politics," *JIH*, 15 (Winter 1985): 497, 499; J. R. Pole, *The Gift of Government: Political Responsibility from the English Restoration to American Independence* (Athens: Univ. of Georgia Press, 1983), xiii; J. Morgan Kousser, "Are Political Acts Unnatural?," *JIH*, 15 (Winter 1985): 468. See also, more generally, Samuel P. Hays, *American Political History as Social Analysis: Essays* (Knoxville: Univ. of Tennessee Press, 1980); and J. Morgan Kousser, "Toward 'Total Political History': A Rational Choice Research Program," *JIH*, 20 (Spring 1990): 521–60.

9. Walter Dean Burnham, "The Turnout Problem," in A. James Reichley, ed., *Elections American Style* (Washington, D.C.: Brookings Institution, 1987), 98.

Chapter One

1. This pattern is nicely captured by the subject and titles of the sequential volumes in Harper and Row's *New American Nation* series covering these years, beginning with Glyndon G. Van Deusen, *The Jacksonian Era, 1828–1848* (1959); continuing through David M. Potter (edited and completed by Don Fehrenbacher), *The Impending Crisis, 1848–1861* (1976); and ending with John A. Garraty, *The New Commonwealth, 1877–1890* (1968). Early criticisms

of this approach appeared in Lee Benson, "Research Problems in American Political Historiography," in Mirra Komarovsky, ed., *Common Frontiers in the Social Sciences* (Glencoe, Ill.: Free Press, 1957), 113–83; and Joel H. Silbey, "The Civil War Synthesis in American Political History," *Civil War History*, 10 (June 1964): 130–40.

2. William N. Chambers and Walter Dean Burnham, eds., *The American Party Systems* (New York: Oxford Univ. Press, 1967; 2d ed. 1975); Paul Kleppner et al., *The Evolution of American Electoral Systems* (Westport, Conn.: Greenwood Press, 1981).

3. Much of this criticism is ably summarized in Richard L. McCormick, "The Realignment Synthesis in American Political History," *JIH*, 13 (Summer 1982): 85–105. On the current approach of voting behavior research to realignment theory, see Everett C. Ladd, "The 1988 Elections: Continuation of the Post New Deal System," *Political Science Quarterly*, 104 (Spring 1989): 1–18. On the other hand, critical election theory is defended, and changes in the nature of popular voting behavior questioned, in the new final chapter of the "encore edition" of Jerome M. Clubb, William H. Flanigan, and Nancy H. Zingale, *Partisan Realignment: Voters, Parties and Government in American History* (Boulder, Colo.: Westview, 1990), 273–98.

4. Lee Benson and I originally developed this concept in work done with Phyllis Field. See Lee Benson, Joel H. Silbey, and Phyllis F. Field, "Toward a Theory of Stability and Change in American Voting Patterns: New York State, 1792–1970," in Joel H. Silbey, Allan G. Bogue, and William H. Flanigan, eds., *The History of American Electoral Behavior* (Princeton, N.J.: Princeton Univ. Press, 1978), 78–105; Lee Benson and Joel H. Silbey, "American Political Eras, 1788–1984: Toward a Normative, Substantive, and Conceptual Framework for the Historical Study of American Political Behavior" (paper presented at the annual Social Science History Association meeting, 1978); and Lee Benson and Joel H. Silbey, "The American Voter, 1854–1860 and 1948–1984" (paper presented at the annual meeting of the Organization of American Historians, 1978).

5. Of course, in characterizing the system as a whole in this way, important variants will occasionally be flattened out. There were always quirks, differences, poor fits, and exceptions to the political nation's dominant central tendency. One can always find a profusion of elements in different local experiences in 19th century America incompatible with the main thrust. But the political nation transcended such variations. The most recent development of this approach is Joel H. Silbey, "Beyond Realignment and Realignment Theory: American Political Eras, 1789–1989," in Byron E. Shafer, ed., *The End of Realignment?* (Madison: Univ. of Wisconsin Press, 1991).

6. See Richard L. McCormick, *The Party Period and Public Policy: American Politics from the Age of Jackson to the Progressive Era* (New York: Oxford University Press, 1986); and Joel H. Silbey, *The Partisan Imperative: The Dynamics of American Politics Before the Civil War* (New York: Oxford Univ. Press, 1985), for strong, if slightly different, assertions of this perspective.

7. Paul Kleppner, *The Third Electoral System, 1853–1892: Parties, Voters, and Political Cultures* (Chapel Hill: Univ. of North Carolina Press, 1979); Joel H.

Silbey, *A Respectable Minority: The Democratic Party in the Civil War Era, 1860–1868* (New York: Norton, 1977).

8. Here I agree with Charles Maier's statement, offered in another context, that "even catastrophic events do not always directly alter the trajectory of institutions." "The Two Postwar Eras and the Conditions for Stability in Twentieth-Century Western Europe," *AHR*, 86 (April 1981): 352.

9. Samuel T. McSeveney, *The Politics of Depression: Political Behavior in the Northeast, 1893–1896* (New York: Oxford Univ. Press, 1972); Kleppner, *Third Electoral System*; Richard L. McCormick, *From Realignment to Reform: Political Change in New York State, 1893–1910* (Ithaca, N.Y.: Cornell Univ. Press, 1981).

10. Richard L. McCormick, "The Party Period and Public Policy: An Exploratory Hypothesis," *JAH*, 66 (Sept. 1979): 281.

11. The "classical republican" underpinning of early American politics is traced in J. G. A. Pocock, *The Machiavellian Moment: Florentine Political Thought and the Atlantic Republican Tradition* (Princeton, N.J.: Princeton Univ. Press, 1975); Bernard Bailyn, *The Origins of American Politics* (Providence, R.I.: Brown Univ. Press, 1968); and Bailyn, *Ideological Origins of the American Revolution* (Cambridge, Mass.: Harvard Univ. Press, 1967). For summaries, see Robert E. Shalhope, "Toward a Republican Synthesis: The Emergence of an Understanding of Republicanism in American Historiography," *William and Mary Quarterly*, 29 (Jan. 1972): 49–80; Shalhope, "Republicanism and Early American Historiography," *William and Mary Quarterly*, 39 (April 1982): 334–56; and Shalhope, *The Roots of Democracy: American Thought and Culture, 1760–1800* (Boston: Twayne, 1990).

Among the many good studies of colonial politics that I have found useful are Gary B. Nash, *The Urban Crucible: Social Change, Political Consciousness, and the Origins of the American Revolution* (Cambridge, Mass.: Harvard Univ. Press, 1979); Patricia Bonomi, *A Factious People: Politics and Society in Colonial New York* (New York: Columbia Univ. Press, 1971); T. H. Breen, *The Character of the Good Ruler: A Study of Puritan Political Ideas in New England, 1630–1730* (New Haven, Conn.: Yale Univ. Press, 1970); Edward Countryman, *A People in Revolution: The American Revolution and Political Society in New York, 1760–1790* (Baltimore: Johns Hopkins Univ. Press, 1981); Jack P. Greene, *The Quest for Power: The Lower Houses of Assembly in the Southern Royal Colonies, 1689–1776* (Chapel Hill: Univ. of North Carolina Press, 1963); and Douglas Greenberg, "The Middle Colonies in Recent American Historiography," *William and Mary Quarterly*, 36 (July 1979): 396–427.

12. Edmund S. Morgan, *Inventing the People: The Rise of Popular Sovereignty in England and America* (New York: Norton, 1988), 304.

13. Ronald P. Formisano, *The Transformation of Political Culture: Massachusetts Parties, 1790s–1840s* (New York: Oxford Univ. Press, 1983); Formisano, "Deferential-Participant Politics: The Early Republic's Political Culture, 1789–1840," *American Political Science Review*, 68 (June 1974): 473–87. Two useful overviews of this political world are M. J. Heale, *The Making of American Politics, 1750–1850* (London: Longman, 1977); and Richard P. McCormick, *The Presidential Game: The Origins of American Presidential Politics* (New York: Oxford Univ. Press, 1982).

14. Formisano, *Transformation*, 6.

15. On politics and society at the moment of George Washington's election, see, most recently, Jack Rakove, "The Structure of Politics at the Accession of George Washington," in Richard Beeman et al., eds., *Beyond Confederation: Origins of the Constitution and American National Identity* (Chapel Hill: Univ. of North Carolina Press, 1987), 261–94.

16. The literature on the politics of the 1790's is immense. A useful overview is John C. Miller, *The Federalist Era, 1789–1801* (New York: Harper & Row, 1960). See also Lance Banning, *The Jeffersonian Persuasion: Evolution of a Party Ideology* (Ithaca, N.Y.: Cornell Univ. Press, 1978); James Banner, *To the Hartford Convention: The Federalists and the Origins of Party Politics in Massachusetts, 1789–1815* (New York: Knopf, 1970); and David Hackett Fischer, *The Revolution of American Conservatism: The Federalist Party in the Era of Jeffersonian Democracy* (New York: Oxford Univ. Press, 1965).

17. Joyce Appleby, *Capitalism and the New Social Order: The Republican Vision of the 1790s* (New York: New York Univ. Press, 1984); Chilton Williamson, *American Suffrage: From Property to Democracy, 1760–1860* (Princeton, N.J.: Princeton Univ. Press, 1960).

18. James Young, *The Washington Community, 1800–1828* (New York: Columbia Univ. Press, 1966); Noble Cunningham, *The Process of Government Under Jefferson* (Princeton, N.J.: Princeton Univ. Press, 1978); Leonard White, *The Federalists: A Study in Administrative History* (New York: Macmillan, 1948). The federal government had 4,837 civilian employees in 1816, 18,038 in 1841; the federal budget was $5,000,000 in 1792, $8,000,000 in 1811, and $24,318,000 in 1840. *Historical Statistics of the United States, Colonial Times to 1970* (Washington, D.C.: Government Printing Office, 1970), 2: 1103–1104.

19. *Historical Statistics*, 2: 1082.

20. Williamson, *American Suffrage*; J. R. Pole, *Political Representation in England and the Origins of the American Republic* (New York: St. Martin's Press, 1966).

21. Richard P. McCormick, "New Perspectives on Jacksonian Politics," *AHR*, 65 (Jan. 1960): 288–301.

22. Gordon Wood, *The Creation of the American Republic, 1776–1789* (Chapel Hill: Univ. of North Carolina Press, 1969), 562. On political leadership in the first half of the 19th century, see Edward Pessen, *Riches, Class and Power Before the Civil War* (Lexington, Mass.: Heath, 1973); and Whitman Ridgway, *Community Leadership in Maryland, 1790–1840: A Comparative Analysis of Power in Society* (Chapel Hill: Univ. of North Carolina Press, 1979).

23. Fischer, *Revolution of American Conservatism*; James Broussard, *The Southern Federalists, 1800–1816* (Baton Rouge: Louisiana State Univ. Press, 1978); Allan G. Bogue and Mark P. Marlaire, "Of Mess and Men: The Boardinghouse and Congressional Voting, 1821–1842," *American Journal of Political Science*, 19 (May 1975): 207–30.

24. On the limits of the Federalists and Republicans as parties, see Ronald P. Formisano, "Federalists and Republicans: Parties, Yes—System, No," in Kleppner et al., *Evolution*, 33–76. See also Richard Hofstadter, *The Idea of a*

Party System: The Rise of Legitimate Opposition in the United States, 1780–1840 (Berkeley: Univ. of California Press, 1969).

25. Rudolph Bell, *Party and Faction in American Politics: The House of Representatives, 1789–1801* (Westport, Conn.: Greenwood Press, 1973); David Bohmer, "The Maryland Electorate and the Concept of a Party System in the Early National Period," in Silbey, Bogue, and Flanigan, *History of Electoral Behavior*, 146–73; Benson, Silbey, and Field, "Toward a Theory of Stability."

26. *The Federalist Papers*, ed. Isaac Kramnick (Harmondsworth, Eng.: Penguin, 1987); Jefferson to Francis Hopkinson, March 13, 1789, in Julian P. Boyd, ed., *The Papers of Thomas Jefferson* (Princeton, N.J.: Princeton Univ. Press, 1958), 14: 650; George Billias, *Elbridge Gerry, Founding Father and Republican Statesman* (New York: McGraw Hill, 1976), 252.

27. Lee Benson, "Discussion," in Patricia Bonomi et al., eds., *The American Constitutional System Under Strong and Weak Parties* (New York: Praeger, 1981), 24.

28. See the arguments summed up in Formisano, "Federalists and Republicans."

29. William Nisbet Chambers, *Political Parties in a New Nation: The American Experience, 1776–1809* (New York: Oxford Univ. Press, 1963), 147.

30. The following works begin the process of detailing these changes and tensions: Douglass C. North, *The Economic Growth of the United States, 1790–1860* (New York: Norton, 1966); George Rogers Taylor, *The Transportation Revolution, 1815–1860* (New York: Rinehart, 1951); Paul Wallace Gates, *The Farmers' Age: Agriculture, 1815–1860* (New York: Holt, Rinehart & Winston, 1960); Don H. Doyle, *The Social Order of a Frontier Community: Jacksonville, Illinois, 1825–1870* (Urbana: Univ. of Illinois Press, 1978); Stuart Blumin, *The Urban Threshold: Growth and Change in a Nineteenth-Century American Community* (Chicago: Univ. of Chicago Press, 1976); Alan Dawley, *Class and Community: The Industrial Revolution in Lynn* (Cambridge, Mass.: Harvard Univ. Press, 1976); and Sean Wilenz, *Chants Democratic: New York City and the Rise of the American Working Class, 1788–1850* (New York: Oxford Univ. Press, 1984).

31. There is a vast literature on the transition from republican values to those of conflict-prone liberalism in this period. One can usefully begin with Drew R. McCoy, *The Elusive Republic: Political Economy in Jeffersonian America* (Chapel Hill: Univ. of North Carolina Press, 1980); John Diggins, *The Lost Soul of American Politics: Virtue, Self-Interest, and the Foundations of Liberalism* (New York: Basic Books, 1984); and Steven Watts, *The Republic Reborn: War and the Making of Liberal America, 1790–1820* (Baltimore: Johns Hopkins Univ. Press, 1987).

32. The "revival" quotation is from Charles Grier Sellers, Jr., *James K. Polk, Jacksonian, 1795–1843* (Princeton, N.J.: Princeton Univ. Press, 1957), 105. On the widening electorate, see Williamson, *American Suffrage*. A good survey of one key battle in this period is in Glover Moore, *The Missouri Controversy, 1819–1821* (Lexington: Univ. of Kentucky Press, 1953).

33. Noble E. Cunningham, *Circular Letters of Congressmen to Their Constitu-*

ents, 1789–1829 (Chapel Hill: Univ. of North Carolina Press, 1978), 3 vols.; Richard P. McCormick, *The Second American Party System: Party Formation in the Jacksonian Era* (Chapel Hill: Univ. of North Carolina Press, 1966). On the election of 1824, see the essay by James F. Hopkins, in Arthur M. Schlesinger, Jr., and Fred L. Israel, eds., *History of Presidential Elections, 1788–1968* (New York: Chelsea House, 1971), 1: 349–409.

34. See Donald B. Cole, *Martin Van Buren and the American Political System* (Princeton, N.J.: Princeton Univ. Press, 1984); John Niven, *Martin Van Buren: The Romantic Age of American Politics* (New York: Oxford Univ. Press, 1983); and Robert Remini, *Martin Van Buren and the Making of the Democratic Party* (New York: Columbia Univ. Press, 1951).

35. On antimasonry in particular, see Kathleen Kutalowski, "Antimasonry Reexamined: Social Bases of the Grass-Roots Party," *JAH*, 71 (Sept. 1984): 269–93, and her other articles cited therein; Michael F. Holt, "The Antimasonic and Know-Nothing Parties," in Arthur M. Schlesinger, Jr., *History of U.S. Political Parties* (New York: Chelsea House, 1973), 1: 583–89; Paul Goodman, *Toward a Christian Republic: Antimasonry and the Great Transition in New England, 1826–1836* (New York: Oxford Univ. Press, 1988); and William Vaughn, *The Antimasonic Party in the United States, 1826–1843* (Lexington: Univ. of Kentucky Press, 1983). On the relation between these movements and early political organization, see Lee Benson, *The Concept of Jacksonian Democracy: New York as a Test Case* (Princeton, N.J.: Princeton Univ. Press, 1961).

36. Michael Wallace, "Ideologies of Party in the Early Republic," (Ph.D. dissertation, Columbia Univ., 1973), 138, 207 (see also his "Changing Concepts of Party in the United States: New York, 1815–1828," *AHR*, 74, Dec. 1968: 453–91); U.S. Congress, *Register of Debates*, 19th Cong., 1st sess., 1546; John Fitzpatrick, ed., *The Autobiography of Martin Van Buren* (Washington, D.C.: American Historical Association, 1918), 2: 125.

37. "Proceedings and Address of the Republican Young Men of the State of New York Assembled at Utica [1828]," (New York, 1828), 11; "Proceedings and Address of the New Jersey State Convention [Jan. 8, 1828]," (Trenton, 1828), 7; Harry L. Watson, *Jacksonian Politics and Community Conflict* (Baton Rouge: Louisiana State Univ. Press, 1981), 23, 81. See also Watson, *Liberty and Power: The Politics of Jacksonian America* (New York: Hill & Wang, 1990).

38. David Krueger, "Party Development in Indiana, 1800–1832" (Ph.D. dissertation, Univ. of Kentucky, 1974), 194–95; "Report of the Proceedings of the Town Meeting in the City of Philadelphia, July 7th, 1828" (n.p., n.d.), 22; Joseph H. Prince, "Address . . . at the Jackson Celebration in Boston" (Boston, 1828), 15.

39. M. Philip Lucas, "The Development of the Second Party System in Mississippi, 1817–1846" (Ph.D. dissertation, Cornell Univ., 1983), 86. On Jacksonian antipartyism, see the printed circular reporting a Jackson meeting in New York City in 1828 in the Azariah Flagg Papers, New York Public Library; and, more generally, Robert Remini, *Andrew Jackson and the Course of American Freedom, 1822–1832* (New York: Harper & Row, 1981).

40. "Journal of the Proceedings of the National Republican Convention

Held at Worcester, October 11, 1932" (Boston, 1832), 37, 62; "Proceedings and Address of the Convention of Delegates . . . at Columbus, Ohio, Dec. 28, 1827, . . . Favorable to the Reelection of John Quincy Adams" (Columbus, 1827), 10; "Address of the Central Committee . . . Friendly to the Election of John Q. Adams [Boston, 1828]" (n.p., n.d.), 2; "Address of the Administration Convention Held in the Capitol at Raleigh, Dec. 20, 1827" (n.p., n.d.), 2, 3; "Address of the Republican Members of the Legislature Friendly to the Elevation of Henry Clay to the Office of President . . ." (Albany, N.Y., 1824), 14; "Proceedings of the National Republican Convention Held at Frankfort, Kentucky, on Thursday, December 9, 1830" (n.p., n.d.), 15.

41. "Address," Administration Convention, Raleigh, 1827, 9; "Proceedings," Town Meeting, Philadelphia, July 7, 1828, 20; "Proceedings," National Republicans, Kentucky, 1830, 19; "Proceedings of the State Convention of the National Republican Young Men . . ." (Hartford, Conn., 1832), 12; Lucas, "Development of Second Party System," 122, 290ff; Watson, *Jacksonian Politics*, 76.

42. James S. Chase, *Emergence of the Presidential Nominating Convention, 1789–1832* (Urbana: Univ. of Illinois Press, 1973), 93.

43. "Address to the People of Connecticut Adopted at the State Convention Held at Middletown, August 7, 1828" (Hartford, 1828), 6, 24; "Republican State Convention [New York, 1828]," Albany, N.Y., *Argus* Extra, Oct. 7, 1828: 37.

44. "Proceedings," Town Meeting, Philadelphia, July 7, 1828, 22; "The Virginia Address" [n.p., [1827]), 7; "Address," Administration Convention, Raleigh, Dec. 20, 1827, 1, 5–6; "Address of the Administration Standing Committee to Their Fellow Citizens of Indiana" (n.p., [1828]), 1, 16.

45. Ronald P. Formisano, "Political Character, Antipartyism, and the Second Party System," *American Quarterly*, 21 (Winter 1969): 683–709; William G. Shade, "Political Pluralism and Party Development: The Creation of a Modern Party System: 1815–1852," in Kleppner et al., *Evolution*, 77–111; Lucas, "Development of Second Party System," 327; Alvin Kass, *Politics in New York State, 1800–1830* (New York: Syracuse Univ. Press, 1965), 19.

46. Watson, *Jacksonian Politics*, 14–15. Major L. Wilson argues that Van Buren's defense of party, at the beginning at least, stressed traditional republican values and arguments rather than the new values of sustained, permanent conflict. "Republicanism and the Idea of Party in the Jacksonian Period," *JER*, 8 (Winter 1988): 419–42.

47. Alfred Balch to Polk, Jan. 6, 1831, in Herbert Weaver, ed., *The Correspondence of James K. Polk* (Nashville, Tenn.: Vanderbilt Univ. Press, 1969), 1: 376; McCormick, *Presidential Game*, 127.

48. "An Address to The People of the United States on the Subject of the Presidential Election . . ." (Washington, D.C., 1832), 5; "Proceedings," National Republican Convention, Kentucky, 1830, 19; "Address and Proceedings of the Ohio State [Democratic] Convention . . . January 9, 1832" (Columbus, 1832), 12; "Proceedings of the Democratic Republican State Convention . . . Concord, June 26, 1832" (Concord, N.H., 1832), 5.

49. *CG*, 23d Cong., 1st sess., 286; Lucas, "Development of Second Party System," 325; Formisano, *Transformation*, 43; J. Mills Thornton, *Politics and Power in a Slave Society: Alabama, 1800–1860* (Baton Rouge: Louisiana State Univ. Press, 1978), 34.

50. Richard P. McCormick argues strongly that the organizing of political parties was due less to battles over any particular set of issues than to the re-newed contest for the Presidency from 1824 on. *Second Party System, passim.*

51. Quoted in Clement L. Grant, "The Public Career of Cave Johnson" (Ph.D. dissertation, Vanderbilt Univ., 1951), 80; *Globe*, March 19, 1835; Lucas, "Development of Second Party System," 330ff; Watson, *Jacksonian Politics*, 198.

52. Milledgeville, Ga., *Federal Union*, April 21, 1835, Jan. 18, 1836. For the Democrats' "Address to the People," see Joel H. Silbey, "Election of 1836," in Schlesinger and Israel, *History of Presidential Elections*, 1: 616–38.

53. *Vicksburg Register*, in *States Rights Banner*, Dec. 25, 1834. On the election of 1836, see Silbey, "Election of 1836," in Schlesinger and Israel, *History*; and Richard P. McCormick, "Was There a 'Whig Strategy' in 1836?," *JER*, 4 (Spring 1984): 47–70.

54. See speech of John Bell in Nashville, Tenn., July 1835, in Silbey, "Election of 1836," in Schlesinger and Israel, *History*, 639; Cincinnati *Daily Gazette*, in *National Intelligencer*, Aug. 1, 1835. See also Albany, N.Y., *Evening Journal*, Feb. 10, 1836; and *National Intelligencer*, Sept. 20, 1835. The attack on Van Buren is in the *Evening Journal*, March 19, 1835.

55. Silbey, "Election of 1836," in Schlesinger and Israel, *History*; Joel H. Silbey, "The Election of 1836," in Arthur S. Link, ed., *Crucial American Elections* (Philadelphia: American Philosophical Society, 1973), 14–29.

56. Clay to Noah Noble, June 20, 1837, Clay to John M. Clayton, June 15, 1838, Clay to Harrison Gray Otis, June 26, 1838, in Robert Seager, ed., *The Papers of Henry Clay* (Lexington: Univ. of Kentucky Press, 1988), lx, 50, 205, 209.

57. *DR*, 2 (June 1838): 316, 317; William Shade, "Society and Politics in Antebellum Virginia's Southside," *Journal of Southern History*, 53 (May 1987): 171–72.

58. Sellers, *Polk*, 325; Webster to Robert C. Winthrop, Aug. 10, 1840, in Harold D. Moser, ed., *The Papers of Daniel Webster* (Hanover, N.H.: Univ. Press of New England, 1928), 5: 53.

59. Michael F. Holt, "The Election of 1840, Voter Mobilization, and the Emergence of the Second American Party System: A Reappraisal of Jacksonian Voting Behavior," in William J. Cooper, Michael F. Holt, and John Mc-Cardell, eds., *A Master's Due: Essays in Honor of David Herbert Donald* (Baton Rouge: Louisiana State Univ. Press, 1985), 55.

60. Roy F. Nichols, *The Invention of the American Political Parties* (New York: Macmillan, 1967); McCormick, *Second Party System*; Benson, *Concept of Jacksonian Democracy*.

61. Robert Johannsen, *Stephen A. Douglas* (New York: Oxford Univ. Press, 1973), 27; Formisano, "Federalists and Republicans."

62. Ronald P. Formisano, *The Birth of Mass Political Parties: Michigan, 1827–1861* (Princeton, N.J.: Princeton Univ. Press, 1971), 22.

63. Walter Dean Burnham, "Elections as Democratic Institutions," in Kay Schlozman, *Elections in America* (Boston: Allen & Unwin, 1987), 34–35.

64. Silbey, "Election of 1836," in Link, *Crucial American Elections*, 26–27. Jackson had received more than 75% of the popular vote in four states in 1828, Adams that much in three (and 74.4% in another).

65. *Congressional Quarterly's Guide to U.S. Elections* (Washington, D.C., 1975).

66. Benson, Silbey, and Field, "Toward a Theory"; Shade, "Society and Politics," 173. The New York state figures are from *Census of the State of New York for 1865* (Albany: Van Benthuysen & Sons, 1867), lxxxiii.

67. Benson, *Concept of Jacksonian Democracy*; Amy Bridges, *A City in the Republic: Antebellum New York and the Origins of Machine Politics* (New York: Cambridge Univ. Press, 1984).

68. Formisano, *Transformation*, 245. See also W. Wayne Smith, "The Whig Party of Maryland, 1826–1856" (Ph.D. dissertation, Univ. of Maryland, 1967), 147; and Elliot R. Barkan, *Portrait of a Party: The Origins and Development of the Whig Persuasion in New York State* (New York: Garland, 1988).

69. Washington *Globe*, Aug. 11, 1838; *Nashville Union*, Nov. 9, 1838.

70. Holt, "Election of 1840," 17; Donald Ratcliffe, "Voter Turnout in Early Ohio," *JER*, 7 (Fall 1987): 250.

71. This emerging system had its limits, to be sure. As Mary P. Ryan writes, "The rise of the common man and the political exclusion of women proceeded in tandem between 1825 and 1840. By the late 1840s, the American public sphere presented a relatively one-dimensional gender picture. Any females along its border were decisively shunted aside, and the composition of the public became masculine. . . . Political energies were focussed on building a masculine fortress in the public sphere." *Women in Public: Between Banners and Ballots, 1825–1880* (Baltimore: Johns Hopkins Univ. Press, 1990), 135.

Chapter Two

1. Speech of Jan. 5, 1837, in Clyde N. Wilson, ed., *The Papers of John C. Calhoun* (Columbia: Univ. of South Carolina Press, 1980), 13: 345; Calhoun to R. M. T. Hunter, June 1839, in ibid., 14: 617. Not that Calhoun eschewed various forms of democratic political conflict. As Lacy K. Ford has written, "Throughout his life, Calhoun and his followers kept South Carolina half-in and half-out of the Jacksonian mainstream, waging a series of heated grassroots campaigns, literally going field-to-field and door-to-door wooing voters, but always, even when acting as a tough partisan, standing as a barrier to the development of a permanent two-party system in South Carolina." *Origins of Southern Radicalism: The South Carolina Upcountry, 1800–1860* (New York: Oxford Univ. Press, 1988), 191–92. It was of course his "standing as a barrier" against a party system that made Calhoun as out of step as he was.

2. *CG*, 26th Cong., 1st sess., *Appendix*, 41; Charles Grier Sellers, Jr., *James*

K. *Polk, Jacksonian, 1795–1843* (Princeton, N.J., Princeton Univ. Press, 1957), 340; Richard P. McCormick, *The Second American Party System: Party Formation in the Jacksonian Era* (Chapel Hill: Univ. of North Carolina Press, 1966).

3. Marc Kruman, *Parties and Politics in North Carolina, 1836–1865* (Baton Rouge: Louisiana State Univ. Press, 1983), 5.

4. *AR*, 1 (Feb. 1845): 115.

5. Ronald Formisano, *The Transformation of Political Culture: Massachusetts Parties, 1790s–1840s* (New York: Oxford Univ. Press, 1983), 23; Richard Buel, Review of Formisano, *Transformation*, *JIH*, 15 (Winter 1985): 537; Harry L. Watson, *Jacksonian Politics and Community Conflict* (Baton Rouge: Louisiana State Univ. Press, 1981), 2.

6. Seward to John Quincy Adams, Nov. 6, 1841, in George E. Baker, ed., *The Works of William H. Seward* (Boston: Houghton-Mifflin, 1884), 3: 455; *CG*, 26 Cong. 1st sess., 190, *Appendix*, 340; Benjamin F. Butler, "Representative Democracy in the United States" (Albany, 1841), 28–29.

7. "A History of the Federal and Democratic Parties in the United States" (Richmond, Ind., 1837), 51; *DR*, 9 (Oct. 1841): 345; *CG*, 26th Cong., 1st sess., *Appendix*, 52; Albany, N.Y., *Argus*, Aug. 12, 1844; *AR*, as quoted in Michael Wallace, "Ideologies of Party in the Early Republic" (Ph.D. dissertation, Columbia Univ., 1973), 325.

8. *Works of Seward*, 3: 261, 294, 305; *CG*, 26th Cong., 2d sess., *Appendix*, 169; *New Hampshire Statesman*, May 22, 1852.

9. Leverett Saltonstall to Mary Saltonstall, Dec. 8, 1839, in Robert E. Moody, ed., *The Papers of Leverett Saltonstall, 1816–1845* (Boston: Massachusetts Historical Society, 1982), 2: 258.

10. *CG*, 25th Cong., 3d sess., *Appendix*, 403.

11. Daniel Walker Howe, *The Political Culture of the American Whigs* (Chicago: Univ. of Chicago Press, 1979); Formisano, *Transformation*.

12. Leverett Saltonstall to Anna E. Saltonstall, Dec. 10, 1839, *Saltonstall Papers*, 2: 259; *Ohio State Journal*, Sept. 24, 1839.

13. "Proceedings of the Whigs of Chester County Favorable to a Distinct Organization of the Whig Party" (West Chester, Pa., 1838), 5; 15; "Speech of S. W. Downs . . . on the Annexation of Texas [1844]" (New Orleans, 1844), 5; *New Hampshire Statesman*, Dec. 21, 1839.

14. Douglas Jaenicke, "American Ideas of Political Party as Theories of Politics: Competing Theories of Liberty and Community" (Ph.D. dissertation, Cornell Univ., 1981), 21.

15. *New Hampshire Statesman*, March 9, 1839.

16. Thurlow Weed to Willis Hall, July 28, 1837, M. L. Davis to Willis Hall, Oct. 3, 1837, Duff Green to Willis Hall, July 29, 1837, in Daniel Ullmann Papers, New York Historical Society.

17. "Great Whig Demonstration in Favor of the Nomination of Gen. Taylor . . . at Philadelphia, February 22, 1848" (n.p., n.d.), 7; Leverett Saltonstall to Anna S. White, Dec. 30, 1838, *Saltonstall Papers*, 2: 146; Caleb Cushing, "To My Constituents" (n.p., [1841]), 12. On Lincoln as a political organizer, see

Joel H. Silbey, "Always a Whig in Politics: The Partisan Life of Abraham Lincoln," *Papers of the Abraham Lincoln Association*, 8 (1986): 21–42.

18. S. H. Laughlin to Polk, Oct. 1, 1839, in Wayne Cutler, ed., *Correspondence of James K. Polk* (Nashville, Tenn.: Vanderbilt Univ. Press, 1979), 5: 259; "History of Federal and Democratic Parties," 52; "To the Electors of Massachusetts" (n.p., [1837], 1; *Ohio State Journal*, Feb. 1, 1839 (see also the issues of April 23, May 3, and Nov. 15, 1839). Interestingly enough, it was this commitment to unity and concert that led Lincoln to use the famous expression "a house divided against itself cannot stand" in the 1840's to condemn Whig factionalism. Wallace, "Ideologies of Party," 330.

19. In April 1838, the party newspaper in Missouri "used the word *Whig* for the first time in reference to a specific state political contest." Before that, the Democrats' opponents had been identified as the "opposition," the "Clay Party," and "Friends of [the] American System." John V. Mering, *The Whig Party in Missouri* (Columbia: Univ. of Missouri Press, 1967), 1–2.

20. *Atlas*, July 6, 1848; J. Mills Thornton, *Politics and Power in a Slave Society: Alabama, 1800–1860* (Baton Rouge: Louisiana State Univ. Press, 1978), 37.

21. Leverett Saltonstall to Mary Saltonstall, Dec. 17, 1838, *Saltonstall Papers*, 2: 133.

22. Quoted in M. Philip Lucas, "The Period of Political Alchemy: Party in the Mississippi Legislature, 1835–1846" (M.A. thesis, Cornell Univ., 1981), 70; *CG*, 24th Cong., 1st sess., 230; Saltonstall to James C. Merrill, Dec. 21, 1839, *Saltonstall Papers*, 2: 267.

23. Thornton, *Politics and Power*, 128; Sellers, *Polk, Jacksonian*, 399.

24. William Nisbet Chambers, "Election of 1840," in Arthur M. Schlesinger, Jr., *History of American Presidential Elections* (New York: Chelsea House, 1971), 1: 645.

25. Michael Holt, "The Election of 1840, Voter Mobilization and the Emergence of The Second American Party System: A Reappraisal of Jacksonian Voting Behavior," in William J. Cooper, Michael F. Holt, and John McCardell, eds., *A Master's Due: Essays in Honor of David Herbert Donald* (Baton Rouge: Louisiana State Univ. Press, 1985), 16–58; *Daily Globe*, Sept. 25, 1840.

26. McCormick, *Second Party System*; Ronald Formisano, "Federalists and Republicans: Parties, Yes—System, No," in Paul Kleppner et al., *The Evolution of American Electoral Systems* (Westport, Conn.: Greenwood Press, 1981); William Shade, "Political Pluralism and Party Development: The Creation of a Modern Party System: 1815–1852, in Kleppner et al.

27. *Southern Banner*, Dec. 14, 1843; *Argus*, Nov. 3, 1846; *Atlas and Argus*, March 31, 1856.

28. M. Philip Lucas, "The Development of The Second Party System in Mississippi, 1817–1846" (Ph.D. dissertation, Cornell Univ., 1983); Watson, *Jacksonian Politics*, 2; Thornton, *Politics and Power*; Kruman, *Parties and Politics*; Paul Bergeron, *Antebellum Politics in Tennessee* (Lexington: Univ. of Kentucky Press, 1982); William Shade, "Society and Politics in Antebellum Virginia's Southside," *Journal of Southern History*, 53 (May 1987): 163–93; Daniel Crofts, *Reluctant Confederates: Upper South Unionists in the Secession Crisis* (Chapel Hill:

Univ. of North Carolina Press, 1989); Thomas E. Jeffrey, *State Parties and National Politics: North Carolina, 1815–1861* (Athens: Univ. of Georgia Press, 1989).

29. Chambers, "Election of 1840," 684; *Atlas*, Oct. 23, 1846.

30. *DR*, 32 (Jan. 1853): 89.

31. Raleigh, N.C., *Register*, May 24, Aug. 2, 1844; *New Hampshire Statesman*, Dec. 16, 1842; Formisano, *Transformation*, 266; Wallace, "Ideologies of Party," 323; Thomas E. Brown, *Politics and Statesmanship: Essays on the American Whig Party* (New York: Columbia Univ. Press, 1985), 169.

32. *AR*, 4 (Nov. 1846): 444–46, 8 (July 1848): 8, 9 (Feb. 1849): 115; *Ohio State Journal*, March 11, 1848.

33. *AR*, 7 (March 1848): 218.

34. "Proceedings of the Democratic Republican Convention of the State of Indiana, Indianapolis, Jan. 8, 1936" (n.p., n.d.), 23; Philip C. Friese, *An Essay on Party: Showing Its Uses, Its Abuses and Its Natural Dissolution* (New York, 1856), 11.

35. Richard Latner, *The Presidency of Andrew Jackson: White House Politics, 1829–1837* (Athens: Univ. of Georgia Press, 1979), 127–28; *DR*, 9 (Nov. 1841): 497; Paulding, Miss., *True Democrat*, Aug. 6, 1845, cited in Lucas, "Development of Second Party System," 21; "Proceedings," Whigs of Chester County, 15; Formisano, *Transformation*, 310.

36. *Argus*, Nov. 9, 1848; *Ohio State Journal*, March 11, 1848.

Chapter Three

1. *Argus*, Aug. 11, 1843; *New Hampshire Statesman*, Feb. 4, 1848. A useful introduction to the history of campaigning practices over the course of American politics is Robert J. Dinkin, *Campaigning in America: A History of Election Practices* (New York: Greenwood Press, 1989), especially chaps. 3 and 4: "The Jacksonian Period, 1824–1852," and "The Golden Age of Parties, 1854–88."

2. *Republican Sentinel*, June 8, 1844; William E. Baringer, "Campaign Techniques in Illinois, 1860," *Illinois State Historical Society Transactions for the Year 1932* (Springfield, 1932): 202–81.

3. Richmond, Va., *Enquirer*, Nov. 5, 1844; *Globe*, Nov. 5, 1844; *Springfield, Mass., Republican*, Sept. 14, 1844; *Indiana State Sentinel*, April 6, 1848.

4. Even as the *New Hampshire Statesman* was still reporting presidential returns in its Dec. 19, 1840, issue, it reminded everyone that it was time to call conventions for the upcoming state elections. See also Milledgeville, Ga., *Federal Union*, Oct. 12, 1841.

5. *Argus*, various issues, 1843 and 1844.

6. Raleigh, N.C., *Register*, Oct. 22, 1844; *Argus*, Sept. 14, 1842; *Republican Sentinel*, Oct. 18, 1844; *The Campaign*, no. 4, June 21, no. 21, Oct. 18, 1848; Albany, N.Y., *Evening Journal*, Aug. 1, 1848; *Louisville Journal*, Aug. 14, Nov. 1, 1852; *New Hampshire Statesman and Journal*, Sept. 4, 1843; Chicago *Weekly Democrat*, June 12, 1844.

7. *Seneca Falls Democrat* in *People's Democratic Guide*, 1 (Sept. 1842): 328; *Richmond Whig*, Oct. 3, 1848. For a similar Whig perspective, see Raleigh *Register*, July 5, 1848.

8. *New York Globe*, April 19, 1847; Dayton, Ohio, *Stars and Stripes*, Oct. 21, 1852; *DR*, 37 (April 1856): 316; Springfield, Mass., *The Extra Journal*, April 20, 1843.

9. "Richard Croker on Politics," in *Tammany Hall Souvenir of the Inauguration of Cleveland and Stevenson* (New York, 1893), 65.

10. *The Grape Shot*, Aug. 26, Sept. 23, 1848; *Atlas*, July 6, 1848.

11. "To the Whigs and Conservatives of the United States," (Washington, D.C., 1840), 2: *Papers for the People*, Oct. 9, 1852: 288; *Ohio State Journal*, Oct. 13, 1848; General Committee of Democratic Whig Young Men of the City and County of New York to "Sir," July 4, 1840, in Miscellaneous Papers, New York Historical Society; *Springfield Daily Republican*, Oct. 31, 1846; *Republican Sentinel*, Oct. 30, 1844; Washington *Globe*, July 30, 1840. According to John V. Mering, Missouri's Whigs in the 1840's "expected too much from organization, largely because they erred in interpreting their past reversals in terms of its absence." *The Whig Party in Missouri* (Columbia: Univ. of Missouri Press, 1967), 50.

12. *Register*, in *The Signal*, Aug. 21, 1852: 127; Albany, N.Y., *Rough Hewer*, Oct. 22, 1840: 286; *Republican Sentinel*, April 20, 1844; *Argus*, Sept. 22, 1852; Ravenna, Ohio, *Campaign Democrat*, Sept. 27, 1855; *Evening Journal*, Aug. 30, 1844.

13. *The Recruit*, Sept. 19, 1848; "Proceedings and Address of the Democratic State Convention of the State of Ohio . . ." (Columbus, 1844), 30.

14. *Ohio State Journal*, Aug. 6, 1856; *Rough and Ready*, Feb. 20, 1847; *Springfield Republican*, Sept. 7, 1844; *Argus*, Sept. 22, 1852.

15. A. O. P. Nicholson to Polk, Nov. 15, 1840, in Wayne Cutler, ed., *The Correspondence of James K. Polk* (Nashville, Tenn.: Vanderbilt Univ. Press, 1979), 5: 586; A. C. Flagg et al. to "Sir," Sept. 6, 1840, in Henry O'Reilly Papers, New York Historical Society; *New Hampshire Statesman*, Jan. 12, 1839.

16. Groton, Mass., *Spirit of the Times*, Sept. 6, 1848; *The Recruit*, July 25, 1848.

17. *Papers for the People*, Sept. 25, 1852: 228; *Evening Journal*, Oct. 21, 23, 1848. The cover of one surviving poll book bears the inscription, "The only fear of an adverse result" is if our friends "will not be at the polls in their full strength." "Minden Poll Book, 1863," (from Montgomery County, N.Y.), in Miscellaneous Collections, New York Historical Society. On poll books generally, see John M. Rozett, "The Social Bases of Party Conflict in the Age of Jackson: Individual Voting Behavior in Greene County, Illinois, 1838–1848, (Ph.D. dissertation, Univ. of Michigan, 1974); Kenneth J. Winkle, *The Politics of Community: Migration and Politics in Antebellum Ohio* (New York: Cambridge Univ. Press, 1988); and Donald DeBats and Paul Bourke's articles "Identifiable Voting in Nineteenth-Century America: Toward a Comparison of Britain and the United States Before the Secret Ballot," *Perspectives in American His-*

tory, 11 (1977–78): 259–88, and "The Structures of Political Involvement in the Nineteenth Century: A Frontier Case," *Perspectives in American History*, n.s. 3 (1986): 209–40.

18. *The Recruit*, Oct. 3, 1848; *New Hampshire Statesman*, Jan. 3, 1847; *Atlas and Argus*, Nov. 11, 1856, Aug. 12, 1857; Charles Grier Sellers, Jr., *James K. Polk: Jacksonian, 1795–1843* (Princeton, N.J.: Princeton Univ. Press, 1957), 366. Justin Morrill kept a list of every document sent to voters in his district. William B. Parker, *The Life and Public Service of Justin Morrill* (Boston: Houghton-Mifflin, 1924), 99. Good discussions of local political organization are in Don H. Doyle, *The Social Order of a Frontier Community: Jacksonville, Illinois, 1825–1870* (Urbana: Univ. of Illinois Press, 1978); and Merle Curti, *The Making of an American Community: A Case Study of Democracy in a Frontier County* (Stanford, Calif.: Stanford University Press, 1959).

19. J. Mills Thornton, *Politics and Power in a Slave Society: Alabama, 1800–1866* (Baton Rouge: Louisiana State Univ. Press, 1988), 143. For a plan similar to Lincoln's on the Democratic side, see Flagg et al. to "Dear Sir," Oct. 14, 1844, in Azariah Flagg Papers, New York Public Library.

20. There are many discussions of the Republican's organizational activities in their first national campaign in the Nathaniel P. Banks Papers, Library of Congress. See, for example, A. Orlando Hart to Banks, Feb. 1, 1856, and Thomas Balch to Banks, Dec. 11, 1856. Roy F. Nichols, *The Invention of the American Political Parties: A Study of Political Improvisation* (New York: Macmillan, 1967), and Robert Marcus, *Grand Old Party: Political Structure in the Gilded Age, 1880–1896* (New York: Oxford Univ. Press, 1971), are good introductions to national party structure in this political nation. An older study containing many important details is George Luetscher, *Early Political Machinery in the United States* (Philadelphia: Univ. of Pennsylvania Press, 1903).

21. *New Hampshire Statesman*, April 9, 1847; "Speeches Delivered at Tammany Hall, New York City, Sept. 2, 1852," *Evening Post Documents No. 10* (n.p., n.d.), 12; *Argus*, July 4, 1838, Nov. 11, 1856; *The Young Guard*, July 4, 1848; Webster to Nicholas Biddle, May 12, 1835, in Charles M. Wiltse, ed., *The Papers of Daniel Webster* (Hanover, N.H.: Univ. Press of New England, 1980), 4: 45; Jabez Hammond, *History of Political Parties in the State of New York* (Syracuse: Hall & Dickson, 1848), 1: 279.

22. *The Signal*, July 1, 1852; Thomas Leonard, *The Power of the Press: The Birth of American Political Reporting* (New York: Oxford Univ. Press, 1986), 167; *AR*, 7 (Jan. 1848): 2. I have borrowed the "barometers of orthodoxy" phrase from James Brewer Stewart, *Joshua R. Giddings and the Tactics of Radical Abolition* (Cleveland: Case-Western Reserve Univ. Press, 1970), 287.

23. S. H. Hammond to ?, April 29, 1855, in Daniel Ullmann Papers, New York Historical Society; *Republican Sentinel*, Oct. 30, 1844; Michael E. McGerr, *The Decline of Popular Politics: The American North, 1865–1928* (New York: Oxford Univ. Press, 1986), 17.

24. Donald DeBats, "Elites and Masses: Political Structure, Communications and Behavior in Ante-Bellum Georgia" (Ph.D. dissertation, Univ. of

Wisconsin, 1973), 236; *Argus*, Aug. 5, 1858. Some newspapers remained independent. They were viewed with suspicion as being deceptive and really in the pay of some party whatever their protestations. See, for example, *Boston Post*, Nov. 1, 1880. William Miles, *The People's Voice: An Annotated Bibliography of American Presidential Campaign Biographies, 1828–1844* (New York: Greenwood Press, 1987).

25. *The Recruit*, June [?], 1848. Among the other such sheets cited were *The Signal*, the *Republican Sentinel*, *The Grape Shot*, and *The Rough Hewer*.

26. W. Burlie Brown, *The People's Choice: The Presidential Image in the Campaign Biography* (Baton Rouge: Louisiana State Univ. Press, 1960), 9.

27. Franklin Townsend (secretary of Whig State Central Committee) to Daniel Ullmann, Oct. 3, 1851, in the Ullman Papers. This was a printed circular, indicating that it was sent to many other Whigs.

28. John D. Morris, "The New York State Whigs, 1843–1842: A Study of Political Organization" (Ph.D. dissertation, Univ. of Rochester, 1970), 155–56; Chauncey M. Depew, *My Memories of Eighty Years* (New York: Scribner's, 1924), 20; Nichols, *Invention of Parties*, 375; Robert J. Haws, "Massachusetts Whigs, 1833–1854" (Ph.D. dissertation, Univ. of Nebraska, 1973), 236. Edwin Morgan, the first Republican national chairman, tried very hard to make fund raising more systematic. See James A. Rawley, *Edwin D. Morgan, 1811–1883: Merchant in Politics* (New York: Columbia Univ. Press, 1955).

29. *Ohio State Journal*, Oct. 1, 1856; Sellers, *Polk, Jacksonian*, 355–77; *Register*, April 10, 1840; *Evening Journal*, July 19, 1844; New York *Tribune*, June 10, 1858; David Turpie, *Sketches of My Own Time* (Indianapolis: Bobbs-Merrill, 1903), 194–95. The most recent survey of the history of political campaigning in America is R. J. Dinkin, *Campaigning in America*.

30. Margaret Leech and Harry J. Brown, *The Garfield Orbit* (New York: Harper & Row, 1978), 173; Reuben Davis, *Recollections of Mississippi and Mississippians* (Boston: Houghton-Mifflin, 1889), 194. As Mary P. Ryan points out, it was here, in such public meetings, that "women as audience" appeared directly in the political sphere from which they were usually shut out. Their participation was neither casual nor occasional, but an expected and regular aspect of the emerging political world, certainly in the urban centers that are the focus of her research. *Women in Public: Between Banners and Ballots, 1825–1880* (Baltimore: Johns Hopkins Univ. Press, 1990), 136.

31. Dayton *Stars and Stripes*, Sept. 16, 1852; *Tribune*, June 10, 1858.

32. Davis, *Recollections*, 111, 194.

33. *Nashville Union*, Oct. 27, 1852; *Springfield Republican*, Oct. 3, 1840, Nov. 6, 1846.

34. *North Carolina Standard*, Oct. 30, 1844; *Southern Banner*, Dec. 21, 1843; *Nashville Union*, Oct. 28, 1844; *Illinois State Register*, Oct. 16, 1840; *Atlas and Argus*, Oct. 25, 1859; *Argus*, Nov. 2, 1847; *Ohio State Journal*, Nov. 1, 1856, Oct. 7, 1858.

35. There is a useful discussion of aspects of this process in William E. Gienapp, "'Politics Seems to Enter into Everything': Political Culture in the

North, 1840–1860," in Stephen E. Maizlish and John J. Kushma, eds., *Essays on American Antebellum Politics, 1840–1860* (College Station: Texas A&M Univ. Press, 1982), 14–69. See also Milledgeville, Ga., *Federal Union*, Oct. 29, 1844; Mobile, Ala., *Register*, Oct. 20, 1840; *New Hampshire Statesman*, Feb. 21, 1845; and *Argus*, Oct. 23, 1844.

36. *Argus*, Oct. 23, 1844, Nov. 4, 1851, Nov. 2, 1852; H. T. Stockbridge to "Sir," Oct. 27, 1840, in the O'Reilly Papers.

37. Ravenna, Ohio, *Campaign Democrat*, Oct. 8, 1855; Concord, N.H., *Tough and Steady*, March 2, 1847; *The Battery*, Oct. 12, 1848; *Atlas and Argus*, Nov. 6, 1860; Albany, N.Y., *Statesman*, Oct. 27, 1856; *Ohio State Journal*, Oct. 6, 1859; Harrisburg, Pa., *Yeoman*, Oct. 8, 1841.

38. William Sulzer, "Tammany's Relation to the Democracy," in *Tammany Hall Souvenir*, 88, 92.

39. *Whig*, Jan. 25, 1848; *Indiana State Sentinel*, Dec. 2, 1847.

40. Jackson's comment is in Andrew Jackson to James Gunn, Feb. 23, 1835, Niles' *Register*, April 4, 1835: 84 (the same comment appears in the Whig *Connecticut Courant*, Aug. 1, 1852); *DR*, 30 (May 1852): 472.

41. James McGregor Burns, *The Vineyard of Liberty* (New York: Knopf, 1982), 594. A very good history of the origins of the convention is James S. Chase, *The Emergence of the Presidential Nominating Convention, 1789–1832* (Urbana: Univ. of Illinois Press, 1973).

42. Owego, N.Y., *Gazette*, in *Argus*, March 14, 1848; Daniel Webster to Edward Everett, March 14, 1836, in *Webster Papers*, 4: 95; "Proceedings of the National Union Republican Convention [1868]" (Chicago, 1868), 105; "Official Proceedings of the National Democratic Convention Held at Baltimore, July 9, 1872" (Boston, 1872), 67; *Cortland Democrat*, in *Atlas*, May 30, 1848.

43. The *Standard* quotation is in Thomas E. Jeffrey, "The Second Party System in North Carolina, 1836–1860" (Ph.D dissertation, Catholic University of America, 1976), 125. Jeffrey's dissertation, now published as *State Parties and National Politics: North Carolina, 1815–1861* (Athens: Univ. of Georgia Press, 1989), contains an excellent description of the evolution of party organization in that state. *DR*, 30 (March 1852): 281, 30 (May 1852): 472; William Gwin to Polk, Nov. 5, 1842, *Correspondence of James Polk*, 6: 129; *Atlas*, Aug. 30, 1843, Jan. 24, 1844, Oct. 30, 1846; "Great Whig Demonstration in Favor of the Nomination of Gen. Taylor . . . at Philadelphia, February 22, 1848" (n.p., n.d.), 2; "Proceedings of the Republican Convention [Virginia, 1839]" (n.p., n.d.), 3.

44. *The Log Cabin*, Sept. 25, 1841.

45. *AR*, 15 (May 1852): 379.

46. Joshua Cunningham to Polk, March 23, 1838, in *Correspondence of James Polk*, 4: 399.

47. Chase, *Emergence of Nominating Convention*, 3.

48. *Republican Sentinel*, April 13, 1844; Dayton, Ohio, *Coon Dissector*, Aug. 2, 1844; Concord, N.H., *Rough and Ready*, Dec. 12, 1846; *Springfield Daily Republican*, Oct. 1, 1846; Sept. 14, 1853, clipping in the Ullmann Papers.

49. "Proceedings and Address of the Democratic County Convention

Held at Galena . . . 22nd February, 1839" (n.p., n.d.), 6; *DR*, 30 (March 1852): 276.

50. *Argus*, Sept. 26, 1846, April 10, 1851, April 18, 1854; *Springfield Daily Republican*, May 28, 1844; *Ohio State Journal*, June 23, 1852.

51. *Republican Sentinel*, May 18, 1844; Chase, *Emergence of Nominating Convention*.

52. "Proceedings of the Democratic National Convention, Held at Baltimore, June 1–5, 1852 . . ." (Washington, D.C., 1852), 6.

53. "Official Proceedings of the National Democratic Convention Held at Baltimore, July 9, 1872" (Boston, 1872), 46; "Official Proceedings of the National Democratic Convention [1880]" (Dayton, Ohio, 1882), 4; *The Campaign*, June 18, 1852; *New York Globe*, July 23, 1847.

54. *New Hampshire Statesman*, Oct. 10, 1845. "Proceedings of the State Convention of the State Rights Democracy of Pennsylvania, Held at Harrisburg on Wednesday, April 13, 1859" (Harrisburg, 1859), 43.

55. Hartford *Connecticut Courant*, Oct. 12, 1844; *New Hampshire Statesman*, Sept. 20, 1851.

56. Gienapp, "Politics Seems to Enter into Everything," 43.

57. *New Hampshire Statesman*, Nov. 7, 1845.

58. Louis Lott to James Barker, Oct. 26, 1854, in the Ullmann Papers; Polk to Robert B. Reynolds, Nov. 18, 1840, Feb. 4, 1841, in *Correspondence of James Polk*, 5: 594, 626–27.

59. Richard M. Woods to Polk, Jan. 28, 1839, in *Correspondence of James Polk*, 5: 37.

60. *Atlas*, Feb. 22, 1848; Cincinnati *The Rail Splitter*, Aug. 29, 1860; New York *Tribune*, July 31, 1858; *New York Globe*, June 10, 1847.

61. *Atlas*, Nov. 14, 16, 1848.

62. Ibid., Feb. 22, 1848; "Address of the Democratic Hickory Club [Philadelphia, 1844]" (n.p., n.d.), 5; *Democratic Review*, 37 (April 1856): 324; *New York Globe*, Nov. 3, 1847.

63. Douglas Jaenicke, "The Jacksonian Integration of Parties into the Constitutional System," *Political Science Quarterly*, 101 (Summer 1986): 216; *AR*, 1 (Feb. 1845): 115; "Proceedings," Republican Convention, Virginia, 1839, 6; *The Democratic Textbook* (New York, 1848), 4.

64. *New York Globe*, Oct. 8, 1847; *Ohio State Journal*, April 12, 1852; *The Log Cabin*, Nov. 9, 1840; *AR*, 8 (July 1848): 1, 8 (Oct. 1848): 334.

65. A. B. James to ?, Aug. 16, 1854, in the Ullmann Papers; *The Log Cabin*, Nov. 9, 1840; *New York Globe*, Sept. 16, 1847.

66. *AR*, 4 (Nov. 1846): 445; *DR*, 37 (April 1856): 317, 38 (July 1856): 527; *Atlas and Argus*, Sept. 10, 1857; Springfield, Mass., *Extra Journal*, April 20, 1843.

67. *The Campaign*, no. 1, May 31, 1848; "The Correspondence Between Hon. Hamilton Fish . . . and Hon. James Hamilton" (n.p., [1856]), 2; "Proceedings of the First Three Republican National Conventions of 1856, 1860 and 1864" (Minneapolis, 1893), 18; "Address and Resolutions Adopted at the Whig State Convention, Worcester, October 3, 1849" (Boston, 1849), 21.

68. Albany, N.Y., *State Register*, Feb. 17, 1851; *New York Daily Globe*, March 30, 1849; *The Log Cabin*, Aug. 17, 1841.

69. *New York Daily Globe*, Jan. 29, 1849; *Atlas*, Nov. 8, 1848; *Papers for the People*, Sept. 25, 1852: 227; "The Address and Proceedings of the Friends of Daniel Webster," (Boston, 1852), 5 ("The decision of a National Party Convention is in no sense conclusive upon the conduct of all the members of that party throughout the country." All celebration of party loyalty "is only a confession of . . . abject servitude"); [Timothy C. Day], "The Humbug and the Reality: An Address to the People of the First Congressional District . . ." (n.p., [1856]), 6.

70. Hammond, *History of Political Parties*, 1: 467.

71. Marc Kruman, *Parties and Politics in North Carolina, 1836−1865* (Baton Rouge: Louisiana State Univ. Press, 1983), 36. See also, more extensively, Steven Hansen, *The Making of the Third Party System: Voters and Parties in Illinois, 1850−1876* (Ann Arbor, Mich.: UMI Research Press, 1980); Paul Bergeron, *Antebellum Politics in Tennessee* (Lexington: Univ. Press of Kentucky, 1982), 143; and Jeffrey, *State Parties*, chap. 4.

72. Richmond, Va., *Enquirer*, March 19, 1844; *Louisville Journal*, Sept. 7, 1852.

73. See, in particular, Marcus, *Grand Old Party*.

74. *Argus*, Sept. 16, 1844; Gerson Harry Smoger, "Organizing Political Campaigns: A Survey of 19th- and 20th-Century Trends" (Ph.D dissertation, Univ. of Pennsylvania, 1982), 42.

75. Flagg et al. to "Dear Sir," Oct. 14, 1844, in the Flagg Papers.

76. William J. Cooper, *The South and the Politics of Slavery* (Baton Rouge: Louisiana State Univ. Press, 1978), 38; William Henry Seward, "Immigrant White Free Labor, or Imported Black African Slave Labor, Speech . . . at Oswego, New York, November 3, 1856" (n.p., n.d.), 6.

Chapter Four

1. The past 20 years have seen several very good studies of political ideas in mid-19th-century America including Daniel Walker Howe, *The Political Culture of the American Whigs* (Chicago: Univ. of Chicago Press, 1979); John Ashworth, *Agrarians and Aristocrats: Party Political Ideology in the United States* (London: Royal Historical Society, 1983); David J. Russo, *The Major Political Issues of the Jacksonian Period and the Development of Party Loyalty in Congress, 1830−1840* (Philadelphia: American Philosophical Society, 1972); Bruce Collins, "The Ideology of the Ante-Bellum Northern Democrats," *Journal of American Studies*, 11 (April 1977): 103−21; and Lawrence Frederick Kohl, *The Politics of Individualism: Parties and the American Character in the Jacksonian Era* (New York: Oxford Univ. Press, 1989). I have drawn on the insights of these writers, even if I do not always agree with them and their approaches. In a class by itself and very helpful is Daniel T. Rodgers, *Contested Truths: Keywords in American Politics Since Independence* (New York: Basic Books, 1987).

In addition, I have benefited from such studies as John P. Diggins, *The Lost Soul of American Politics: Virtue, Self Interest and the Foundations of Liberalism*

(New York: Basic Books, 1984); Major L. Wilson, *Space, Time and Freedom: The Quest for Nationality and the Irresistible Conflict, 1845–1861* (Westport, Conn.: Greenwood Press, 1974); Robert Wiebe, *The Opening of American Society: From the Adoption of the Constitution to the Eve of Disunion* (New York: Knopf, 1984); and Sean Wilentz, *Chants Democratic: New York City and the Rise of the American Working Class, 1788–1850* (New York: Oxford Univ. Press, 1984).

2. *AR*, 8 (Aug. 1848): 221.

3. *Argus*, Oct. 30, 1849, Jan. 14, 1856; Newburgh, N.Y., *Telegraph*, April 22, 1858; *New York Daily Globe*, Jan. 1, 1847, Jan. 9, 1849; New York *Courier and Enquirer*, July 28, 1858; *CG*, 25th Cong., 2d sess., 421.

4. *Ohio State Journal*, May 14, 1852.

5. James K. Polk to Marcy, March 1, 1845, in William L. Marcy Papers, Library of Congress; Charles Grier Sellers, Jr., *James K. Polk, Continentalist, 1843–1846* (Princeton, N.J.: Princeton University Press, 1966), 324, 346; "Address and Resolves of the Democratic Members of the Massachusetts Legislature of 1838 . . ." (n.p., n.d.), 2. When Franklin Pierce was called an "inflexible" Democrat who belonged to "the strictest sect," it was considered a high compliment. *The Campaign*, no. 4, July 3, 1852.

6. "Proceedings of a Convention of the People of Maine . . ." (n.p., [1828]), 6. Some scholars argue that parties were essentially electoral machines, concerned only to get their men into office, and that there was little substance to their arguments. Their rhetoric, in this view, was designedly deceptive. As Edward Pessen writes, "The great major parties were in a large sense great hoaxes" because of their failure to take meaningful positions about the problems of their society. "We Are All Jeffersonians, We Are All Jacksonians: Or a Pox on Stultifying Periodizations," *JER*, 1 (Spring 1981): 25.

On parties as essentially electoral machines, see Richard P. McCormick, *The Second American Party System: Party Formation in the Jacksonian Era* (Chapel Hill: Univ. of North Carolina Press, 1967). In contrast, David Singal contends that Richard Hofstadter's "endorsement of the two-party system [in *The Idea of a Party System* and elsewhere] is premised on the assumption that the parties would always take substantive issues seriously and would reflect real social divisions in their respective programs." "Beyond Consensus: Richard Hofstadter and American Historiography," *AHR*, 89 (Oct. 1984): 996. For a middle ground on this issue, see Thomas E. Jeffrey, *State Parties and National Politics, 1815–1861* (Athens: Univ. of Georgia Press, 1989).

7. Wilentz, *Chants Democratic*, 14. See also Lee Benson, *The Concept of Jacksonian Democracy: New York as a Test Case* (Princeton, N.J.: Princeton Univ. Press, 1967), 216; and Ashworth, *Agrarians and Aristocrats*, 271.

8. Samuel P. Hays, "Politics and Society: Beyond the Political Party," in Paul Kleppner et al., *The Evolution of American Electoral Systems* (Westport, Conn.: Greenwood Press, 1981), 255–56; Rodgers, *Contested Truths*, 4.

9. Steuben, N.Y., *Courier*, Sept. 8, 1858; *DR*, 40 (Oct. 1857): 296.

10. Michael Holt, *The Political Crisis of the 1850s* (New York: Wiley, 1978), 32; "Proceedings of the Whig State Convention Held at Utica . . . August, 1840" (Albany, N.Y., 1840), 13. See also Ashworth, *Agrarians and Aristocrats*, 2–4.

11. Major L. Wilson, *The Presidency of Martin Van Buren* (Lawrence: Univ. of Kansas Press, 1984), 200; Howe, *Political Culture*, 14. See also Michael F. Holt, "The Election of 1840, Voter Mobilization, and the Emergence of the Second American Party System: A Reappraisal of Jacksonian Voting Behavior," in William J. Cooper et al., eds., *A Master's Due: Essays in Honor of David Herbert Donald* (Baton Rouge: Louisiana State Univ. Press, 1985), 16–58.

12. Wiebe, *Opening of American Society*, xiii; Collins, "Ideology of Northern Democrats," 116; Ashworth, *Agrarians and Aristocrats*, 170, 174. There were, of course, those on the margins of this society who vigorously disputed the ideological consensus and sought to break the dominant rhetorical mode. See Chap. 11, below.

13. These comments are based on my reading of the scholars cited in note 1, above.

14. R. Laurence Moore, "Insiders and Outsiders in American Historical Narrative and American History," *AHR*, 87 (April 1982): 410; *AR*, 4 (Nov. 1846): 445.

15. "Proceedings of the Democratic National Convention Held at Baltimore, June 1–5, 1852 . . ." (Washington, D.C., 1852), 61; Howe, *Political Culture*, 20.

16. *The Campaign*, no. 17, Oct. 2, 1852: 259.

17. *Utica Observer*, in *Argus*, Aug. 15, 1839.

18. "Great and Important Meeting of Democratic Republicans," ([New York, 1839]), 29; "Address of the Democratic Central Committee to the People of Pennsylvania" (Harrisburg, 1838), 3; "Proceedings and Address of the Democratic State Convention of the State of Ohio [1844]," (Columbus, 1844), 9; "Proceedings of the Republican Convention," ([Virginia, 1839]), 10; Polk to William Smith et al., Aug. 31, 1839, in Wayne Cutler, ed., *The Correspondence of James K. Polk* (Nashville, Tenn.: Vanderbilt Univ. Press, 1979), 5: 219–20; "Address to the Democratic Republican Electors of the State of New York" (Washington, D.C., 1840), 13.

19. "Address," Democratic Committee to People of Pennsylvania, 3; "Letter of the Hon. John C. Calhoun [to] Democratic Republican Electors of the City of New York . . ." (New York, 1850), 4; *Republican Sentinel*, Aug. 3, 1844; *The People's Democratic Guide*, 1 (1841–42): preface, unpaginated; "Proceedings," Republican Convention, Virginia, 1839, 22.

20. *The Log Cabin*, July 4, Oct. 17, Dec. 26, 1840; *AR*, 3 (May 1846): 460; *The Battery*, July 27, 1848: 61; R. McKinley Ormsby, *A History of the Whig Party* (Boston, 1859), 185; "Proceedings of a State Convention of the Whig Young Men of Connecticut . . . February 26, 1840" (Hartford, 1840), 40.

21. *DR*, 36 (Nov. 1855): 393; *CG*, 25th Cong., 2d sess., *Appendix*, 275; *Argus*, May 9, 1844, Feb. 12, 1859.

22. "The Grounds of Difference Between the Contending Parties," *Whig Almanac, 1843* (New York, 1843): 16; *AR*, 10 (Nov. 1849): 443, 15 (Feb. 1852): 125; Albany, N.Y., *State Register*, April 2, 1850; Howe, *Political Culture*, 130.

23. Sean Wilentz, "On Class and Politics in Jacksonian America," *Reviews in American History*, 10 (Dec. 1982): 58; *CG*, 26th Cong., 1st sess., *Appendix*,

346; *Argus*, Aug. 7, 1841; Howe, *Political Culture*, 139; Kohl, *Politics of Individualism*.

24. "Address of the Central Hickory Club to the Republican Citizens of the United States [1832]" (Washington, D.C., 1832), 7; *Atlas and Argus*, July 8, 1856; *DR*, 22 (June 1848): 496, 28 (April 1851): 295; Samuel S. Bloom, "Why Are You a Democrat? Tersely Answered" (Cincinnati, 1880), 45; *Republican Sentinel*, April 6, 1844; *Atlas*, March 29, 1845.

25. *Atlas*, Oct. 4, 1843; *DR*, 32 (Feb. 1853): 105; Howe, *Political Culture*, 20, 198; *AR*, 16 (Sept. 1852): 275; Kohl, *Politics of Individualism*, 68; "Proceedings," Whig Convention, Utica, N.Y., 1840, 9.

26. *AR*, 9 (March 1849): 298, 15 (Jan. 1852): 10; Kohl, *Politics of Individualism*, 68; Ashworth, *Agrarians and Aristocrats*, 198; Michael A. Morrison, "Westward the Curse of Empire: Texas Annexation and the American Whig Party," *JER*, 10 (Summer 1990): 221–49.

27. *Papers for the People*, June n.d. (no. 1), 1852: 10–11.

28. Washington, D.C., *Evening Star*, Nov. 10, 1856; *The Campaign*, no. 13, Aug. 23, 1848: 193.

29. John A. Dix, speech to Tammany, in *The Campaign*, no. 6, July 17, 1852; *Argus*, June 9, 1837; James K. Polk to Henry Horn et al., in *Niles' Register*, April 11, 1838: 374; *New York Globe*, Jan. 12, 1849; "Resolutions of Democrats in the First Congressional District of Michigan, June 6, 1843," *Detroit Free Press*, June 8, 1843; *DR*, 2 (May 1838): 113; printed circular, Chautauqua County Correspondence Committee, July 134, 1840, in Henry O'Reilly Papers, New York Historical Society.

30. *New York Daily Globe*, Oct. 31, 1848; Kirk H. Porter and Donald Bruce Johnson, eds., *National Party Platforms, 1840–1964*, 2d ed. (Urbana: Univ. of Illinois Press, 1967), 2; *The Signal*, July 4, 1852: 56; New York *Evening Post*, March 8, 1841.

31. "Great Whig Demonstration in Favor of the Nomination of Gen. Taylor . . . at Philadelphia, February 22, 1848" (n.p., n.d.), 3; Irving Bartlett, *Daniel Webster* (New York: Norton, 1978), 153; *AR*, 15 (Feb. 1852): 134; *Ohio State Journal*, June 21, 1852; Seward, speech to Orleans County Whig Meeting, Aug. 21, 1848, in George Baker, ed., *The Works of William H. Seward* (New York: Redfield, 1853), 3: 410 *New Hampshire Statesman*, July 30, 1847.

32. *AR*, 5 (April 1847): 325. On foreign policy differences more generally, see Howe, *Political Culture*; Joel H. Silbey, *The Shrine of Party: Congressional Voting Behavior, 1841–1852* (Pittsburgh: Univ. of Pittsburgh Press, 1967), chaps. 5–6; and Morrison, "Westward the Curse of Empire."

33. "Speeches of Messrs. Weller, Orr, Lane and Cobb Delivered in Phoenix and Depot Halls, Concord, N. H. . . ." (n.p., [1856]), 17. See Oscar Handlin, *Boston's Immigrants: A Study in Acculturation*, rev. ed. (New York: Atheneum, 1959), and Ray Billington, *The Protestant Crusade, 1800–1860* (New York: Macmillan, 1938), for good introductions to the immigrant "menace."

On the political controversies stimulated by immigration, ethnicity, and religion, see especially Holt, *Political Crisis*; Robert Kelley, *The Cultural Pattern in American Politics: The First Century* (New York: Knopf, 1979); and Paul Kleppner, *The Cross of Culture: A Social Analysis of Midwestern Politics, 1850–1900* (New York: Free Press, 1970).

34. "Speech of Hon. Stephen A. Douglas, of Illinois, . . . Richmond, Virginia, July 9, 1852" (n.p., n.d.), 5; *Atlas and Argus*, May 26, 1860; *DR*, 37 (Jan. 1856): 11; *CG*, 26th Cong., 2nd sess., *Appendix*, 269, 271; "Proceedings," Democratic Convention, Ohio, 1844, 8; *The Young Guard*, July 29, 1848; *Argus*, Oct. 11, 1844; *Coon Dissector*, June 14, 1844; Washington, D.C., *Globe*, Aug. 31, 1844.

35. *DR*, 30 (March 1852): 273, 40 (Aug. 1857): 102; Benjamin Barstow, "A Letter to the Hon. James Buchanan" (Concord, N.H., 1857), 13–15; *Atlas*, Oct. 4, 1843.

36. William Seward to B.S. Esq., Nov. 2, 15, 1840, in Seward, *Works*, 3: 387, 389; "The Crisis! An Appeal to Our Countrymen, on the Subject of Foreign Influence in the United States" (New York, 1844), 10; Dayton, Ohio, *That Same Old Coon*, Aug. 31, 1844; *AR*, 13 (Jan. 1851): 2; *The Signal*, Oct. 30, 1852: 281; William G. Brownlow, *A Political Register . . .* (Jonesborough, Tenn., 1844), 110.

37. "Address of the National Democratic Republican Committee" (n.p., 1848), 3; *The Young Guard*, July 4, Aug. 26, 1848; *DR*, 36 (Oct. 1855): 342.

38. *Ohio State Journal*, June 11, 1844; *The Campaign*, no. 11, Aug. 21, 1852: 176; Washington, D.C., *Union*, Aug. 18, 1852.

38. *Ohio State Journal*, June 11, 1844; *The Campaign*, no. 11, Aug. 21, 1852: 176; Washington, D.C., *Union*, Aug. 18, 1852.

39. The rest of the paragraph says that "it would be followed by a strong Federal Government, a high tariff, a mammoth Federal bank, a system of internal improvements . . . and by all the concomitants of Federal ursurpation." William R. King et al., "To the Democratic Republican Party of Alabama" (n.p., [1840]), 6.

40. Isaac Holmes to Cobb, Aug. 21, 1847, in Ulrich B. Phillips, ed., *The Correspondence of Robert Toombs, Alexander Holmes Stephens and Howell Cobb, Annual Report of the American Historical Association for the Year 1911* (Washington, D.C., 1913), 88; *Charleston* [S.C.] *Mercury*, Feb. 22, 1848; Mobile, Ala., *Register*, Nov. 12, 1842, April 12, 1843. On Calhoun see, most recently, John Niven, *John C. Calhoun* (Baton Rouge: Louisiana State Univ. Press, 1988). On the South's sectional politics, see William J. Cooper, *The South and the Politics of Slavery, 1828–1856* (Baton Rouge: Louisiana State Univ. Press, 1978); and Joel H. Silbey, "The Southern National Democrats, 1846–1861," in *The Partisan Imperative: The Dynamics of American Politics Before the Civil War* (New York: Oxford Univ. Press, 1985), 116–26.

41. The best introduction to Democratic attitudes toward the territories is Robert Johannsen, *Stephen A. Douglas* (New York: Oxford Univ. Press, 1973). The Whig positions can be followed in a number of places. See especially Howe, *Political Culture*; Cooper, *South and Politics of Slavery*; and Holman Hamilton, *Zachary Taylor: Soldier in the White House* (Indianapolis: Bobbs-Merrill, 1951). Eric Foner, *Free Soil, Free Labor, Free Men: The Ideology of the Republi-*

can Party Before the Civil War (New York: Oxford Univ. Press, 1970), is the best introduction to the Republicans' views on the extension of slavery.

42. Speech, Douglas, Richmond, July 9, 1852, 1; Porter and Johnson, *National Party Platforms*, 2; Washington *Globe*, June 8, 1844.

43. Porter and Johnson, *National Party Platforms*, 8ff; *The Signal*, Sept. 4, 1852; 165; *AR*, 11 (Feb. 1850): 113.

44. Charles Grier Sellers, Jr., *James K. Polk, Jacksonian, 1795–1843* (Princeton, N.J.: Princeton University Press, 1957), 361; undated notes, late 1830's, in Daniel Ullmann Papers, New York Historical Society.

45. "Address and Resolutions Adopted at the Whig State Convention, Worcester, October 3, 1849 . . ." (Boston, 1849), 1; *Atlas and Argus*, March 31, 1856; Polk to Samuel H. Laughlin, March 9, 1841, *Correspondence of James Polk*, 5: 653. See also Sellers, *Polk, Jacksonian*, 439.

46. Thomas E. Jeffrey, "The Second Party System in North Carolina" (unpublished Ph.D. dissertation, Catholic University of America, 1976), 3, 24, chap. 7; Jeffrey, *State Parties and National Politics: North Carolina, 1815–1861* (Athens: Univ. of Georgia Press, 1989), 165; *That Same Old Coon*, Aug. 10, 1844; *The Rough Hewer*, Aug. 27, 1840: 217.

47. Samuel Kernall, "The Early Nationalization of Political News in America," in *Studies in American Political Development 1*, (New Haven, Conn.: Yale Univ. Press, 1986): 255–78; "Proceedings of the State Convention of the Whig Young Men of Massachusetts . . . September 11, 1839" (Boston, 1839), 24.

48. Printed circular, Chautauqua County Correspondence Committee, July 13, 1840, in the O'Reilly Papers; Marc Kruman, *Parties and Politics in North Carolina, 1836–1865* (Baton Rouge: Louisiana State Univ. Press, 1983), 138–39.

49. Porter and Johnson, *National Party Platforms*, 67–68. For some flavor of this continuity, follow the editorials in a Democratic newspaper like the New York *World*. See, for example the issues of Oct. 2, 1863, and Nov. 11, 1864.

50. See Chap. 7, below.

51. Porter and Johnson, *National Party Platforms*, 73–74; Foner, *Free Soil*. Good introductions to the Republican party in the post–Civil War era are Paul Kleppner, *The Third Electoral System, 1853–1892: Parties, Voters and Political Culture* (Chapel Hill: Univ. of North Carolina Press, 1979); and Richard Jensen, *The Winning of the Midwest: Social and Political Conflict, 1888–1896* (Chicago: Univ. of Chicago Press, 1971).

52. *Louisville Journal*, Sept. 8, 1852.

Chapter Five

1. Raleigh *Register*, June 23, 1840.

2. Daniel Walker Howe, "British Historians on the Second American Party System," *Reviews in American History*, 13 (Sept. 1985): 372; *CG*, 25th Cong., 3d sess., 54.

3. Charles Grier Sellers, Jr., "Election of 1844," in Arthur M. Schlesinger, Jr., ed., *History of American Presidential Elections* (New York: Chelsea House, 1971), 1: 786. As J. Willard Hurst has put it, "A good deal of melodrama is

inherent in a politics which must interest a wide public; there must be heroes and villains and plenty of action or the appearance of action." *Law and the Conditions of Freedom in the Nineteenth-Century United States* (Madison: Univ. of Wisconsin Press, 1956), 102n. See also Daniel T. Rodgers, *Contested Truths: Keywords in American Politics Since Independence* (New York: Basic Books, 1987), 90.

4. *Argus*, March 27, 1844.

5. Howe, "British Historians," 372–73. The Whigs labeled themselves the "Democratic-Whig Party" in their first national convention in 1839. *Proceedings of the Democratic Whig National Convention . . . (Harrisburg, 1839)*.

6. J. Mills Thornton, *Politics and Power in a Slave Society: Alabama, 1800–1860* (Baton Rouge: Louisiana State Univ. Press, 1978), 200, 348, 445.

7. *DR*, 7 (Jan. 1840): preface; "Proceedings of a Convention of Democratic Young Men . . . of Pennsylvania . . . Opposed to Martin Van Buren . . ." (Reading, 1838), 23; "Speech of R. Wickliffe, Jr. [of Kentucky] Delivered in the National Convention of the Whig Young Men of the United States. . . ." (Lexington, 1841), 4; *Advance Guard of Democracy*, Oct. 16, 1840; *Argus*, Sept. 4, 1840; John C. Smith, Jr., to Welles, March 7, 1842, in Gideon Welles Papers, New York Public Library; *Argus*, June 28, 1844; *DR*, 23 (Nov. 1848): 381; *Ohio State Journal*, Nov. 7, 1848; "To the People of Ohio. Proceedings and Address of the Democratic State Convention Held at Columbus, May 10, 1848" (Columbus, 1848), 15.

8. Thornton, *Politics and Power*, xvii; Michael F. Holt, *The Political Crisis of the 1850s* (New York: Wiley, 1978), 38; "To the People of Ohio . . . 1848," 15; "Speeches Delivered at Tammany Hall, New York City, September 2, 1852 . . . ," *Evening Post Documents No. 10* (n.p., n.d.), 10.

9. "Journal of the Proceedings of the National Republican Convention Held at Worcester, October 11, 1832," (Boston, 1832), 14; [Joseph F. Atwill], "The CRISIS! An Appeal to Our Countrymen, on the Subject of Foreign Influence in the United States" (New York, 1844), 10.

10. *DR*, 7 (June 1840): 485; William Winans to Messrs. Edmund Smith et al., Sept. 2, 1840, in Ray Holder, ed., "Long Live 'Tippecanoe'! Letters of a Mississippi Whig, 1840–1841," *Journal of Mississippi History*, 45 (Feb. 1983): 46.

11. Raleigh *North Carolina Standard*, Oct. 17, 1840; *Ohio State Journal*, June 20, 1856.

12. *DR*, 27 (Nov. 1850): 387, 14 (June 1844): 563, 38 (Aug. 1856): 3; *Papers for the People*, Sept. 11, 1852: 196; "To the True Democracy of Monroe and Orleans Counties, August 1, 1840," printed circular in Henry O'Reilly Papers, New York Historical Society; *Argus*, May 25, 1841; *Atlas*, Oct. 29, 1846; Polk to Andrew Jackson Donelson, Dec. 18, 1837, in Herbert Weaver, ed., *Correspondence of James K. Polk* (Nashville, Tenn.: Vanderbilt Univ. Press, 1977), 4: 296; *The Campaign*, Oct. 27, 1848: 374; "Voice of the Southwest: Proceedings of the Democratic State Convention of Tennessee at Nashville, February 11, 1840" (Nashville, 1840), 9; *CG*, 25th Cong., 2d sess., *Appendix*, 48.

13. *CG*, 26th Cong., 2d sess., *Appendix*, 155; [Charles G. Green and Benjamin F. Hallet], "Whigery Is Federalism" ([Boston, 1840]), 18, 23.

14. *Republican Sentinel*, April 6, June 29, Oct. 28, 1844; James K. Polk to

Henry Horn et al., July 14, 1838, in *Niles' Register*, Aug. 11, 1838: 374; *The Recruit*, Sept. 12, 1848; "Speeches at Tammany . . . 1852," 3; Richard Rush, "To the Democratic Citizens of Pennsylvania," (n.p., Sept. 1844), 8.

15. *North Carolina Standard*, April 5, 1843; *The Campaign*, no. 5, July 10, 1852; William Allen, "Mr. Clay's Declaration of Principles. . . ." (Washington, D.C., 1842), 7.

16. Allen, "Mr. Clay's Declaration," 1; *CG*, 26th Cong., 1st sess., *Appendix*, 537; "To the True Democracy . . ."; *Coon Dissector*, July 12, 1844; *The Recruit*, Oct. 24, 1848; *Argus*, Jan. 25, 1837; Washington, D.C., *Globe*, July 10, 1844.

17. *Illinois State Register*, May 25, 1838; *CG*, 25th Cong., 2d sess., *Appendix*, 53, 26th Cong., 1st sess., *Appendix*, 429; *Proceedings of the National Democratic Convention Held at Baltimore, May 5, 1840* (Baltimore, 1840), 4; *Atlas*, Oct. 29, 1846, Sept. 18, 1848; *Nashville Union*, June 15, 1840.

18. *Argus*, Nov. 27, 1852, May 5, 1855; Allen, "Mr. Clay's Declaration," 1; *CG*, 25th Cong., 2d sess., 421.

19. *CG*, 26th Cong., 2d sess., *Appendix*, 272; "To the People of Pennsylvania" (n.p., [1848]), 1; "Address of the Democratic Republican Young Men's General Committee of the City of New York . . . 1840" (New York, 1840), 4; *DR*, 8 (Aug. 1840): 174; *The Campaign*, no. 9, July 26, 1848: 141, no. 23, Oct. 25, 1848: 355; *Illinois State Register*, Aug. 11, 1843; "Address of the Democratic Convention [Nashville, Tenn., Nov. 1843]," (n.p., n.d.), 8. Throughout the 1840 presidential campaign, the Albany *Argus* headed its review of the stakes at issue with such titles as "Another Infamous Federal Forgery," "Hatred of Federalism Toward Foreigners," "More Ruin," "They Are Burying the Constitution," and "Gen. Harrison's Black Cockade Federalism."

20. Washington *Globe*, Oct. 26, 1844; Churchill C. Cambreleng to Messrs. George Seaman et al., Oct. 9, 1838, in *Niles' Register*, Nov. 3, 1838: 155; *The Yeoman*, April 30, 1841.

21. *The Young Guard*, Oct. 21, 1848; *Proceedings, Democratic National Convention, 1840*, 23; "A Refutation of Andrew Stewart's Fabrication Against General Lewis Cass" ([Washington, D.C.], 1848), 2; *The Recruit*, July 8, 1848; *The Campaign*, no. 20, Oct. 11, 1848: 307; *Argus*, July 30, 1838; *The Yeoman*, Oct. 8, 1841.

22. *AR*, 5 (April 1847): 325; *Argus*, Oct. 28, 1847; *Rough and Ready*, Dec. 26, 1846, Feb. 6, 1847; "Taylor Whiggery Exposed" ([Washington, D.C.], 1848), 3.

23. *DR*, 38 (Oct. 1856): 183, 40 (July 1857): 4, 40 (Aug. 1857): 103; *Atlas and Argus*, May 21, 1860.

24. *Richmond Whig*, Oct. 27, 1840.

25. "The Northern Man with Southern Principles and the Southern Man with American Principles, . . ." (Washington, D.C., 1840), 32; *AR*, 1 (Jan. 1845): 18, 16 (July 1852): 4, 79; *CG*, 25th Cong., 1st sess., 251; Troy, Ohio, *Investigator and Expositer*, 1.13 (July 1840): 177; *Illinois State Journal*, Aug. 31, 1852); *That Same Old Coon*, June 29, 1844.

26. *The Signal*, Oct. 16, 1852: 254; R. McKinley Ormsby, *A History of the Whig Party* (Boston, 1859), 285; *AR*, 16 (July 1852): 10; *Louisville Journal*, in

The Signal, Aug. 28, 1852; "To the People of Michigan," (n.p., [Aug. 20, 1844]), 2, 8.

27. *AR*, 15 (Feb. 1852): 135; *National Intelligencer*, Sept. 7, 1848; *New Hampshire Statesman*, Oct. 13, 1838; Daniel Walker Howe, *The Political Culture of the American Whigs* (Chicago: Univ. of Chicago Press, 1979), 35.

28. "Young Men's Whig State Convention" ([Connecticut, 1840]), 4; *CG*, 26th Cong., 1st sess., *Appendix*, 719; *AR*, 1 (Jan. 1845): 19, 16 (Aug. 1852): 102.

29. *Proceedings, Democratic Whig Convention, 1839* 13; *AR*, 1 (Jan. 1845): 2; *CG*, 26th Cong., 1st sess., 243; William G. Brownlow, *A Political Register* (Jonesborough, Tenn., 1844), 125.

30. *AR*, 3 (May 1846): 461, 15 (Feb. 1852): 124, 16 (Aug. 1852): 137; *Louisville Journal*, Nov. 9, 1852; Hartford *Connecticut Courant*, July 31, 1852.

31. *AR*, 1 (Jan. 1845): 15, 3 (May 1846): 461, 463, 15 (May 1852): 382; 16 (Aug. 1852), 132; *The Log Cabin*, June 13, 1840.

32. *The Log Cabin*, Sept. 5, 1840; *AR*, 16 (July 1852): 10; "Whig Textbook, or Democracy Unmasked," (Washington, D.C., [1844]), 30; *Richmond Whig*, June 4, 1844.

33. *The Rail Splitter*, Aug. 15, 1860. The 1860's remarks are quoted in Joel H. Silbey, *A Respectable Minority: The Democratic Party in the Civil War Era, 1860–1868* (New York: Norton, 1978), 167n.

34. Roy F. Nichols and Jeanette P. Nichols, "Election of 1852," in Schlesinger, *American Presidential Elections*, 2: 921–1003.

35. Ibid.; Kirk H. Porter and Donald Bruce Johnson, *National Party Platforms, 1840–1964* (Urbana: Univ. of Illinois Press, 1967), 16–21.

36. *Nashville Union*, Oct. 27, 1852; "Speech of Hon. John A. Dix, of New York, at the Mass Meeting [Newburgh] . . . 26th of July, 1852" (n.p., n.d.), 1; *DR*, 31 (July 1852): 88; *Papers for the People*, Oct. 9, 1852: 276–77.

37. *The Campaign*, no. 8, July 31, 1852: 124; *Stars and Stripes*, Sept. 9, 1852; *Papers for the People*, Aug. 14, 1852: 132–33.

38. *The Campaign*, no. 7, July 24, 1852; *Papers for The People*, July 31, 1852: 91–92; "Letter from Hon. Harry Hibbard, . . ." (n.p., [1852]), 4.

39. *The Campaign*, no. 9, Aug. 7, 1852: 129–30, no. 12, Aug. 28, 1852: 178; *Papers for The People*, Aug. 28, 1852: 158. The Democrats, on the other hand, had "rushed to the defense" of the alien and Catholic, "no matter at what cost or at what sacrifice." *The Campaign*, no. 11, Aug. 21, 1852: 166.

40. Washington, D.C., *Union*, Aug. 28, 1852; *Stars and Stripes*, Sept. 30, Oct. 7, 1852; *The Campaign*, no. 11, Aug. 21, 1852: 167.

41. *The Campaign*, no. 1, June 12, 1852: 1, no. 4, July 3, 1852: 49, no. 18, Oct. 9, 1852: 273; Speech, John Dix, 2; "Sketches of the Lives of Franklin Pierce and Wm. R. King . . ." ([Washington, D.C.]), 1852), 8.

42. *AR*, 15 (April 1852): 294, 16 (Sept. 1852): 194–95; *Ohio State Journal*, July 15, Sept. 13, 1852.

43. *AR*, 16 (July 1852): 10; *The Signal*, July 1, Oct. 30, 1852.

44. *Ohio State Journal*, Oct. 28, 1852; *New Hampshire Statesman*, Oct. 9, 1852; *The Signal*, Aug. 14, 1852; *Illinois State Journal*, Aug. 3, 1852.

45. Robert Wiebe, *The Opening of American Society, from the Adoption of the Constitution to the Eve of Disunion* (New York: Knopf, 1984), 295; Thomas W. Thomas to Cobb, June 5, 1848, in Ulrich B. Phillips, ed. *The Correspondence of Robert Toombs, Alexander Holmes Stephens and Howell Cobb: Annual Report of the American Historical Association for the Year 1911* (Washington, D.C., 1913), 107.

46. Kenneth Lynn, "The Regressive Historians," *American Scholar*, 47 (Autumn 1978): 473.

Chapter Six

1. *The Signal*, Oct. 2, 1852; *Atlas and Argus*, Aug. 30, 1856, March 19, 1860; *Republican Sentinel*, May 11, 1844; *Stars and Stripes*, Sept. 30, 1852; *The Rail Splitter*, Aug. 22, 1860.

2. Washington, D.C., *Union*, June 24, 1848; *DR*, 33 (July 1853): 85; "Speech of the Hon. John Minor Botts . . . Delivered at the Academy of Music . . . 22nd February, 1859 . . ." (New York, 1859), 12.

3. Washington, D.C., *United States Telegraph*, Nov. 17, 1836; *Union*, June 24, 1848; "Address to the People of Massachusetts" (n.p., [1851]), 12; *Atlas*, Sept. 20, 1843, Jan. 2, 1854.

4. *United States Telegraph*, June 24, 1848; "Proceedings of a Convention of Democratic Young Men . . . of Pennsylvania . . . Opposed to Martin Van Buren . . ." (Reading, 1838), 14; "Proceedings of a State Convention of Delegates Friendly to the Election of William Henry Harrison . . ." (Albany, 1836), 15–16; *DR*, 5 (April 1839): 359; "State of New York. Republican Legislative Address and Resolutions. 1836" (n.p., n.d.), 2; Mobile, Ala., *Register*, Nov. 6, 1838. Republicans turned out to be no better. They were a "scheming, . . . sneaking, double-faced bargaining coalition of factions." *Atlas and Argus*, Sept. 15, 1856.

5. "Address of the Democratic Hickory Club [of] Philadelphia, to Recommend Martin Van Buren as the Presidential Candidate for 1844" (n.p., n.d.), 1; *DR*, 14 (Jan. 1844): 89; *Atlas*, Sept. 20, 1843.

6. *DR*, 8 (Sept. 1840): 200, 11 (July 1842): 95; 14 (Jan. 1844): 89; *Advance Guard of Democracy*, May 22, 1840, June 5, 1840: 81, Sept. 18, 1840: 314; *The Yeoman*, Oct. 8, 1841; *Republican Sentinel*, March 16, 1844; *Argus*, Nov. 12, 1840; "Address of the Democratic Republican Young Men's General Committee of the City of New York . . . 1840" (New York, 1840), 3.

7. *Advance Guard*, June 26, 1840: 133; Chatauqua County, New York Correspondence Committee, printed circular, July 13, 1840, in Henry O'Reilly Papers, New York Historical Society; *Atlas*, May 17, 1843; *North Carolina Standard*, Oct. 7, 1840.

8. Mobile *Register*, Nov. 16, 1840; "Address of the Democratic Association of Norwich" ([Connecticut, 1844–45?]), 10; *New York Globe*, March 18, 1847; Richmond, Va., *Enquirer*, Oct. 23, 1844; Chicago *Weekly Democrat*, Oct. 23, 1844.

9. *The Campaign*, no. 3, June 14, no. 5, June 28, no. 18, Sept. 27, no. 19, Oct. 4, 1848; *The Young Guard*, Aug. 19, Oct. 7, 1848; "Taylor Whiggery Exposed" (n.p., 1848), 8; "The Democratic Policy and Its Fruits" (n.p., 1848), 7; *Illinois*

State Register, June 23, 1848; Milledgeville, Ga., *Federal Union*, Nov. 7, 1848; *Nashville Union*, Nov. 10, 1848; Washington, D.C., *Union*, June 22, 1848.

10. "To the People of Michigan" ([Detroit, 1844]), 1; *That Same Old Coon*, June 29, 1844; *Richmond Whig*, July 14, 1840, Nov. 12, 1844; *The Battery*, Nov. 2, 1848: 288; Groton, Mass., *Spirit of the Times*, Dec. 30, 1848. The Democrats and Whigs attacked the Free Soil party in 1848 in the same terms, with the latter responding in kind. See, as examples, *The Recruit*, Aug. 22, 1848; *The Campaign*, no. 6, July 5, 1848; and *The Barnburner*, Aug. 11, 26, Sept. 2, 1848.

11. *Richmond Whig*, July 28, 1840, Oct. 1, 1852; "Great Whig Demonstration in Favor of the Nomination of Gen. Taylor . . . at Philadelphia, February 22, 1848" (n.p., n.d.), 7; Louisville, Ky., *Journal*, Aug. 3, 1852.

12. Troy, Ohio, *Investigator and Expositor*, 1.3, (Sept. 1839): 42; Henry B. Stanton to Randall, Nov. 11, 1850, in Henry S. Randall Papers, New York Historical Society; J. W. Edmonds to Flagg, Nov. 12, 1839, in Azariah C. Flagg Papers, New York Public Library.

13. "Proceedings of the State National Democratic Convention of Iowa . . . 1860" (Davenport, 1860), 8; *Atlas*, Feb. 22, 1843; *New York Daily Globe*, Nov. 15, 1848.

14. *The Grape Shot*, Aug. 12, 1848; *DR*, 6 (Dec. 1839): 507.

15. *Ohio State Journal*, May 30, 1844. For the persistent difficulties over state-level issues that divided and frustrated parties in one major state, see Thomas E. Jeffrey, *State Parties and National Politics: North Carolina, 1815–1861* (Athens: Univ. of Georgia Press, 1989).

16. *Southern Banner*, Dec. 14, 1843; *AR*, 2 (July 1845): 2; *Federal Union*, July 27, 1841.

17. *Illinois State Register*, April 28, 1848; Wooster Sherman to Chairman, Tammany Committee, Nov. 3, 1859, in Isaac V. Fowler Papers, New York Historical Society; Richmond *Enquirer*, Oct. 17, 1843; *Richmond Whig*, Feb. 15, 1848; *Atlas*, July 26, 1843.

18. Portland *Eastern Argus*, May 27, 1847, quoted in Richard R. Westcott, "A History of Maine Politics, 1840–1857: The Origins of the Republican Party" (Ph.D. dissertation, Univ. of Maine, 1966), 87; "Address and Resolutions Adopted at the Whig State Convention, Worcester, October 3, 1849 . . ." (Boston, 1849), 21; *Nashville Union*, July 3, 1846.

19. Major L. Wilson, *Space, Time and Freedom: The Quest for Nationality and the Irrepressible Conflict, 1815–1861* (Westport, Conn.: Greenwood Press, 1974), 138; Joel H. Silbey, *A Respectable Minority: The Democratic Party in the Civil War Era, 1860–1868* (New York: Norton, 1978), 106ff.

20. Richard Jensen, *The Winning of the Midwest: Social and Political Conflict, 1888–1896* (Chicago: Univ. of Chicago Press, 1971), 190; *Argus*, Aug. 4, 1851; Preston King to Flagg, Nov. 22, 1837, in the Flagg Papers; "Address and Resolutions Adopted at the Whig State Convention, Worcester, October 3, 1849" (Boston, 1849), 21.

21. *Argus*, Sept. 13, 1853; *The Yeoman*, June 25, 1841; *AR*, 15 (March 1852): 266; "Great Whig Demonstration," 1848, 21.

22. Richmond *Enquirer*, July 1844, as quoted in Charles Grier Sellers, Jr.,

James K. Polk, Continentalist, 1843–1846 (Princeton, N.J.: Princeton Univ. Press, 1966), 137; "Great Whig Demonstration," 1848, 11; "Taylor Whiggery Exposed," 5; Johnson speech at Fayetteville, Tenn., Oct. 1, 1860, in LeRoy P. Graf and Ralph W. Haskins, *The Papers of Andrew Johnson* (Knoxville: Univ. of Tennessee Press, 1972), 3: 665; Raleigh *Register*, May 27, 1848.

23. *New Hampshire Statesman*, May 18, 1839, June 19, 26, 1852; *Illinois State Journal*, July 9, 1852; *National Intelligencer*, June 14, 1848; Mobile *Register*, Oct. 25, 1838; *Illinois State Register*, July 31, 1846; *Springfield*, Mass., *Republican*, Nov. 9, 1844; *Richmond Whig*, Oct. 22, 1852.

24. *AR*, 15 (May 1852): 380; "Proceedings of the Democratic National Convention Held at Baltimore, June 1–5, 1852 . . ." (Washington, D.C., 1852), 48.

25. *Ohio State Journal*, Feb. 25, 1840; Edward Pessen, *The Log Cabin Myth: The Social Background of the Presidents* (New Haven, Conn.: Yale Univ. Press, 1984).

26. Anthony Upton, "The Road to Power in Virginia in the Early Nineteenth Century," *Virginia Magazine of History and Biography*, 62 (July 1954): 280; Sidney Aronson, *Status and Kinship in the Higher Civil Service: Standards of Selection in the Administrations of John Adams, Thomas Jefferson and Andrew Jackson* (Cambridge, Mass.: Harvard University Press, 1964), 62; J. R. Pole, "Representation and Authority in Virginia from the Revolution to Reform," *Journal of Southern History*, 24 (Feb. 1958): 48.

27. For particularly useful descriptions of local, state, and regional leadership patterns, see Whitman Ridgway, *Community Leadership in Maryland, 1790–1840: A Comparative Analysis of Power in Society* (Chapel Hill: Univ. of North Carolina Press, 1979); J. Mills Thornton, *Politics and Power in a Slave Society: Alabama, 1800–1860* (Baton Rouge: Louisiana State Univ. Press, 1978); Harry Watson, *Jacksonian Politics and Community Conflict: The Emergence of the Second American Party System in Cumberland County, North Carolina* (Baton Rouge: Louisiana State Univ. Press, 1981); Stuart Blumin, *The Urban Threshold: Growth and Change in a Nineteenth-Century American Community* (Chicago: Univ. of Chicago Press, 1976); and Edward Pessen, *Riches, Class and Power Before the Civil War* (Lexington, Mass.: Addison-Wesley, 1973). On members of Congress, see Allan G. Bogue, Jerome M. Clubb, Carroll R. McKibbin, and Santa Traugott, "Members of the House of Representatives and the Processes of Modernization, 1789–1960," *JAR*, 63 (Sept. 1976): 275–302; and Daniel P. Jordan, *Political Leadership in Jefferson's Virginia* (Charlottesville: Univ. Press of Virginia, 1983). Much of this material is summarized in M. J. Heale, *The Making of American Politics, 1750–1850* (London: Longman, 1977), 157.

28. Marc Kruman, *Parties and Politics in North Carolina, 1836–1865* (Baton Rouge: Louisiana State Univ. Press, 1983), 46–47; Merle Curti, *The Making of an American Community: A Case Study of Democracy in a Frontier County* (Stanford, Calif.: Stanford Univ. Press, 1959), 38. See also Don Harrison Doyle, *The Social Order of a Frontier Community: Jacksonville, Illinois, 1825–1870* (Urbana: Univ. of Illinois Press); Richard S. Alcorn, "Leadership and Stability in Mid-Nineteenth Century America: A Case Study of an Illinois Town," *JAR*, 61

(Dec. 1974): 685–702; and Randolph Campbell and Richard G. Lowe, *Wealth and Power in Antebellum Texas* (College Station: Texas A&M Univ. Press, 1977). Also consult these studies by Ralph Wooster: *The People in Power: Courthouse and Statehouse in the Lower South, 1850–1860* (Knoxville: Univ. of Tennessee Press, 1969); *Politicians, Planters and Plain Folk: Courthouse and Statehouse in the Upper South, 1850–1860* (Knoxville: Univ. of Tennessee Press, 1975); and *The Secession Conventions of the South* (Princeton, N.J.: Princeton Univ. Press, 1962).

29. Alexandra McCoy, "The Political Affiliation of American Economic Elites: Wayne County, Michigan, 1844, 1860, as a Test Case" (Ph.D. dissertation, Wayne State Univ., 1961); Kathleen Smith Kutalowski, "Antimasonry Reexamined: Social Bases of the Grass Roots Party," *JAH*, 71 (Sept. 1984): 269–83; Watson, *Jacksonian Politics*.

30. The quotation is from Ronald P. Formisano, *The Transformation of Political Culture: Massachusetts Parties, 1790s–1840s* (New York: Oxford Univ. Press, 1983), 105. As the columnist George Will has written, "Among the weaknesses incidental to humanity is a reluctance to credit eminent persons with commonplace motives." *Ithaca Journal*, Dec. 3, 1982. See also Edward Pessen, "How Different from Each Other Were the Antebellum North and South?," *AHR*, 85 (Dec. 1980): 1119–49; and Lawrence F. Kohl, "The Concept of Social Control and the History of Jacksonian America," *JER*, 5 (Spring 1985): 21–34.

31. William Freehling, "Spoilsmen and Interests in the Thought and Career of John C. Calhoun, *JAR*, 52 (June 1965): 26–27, 29; McLean to Teesdale, March 8, 1856, in William Salter, ed., "Letters of John McLean to John Teesdale" *Bibliotheca Sacra*, 36 (Oct. 1879): 739.

32. On republicanism and its role in the 1840's and 1850's, see Michael Holt, *The Political Crisis of the 1850s* (New York: Wiley, 1978); and Pessen, "How Different Were the Antebellum North and South?"; Martin Van Buren's recent biographers are good on this. See Donald B. Cole, *Martin Van Buren and the American Political System* (Princeton, N.J.: Princeton Univ. Press, 1984); and John Niven, *Martin Van Buren: The Romantic Age of American Politics* (New York: Oxford Univ. Press, 1983).

33. William Badgley to Ullmann, Oct. 25, 1851, in Daniel Ullmann Papers, New York Historical Society; "The Lecompton Question. Governor Wise's . . . Letters . . . (n.p., [1857–58]), 13–14; Giovanni Sartori, *Parties and Party Systems: A Framework for Analysis* (London: Cambridge Univ. Press, 1976), 25.

34. "Lecompton Question," 51; *New York Tribune*, July 24, 1858; *Ohio State Journal*, Feb. 25, 1840, Nov. 1, 1848.

35. Hendrik Booraem, *The Formation of the Republican Party in New York: Politics and Conscience* (New York: New York Univ. Press, 1983), 95.

36. Ibid., 92; Thornton, *Politics and Power*, 116, 151, 201, 331. Sometimes convention delegates did not follow the dictates of electability and accept the leaders' choice. "The fact is, the county delegates made the nominations as they pleased," Lincoln complained. Letter to John T. Stuart, March 26, 1840, in Roy P. Basler, ed., *The Collected Works of Abraham Lincoln* (New Brunswick, N.J.: Rutgers Univ. Press, 1953), 1: 208.

37. Thornton, *Politics and Power*, 201.

38. King to Jabez D. Hammond, Aug. 11, 1852, in Preston King Papers, New York Historical Society; W. D. Moseley to Polk, Nov. 29, 1832, in Herbert Weaver, ed., *The Correspondence of James K. Polk* (Nashville, Tenn.: Vanderbilt Univ. Press, 1969), 1: 546.

39. Robert Wiebe, *The Opening of American Society, from the Adoption of the Constitution to the Eve of Disunion* (New York: Knopf, 1984), 295.

Chapter Seven

1. William J. Cooper, *Liberty and Slavery: Southern Politics to 1860* (New York: Knopf, 1983), 200.

2. *New York Evening Post*, Sept. 25, 1858, as quoted in Richard A. Heckman, "The Douglas-Lincoln Campaign of 1858" (Ph.D. dissertation, Univ. of Indiana, 1960), 70.

3. See William Gienapp, "'Politics Seems to Enter into Everything': Political Culture in the North, 1840–1860," in Stephen E. Maizlish and John J. Kushma, eds., *Essays on American Antebellum Politics, 1840–1860* (College Station: Texas A&M Univ. Press, 1982), 14–69.

4. "The Parties of the Day. Speech of William H. Seward at Auburn, October 21, 1856" (Washington, D.C. 1857), 3, 4; "Speech of John H. George, Esq., of Concord at the Mass Convention of the Democracy of New Hampshire . . . June 10, 1852" (n.p., n.d.), 4.

5. "Speech of General J. Watson Webb at the Great Mass Meeting on the Battle Ground of Tippecanoe" (New York, 1856), 9; William J. Duane to William Lyon Mackenzie, July 16, 1839, in Lillian Gates, "*Mackenzie's Gazette*: An Aspect of W. L. Mackenzie's American Years," *Canadian Historical Review*, 46 (Dec. 1965): 342; Don S. Fehrenbacher, *The Dred Scott Case: Its Significance in American Law and Politics* (New York: Oxford Univ. Press, 1981), 479. For an excellent description of this feeling, see Paula Baker, "The Domestication of Politics: Women and American Political Society, 1780–1920," *AHR*, 89 (June 1984): 620–47.

6. *CG*, 30th Cong., 1st sess., *Appendix*, 775; Seward to John C. Clark, Nov. 4, 1843, in George Baker, ed., *The Works of William H. Seward* (New York: Redfield, 1853), 3: 391.

7. *CG*, 30th Cong., 1st sess., *Appendix*, 775; *The Recruit*, Sept. 19, 1848; Nahum Capen, *The History of Democracy in the United States* (Boston: H. Wentworth, 1852), 1: 1; Sumner, as quoted in Richard Hofstadter, *The Idea of a Party System* (Berkeley: Univ. of California Press, 1969), 269. Such paeans were a regular feature of public political discourse for the rest of the 19th century. As the editor of the New York *Nation* summed up in the May 29, 1866 issue, his generation believed that parties were "essential instruments in the conduct of public affairs."

8. Morton Keller, "The Politicos Reconsidered," *Perspectives in American History*, 1 (1967): 405.

9. Edward Spann, *New Metropolis: New York City, 1840–1857* (New York:

Columbia Univ. Press, 1981), 335; William R. Brock, *Parties and Political Conscience: American Dilemmas, 1840–1850* (Millwood, N.Y.: KTO Press, 1979), 35.

10. *CG*, 26th Cong., 1st sess., 44; *Argus*, June 5, 1844; *AR*, 5 (June 1847): 621, 9 (June 1849): 553.

11. Cave J. Couts to Polk, Jan. 13, 1841, in Wayne Cutler, ed., *The Correspondence of James K. Polk* (Nashville: Vanderbilt Univ. Press, 1979), 5: 65; "Official Proceedings of the National Democratic Convention Held in Cincinnati, June 2–6, 1856)" (Cincinnati, 1856), 22; Michael Wallace, "Ideologies of Party in the Early Republic" (Ph.D. dissertation, Columbia Univ., 1973), 150; *New York Courier and Enquirer*, July 28, 1858; Roy F. Nichols, *Franklin Pierce: Young Hickory of the Granite Hills*, 2d ed. (Philadelphia: Univ. of Pennsylvania Press, 1958), 47; James W. Neilson, *Shelby M. Cullom, Prairie State Politician* (Urbana: Univ. of Illinois Press, 1962), 292.

12. Brand Whitlock, *Forty Years of It* (New York: Appleton & Co., 1914), 27, 32.

13. *DR*, 12 (May 1843): 485; *New Hampshire Statesman*, Feb. 17, 1843; *New York Daily Globe*, Jan. 29, 1849; *Ohio State Journal*, July 2, 1859.

14. Ronald Formisano, *The Transformation of Political Culture: Massachusetts Parties, 1790s–1840s* (New York: Oxford Univ. Press, 1983), 280; Melvin Philip Lucas, "The Development of the Second Party System in Mississippi, 1817–1846" (Ph.D. dissertation, Cornell Univ., 1983), 467. Horace Greeley, lamenting the Democrats' pull on their adherents, said that "they may have a roast baby for breakfast every morning, with missionary steaks for dinner, and yet rule the country forever." Letter to J. S. Pike, April 28, 1850, quoted in Jeter Isely, *Horace Greeley and the Republican Party, 1853–1861: A Study of the New York Tribune* (Princeton, N.J.: Princeton Univ. Press, 1947), 34.

15. Joseph Harrison, "*Sic et Non*: Thomas Jefferson and Internal Improvement," *JER*, 7 (Winter 1987): 335–49. On early sectionalism one can begin with William J. Cooper, *The South and the Politics of Slavery, 1828–1856* (Baton Rouge: Louisiana State Univ. Press, 1978), and come up to Richard P. McCormick, "The Jacksonian Strategy," *JER*, 10 (Spring 1990): 1–17. Older but still useful studies are Donald Robinson, *Slavery in the Structure of American Politics, 1765–1820* (New York: Harcourt Brace, Jovanovich, 1970); Charles Sydnor, *The Development of Southern Sectionalism, 1819–1848* (Baton Rouge: Louisiana State Univ. Press, 1948); and Glover Moore, *The Missouri Controversy, 1819–1821* (Lexington: Univ. of Kentucky Press, 1953).

16. Kenneth S. Greenberg, *Masters and Statesmen: The Political Culture of American Slavery* (Baltimore: Johns Hopkins Univ. Press, 1985); James Oakes, "From Republicanism to Liberalism: Ideological Change and the Crisis of the Old South," *American Quarterly*, 37 (Fall 1985): 551–71; Joel H. Silbey, *The Partisan Imperative: The Dynamics of American Politics Before the Civil War* (New York: Oxford Univ. Press, 1985). The most compelling and sophisticated analysis of southern political thought and behavior in the ante-bellum period in all its complexity is now William H. Freehling, *The Road to Disunion: Secessionists at Bay, 1776–1854* (New York: Oxford Univ. Press, 1990).

17. "Responsible leaders of both parties sought to enforce the norm that banned the slavery issue from national politics." McCormick, "Jacksonian Strategy," 15. The quotations in the text are in Lacy K. Ford, Jr., *Origins of Southern Radicalism: The South Carolina Upcountry, 1800–1860* (New York: Oxford Univ. Press, 1988), 191; Cooper, *Politics of Slavery*, 41–42, 164–65.

18. Mobile *Register*, Dec. 19, 1842; Milledgeville, Ga., *Federal Union*, May 16, 1843; Little Rock *Arkansas Banner*, Feb. 20, 1844; J. Mills Thornton, III, *Politics and Power in a Slave Society: Alabama 1800–1860* (Baton Rouge: Louisiana State Univ. Press, 1978), 445. Compare Joel H. Silbey, "John C. Calhoun and the Limits of Southern Congressional Unity," *The Historian*, 30 (Nov. 1967): 58–71; M. Philip Lucas, "'To Carry Out Great Fundamental Principles': The Antebellum Southern Political Culture," *Journal of Mississippi History*, 52 (Feb. 1990): 1–22; and Daniel W. Crofts, *Reluctant Confederates: Upper South Unionists in the Secession Crisis* (Chapel Hill: Univ. of North Carolina Press, 1989). South Carolina was the exception: "Though loosely aligned with the Democratic party, [it] remained largely outside the national party system." What political opposition there was "emerged on an *ad hoc* basis from a variety of quarters, but never coalesced into anything resembling an organized opposition party." Ford, *Origins of Southern Radicalism*, 183.

19. *AR*, 11 (June 1850): 555; Chaplain Morrison, *The Democratic Party and Sectionalism: The Wilmot Proviso Controversy* (Chapel Hill: Univ. of North Carolina Press, 1967); Richard Sewell, *Ballots for Freedom: Antislavery Politics in the United States, 1837–1860* (New York: Oxford Univ. Press, 1976); Vernon L. Volpe, *Forlorn Hope of Freedom: The Liberty Party in the Old Northwest, 1838–1848* (Kent, Ohio: Kent State Univ. Press, 1990).

20. Joseph Rayback, *Free Soil: The Election of 1848* (Lexington: Univ. of Kentucky Press, 1971); John Mayfield, *Rehearsal for Republicanism: Free Soil and the Politics of Antislavery* (Port Washington, N.Y.: Kennikat, 1980); Frederick Blue, *The Free Soilers: Third Party Politics, 1848–1854* (Urbana: Univ. of Illinois Press, 1973); John Niven, *Martin Van Buren: The Romantic Age of American Politics* (New York: Oxford Univ. Press, 1983); Donald B. Cole, *Martin Van Buren and the American Political System* (Princeton, N.J.: Princeton Univ. Press, 1984).

21. Cooper, *Politics of Slavery*, 165; "An Appeal to the People of Massachusetts on the Texas Question" (Boston, 1844), 15, 19; *Republican Sentinel*, June 8, 1844. "The most important factor affecting the Free Soil election was party loyalty." Rayback, *Free Soil*, 288.

22. Isaac Holmes to Cobb, Aug. 21, 1847, in Ulrich B. Phillips, ed., *The Correspondence of Robert Toombs, Alexander Holmes Stephens and Howell Cobb: Annual Report of the American Historical Association for 1911* (Washington, D.C., 1913), 88; New York *Evening Post*, Oct. 14, 1848; *The Young Guard*, Aug. 26, 1848; Raleigh *Register*, April 8, 1848; "Address Adopted by the Whig State Convention . . . Worcester, September 13, 1848" (n.p., n.d.), 13; Brock, *Parties and Political Conscience*, 207; Portland *Daily Advertiser*, Nov. 13, 1848, as quoted in Richard R. Westcott, "A History of Maine Politics, 1840–1856: The Formation of the Republican Party" (Ph.D. dissertation, Univ. of Maine, 1967), 116; *Ohio State Journal*, April 21, June 16, 1848.

23. "Speech of the Hon. Daniel Webster, Delivered at Marshfield, Sept. 1, 1848" (n.p., n.d.), 4; Bradish speech at the Young Men's Henry Clay Association Meeting, New York City, Feb. 12, 1848, as quoted in Louis B. Gimelli, "Luther Bradish, 1783–1863" (Ph.D. dissertation, New York Univ., 1964), 240; "Address Adopted by the Whig Convention," 12.

24. Niven, *Van Buren*, 585; John Wentworth to Kimberly, June 27, 1848, in E. S. Kimberly Papers, Chicago Historical Society; *Chicago Democrat*, Dec. 22, 1848.

25. Quoted in Rayback, *Free Soil*, 232; Washington, D.C., *Union*, June 17, 1847.

26. Alfred E. Burr to Welles, Aug. 9, 1849, in Gideon Welles Papers, Connecticut Historical Society; *New York Daily Globe*, Nov. 2, 1848.

27. *The Recruit*, July 19, 1848; *The Young Guard*, Aug. 19, 1848; *Federal Union*, Jan. 30, 1849. William Freehling's characterization is particularly apt: "The southern attachment to national parties, at a moment when neither party served the region's anti-Proviso frenzy, showed the strength of the two-party system in the South. . . . By saying no to Calhoun, national party leaders, speaking for a million southern voters out in the countryside, declared that party shrines remained too holy to be abandoned over this probably temporary crisis." *Road to Disunion*, 479–80.

28. *AR*, 9 (June 1849): 553, 14 (Nov. 1851): 434; *New York Daily Globe*, Jan. 29, 1849; Natchez *Daily Courier*, Oct. 26, 1852.

29. The best introduction to the renewal of sectional conflict and the subsequent political realignment is Michael F. Holt, *The Political Crisis of the 1850s* (New York: Wiley, 1978).

30. Arthur Holmes, *Parties and Their Principles: A Manual of Political Intelligence* (New York: Appleton & Co., 1859), 319.

31. Such realignments have been a cyclical phenomenon in American electoral history—or at least in part of it. See, most recently, Joel H. Silbey, "Beyond Realignment and Realignment Theory: American Political Eras, 1789–1989," in Byron Shafer, ed., *The End of Realignment?* (Madison: Univ. of Wisconsin Press, 1991), 3–23. On the realignment of the 1850's, see William Gienapp, *The Origins of the Republican Party, 1852–1856* (New York: Oxford Univ. Press, 1987).

32. "Speech of Hon. Horatio Seymour, Delivered at Tammany Hall, . . . Sep. 28, 1855" (n.p., n.d.), 9; Silbey, *Partisan Imperative, passim*.

33. See above, in the discussions of organization, argument, and commitment. On Whig antipartyism, see Daniel Walker Howe's excellent and nuanced *The Political Culture of the American Whigs* (Chicago: Univ. of Chicago Press, 1979).

34. Gienapp, *Origins of Republican Party*, chap. 1; "Correspondence Between Hon. Hamilton Fish . . . and Hon. James A. Hamilton" (n.p., [1856]), 1; George E. Baker to Seward, Oct. 19, 1855, in William Henry Seward Papers, New York Historical Society. See also "Speech of the Hon. John Minor Botts . . . Sept. 19, 1853," (Newark, N.J., 1853).

35. See below, Chap. 11.

36. Crofts, *Reluctant Confederates*, chap. 2. The quote is at p. 37. See also Thomas E. Jeffrey, *State Parties and National Politics: North Carolina, 1815–1861* (Athens: Univ. of Georgia Press, 1989), chap. 11.

37. The Democrats certainly believed that such expressions by the Whigs were tactical, not ideological, a phony "indifference to party." The Whig "delicacy which rejects party machinery, and deplores every manifestation of party spirit seems peculiar to minorities." *Atlas*, June 2, 1846.

38. Vincent P. DeSantis, *Republicans Face the Southern Question: The New Departure Years, 1877–1897* (Baltimore: Johns Hopkins Univ. Press, 1959); Stanley P. Hirshon, *Farewell to the Bloody Shirt: Northern Republicans and the Southern Negro, 1877–1893* (Bloomington: Indiana Univ. Press, 1962); Richard H. Abbott, *The Republican Party and the South* (Chapel Hill: Univ. of North Carolina Press, 1986). On the solid South see, most recently, Dewey Grantham, *The Life and Death of the Solid South* (Lexington: Univ. of Kentucky Press, 1988).

Chapter Eight

1. New York *Journal of Commerce*, in Albany *Evening Journal*, Nov. 7, 1838. In the 1840's, one state held gubernatorial, congressional, and/or state legislative elections in March; three more did so in April and May; one did in July; nine did in August; ten held theirs in October; and only nine scheduled their nonpresidential elections in November. Until 1845, the date of the presidential election also varied across the calendar. Congress then set it in November, on "the Tuesday next after the first Monday of the year in which they are to be appointed." See Richard P. McCormick, *The Presidential Game: The Origins of American Presidential Politics* (New York: Oxford Univ. Press, 1982), 208.

2. Natchez, Miss., *Daily Courier*, Oct. 26, 1852.

3. Chilton Williamson, *American Suffrage: From Property to Democracy, 1760–1860* (Princeton, N.J.: Princeton Univ. Press, 1960); Kirk H. Porter, *A History of Suffrage in the United States* (Chicago: Univ. of Chicago Press, 1918); Leon E. Aylesworth, "The Passing of Alien Suffrage," *American Political Science Review*, 25 (Feb. 1931): 114–16; J. Mills Thornton, *Politics and Power in a Slave Society: Alabama, 1800–1860* (Baton Rouge: Louisiana State Univ. Press, 1978), 70.

4. *CG*, 26th Cong., 2d sess., *Appendix*, 246; Baltimore *Sun*, Oct. 7, 1846; Concord, N.H. *Tough and Steady*, March 2, 1847.

5. Don H. Doyle, *The Social Order of a Frontier Community: Jacksonville, Illinois, 1825–1870* (Urbana: Univ. of Illinois Press, 1978), 172. The bitter debate over a registration law in one state is a theme in Joel H. Silbey, *The Partisan Imperative: The Dynamics of American Politics Before The Civil War* (New York: Oxford Univ. Press, 1985), 127–65.

6. Kenneth Winkle, *The Politics of Community: Migration and Politics in Antebellum Ohio* (New York: Cambridge Univ. Press, 1988).

7. Daniel Walkowitz, *Worker City, Company Town: Iron and Cotton Worker Protest in Troy and Cohoes, New York, 1855–1884* (Urbana: Univ. of Illinois Press, 1978), 254; William Gienapp "'Politics Seems to Enter into Everything': Politi-

cal Culture in the North, 1840–1860," in Stephen E. Maizlish and John J. Kushma, eds., *Essays on American Antebellum Politics, 1840–1860* (College Station: Texas A&M Univ. Press, 1982), 14–69; Jean Baker, "From Belief into Culture: Republicanism in the Antebellum North," *American Quarterly*, 37 (Fall 1985): 548; Jean Baker, "The Ceremonies of Politics: Nineteenth-Century Rituals of National Affirmation," in William J. Cooper, Michael F. Holt, and John McCardell, eds., *A Master's Due: Essays in Honor of David Herbert Donald* (Baton Rouge: Louisiana State Univ. Press, 1985), 161–78.

8. Gienapp, "Politics Enters into Everything"; Paul F. Bourke and Donald A. DeBats, "Identifiable Voting in Nineteenth Century America: Toward a Comparison of Britain and the United States Before the Secret Ballot," *Perspectives in American History*, 11 (1977–78): 257–88; Paul Goodman, "The Social Bases of New England Politics in Jacksonian America," *JER*, 6 (May 1986): 29.

9. Bourke and Debats, "Identifiable Voting," 274–75; *CG*, 40th Cong., 1st sess., 101.

10. Jasper B. Shannon and Ruth McQuown, *Presidential Politics in Kentucky, 1824–1948* (Lexington, Ky.: Bureau of Government Research, 1950), 2–67; Walter Dean Burnham, "The Appearance and Disappearance of the American Voter," in Burnham, *The Current Crisis in American Politics* (New York: Oxford Univ. Press, 1982), 160–61.

11. M. Philip Lucas, "The Development of the Second Party System in Mississippi, 1817–1846" (Ph.D. dissertation, Cornell Univ., 1984), 464–65; Kenneth Winkle, "A Social Analysis of Voter Turnout in Ohio, 1850–1860," *JIH*, 13 (Winter 1983): 411–35; John M. Rozett, "The Social Bases of Party Conflict in the Age of Jackson: Individual Voting Behavior in Greene County, Illinois, 1838–1848" (Ph.D. dissertation, Univ. of Michigan, 1974), 26. Winkle shows that residential distance from the polls affected turnout rates. *Politics of Community*, 129–31.

12. The presidential returns are from Walter Dean Burnham, "Voter Participation in Presidential Elections, by State, 1824–1968," in *Historical Statis-*

TABLE TO NOTE 12

Mississippi Turnout, 1838–45

Year	Election	Percentage of eligible voters	Year	Election	Percentage of eligible voters
1838	Congress	66.0%	1843	Governor	81.6%
1839	Governor	89.5		Congress	74.4
	Congress	89.0		Legislature	77.9
	Legislature	84.6	1844	President	89.6
1840	President	88.2	1845	Governor	80.8
1841	Governor	81.8		Congress	83.7
	Congress	81.6		Legislature	80.4
	Legislature	77.9			

SOURCE: M. Philip Lucas, "The Development of the Second Party System in Mississippi, 1817–1846" (Ph.D. dissertation, Cornell Univ., 1983), 464.

tics of the United States, Colonial Times to 1970 (Washington, D.C.: Government Printing Office, 1975), 2: 1071–1077. See also Paul Kleppner, *Who Voted: The Dynamics of Electoral Turnout, 1870–1980* (New York: Praeger, 1982). The Georgia figures are from Donald DeBats, "Elites and Masses: Political Structure, Communications and Behavior in Ante-Bellum Georgia" (Ph.D. dissertation, Univ. of Wisconsin, 1973), 478–80. Lucas's figures for Mississippi are shown in the accompanying table.

13. Gerald Ginsburg has raised questions about the high levels of these figures. See "Computing Antebellum Turnout: Methods and Models," *JIH*, 16 (Spring 1986): 579–611. But see also the strong response by Walter Dean Burnham, "Those High Nineteenth-Century American Voting Turnouts: Fact or Fiction?," ibid., 613–44.

14. Albany *Evening Journal*, Oct. 1, 1838; Edward Everett to Webster, Jan. 3, 1845, in Charles M. Wiltse, ed., *The Papers of Daniel Webster, Correspondence* (Hanover, N.H.: Univ. Press of New England, 1984), 6: 68; Raleigh *Register*, Nov. 15, 1844. The most recent examination of corruption during part of the period is Mark Summers, *The Plundering Generation: Corruption and the Crisis of the Union, 1849–1861* (New York: Oxford Univ. Press, 1987), a gold mine of information.

15. Summers, *Plundering Generation*, 14. The charges of election corruption are put in context in Howard W. Allen and Kay Warren Allen, "Vote Fraud and Data Validity," in Jerome M. Clubb, William H. Flanigan, and Nancy H. Zingale, *Analyzing Electoral History: A Guide to the Study of American Voting Behavior* (Beverly Hills, Calif.: Sage, 1981), 153–93; and in Walter Dean Burnham, "Theory and Voting Research," *American Political Science Review*, 67 (Sept. 1974): 1002–1023, and the comments by Philip Converse and Gerald Kramer that follow. A quite different perspective, suggesting that electoral fraud was more serious than the Allens and Burnham believe, at least during the last decades of the 19th century, is Peter Argersinger, "New Perspectives on Election Fraud in the Gilded Age," *Political Science Quarterly*, 100 (Winter 1985–86): 669–87. All of these works provide extensive bibliographies of the secondary literature.

16. Gienapp, "Politics Seem to Enter into Everything," 26; Reuben E. Davis, *Recollections of Mississippi and Mississippians* (Boston: Houghton, Mifflin, 1889), 112; Roy Basler, ed., *The Collected Works of Abraham Lincoln* (New Brunswick, N.J.: Rutgers Univ. Press, 1953), 1: 212; Gary W. Cox and J. Morgan Kousser, "Turnout and Rural Corruption: New York as a Test Case," *American Journal of Political Science*, 25 (Nov. 1981): 646–63.

17. Burnham, "Appearance and Disappearance," 131.

18. Kleppner, *Who Voted*, 30; Winkle, *Politics of Community*, 3; Robert Doherty, *Society and Power: Five New England Towns, 1800–1860, a Comparative Study* (Amherst: Univ. of Massachusetts Press, 1977), 81; Kenneth Winkle, "Lincoln's Springfield Revisited: Community and Politics in the Antebellum Midwest" (unpublished paper, 1985), 2.

19. Paul Bourke and Donald DeBats, "Individuals and Aggregates: A Note on Historical Data and Assumptions," *Social Science History* 4 (Spring

1980): 241; Winkle, "Social Analysis of Voter Turnout," 416, 420; Winkle, "Lincoln's Springfield," 7−8.

20. Winkle, "Lincoln's Springfield," 10; William Shade, "Society and Politics in Antebellum Virginia's Southside," *Journal of Southern History*, 53 (May 1987): 177; Daniel H. Calhoun, "From Collinearity to Structure: San Francisco and Pittsburgh, 1860," *Historical Methods Newsletter*, 12 (Summer 1981): 119.

21. Winkle, "Lincoln's Springfield," 10; Kleppner, *Who Voted*, 143.

22. Kleppner, *Who Voted*, 24. See also William Claggett, "Turnout and Core Voters in the Nineteenth and Twentieth Centuries: A Reconsideration," *Social Science Quarterly*, 62 (Sept. 1981): 443−49.

23. Thornton, *Politics and Power*, 159. The national and state totals returns, here and below, are drawn from *Congressional Quarterly's Guide to U.S. Elections* (Washington, D.C., 1975). Such vote stability at the local level is the theme of several state studies, including Philip C. Davis, "The Persistence of Partisan Alignment: Issues, Leaders and Votes in New Jersey, 1840−1860" (Ph.D. dissertation, Washington Univ., 1978); Marc Kruman, *Parties and Politics in North Carolina, 1836−1865* (Baton Rouge: Louisiana State Univ. Press, 1983); Donald J. Ratcliffe, "Politics in Jacksonian Ohio: Reflections on the Ethnocultural Interpretation," *Ohio History*, 88 (Winter 1979): 14; and Lee Benson, Joel H. Silbey, and Phyllis F. Field, "Toward a Theory of Stability and Change in American Voting Behavior: New York State, 1792−1970, as a Test Case," in Joel H. Silbey, Allan G. Bogue, and William H. Flanigan, eds., *The History of American Electoral Behavior* (Princeton, N.J.: Princeton Univ. Press, 1977), 78−105.

24. Samuel P. Hays, review of Stephen Thernstrom, *The Other Bostonians*, in *Journal of Social History*, 9 (Spring 1974): 413; Don Doyle, "Social Theory and New Communities in Nineteenth Century America," *Western Historical Quarterly*, 8 (April 1977): 160−61.

25. Edward D. Mansfield, *Personal Memories, Social, Political and Literary . . . 1803−1843* (Cincinnati, Ohio: R. Clarke & Co., 1879), 235; *Illinois State Register*, Oct. 23, 1840; Paul Kleppner, *The Third Electoral System, 1853−1892: Parties, Voters, and Political Cultures* (Chapel Hill: Univ. of North Carolina Press, 1979); Gienapp, "Politics Seems to Enter into Everything"; Paul Kleppner et al., *The Evolution of American Electoral Systems* (Westport, Conn.: Greenwood Press, 1981). Lucas, in his study of Mississippi political development between 1835 and 1845, notes the sharp decline in the number of electoral precincts (the smallest voting unit) significantly shifting their support for either party between successive elections after 1838. He concludes that "the precinct level data [are] consistent with the contention that voters adopted party loyalties by the late 1830's and did not abandon them thereafter." "Development of Second Party System," 492−93.

26. The national correlations are drawn from Gerald Pomper, *Elections in America* (New York: Longman's, 1980), 229ff. See also Kleppner et al., *Evolution of Electoral Systems*.

27. Benson, Silbey, and Field, "Toward a Theory"; Davis, "Persistence of

Partisan Alignment," 61; DeBats, "Elites and Masses," 498–99; Kruman, *Parties and Politics*, 44.

28. Davis, "Persistence of Partisan Alignment," 61; Lucas, "Development of Second Party System," 480; "Proceedings of the State Convention of the Whig Young Men of Massachusetts . . . September 11th, 1839" (Boston, 1839), 25.

29. Thomas P. Alexander, "The Dimension of Voter Partisan Constancy in Presidential Elections from 1840 to 1860," in Maizlish and Kushma, *Essays on Antebellum Politics*, 70–121 (the quotation is at p. 113); Kleppner et al., *Evolution of Electoral Systems*, 18; George Merriam, *The Life and Times of Samuel Bowles* (New York: Century Co., 1885), 2: 222; Horatio Seymour to Randall, Oct. 5, 1868, in H. S. Randall Papers, New York Historical Society.

30. *Ohio State Journal*, July 15, 1852; Walter Dean Burnham, "Party Systems and the Political Process," in William N. Chambers and Walter Dean Burnham, *The American Party Systems: Stages of Political Development*, 2d ed. (New York: Oxford Univ. Press, 1975), 295.

31. Alexander, "Voter Constancy," 70; Kleppner, "Critical Realignments," in Kleppner et al., *Evolution of Electoral Systems*, 18.

32. The index of competition was developed by Paul David in *Party Strength in the United States, 1872–1970* (Charlottesville: Univ. Press of Virginia, 1972). It is based on computing how much the losing party needs to gain in order to win. See its use in Joel H. Silbey, *A Respectable Minority: The Democratic Party in the Civil War Era, 1860–1868* (New York: Norton, 1977), 20. Intensely competitive states had an index of .95 or better, moderately competitive states an index of .90 to .949, one-party dominant lay between .85 and 89.9, and safe fell below .85. The grounds for the competitiveness varied within the different states. In some, individual counties were highly competitive throughout. In others, each party had a large enough share of one-sided races to yield an overall pattern of competitiveness.

33. David W. Brady, *Critical Elections and Congressional Policy Making* (Stanford, Calif.: Stanford University Press, 1988). In these years, the total national distribution of House seats gave each party a large bloc.

34. On realignment see, among many, Kleppner et al., *Evolution of Electoral Systems*; William Gienapp, *The Origins of the Republican Party, 1852–1856* (New York: Oxford Univ. Press, 1988); and Michael F. Holt, *The Political Crisis of the 1850s* (New York: Wiley, 1978).

35. Robert William Fogel, *Without Consent or Contract: The Rise and Fall of American Slavery* (New York: Norton, 1989), 382–83; Silbey, *Respectable Minority: passim*; Kleppner, *Third Electoral System*.

36. The "anatomy" of the post–Civil War stalemate is well described in Samuel T. McSeveney, *The Politics of Depression: Voting Behavior in the Northeast, 1893–1896* (New York: Oxford Univ. Press, 1974), chap. 1.

37. Kleppner, "Critical Realignments"; Walter Dean Burnham, "The Changing Shape of the American Political Universe," chap. 1 of Burnham, *Current Crisis of American Politics*; Brady, *Critical Elections*.

38. Paul Kleppner, "Voters and Parties in the West, 1876–1900," *Western Political Quarterly*, 14 (Jan. 1983): 55, 57.

39. Mansfield, *Personal Memories*, 321.

Chapter Nine

1. New York *Tribune*, Sept. 11, 1852.

2. Raleigh *Register*, January 24, 1849.

3. Joel H. Silbey, *A Respectable Minority: The Democratic Party in the Civil War Era, 1860–1868* (New York: Norton, 1977), 5. Lawrence Frederick Kohl, *The Politics of Individualism: Parties and the American Character in the Jacksonian Era* (New York: Oxford Univ. Press, 1989), 5, 225, and *passim*, opts for an individualistic, psychological explanation of party choice. The literature on 19th-century popular voting behavior is immense. Three historiographic articles that frame that literature are good places to begin: Peter H. Argersinger and John W. Jeffries, "American Electoral History: Party Systems and Voting Behavior," *Research in Micropolitics*, 1 (1986): 1–34; William G. Shade, "Parties and Politics in Jacksonian America," *Pennsylvania Magazine of History and Biography*, 110 (Oct. 1986): 483–508; and Daniel Feller, "Politics and Society: Toward a Jacksonian Synthesis," *JER*, 10 (Summer 1990): 135–61.

4. Shade, "Parties and Politics," 503. See also Daniel W. Crofts, *Reluctant Confederates: Upper South Unionists in the Secession Crisis* (Chapel Hill: Univ. of North Carolina Press, 1989), 48.

5. Melvyn Hammarberg, *The Indiana Voter: The Historical Dynamics of Party Allegiance During the 1870s* (Chicago: Univ. of Chicago Press, 1977), 1.

6. Ronald P. Formisano, *The Transformation of Political Culture: Massachusetts Parties, 1790s–1840s* (New York: Oxford Univ. Press, 1983), 279; William G. Shade, "Society and Politics in Antebellum Virginia's Southside," *Journal of Southern History*, 53 (May 1987): 193.

7. Richard L. McCormick, *The Party Period and Public Policy: American Politics from the Age of Jackson to the Progressive Era* (New York: Oxford Univ. Press, 1986), 120. In general, see Drew R. McCoy, *The Elusive Republic: Political Economy in Jeffersonian America* (Chapel Hill: Univ. of North Carolina Press, 1980); Steven Watts, *The Republic Reborn: War and the Making of Liberal America, 1790–1820* (Baltimore: Johns Hopkins Univ. Press, 1987); Sean Wilentz, *Chants Democratic: New York City and the Rise of the American Working Class, 1788–1850* (New York: Oxford Univ. Press, 1984); and Kohl, *Politics of Individualism*.

8. Carter Goodrich, *Government Promotion of American Canals and Railroads, 1800–1890* (New York: Columbia Univ. Press, 1960); George Rogers Taylor, *The Transportation Revolution, 1815–1860* (New York: Rinehart, 1951); Robert William Fogel, *Without Consent or Contract: The Rise and Fall of American Slavery* (New York: Norton, 1989), chaps. 9 and 10.

9. Harry Watson, *Jacksonian Democracy and Community Conflict: The Emergence of the Second American Party System in Cumberland County, North Carolina* (Baton Rouge: Louisiana State Univ. Press, 1981); Watson, "Conflict and Collaboration: Yeomen, Slaveholders and Politics in the Antebellum South," *So-*

cial History, 10 (Oct. 1985): 273–98; William G. Shade, *Banks or No Banks: The Money Issue in Western Politics, 1832–1865* (Detroit: Wayne State Univ. Press, 1972); Shade, "Society and Politics," 192–93; James Oakes, "The Politics of Economic Development in the Antebellum South," *JIH*, 15 (Autumn 1984): 305–16; Oakes, *Slavery and Freedom: An Interpretation of the Old South* (New York: Knopf, 1990). Compare Crofts, *Reluctant Confederates*, 48; and Marc Kruman, *Parties and Politics in North Carolina, 1836–1865* (Baton Rouge: Louisiana State Univ. Press, 1983), 17.

10. Don H. Doyle, "The Social Functions of Voluntary Associations in a Nineteenth Century American Town," *Social Science History*, 1 (Spring 1977): 341; *New York Weekly Tribune*, March 22, 1851. In general, the starting points on this development are Lee Benson, *The Concept of Jacksonian Democracy: New York as a Test Case* (Princeton, N.J.: Princeton Univ. Press, 1961); and Ronald Formisano, *The Birth of Mass Political Parties: Michigan, 1837–1861* (Princeton, N.J.: Princeton Univ. Press, 1971).

11. Paul Kleppner, *The Third Electoral System, 1853–1892: Parties, Voters and Political Cultures* (Chapel Hill: Univ. of North Carolina Press, 1979), 58. On these matters see, most recently, the essays in Mark A. Noll, ed., *Religion and American Politics: From the Colonial Period to the 1980s* (New York: Oxford Univ. Press, 1990).

12. Robert Kellley, *The Cultural Pattern in American Politics: The First Century* (New York: Knopf, 1979); Owen Ireland, "The Crux of Politics: Religion and Party in Pennsylvania, 1778–1789," *William and Mary Quarterly*, 42 (Oct. 1985): 453–75.

13. William Shade, "Pennsylvania Politics in the Jacksonian Period: A Case Study, Northampton County, 1824–1844," *Pennsylvania History*, 39 (July 1972): 329; John Rozett, "The Social Bases of Party Conflict in the Age of Jackson: Individual Voting Behavior in Greene County, Illinois, 1838–1845," (Ph.D. dissertation, Univ. of Michigan, 1974), 173; Benson, *Concept of Jacksonian Politics*; Formisano, *Transformation*, 293; Paul Goodman, "The Politics of Industrialism: Massachusetts, 1830–1870," in Richard Bushman et al., eds., *Uprooted Americans* (Boston: Little, Brown, 1979), 170; Kleppner, *Third Electoral System*, 61; Robert B. Swierenga, "Ethnoreligious Political Behavior," in Noll, ed., *Religion and American Politics*, 157.

14. Natchez *Courier*, Nov. 6, 1844, in *Mississippi Free Trader*, Nov. 9, 1844; Watson, *Jacksonian Democracy*, 213; Kruman, *Parties and Politics*, 15; Kleppner, *Third Electoral System*, 62.

15. Kleppner, *Third Electoral System*; Daniel Walker Howe, *The Political Culture of the American Whigs* (Chicago: Univ. of Chicago Press, 1979), 167; Kohl, *Politics of Individualism*; *DR*, 36 (Oct. 1855): 342, 36 (Jan. 1856): 11.

16. Kleppner, *Third Electoral System*, 60ff, and Howe, *Political Culture of American Whigs, passim*, describe the Whig community.

17. Kleppner, *Third Electoral System*, 60.

18. J. Mills Thornton, *Politics and Power in a Slave Society: Alabama, 1800–1860* (Baton Rouge: Louisiana State Univ. Press, 1978), especially

55–59; Oakes, *Slavery and Freedom*; Formisano, *Transformation.* See also Oakes "Politics of Economic Development"; and John Mack Faragher, *Sugar Creek: Life in the Illinois Prairie* (New Haven, Conn.: Yale Univ. Press, 1986), 190–96.

19. David Montgomery, "The Shuttle and the Cross: Weavers and Artisans in the Kensington Riots of 1844," *Journal of Social History*, 5 (Summer 1972): 411–12; Susan Hirsch, *Roots of the American Working Class: The Industrialization of Crafts in Newark, 1815–1860* (Philadelphia: Univ. of Pennsylvania Press, 1978), 106.

20. Michael Feldberg, *The Philadelphia Riots of 1844: A Study of Ethnic Conflict* (Westport, Conn.: Greenwood Press, 1975), 58. On the larger issues here, see Lee Benson, "Marx's General and Middle Range Theories of Social Conflict," in Robert K. Merton et al., eds., *Qualitative and Quantitative Social Research: Papers in Honor of Paul F. Lazarsfeld* (New York: Free Press, 1979), 206; and Daniel Walker Howe's fine essay "Religion and Politics in the Antebellum North," in Noll, ed., *Religion and American Politics*, 121–45.

21. Michael Kazin, "Struggling with the Class Struggle: Marxism and the Search for a Synthesis of U.S. Labor History," *Labor History*, 28 (Fall 1987): 508. See also Nick Salvatore, "Response to Sean Wilentz, 'Against Exceptionalism: Class Consciousness and the American Labor Movement, 1790–1920,'" *International Labor and Working Class History*, no. 26 (Fall 1984): 25–30; and Richard Oestereicher, "Urban Working-Class Political Behavior and Theories of American Electoral Politics, 1870–1940," *JAH*, 74 (March 1988): 1257–1286. Some historians place a much different emphasis on the relationship between ethnicity and class in shaping individual and group voting behavior. See, for example, most recently, Grace Palladino, *Another Civil War: Labor, Capital, and the State in the Anthracite Regions of Pennsylvania, 1840–68* (Urbana: Univ. of Illinois Press, 1990), 70ff; and more generally, Feller, "Politics and Society."

22. Ronald P. Formisano, "Toward a Reorientation of Jacksonian Politics: A Review of the Literature, 1959–1975," *JAH*, 63 (June 1976): 62; Shade, "Society and Politics," 190; Stuart Blumin, *The Urban Threshold: Growth and Change in a Nineteenth Century American City* (Chicago: Univ. of Chicago Press, 1976), 184. See also Blumin, *The Emergence of the Middle Class: Social Experience in the American City, 1760–1900* (Cambridge: Cambridge Univ. Press, 1989), and David A. Gerber, *The Making of an American Pluralism: Buffalo, New York, 1825–1850* (Urbana: Univ. of Illinois Press, 1989), for thoughtful attempts to work out the relationship between cultural and class factors in mid-19th century urban politics.

A number of historians argue that issues other than slavery played only a limited role in southern political life, that whatever the situation elsewhere in the nation, class-rooted divisions anchored in slavery shaped Democratic-Whig conflict below the Mason-Dixon Line. As James Oakes has recently written: "To be sure, the political split between slaveholders and non-slaveholders was rarely neat and never absolute. Class divisions were frequently obscured by shared convictions, conflicting impulses, changes over time, and always, exceptions to the rule. Nevertheless, what remains unusual, almost unique, about politics in the Old South is not its predictable obscurities and inconsistencies but its unusual clarity. With the slaves politically silenced and with a relatively homogeneous white population, racial, ethnic, and religious tensions were unlikely to mask fundamental class divisions." Thus, while the impulses present in the larger political world had an "inescapable influence" on southern politics, "as always slavery altered the meaning and significance of every conflict that fell within the scope of southern society." *Slavery and Freedom*, 124–25. Oakes also points out that "slavery itself became the major dividing line in southern politics only indirectly"; and, finally, that all of this was framed within the conventions and practices of a vigorous two-party political system there. P. 124, and *passim*.

23. Michael Holt, "The Election of 1840, Voter Mobilization, and the Emergence of the Second American Party System: A Reappraisal of Jacksonian Voting Behavior," in William J. Cooper, Michael F. Holt, and John McCardell, eds., *A Master's Due: Essays in Honor of David Herbert Donald* (Baton Rouge: Louisiana State Univ. Press, 1985), 16–58.

24. Benson, *Concept of Jacksonian Democracy*; Oakes, "Politics of Economic Development."

25. Kleppner, *Third Electoral System*, is particularly sensitive to the importance of contextual factors.

26. Ibid., *passim*.

27. Paula Baker, "The Culture of Politics in the Late Nineteenth Century: Community and Political Behavior in Rural New York," *Journal of Social History*, 18 (Winter 1984): 167–93; Donald DeBats, "Before the Decline: The Reach and Meaning of Politics in Nineteenth Century America" (unpublished paper, 1984), 51. Melvyn Hammarberg stresses the importance of the web of communicating and reinforcing institutions that kept people alert and ready to choose. Indianans who lived isolated lives in the 1880's showed comparatively little commitment and partisanship. *Indiana Voter*.

28. Thornton, *Politics and Power*, 151, 159.

29. Kathleen Conzen, *Immigrant Milwaukee, 1836–1860: Accommodation and Community in a Frontier City* (Cambridge, Mass.: Harvard Univ. Press, 1976), 223.

30. *CG*, 41st Cong., 2d sess., 3664; Don H. Doyle, *The Social Order of a Frontier Community: Jacksonville, Illinois, 1825–1870* (Urbana: Univ. of Illinois Press, 1978), 143; *Nashville Union*, Oct. 28, 1848; *Illinois State Register*, Sept. 10, 1852.

31. Richard P. McCormick, *The Presidential Game: The Origins of American Presidential Politics* (New York: Oxford Univ. Press, 1982), 12; *AR*, 9 (June 1849): 553.

32. William Gienapp, *The Origins of the Republican Party, 1852–1856* (New York: Oxford Univ. Press, 1987), 66; Fogel, *Without Consent or Contract*, 356–57.

33. Fogel, *Without Consent or Contract*, 362; Michael F. Holt, *The Political Crisis of the 1850s* (New York: Wiley, 1978), 164; *CG*, 34th Cong., 1st sess., 190.

34. The Whigs' 1852 strategy is discussed in Gienapp, *Origins of Republican Party*, 20–31.

35. Holt, *Political Crisis of 1850s*, is excellent on the rising sectional antagonisms.

36. Don S. Fehrenbacher, *Chicago Giant: A Biography of 'Long John' Wentworth* (Madison, Wis.: American History Research Center, 1957), 139; William Gienapp, "Who Voted For Lincoln?," in John L. Thomas, ed., *Abraham Lincoln and the American Political Tradition* (Amherst: Univ. of Massachusetts Press, 1986), 59; *CG*, 34th Cong., 1st sess., 199.

37. Kleppner, *Third Electoral System*, 76ff; Dale Baum, *The Civil War Party System: The Case of Massachusetts, 1848–1876* (Chapel Hill: Univ. of North Carolina Press, 1984), 73–100. Baum is more hesitant than I am about the power of ethnoculture influences to shape party choice.

38. Kleppner, *Third Electoral System*, 196–97.

39. For an excellent case study tracing the basis of partisan divisions in a single locality and linking them to existing patterns of elite and neighborhood conflict, see Robert C. Kenzer, *Kinship and Neighborhood in a Southern Community: Orange County, North Carolina, 1849–1881* (Knoxville: Univ. of Tennessee Press, 1987).

40. "Address of the Democratic Republican Young Men's General Committee of the City of New York . . . 1840" (New York, 1840), 3; Richard Jensen, *The Winning of the Midwest: Social and Political Conflict, 1888–1896* (Chicago: Univ. of Chicago Press, 1971), 2–4; Albert C. Parker, "Empire Stalemate: Voting Behavior in New York State, 1860–1892" (Ph.D. dissertation, Washington Univ., 1975), 94.

41. *Cincinnati Commercial*, Sept. 21, 1852, as quoted in William Gienapp, "'Politics Seems to Enter into Everything': Political Culture in the North, 1840–1860," in Stephen E. Maizlish and John J. Kushma, eds., *Essays on American Antebellum Politics, 1840–1860* (College Station: Texas A&M Univ. Press, 1982), 59; Ralph M. Aderman, ed., *The Letters of James Kirke Paulding* (Madison: Univ. of Wisconsin Press, 1962), 141.

Chapter Ten

1. *New York Times*, Feb. 13, 1981.

2. John M. Murrin, "The Great Inversion, or Court Versus Country: A Comparison of the Revolution Settlements in England (1688–1721) and America (1776–1816)," in J. G. A. Pocock, *Three British Revolutions, 1641, 1688, 1776* (Princeton, N.J.: Princeton Univ. Press, 1980), 430; *AR*, 12 (July 1850): 1.

3. Oscar Handlin and Mary Flug Handlin, *Commonwealth: A Study of the Role of Government in the American Economy: Massachusetts, 1774–1861* (Cambridge, Mass.: Harvard Univ. Press, 1947); Robert Lively, "The American System: A Review Article," *Business History Review*, 29 (March 1955): 81–96; Harry Scheiber, "Government and the Economy: Studies of the 'Commonwealth' Policy in Nineteenth-Century America," *JIH*, 3 (Summer 1972): 135–51.

4. J. Willard Hurst, *Law and Economic Growth: The Legal History of the Lumber Industry in Wisconsin, 1836–1915* (Cambridge, Mass.: Harvard Univ. Press, 1964), 6.

5. L. Ray Gunn, *The Decline of Authority: Public Economic Policy and Political Development in New York, 1800–1860* (Ithaca, N.Y.: Cornell Univ. Press, 1988), 3; Samuel P. Hays, "Society and Politics: Politics and Society," *JIH*, 15 (Winter 1985): 485; Loren Beth, *The Development of the American Constitution, 1877–1917* (New York: Harper & Row, 1971), 74.

6. Robert Rantoul, "Oration . . . on the Fourth of July, 1836" (Boston, 1836), 42.

7. Lively, "American System," 81; Scheiber, "Government and the Economy"; George Rogers Taylor, *The Transportation Revolution, 1815–1860* (New York: Rinehart, 1951); Paul Wallace Gates, *The Farmers' Age: Agriculture, 1815–1860* (New York: Holt, Rinehart, 1960).

8. Paul Wallace Gates, *History of Public Land Law Development* (Washington, D.C.: Government Printing Office, 1968), is a gold mine of information on differences over policy throughout the 19th century.

9. Harry Scheiber, "Federalism and the American Economic Order, 1789–1910," *Law and Society Review*, 10 (Fall 1975): 63. On the federal side, Stanley Kutler, *Privilege and Creative Destruction: The Charles River Bridge Case* (Philadelphia: Lippincott, 1971).

10. Philip Paludan, *"A People's Contest": The Union and Civil War, 1861–1865* (New York: Harper & Row, 1988), 143.

11. J. Willard Hurst, *Law and the Conditions of Freedom in the Nineteenth-Century United States* (Madison: Univ. of Wisconsin Press, 1956), 10, 43. Compare Theodore Lowi, *The End of Liberalism: Ideology, Policy and the Crisis of Public Authority* (New York: Norton, 1969); and Carter Goodrich, *Government Promotion of American Canals and Railroads, 1810–1890* (New York: Columbia Univ. Press, 1960). Harry Scheiber, *The Ohio Canal Era: A Case Study of the Government and the Economy, 1820–1861* (Athens: Ohio Univ. Press, 1968), is a model case study of the development efforts undertaken in one state by government and private enterprise.

12. Peter Wallenstein, *From Slave South to New South: Public Policy in Nineteenth-Century Georgia* (Chapel Hill: Univ. of North Carolina Press, 1986), 63; William R. Brock, *Investigation and Responsibility: Public Responsibility in the United States, 1865–1900* (Cambridge: Cambridge Univ. Press, 1984); Gerald R. Grob, "The Political System and Social Policy in the Nineteenth Century: Legacy of the Revolution," *Mid-America*, 58 (Jan. 1976): 5–19.

13. Ruth Elson, *Guardians of Tradition: American Schoolbooks of the Nineteenth Century* (Lincoln: Univ. of Nebraska Press, 1964); Michael Katz, *The Irony of Early School Reform: Educational Innovation in Mid-Nineteenth-Century Massachusetts* (Cambridge, Mass.: Harvard Univ. Press, 1968); Robert Hampel, *Temperance and Prohibition in Massachusetts, 1813–1852* (Ann Arbor, Mich.: UMI Research Press, 1982).

14. Hurst, *Law and Economic Growth*, 140; Richard L. McCormick, "The

Party Period and Public Policy: An Exploratory Hypothesis," *JAH*, 66 (Sept. 1979): 284; Brock, *Investigation and Responsibility*, 56.

15. Leonard White, *The Jacksonians: A Study in Administrative History, 1829–1861* (New York: Macmillan, 1954); White, *The Republican Era, 1869–1901* (New York: Macmillan, 1958). *Historical Statistics of the United States, Colonial Times to 1970* (Washington, D.C.: Government Printing Office, 1975), 2: 1102–1104; Wallace Farnham, "The 'Weakened Spring of Government': A Study in Nineteenth Century American History," *AHR*, 68 (April 1963): 662–90; Matthew A. Crenson, *The Federal Machine: Beginnings of Bureaucracy in Jacksonian America* (Baltimore: Johns Hopkins Univ. Press, 1975); Morton Keller, *Affairs of State: Public Life in Late Nineteenth-Century America* (Cambridge, Mass.: Harvard Univ. Press, 1977), 98–99.

16. William J. Hartman, "Politics and Patronage: The New York Customs House, 1852–1902" (Ph.D. dissertation, Columbia Univ., 1952); Malcolm J. Rohrbaugh, *The Land Office Business: The Settlement and Administration of the Public Lands, 1789–1837* (New York: Oxford Univ. Press, 1971); Milton Conover, *The General Land Office: Its History, Activities and Organization* (Baltimore: Johns Hopkins Univ. Press, 1923), 25; Gates, *History of Public Land Law*. But, again, most of the Land Office's employees were deployed in regional offices throughout the Union. It had fewer than 20 employees in Washington.

17. Keller, *Affairs of State*; William E. Nelson, *The Roots of American Bureaucracy, 1830–1890* (Cambridge, Mass.: Harvard Univ. Press, 1982); Richard N. Current, *Those Terrible Carpetbaggers* (New York: Oxford Univ. Press, 1988), 149. Richard Bensel, *Yankee Leviathan: The Origins of Central State Authority in America, 1859–1877* (New York: Cambridge Univ. Press, 1991), tracks the growth—and then decline—of the American national state's capacity during the Civil War and Reconstruction eras.

18. Keller, *Affairs of State*, 183, 311.

19. Ibid., 121. Webster was Secretary of State twice; Crittenden was a senator three different times and Attorney-General twice. Richard Bensel argues for a more robust view of the development of the Confederate state during the war than is usually offered. See his "Southern Leviathan: The Development of Central State Authority in the Confederate States of America," in *Studies in American Political Development: An Annual*, 2 (New Haven, Conn.: Yale Univ. Press, 1987): 68–136.

20. Scheiber, "Federalism"; J. Mills Thornton, *Politics and Power in a Slave Society: Alabama, 1800–1860* (Baton Rouge: Louisiana State Univ. Press, 1978), 83; Albert Kirwan, *John J. Crittenden: The Struggle for the Union* (Lexington: Univ. of Kentucky Press, 1962), 235; Marc Kruman, *Parties and Politics in North Carolina, 1836–1865* (Baton Rouge: Louisiana State Univ. Press, 1983), 45.

21. Gunn, *Decline of Authority*; Lee Benson, *Merchants, Farmers and Railroads: Railroad Regulation and New York Politics, 1850–1887* (Cambridge, Mass.: Harvard Univ. Press, 1955).

22. Nelson, *Roots of Bureaucracy*, 12; Michael Katz, *In The Shadow of the Poorhouse: A Social History of Welfare in America* (New York: Basic Books, 1982),

chap. 1; Michael B. Katz, *Poverty and Policy in American History* (San Diego, Calif.: Academy Press, 1983), 7.

23. Richard Yates and Catherine Yates Pickering, *Richard Yates, Civil War Governor* (Danville, Ill.: Interstate Printers, 1966); Arthur C. Cole, *The Era of the Civil War, 1848–1870* (Springfield: Illinois Centennial Commission, 1919); William Hesseltine, *Lincoln and the War Governors* (Gloucester, Mass.: Peter Smith, 1972); Keller, *Affairs of State*, 114.

24. The dates of congressional sessions are listed in *Biographical Directory of the United States Congress, 1774–1989* (Washington, D.C.: Government Printing Office, 1989); the number of bills are in *Historical Statistics*, 2: 1081–1082. The life and role of congressmen in part of this period are caught in Allan G. Bogue, *The Congressman's Civil War* (New York: Cambridge Univ. Press, 1989). The sense of an increased, and often overwhelming, workload after the Civil War is conveyed in James A. Garfield, "A Century of Congress," *Atlantic Monthly*, 40 (July 1877): 49–64.

25. Margaret Susan Thompson, "Corruption—Or Confusion? Lobbying and Congressional Government in the Early Gilded Age," *Congress and the Presidency*, 10 (Autumn 1983): 169–93; Thompson, *The 'Spider Web': Congress and Lobbying in the Age of Grant* (Ithaca, N.Y.: Cornell Univ. Press, 1985), 42ff; Douglas E. Bowers, "From Log Rolling to Corruption: The Development of Lobbying in Pennsylvania, 1815–1861," *JER*, 3 (Winter 1983): 443. The Pennsylvania legislature passed about 190 bills a session in the 1830's, 358 by 1845, and 725 by 1860.

26. Allan G. Bogue, Jerome M. Clubb, and Carroll McKibben, "Members of the House of Representatives and the Process of Modernization, 1789–1860," *JAH*, 63 (Sept. 1976): 275–302; Nelson Polsby, "The Institutionalization of the U.S. House of Representatives," *American Political Science Review*, 62 (March 1968): 146; Thompson, *Spider Web*, 78; H. Douglas Price, "Congress and the Evolution of Legislative 'Professionalism,'" in Norman Ornstein, ed., *Congress in Change: Evolution and Reform* (New York: Praeger, 1975), 2–23.

27. *Biographical Directory*; Thompson, *Spider Web*, 87.

28. Kruman, *Parties and Politics*, 51–52; Gunn, *Decline of Authority*, 79; Ballard C. Campbell, *Representative Democracy: Public Policy and Midwest Legislatures in the Late Nineteenth Century* (Cambridge, Mass.: Harvard Univ. Press, 1980), 32. See also Donald A. DeBats, "An Uncertain Arena: The Georgia House of Representatives, 1808–1861," *Journal of Southern History*, 56 (Aug. 1990): 428–33; and Robert W. Cherny, *Populism, Progressivism, and the Transformation of Nebraska Politics, 1885–1915* (Lincoln: Univ. of Nebraska Press, 1981), 30.

29. This is the main point of Thompson, *Spider Web*. See also Polsby, "Institutionalization"; Nelson W. Polsby et al., "The Growth of the Seniority System in the U.S. House of Representatives," *American Political Science Review*, 63 (Aug. 1969): 787–807; and DeBats, "Uncertain Arena," 437–40.

30. McCormick, "Party Period," 206.

31. Paul Bergeron, *The Presidency of James K. Polk* (Lawrence: Univ. of Kansas Press, 1987), 143ff; Philip Palumbo, "The Rules of the Game: Local

Republican Political Culture in the Gilded Age," *Historian*, 47 (Aug. 1985): 495; Kermit Hall, *The Politics of Justice: Lower Federal Judicial Selection and the Second Party System, 1829–1861* (Lincoln: Univ. of Nebraska Press, 1979), 62; Farnham, "Weakened Spring," 665, 668.

32. Joel H. Silbey, *The Partisan Imperative: The Dynamics of American Politics Before the Civil War* (New York: Oxford Univ. Press, 1985), 17ff; Leonard Richards, *The Life and Times of Congressman John Quincy Adams* (New York: Oxford Univ. Press, 1986), 56.

33. *CG*, 34th Cong., 1st sess., 185. The Washington and New York party newspapers were filled with reports of these caucus meetings.

34. Ronald P. Formisano, *The Transformation of Political Culture: Massachusetts Parties, 1790s–1840s* (Princeton, N.J.: Princeton Univ. Press, 1983), 309; Kruman, *Parties and Politics*, 52–53; Rodney O. Davis, "Partisanship in Jacksonian State Politics: Party Divisions in the Illinois State Legislature, 1834–1841," in Robert P. Swierenga, *Quantification in American History: Theory and Research* (New York: Atheneum, 1971), 149–62; Thornton, *Politics and Power*, 94, 97.

35. Campbell, *Representative Democracy*, 197.

36. Silbey, *Partisan Imperative*, 17; William Shade et al., "Partisanship in the United States Senate, 1869–1901," *JIH*, 4 (Autumn 1973): 185–205; David W. Brady et al., "The Decline of Party in the U.S. House of Representatives, 1887–1968," *Legislative Studies Quarterly*, 4 (Aug. 1979): 381–407. Margaret Susan Thompson suggests that the Grant years were characterized by more fluidity in party voting than is argued here. Thompson, *Spider Web*, 114–15. There is no doubt that there were ups and downs throughout, but the basic line was partisan.

37. Bowers, "From Log-Rolling to Corruption," 451n; Formisano, *Transformation*, 330. See also Peter Levine, *The Behavior of State Legislative Parties in the Jacksonian Era: New Jersey, 1829–1844* (Rutherford: Fairleigh Dickinson Univ. Press, 1977); and Thornton, *Politics and Power*, chap. 2.

38. Herbert Ershkowitz and William G. Shade, "Consensus or Conflict? Political Behavior in the State Legislatures During the Jacksonian Era," *JAH*, 58 (Dec. 1971): 613, 621.

39. Kruman, *Parties and Politics*, 53; M. Philip Lucas, "The Development of the Second Party System in Mississippi, 1817–1846" (Ph.D. dissertation, Cornell Univ., 1984), chaps. 11–14.

40. Such battles at the congressional level are traced in Joel H. Silbey, *The Shrine of Party: Congressional Voting Behavior, 1841–1852* (Pittsburgh: Univ. of Pittsburgh Press, 1967). See also Scheiber, *Ohio Canal Era*. Donald DeBats is particularly insistent on this partisan weakening on important policy matters. See "Uncertain Arena," 444ff.

41. Campbell, *Representative Democracy*, 175; DeBats, "Uncertain Arena," 440. This was further buttressed by the fact that in many state legislatures new members were often from the same party as the men they replaced. DeBats, "Uncertain Arena," 435.

42. Bogue, *Congressmen's Civil War*, 44–45. Bergeron, *Presidency of Polk*, provides many illustrations of the point.

43. Hall, *Politics of Justice*, especially xvi, 77.

44. Joel H. Silbey, *A Respectable Minority: The Democratic Party in the Civil War Era, 1860–1868* (New York: Norton, 1977); Emory Thomas, *The Confederate Nation, 1861–1865* (New York: Harper & Row, 1979). Kruman, *Parties and Politics*, covers North Carolina's political experience during the war with great clarity.

45. Don Fehrenbacher, *Prelude to Greatness: Lincoln in the 1850s* (Stanford, Calif.: Stanford Univ. Press, 1962), 8.

46. Samuel P. Hays, *The Response to Industrialism, 1877–1914* (Chicago: Univ. of Chicago Press, 1957), Thomas P. Cochran and William Miller, *The Age of Enterprise: A Social History of Industrial America* (New York: Macmillan, 1942), and Robert Wiebe, *The Search for Order, 1877–1920* (New York: Hill & Wang, 1967), introduce the economic and political changes under way.

47. Farnham, "Weakened Spring," 668; Thompson, "Confusion—or Corruption," 174; Thompson, *Spider Web*, 216.

48. Thompson, "Confusion—or Corruption," 185; Thompson, *Spider Web*, 144, 147.

49. Jerome Sternstein, "The Problem of Corruption in the Gilded Age: The Case of Nelson W. Aldrich," in Abraham S. Eisenstadt, ed., *Before Watergate: Problems of Corruption in American Society* (Brooklyn, N.Y.: Brooklyn College Press, 1978), 144, 145; Ari Hoogenboom, "Did Gilded Age Scandals Bring Reform?," in ibid., 141.

50. Keller, *Affairs of State*, 245; Brock, *Investigation and Responsibility*, 51.

51. Hays, *Response to Industrialism*, Wiebe, *Search for Order*, and Cochran and Miller, *Age of Enterprise*, are all very good on this antipartisan interest-group development.

52. Farnham, "Weakened Spring," 673. See also Bensel, *Yankee Leviathan*.

53. William G. Shade, "'Revolutions May Go Backwards': The American Civil War and the Problem of Political Development," *Social Science Quarterly*, 55 (Dec. 1974), 756; Morton Keller, "Powers and Rights: Two Centuries of American Constitutionalism," *JAH*, 74 (Dec. 1987): 681.

Chapter Eleven

1. William E. Gienapp, *The Origins of the Republican Party, 1852–1856* (New York: Oxford Univ. Press, 1988); Samuel T. McSeveney, *The Politics of Depression: Voting Behavior in the Northeast, 1893–1896* (New York: Oxford Univ. Press, 1972); William Nisbet Chambers and Walter Dean Burnham, *The American Party Systems: Stages of Political Development* (New York: Oxford Univ. Press, 1967).

2. *The Grape Shot*, Dec. 7, 1848; Daniel Walker Howe, *The Political Culture of the American Whigs* (Chicago: Univ. of Chicago Press), 43. The battles of Cass and the others are described in Arthur M. Schlesinger, Jr., ed., *The History of American Presidential Elections* (New York: Chelsea House, 1971), 4 vols. On John Quincy Adams, see Samuel Flagg Bemis, *John Quincy Adams and the Union* (New York: Knopf, 1956); and Leonard Richards, *The Life and Times*

of Congressman John Quincy Adams (New York: Oxford Univ. Press, 1986).

3. Donald B. Cole, *Martin Van Buren and the American Political System* (Princeton, N.J.: Princeton Univ. Press, 1984), and John Niven, *Martin Van Buren and the Romantic Age of American Politics* (New York: Oxford Univ. Press, 1983), effectively cover the Barnburner episode.

4. John Niven, *John C. Calhoun and the Price of Union* (Baton Rouge: Louisiana State Univ. Press, 1988), is the most recent biography of the antiparty southern leader. The other groups referred to are introduced in Richard Sewell, *Ballots for Freedom: Antislavery Politics in the United States, 1837–1860* (New York: Oxford Univ. Press, 1976); Vernon L. Volpe, *Forlorn Hope of Freedom: The Liberty Party in the Old Northwest, 1838–1848* (Kent, Ohio: Kent State Univ. Press, 1990); John Sproat, *The "Best Men": Liberal Reformers in the Gilded Age* (New York: Oxford Univ. Press, 1968); Geoffrey Blodgett, *The Gentlemen Reformers: Massachusetts Democrats in the Cleveland Era* (Cambridge, Mass.: Harvard Univ. Press, 1966); and Gerald McFarland, *Mugwumps, Morals and Politics, 1884–1920* (Amherst: Univ. of Massachusetts Press, 1975).

5. Ronald G. Walters, *American Reformers, 1815–1860* (New York: Hill & Wang, 1978); Walters, *The Antislavery Appeal: American Abolitionism After 1830* (Baltimore: Johns Hopkins Univ. Press, 1976).

6. Edward Pessen, *Most Uncommon Jacksonians: The Radical Leaders of the Early Labor Movement* (Albany: State Univ. of New York Press, 1967). The articles on various third parties by Paul Kleppner, Michael Holt, and George Tindall in Arthur M. Schlesinger, Jr., *History of U.S. Political Parties* (New York: Chelsea House, 1981), introduce the vast literature on the subject. There are illuminating insights about the challengers in Lee Benson, *The Concept of Jacksonian Democracy: New York as a Test Case* (Princeton, N.J.: Princeton Univ. Press, 1961); Benson, *Merchants, Farmers and Railroads: Railroad Regulation and New York Politics, 1850–1880* (Cambridge, Mass.: Harvard Univ. Press, 1955); Paul Kleppner, *The Third Electoral System, 1853–1892* (Chapel Hill: Univ. of North Carolina Press, 1979); Leon Fink, *Workingmen's Democracy: The Knights of Labor and American Politics* (Urbana: Univ. of Illinois Press, 1983); and Lawrence Goodwyn, *Democratic Promise: The Populist Movement in America* (New York: Oxford Univ. Press, 1976).

7. In addition to Walters and Kleppner on these general themes, there is much on the rhetoric of class-rooted protest in Sean Wilentz, *Chants Democratic: New York City and the Rise of the American Working Class, 1788–1850* (New York: Oxford Univ. Press, 1984). See also Amy Bridges, *A City in the Republic: Antebellum New York and the Origins of Machine Politics* (New York: Cambridge Univ. Press, 1984).

8. Walters, *Anti-Slavery Appeal*, 16.

9. On the politicizing of antislavery, in addition to Sewell, *Ballots for Freedom*, Volpe, *Forlorn Hope of Freedom*; and Walters, *Antislavery Appeal*, see Alan Kraut, "Partisanship and Principles: The Liberty Party in Antebellum Political Culture," in Kraut, ed., *Crusaders and Compromisers: Essays on the Relationship of the Antislavery Struggle to the Antebellum Party System* (Westport, Conn.: Greenwood Press, 1983), 71–99; and Phyllis Field and Alan Kraut, "Politics

Versus Principle: The Partisan Response to 'Bible Politics' in New York State,"
Civil War History, 25 (June 1979): 101–18.

10. Union Labor platform of 1888, in Kirk H. Porter and Donald Bruce
Johnson, eds., *National Party Platforms, 1840–1964* (Urbana: Univ. of Illinois
Press, 1966), 84.

11. Ibid., 7.

12. The first quotation is from the Know-Nothing platform of 1856 in
ibid., 23, the second from the Socialist Labor 1892 platform, ibid., 95; the
other two are in ibid., 5, 52.

13. *New York Daily Globe*, Nov. 6, 1848; Kleppner, *Third Electoral System*,
257; Kleppner, "Greenback and Prohibition Parties," in Schlesinger, *History of
Parties*, 2: 1590; George Washington Doane, "The Young American . . . Address at Burlington College, July 4, 1853 . . ." (Philadelphia, 1853), 13; *The
Grape Shot*, Sept. 30, 1848.

14. Porter and Johnson, *National Party Platforms*, 51–52; *The Battery*, Aug.
31, 1848; Kleppner, *Third Electoral System*, 245.

15. Untitled printed circular, Oct. 31, 1844, in American Republican
Party Papers, New York Historical Society; *DR*, 35 (March 1855): 157–58;
Kleppner, "Greenback and Prohibition Parties," in Schlesinger, *History of Par-
ties*, 2: 1615.

16. J. Mills Thornton, *Politics and Power in a Slave Society: Alabama,
1800–1860* (Baton Rouge: Louisiana State Univ. Press, 1978), 371; *New York
Daily Globe*, Dec. 27, 1848; *DR*, 6 (Dec. 1839): 506.

17. Bradish to Daniel D. Barnard, July 30, 1856, as quoted in Louis B.
Gimelli, "Luther Bradish, 1783–1863" (Ph.D. dissertation, New York Univ.
1964), 256; Porter and Johnson, *National Party Platforms*, 45 (Prohibition party
platform, 1872).

18. *New York Daily Globe*, Aug. 19, Nov. 7, 1848; *The Barnburner*, Sept. 2,
1848.

19. Garrison to James Miller McKim, Oct. 14, 1856, in Louis Ruchames,
ed., *The Letters of William Lloyd Garrison* (Cambridge, Mass.: Harvard Univ.
Press, 1976), 4: 405–6.

20. Porter and Johnson, *National Party Platforms*, 71, 85, 90, (Prohibition
party, 1884; United Labor party, 1888; People's party, 1892); Lawrence Fried-
man, *Gregarious Saints: Self and Community in American Abolition, 1830–1870*
(New York: Cambridge Univ. Press, 1982), 235.

21. Richards, *Congressman Adams*; Thornton, *Politics and Power*, 78.

22. See Chap. 1, above.

23. On the Liberal Republicans, with all of their ambivalence, see Sproat,
Best Men; Robert Kelley, *The Transatlantic Persuasion: The Liberal Democratic
Mind in the Age of Gladstone* (New York: Knopf, 1969); Matthew T. Downey,
"Horace Greeley and the Politicians: The Liberal Republican Convention in
1872," *JAH*, 53 (March 1967): 727–50; and Richard Allan Gerber, "The Liberal Republicans of 1872 in Historiographical Perspective," *JAH*, 62 (June
1975): 40–73.

24. "Central Van Buren Convention" (n.p., [May 15, 1844]), 3–4; *The Campaign*, no. 4, June 21, 1848; Michael Holt, "Antimasonic and Know-Nothing Parties," in Schlesinger, *History of Parties*, 1: 604.

25. *The Barnburner*, July 29, 1848; Sewell, *Ballots for Freedom*, 81; American Republican party circular, Oct. 31, 1844; *New York Daily Globe*, July 19, 1848. The most recent general treatments of third parties throughout American history are Daniel Mazmanian, *Third Parties in Presidential Elections* (Washington, D.C.: Brookings Institution, 1974); and Steven J. Rosenstone, *Third Parties in America: Citizen Response to Major Party Failure* (Princeton, N.J.: Princeton Univ. Press, 1984).

26. David Scobey, "Boycotting the Politics Factory: Labor Radicalism and the New York City Mayoral Election of 1884," *Radical History Review*, no. 28–30 (Sept. 1984): 317.

27. The range of the third parties' electoral activities can be traced in *Congressional Quarterly's Guide to U.S. Elections* (Washington, D.C., 1975).

28. Ibid. The increasing legal difficulties of third parties in the 1880's and early 1890's are discussed in three works by Peter Argersinger: *Populism and Politics: William Alfred Pfeffer and the People's Party* (Lexington: Univ. of Kentucky Press, 1974); "New Perspectives on Election Fraud in the Gilded Age," *Political Science Quarterly*, 100 (Winter 1985–86): 669–87; and "'A Place on the Ballot': Fusion Politics and Antifusion Laws," *AHR*, 85 (April 1980): 287–306.

29. There is a great deal of work on the Free Soilers and the election of 1848. In addition to Sewell, *Ballots for Freedom*, see, in particular, Frederick Blue, *The Free Soilers: Third Party Politics, 1848–54* (Urbana: Univ. of Illinois Press, 1973); Joseph Rayback, *Free Soil: The Election of 1848* (Lexington: Univ. of Kentucky Press, 1970); and John Mayfield, *Rehearsal for Republicanism: Free Soil and the Politics of Antislavery* (Port Washington, N.Y.: Kennikat Press, 1980).

30. Kraut, "Partisanship and Principles," 80, 90. The Indiana prohibitionists' quotation is from Kleppner, "Greenback and Prohibition Parties," in Schlesinger, *History of Parties*, 2: 1594–1697.

31. Kraut, "Partisanship and Principles," 90.

32. In addition to Kleppner's discussion of the Prohibitionists in *The Third Electoral System*, see also his essay "Partisanship and Ethnoreligious Conflict: The Third Electoral System, 1853–1892," in Kleppner et al., *The Evolution of American Electoral Systems* (Westport, Conn.: Greenwood Press, 1981), 113–46.

33. Porter and Johnson, *National Party Platforms*, 4–8; Kleppner, *Third Electoral System*, 253.

34. The ambivalence within these movements has led some scholars to label them more as pressure groups than real political parties. See, for example, Benson, *Concept*, 110.

35. Tindall, "Peoples' Party'" in Schlesinger, *History of Parties*, 2: 1701.

36. Sheldon Stromquist, "Different Universes: Working Class Political Behavior in Local and National Elections During the 1890s" (paper presented at

the annual meeting of the Organization of American Historians, 1986), 28. The battle over different strategies is a constant theme of all studies of the political challengers.

37. New York *Herald*, Aug. 30, 1878; Paula Baker, "The Domestication of Politics: Women and American Political Society," *AHR*, 89 (June 1984): 620–47. See also Kraut and Field, "Politics Versus Principle."

38. "Address and Resolutions Adopted at the Whig State Convention, Worcester, October 3, 1849 . . ." (Boston, 1849), 19; *Papers for the People*, June ?, 1852 (no. 1): 4; "Proceedings of the Republican Convention ([Virginia, 1839]), 19.

39. Kleppner points out, however, that the third parties' share of the national vote was increasing from 1876 to 1892. *Third Electoral System*, 239.

40. *Guide to Elections*. On George, see Scobey, "Boycotting the Politics Factory." On the Greenbacker support, see Kleppner, *Third Electoral System*, 267–79.

41. *Guide to Elections*. The George figures are from *The Tribune Almanac . . . 1888* (New York: Tribune Co., 1888).

42. John F. Reynolds, *Testing Democracy: Electoral Behavior and Progressive Reform in New Jersey, 1880–1920* (Chapel Hill: Univ. of North Carolina Press, 1988), 44–45; Argersinger, "A Place on the Ballot." The overall close competitive structure of national politics after the Civil War is discussed in Samuel T. McSeveney, *The Politics of Depression: Voting Behavior in the Northeast, 1893–1896* (New York: Oxford Univ. Press, 1972), chap. 1.

43. Kleppner, *Evolution of Electoral Systems*, 128.

44. Ray Shortridge, "Voting for Minor Parties in the Antebellum Midwest," *Indiana Magazine of History*, 74 (June 1978): 117–34; Kleppner, *Third Electoral System*, 238ff; David C. Hammack, *Power and Society: Greater New York at the Turn of the Century* (New York: Columbia Univ. Press, 1982), 112ff, 174–76; Thomas P. Alexander, "Harbinger of the Collapse of the Second Party System: The Free Soil Party of 1848," in Lloyd E. Ambrosius, ed., *Presidents, Parties and People: American Politics During the Civil War Era* (Lincoln: Univ. of Nebraska Press, 1990), 17–54.

45. Argersinger, *Pfeffer*, 79, 304; Richard L. McCormick, *From Realignment to Reform: Political Change in New York State, 1893–1910* (Ithaca, N.Y.: Cornell Univ. Press, 1981), 35; Joel H. Silbey "After 'The First Northern Victory': The Republican Party Comes to Congress, 1855–1856," *JIH*, 20 (Summer 1989): 1–24.

46. Benson, *Concept*, 112.

47. William Nisbet Chambers and Walter Dean Burnham, eds., *The American Party Systems: Stages of Political Development* 2d ed. (New York: Oxford Univ. Press, 1975), 4; Mayfield, *Rehearsal for Republicanism*, 138.

48. Fink, *Workingmen's Democracy*, 225; Alexander, "Harbinger of Collapse"; Kleppner, *Evolution of Electoral Systems*, 119–20.

49. Fink, *Workingmen's Democracy*, 225. Women's participation in the public politics of this political nation seems to fit this role and, perhaps, move somewhat beyond it. Not all women who became involved in the public sphere

challenged the conventional norms of the political nation. As earlier noted, many women played a continuing role in the ceremonials and rituals of American politics, in public meetings and election rallies. At the same time, many also added "their voice to public discourse." They made attempts to participate in the debates over and the framing of public policy. Much of their advocacy fell within the boundaries of the outsiders' political programs. They often took the lead in organizing pressure groups on behalf of some reform. Frustrated in their efforts to win the right to vote themselves, a campaign that preoccupied many women's groups throughout these years, they were more successful, in Mary Ryan's words, in "winning concessions here and there, imprinting their ideas on public debates, and adding their perspective to the array of conflicting interests that influenced policy decisions." *Women in Politics: Between Banners and Ballots, 1825–1880* (Baltimore: Johns Hopkins Univ. Press, 1990), especially 126, 168, 173. See also Ellen C. DuBois, "Outgrowing the Compact of the Fathers: Equal Rights, Woman Suffrage and the United States Constitution, 1820–1878," *JAH*, 74 (Dec. 1987): 836–56; Lori D. Ginzberg, "'Moral Suasion Is Moral Balderdash': Women, Politics and Social Activism in the 1850s," *JAH*, 73 (Dec. 1986): 601–22; and Ginzberg, *Women and the Work of Benevolence: Morality, Politics and Class in the 19th Century United States* (New Haven: Yale Univ. Press, 1990).

Chapter Twelve

1. The survival of the partisan nation is one of the main themes of Joel H. Silbey, *A Respectable Minority: The Democratic Party in the Civil War Era, 1860–1868* (New York: Norton, 1978). See also Michael Les Benedict, "The Party Going Strong: Congress and Elections in the Mid-19th Century," *Congress and the Presidency*, 9 (Winter 1981–82): 37–60.

2. Samuel S. Cox, "Grant or Greeley, Speech . . . on the Issues of the Presidential Campaign of 1872" (New York, 1872), 4; "Republican Addresses and Platform. Addresses of Hon. Edwin D. Morgan and Hon. Roscoe Conkling at the Republican State Convention . . . Utica, Sept. 23, 1874" (n.p., [1874]), 5–6.

There is an enormous scholarly literature on post–Civil War politics. Among the studies I found most illuminating are Morton Keller, *Affairs of State: Public Life in Late Nineteenth-Century America* (Cambridge, Mass.: Harvard Univ. Press, 1977); Paul Kleppner, *The Third Electoral System: 1853–1892* (Chapel Hill: Univ. of North Carolina Press, 1979); Richard Jensen, *The Winning of the Midwest: Social and Political Conflict, 1888–96* (Chicago: Univ. of Chicago Press, 1971); Samuel T. McSeveney, *The Politics of Depression: Voting Behavior in the Northeast, 1893–1896* (New York: Oxford Univ. Press, 1972); Loren Beth, *The Development of the American Constitution, 1877–1917* (New York: Harper & Row, 1971); Michael McGerr, *The Decline of Popular Politics: The American North, 1865–1928* (New York: Oxford Univ. Press, 1986); and Geoffry Blodgett, "A New Look at the American Gilded Age," *Historical Reflections*, 1 (Winter 1974): 231–46.

3. "Speech [at the Young Men's Democratic Club], Nov. 20, 1874" (n.p.,

n.d.), 4; "Speeches of Warner Miller . . . New York, October 22, 1887 . . . Brooklyn, October 29, 1887" (New York: Republican Publishing Co., 1888), 4.

4. "Official Proceedings of the National Democratic Convention, . . . 1880" (Dayton, Ohio, 1882), 4; "Remarks of Hon. Clarkson N. Potter at Tammany Hall, July 4, 1871" (New York, 1871), 6; *The Campaign Book of the Democratic Party, 1886* (Washington, D.C., 1886), 228.

5. "New York State Democratic Convention . . . Held at Syracuse, April 20, 1880" (New York, 1880), 13; "Senator Thurman's Speech at Cincinnati, Sept. 10, 1870 . . ." (n.p., n.d.), 3; "Remarks of Hon. Clarkson N. Potter at Tammany Hall, July 4, 1871" (New York, 1871), 3; speech of John Quincy Adams, 1870, quoted in Dale Baum, *The Civil War Party System: The Case of Massachusetts, 1848–1876* (Chapel Hill: Univ. of North Carolina Press, 1984), 154; *Brooklyn Eagle*, Aug. ?, 1883, clipping in vol. 1 of Samuel J. Tilden Scrapbooks, New York Public Library.

6. Keller, *Affairs of State*, 33; *CR*, 43rd Cong., 1st sess., *Appendix*, 248; Baum, *Civil War Party System*, 125; "Stand by the Republican Colors! Speech of Hon. Henry Wilson of Massachusetts at Great Falls, New Hampshire, February 24, 1872" (n.p., n.d.), 8. For an interesting exploration of the way some Americans reacted to all of this, see Alan Dawley and Paul Faler, "Working Class Culture and Politics in the Industrial Revolution: Sources of Loyalism and Rebellion," *Journal of Social History*, 9 (Spring 1976): especially 476.

7. "First Roar of the Democratic Gun! Ovation to Ohio's Next Governor, Hon. Thos. Ewing. Washington, D.C., June 6, 1879," (Washington, D.C., 1879), 6; [Horace J. Subers], "The Democratic Party and the South" (n.p., [1880]), 3; "Speeches of Ex-Gov. Horatio Seymour & Hon. Samuel J. Tilden, Before the Democratic State Convention at Albany, March 11, 1868," *World* tracts no. 1 (n.p., n.d.), 15; *CR*, 44th Cong., 1st sess., *Appendix*, 29; "Official Proceedings of the National Democratic Convention . . . 1876" (St. Louis, Mo., 1876), 65.

8. On southern politics generally, see C. Vann Woodward, *Origins of the New South, 1877–1913* (Baton Rouge: Louisiana Univ. Press, 1951). On parties and voters in particular, see Kleppner, *Third Electoral System*, especially 98–120; and J. Morgan Kousser, *The Shaping of Southern Politics: Suffrage Restriction and the Establishment of the One-Party South, 1880–1910* (New Haven, Conn.: Yale Univ. Press, 1974).

9. Robert Marcus, *Grand Old Party: Political Structure in the Gilded Age, 1880–1896* (New York: Oxford Univ. Press, 1971), 11. Conkling is quoted in Thomas Reeves, *Gentleman Boss: The Life of Chester Alan Arthur* (New York: Knopf, 1975), 174.

10. Keller, *Affairs of State*, 241; *Historical Statistics of the United States, Colonial Times to 1970* (Washington, D.C.: Government Printing Office, 1975), 2: 1072.

11. See *Congressional Quarterly's Guide to U.S. Elections* (Washington, D.C., 1975). McSeveney, *Politics of Depression*, chap. 1, offers a clear and concise discussion of the competitive electoral structure in these years. For a far-ranging discussion of the South's electoral system, see Kousser, *Shaping of Southern Politics*.

12. Allan Peskin, *Garfield: A Biography* (Kent, Ohio: Kent State Univ. Press, 1978), 386. The Reading, Pa., *Daily Eagle* told its readers on Nov. 7, 1879, that New York was "the most uncertain state in politics. No political party can rely on it one year with another." In Tilden Scrapbooks, 1. The situation is well covered in Kleppner, *Third Electoral Era*.

13. Reuben Davis, *Recollections of Mississippi and Mississippians* (Boston: Houghton, Mifflin, 1889), 193; McSeveney, *Politics of Depression*, 7.

14. Kleppner, *Third Electoral System*, 196.

15. Jensen, *Winning of Midwest*, 7; "Republican Addresses and Platform . . . 1874," 12.

16. "Speech of Hon. Columbus Delano Delivered at Raleigh, North Carolina, July 24, 1872" (n.p., n.d.), 7; "Official Proceedings of the National Democratic Convention Held at Baltimore, July 9, 1872" (Boston, 1872), 59; "Monopoly Rule, Speech of Col. Llewellyn Baber at Lancaster, Ohio, August 10, 1871" (n.p., n.d.), 16; Cox, "Grant or Greeley," 8; "Issues of the Day, Speech of Hon. Roscoe Conkling of New York . . . at Cooper Institute . . . July 23, 1872" (n.p., n.d.), 20.

17. Delano speech, Raleigh, July 24, 1827, 2; "Speech Delivered by Hon. Lyman Tremain . . . at Cooper Institute, . . . Sept. 18, 1872" (n.p., n.d.), 4, 5; "Proceedings of the Ninth Republican National Convention . . ." (Chicago, 1888), 9.

18. "Address of the Democratic State Central Committee," (n.p., [1876]), 3; "Speech of Stanley Matthews at Athens, Ohio, August 25, 1877, on Political Questions" (Cincinnati, Ohio, 1877), 49–50; Allan Peskin, "Who Were the Stalwarts? Who Were Their Rivals? Republican Factions in the Gilded Age," *Political Science Quarterly*, 99 (Winter 1984–85): 707. There is a great deal on organizational activities in Peskin, *Garfield*, and Reeves, *Gentleman Boss*. Party organization in two states in this era is excellently covered in Albert V. House, "The Democratic State Central Committee of Indiana in 1880: A Case Study in Party Tactics and Finance," *Indiana Magazine of History*, 58 (Sept. 1962): 179–210; and John R. Williams, "*Testing the Iron Law of Oligarchy:* The Formal Structure of the New Jersey Democratic Party in the 1880s," *Shippensburg State College Review*, May 1971: 15–23. Throughout, the same paeans to organization as had been expressed since the late 1830's were a constant feature of political rhetoric. See, as one example, "Address of the State Committee to the Liberal Republicans of New York" (n.p., [1872]), 36.

19. Keller, *Affairs of State*, 536–37; Alexander J. Flick, *Samuel J. Tilden: A Study in Political Sagacity* (New York: Dodd, Mead, 1939), 249; Peskin, *Garfield*, 504–5.

20. Jensen, *Winning of Midwest*, 6; The *Campaign Book of the Democratic Party* (Washington, D.C., 1882), 222; Arthur J. C. Sowdon, "Political Duties. An Essay, . . . February 14, 1878" (n.p., n.d.), 14; "Senator Chandler's Last Speech Delivered at Chicago, Oct. 31, 1879" (Chicago, 1879), 26.

21. "Oration Delivered by the Hon. Fernando Wood at Tammany Hall, N.Y., July 4th 1876" (New York, 1876), 7–8; "Speech [of Roscoe Conkling], Republican State Convention at Saratoga, September 26, 1878" (n.p., n.d.), 7;

"First Roar of the Democratic Gun," 7; Proceedings of the Eighth Republican National Convention" (Chicago, 1884), 7.

22. Herbert Gutman, *Work, Culture and Society in Industrializing America: Essays in American Working Class and Social History* (New York: Knopf, 1976), 57. On the urban political machines, one can begin with Seymour Mandelbaum, *Boss Tweed's New York* (New York: Wiley, 1965); Alexander Callow, *The Tweed Ring* (New York: Oxford Univ. Press, 1966); Leo Hershkowitz, *Tweed's New York: Another Look* (Garden City, N.Y.: Anchor Press, 1977); and Steven P. Erie, *Rainbow's End: Irish-Americans and the Dilemmas of Urban Machine Politics, 1840–1985* (Berkeley: Univ. of California Press, 1988).

23. Keller, *Affairs of State*, 541–42.

24. James Kehl, *Boss Rule in the Gilded Age: Matt Quay of Pennsylvania* (Pittsburgh: Univ. of Pittsburgh Press, 1981), Reeves, *Gentleman Boss*, Peskin, "Who Were the Stalwarts?," Keller, *Affairs of State*, and Marcus, *Grand Old Party*, are all insightful on the culture and perspective of the political boss.

25. *CG*, 43rd Cong., 2d sess., *Appendix*, 191; Yates, as quoted in Rothman, *Politics and Power*, 19. On Congress in this period, one can begin with David Rothman, *Politics and Power: The United States Senate, 1869–1901* (Cambridge, Mass.: Harvard Univ. Press, 1966); and Margaret Susan Thompson, *The 'Spider Web': Congress and Lobbying in the Age of Grant* (Ithaca, N.Y.: Cornell Univ. Press, 1985). The best introduction to the state legislative experience is Ballard C. Campbell, *Representative Democracy: Public Policy and Midwestern Legislatures in the Late Nineteenth Century* (Cambridge, Mass.: Harvard Univ. Press, 1980).

26. Useful introductions to the causes and nature of this new political restlessness are Samuel P. Hays, *The Response to Industrialism, 1877–1914* (Chicago: Univ. of Chicago Press, 1957); and Robert Wiebe, *The Search for Order, 1877–1920* (New York: Hill & Wang, 1967).

27. Hays, *Response to Industrialism*; Wiebe, *Search for Order*. Keller, *Affairs of State*, has a great deal on the social and economic changes as well.

28. George Miller, *Railroads and the Granger Laws* (Madison: Univ. of Wisconsin Press, 1971), is a model study of some of these business stirrings early in the period. See also Gerald D. Nash, "Origins of the Interstate Commerce Act of 1887," *Pennsylvania History*, 24 (July 1957): 181–90; and Edward A. Purcell, "Ideas and Interests: Businessmen and the Interstate Commerce Act," *JAH*, 54 (Dec. 1967): 561–78.

29. Keller, *Affairs of State*, 319ff; Lee Benson, *Merchants, Farmers and Railroads: Railroad Regulation and New York State Politics, 1850–1887* (Cambridge, Mass.: Harvard Univ. Press, 1955). As William Brock has written, "Comparing 1900 with 1870, one finds that in every field the states did more, spent more, and employed far more people." *Investigation and Responsibility: Public Responsibility in the United States, 1865–1900* (New York: Cambridge Univ. Press, 1984).

30. Louis Galambo, "The Emerging Organizational Synthesis in Modern American History," *Business History Review*, 441 (Autumn 1970): 284.

31. The work of Samuel P. Hays provides a key overview to this emerging

political economy. See, in addition to *Response to Industrialism*, his essay "Political Parties and the Community-Society Continuum," in William N. Chambers and Walter Dean Burnham, eds., *The American Party Systems: Stages of Political Development* (New York: Oxford Univ. Press, 1967), 152–81; "Politics and Society: Society and Politics," *JIH*, 15 (Winter 1985): 481–99; and *American Political History as Social Analysis: Essays* (Knoxville: Univ. of Tennessee Press, 1980). See also Martin J. Sklar, *The Corporate Reconstruction of American Capitalism, 1890–1916: The Market, the Law, and Politics* (New York: Cambridge Univ. Press, 1988).

32. Keller, *Affairs of State*, 319.

33. Hays, "Politics and Society," 491; Kleppner, "Partisanship and Ethnoreligious Conflict: The Third Electoral System, 1853–1892," in Paul Kleppner et al., *The Evolution of American Electoral Systems* (Westport, Conn.: Greenwood Press, 1981), 140.

34. Kleppner, "Partisanship," 140.

35. James McGregor Burns, *The Workshop of Democracy* (New York: Knopf, 1985), 213.

36. Ibid., 206; Keller, *Affairs of State*, 289.

37. Political parties, Hays points out, "blunted, modified, compromised and reformulated" demands to meet their own needs. "Politics and Society," 491.

38. Galambos, "Emerging Organizational Synthesis"; Wiebe, *Search for Order*.

39. Hays, *Response to Industrialism*; Wiebe, *Search for Order*; Austin Ranney, *Curing the Mischief of Faction: Party Reform in America* (Berkeley: Univ. of California Press, 1974).

40. Hays, *Response to Industrialism*, and Wiebe, *Search for Order*, cover this ground, although there is some variation in emphases.

41. George Washington Curtis, "The Reason and Result of Civil Service Reform. An Address . . . May 29, 1888" (New York, 1888), 22; Matthew Hale, "Conditions and Limits of Party Fealty" (New York, 1880), 9; *CR*, 45th Cong., 2d sess., *Appendix*, 189; "Official Proceedings of the Anti-Third Term Republican Convention . . . 1880" (n.p., n.d.), 9; William Everett, "Speech at a Meeting of the Independents of Quincy, Mass., 13 September, 1884" (n.p., n.d.), 2; "Chapters for the Times . . . by a Berkshire Farmer" (Lee, Mass., 1884), 3; "Report of the National Executive Committee of Republicans and Independents, Presidential Campaign of 1884" (New York, 1885), 23; Richard L. McCormick has a chapter, "Antiparty Thought in the Gilded Age," in *The Party Period and Public Policy: American Politics from the Age of Jackson to the Progressive Era* (New York: Oxford Univ. Press, 1986), 228–59.

42. "Address of Carl Schurz at Brooklyn, N.Y., August 5, 1884" (n.p., n.d.), 28. Robert Marcus has suggested about charges of corruption at the polls that when electoral competition is as close as it was in this period, "men tend to dwell on the minor episodes that seem to make up a definable margin of victory." *Grand Old Party*, 145.

43. Gerald McFarland, *Mugwumps, Morals and Politics, 1884–1920* (Am-

herst: Univ. of Massachusetts Press, 1975); Geoffrey Blodgett, *The Gentle Reformers: Massachusetts Democrats in the Cleveland Era* (Cambridge, Mass.: Harvard Univ. Press, 1966).

44. "Proceedings of the Republican National Convention [Cincinnati, 1876]" (Concord, 1876), 98. On election fraud and efforts to control it, see Paul Kleppner, *Who Voted: The Dynamics of Electoral Turnout, 1870–1980* (New York: Praeger, 1982), 59; and Albie Burke, "Federal Regulation of Congressional Elections in Northern Cities, 1871–94," *American Journal of Legal History*, 14 (Jan. 1970): 17–34.

45. Andrew D. White, "A Letter to the Republican Club of the City of New York . . . February 12, 1887" (n.p., n.d.); Clarkson N. Potter, "The Dangers & the Duty of the Democracy. A Letter to the Hon. Francis Kernan" (New York, 1876), 10. On the Half-Breeds generally, see Benson, *Merchants, Farmers and Railroads*; and Richard E. Welch, Jr., *George Frisbie Hoar and the Half-Breed Republicans* (Cambridge, Mass.: Harvard Univ. Press, 1971).

46. On some of the changes beginning to occur among the voters, see Benson, *Merchants, Farmers and Railroads*, 185; Kleppner, *Third Electoral System*; Kleppner, *Continuity and Change in Electoral Politics, 1893–1928* (New York: Oxford Univ. Press, 1986); Michael McGerr, *The Decline of Popular Politics: The American North, 1865–1928* (New York: Greenwood Press, 1986); and John F. Reynolds, *Testing Democracy: Electoral Behavior and Progressive Reform in New Jersey, 1880–1920* (Chapel Hill: Univ. of North Carolina Press, 1988).

47. Cleveland's acceptance letter, in "Official Proceedings of the National Democratic Convention . . ." (New York, 1884), 293.

48. For a useful overview of one state's politics as the 1890's began, see Richard L. McCormick, *From Realignment to Reform: Political Change in New York State, 1893–1910* (Ithaca, N.Y.: Cornell Univ. Press, 1981). His first chapter is titled "Nineteenth-Century Politics in Decline."

49. Marcus, *Grand Old Party*, 5.

50. Jensen, *Winning of Midwest*, 33, 175. In 1888, too, there were signs of the future, since some new industrialists spend a great deal of money to defeat the low-tariff Grover Cleveland.

51. McSeveney, *Politics of Depression*, and Kleppner, *Third Electoral System*, cover the 1893–94 elections magnificently. McCormick, *From Realignment to Reform*, details the impetus for change they triggered.

52. *Congressional Quarterly's Guide to U.S. Elections*, 279, 662–71.

53. See, as one example, Roger Wyman, "Wisconsin Ethnic Groups and the Election of 1890," *Wisconsin Magazine of History*, 51 (Summer 1968): 269–93.

54. McSeveney, *Politics of Depression*; Kleppner, *Continuity and Change*, chaps. 1–4.

55. *Historical Statistics*, 2: 1079–1080, 1083. On the election of 1896, see Paul Glad, *McKinley, Bryan and the People* (Philadelphia: Lippincott, 1964).

56. McSeveney, *Politics of Depression*, 87; Kleppner, *Continuity and Change*, 76; Reynolds, *Testing Democracy*, 73.

57. Kleppner, *Continuity and Change*.

Chapter Thirteen

1. In a situation of frequent, sometimes violent, confrontation, "the ballot was added to the strike; the nominating convention to the riot; partisan insurgency to protest; and party to class." Amy Bridges, "Rethinking the Origins of Machine Politics," in John M. Mollenkopf, ed., *Power, Culture, and Place: Essays on New York City* (New York: Russell Sage Foundation, 1987), 66.

2. On the "System of 1896," see Walter Dean Burnham, "The System of 1896: An Analysis," in Paul Kleppner et al., *The Evolution of American Electoral Systems* (Westport, Conn.: Greenwood Press, 1981), 147–202; and, most recently, in *Social Science History*, 10 (Fall 1986), Richard L. McCormick, "Walter Dean Burnham and 'The System of 1896,'" 245–62, and Walter Dean Burnham, "Periodization Schemes and 'Party Systems': The 'System of 1896' as a Case in Point," 263–314.

3. On the Progressives, see Arthur S. Link and Richard L. McCormick, *Progressivism* (Arlington Heights, Va.: Harlan Davidson, 1983); and more generally, Stephen Skowronek, *Building a New American State: The Expansion of National Administrative Capacities, 1877–1920* (New York: Cambridge Univ. Press, 1982). On the transformations under way in the South, see J. Morgan Kousser, *The Shaping of Southern Politics: Suffrage Restriction and the Establishment of the One-Party South, 1880–1910* (New Haven, Conn.: Yale Univ. Press, 1974); in a midwestern state, Philip R. VanderMeer, *The Hoosier Politician: Officeholding and Political Culture in Indiana, 1896–1920* (Urbana: Univ. of Illinois Press, 1984); and in two key industrial states from the 1890's to the First World War, Richard L. McCormick, *From Realignment to Reform: Political Change in New York State, 1893–1910* (Ithaca, N.Y.: Cornell Univ. Press, 1981); and John F. Reynolds, *Testing Democracy: Electoral Behavior and Progressive Reform in New Jersey, 1880–1920* (Chapel Hill: Univ. of North Carolina Press, 1988). It should be noted that neither McCormick nor Reynolds accepts my argument that 1893 clearly marked the end of the partisan political era. Both prefer an early-20th-century date.

The larger themes of change over the 20th century are introduced in Samuel P. Hays, *American Political History as Social Analysis* (Knoxville: Univ. of Tennessee Press, 1980); Hays, "Introduction—The New Organizational Society," in Jerry Israel, ed., *Building the Organizational Society: Essays on Associational Activities in Modern America* (New York: Free Press, 1972), 1–16; and Walter Dean Burnham, *The Current Crisis in American Politics* (New York: Oxford Univ. Press, 1982).

4. Michael E. McGerr, *The Decline of Popular Politics: The American North, 1865–1928* (New York: Oxford Univ. Press, 1986), provides an excellent examination of the processes underlying the political changes. See also Richard Jensen, "Armies, Admen and Crusaders: Types of Presidential Election Campaigns," *History Teacher*, 2 (Jan. 1969): 33–50.

5. James McGregor Burns, *The Power to Lead: The Crisis of the American Presidency* (New York: Simon & Schuster, 1984), 140; Lewis Gould, *Reform and Regulation: American Politics from Roosevelt to Wilson*, 2d ed. (New York: Knopf, 1986), 22.

6. Richard Jensen, "Party Coalitions and the Search for Modern Values, 1820–1970," in Seymour Martin Lipset, ed., *Emerging Coalitions in American Politics* (San Francisco: Institute for Contemporary Studies, 1978), 27.

7. Link and McCormick, *Progressivism*; Robert Wiebe, *Businessmen and Reform: A Study of the Progressive Movement* (Cambridge, Mass.: Harvard Univ. Press, 1962). The literature on the shift in governance beginning with Progressivism is enormous. One can start with Israel, *Building the Organizational Society*. A recent overview is Sean Cashman, *America in the Age of the Titans: From the Rise of Theodore Roosevelt to the Death of FDR* (New York: New York Univ. Press, 1988).

8. Daniel T. Rodgers, "In Search of Progressivism," *Reviews in American History*, 10 (Dec. 1982): 114; John F. Reynolds and Richard L. McCormick, "Outlawing 'Treachery': Split Tickets and Ballot Laws in New York and New Jersey, 1880–1914," *JAH*, 72 (March 1986): 856.

9. The role of the urban political machines is described in John D. Buenker, *Urban Liberalism and Progressive Reform* (New York: Scribners, 1973); and J. Joseph Huthmacher, *Senator Robert F. Wagner and the Rise of Urban Liberalism* (New York: Atheneum, 1968). On the New Deal voter realignment, see Walter Dean Burnham, *Critical Elections and the Mainsprings of American Politics* (New York: Oxford Univ. Press, 1970); and Kristi Anderson, *The Creation of a Democratic Majority* (Chicago: Univ. of Chicago Press, 1979). On the New Deal revolution in government, see, among many, Albert U. Romasco, *The Politics of Recovery: Roosevelt's New Deal* (New York: Oxford Univ. Press, 1983); and Ellis Hawley, *The New Deal and the Problem of Monopoly* (Princeton, N.J.: Princeton Univ. Press, 1966).

10. McGerr, *Decline of Politics*, covers the shift in the press in the first quarter of the 20th century. See also James McGregor Burns, *The Workshop of Democracy: The American Experiment*, 2 (New York: Knopf, 1985): 521.

11. Among the many books on the impact of television on contemporary American politics, see Austin Ranney, *Channels of Power: The Impact of Television on American Politics* (New York: Basic Books, 1983); Doris Graber, *Mass Media and American Politics*, 3d ed. (Washington, D.C.: Congressional Quarterly Press, 1988); James David Barber, *The Pulse of Politics: The Rhythm of Presidential Elections in the Twentieth Century* (New York: Norton, 1980).

12. Kenneth Boulding, *The Organizational Revolution: A Study in the Ethics of Economic Organization* (New York: Harper, 1953), is a good place to begin. See also Theodore J. Lowi, *The End of Liberalism: Ideology, Policy and the Crisis of Public Authority* (New York: Norton, 1968); and James Q. Wilson, "The Rise of the Bureaucratic State," *The Public Interest*, 41 (Fall 1975): 77–103. On Congress, see David W. Brady, Joseph Cooper, and Patricia A. Hurley, "The Decline of Party in the U.S. House of Representatives, 1887–1968," *Legislative Studies Quarterly*, 4 (Aug. 1979): 381–407.

13. Austin Ranney, *Curing the Mischiefs of Faction: Party Reform in America* (Berkeley: Univ. of California Press, 1974).

14. Lowi, *End of Liberalism*.

15. *New York Times Week in Review*, Aug. 3, 1980; E19; "Stability and

Change in 1960: A Reinstating Election," in Angus Campbell et al., *Elections and the Political Order* (New York: Wiley, 1966), 78–95; Richard Jensen, "The Last Party System: Decay of Consensus, 1932–1980," in Kleppner et al., *Evolution of Electoral Systems*, 219. On the decline of party conventions, see Byron Shafer, *Bifurcated Politics: Evolution and Reform in the National Party Convention* (Cambridge, Mass.: Harvard Univ. Press, 1988); and William Crotty, *Decisions for Democrats: Reforming the Party Structure* (Baltimore: Johns Hopkins Univ. Press, 1978).

16. Benjamin Ginsberg, *The Consequences of Consent: Elections, Citizen Control, and Popular Acquiescence* (New York: Random House, 1982); Austin Ranney, *The Federalization of Presidential Primaries* (Washington, D.C.: American Enterprise Institute, 1978), 24.

17. Paul Kleppner, *Who Voted: The Dynamics of Electoral Turnout, 1870–1980* (New York: Praeger, 1982).

18. The "party of nonvoters" usage is from Walter Dean Burnham, "The Appearance and Disappearance of the American Voter" (unpublished paper, American Bar Association Conference on Voting Participation, 1978), 50. See also Everett C. Ladd, *Where Have All The Voters Gone? The Fracturing of America's Political Parties*, 2d ed. (New York: Norton, 1982).

19. Walter Dean Burnham, comp., *Politics/America: The Cutting Edge of Change* (New York: Van Nostrand, 1973), 39; Everett C. Ladd, Jr., "As the Realignment Turns: A Drama in Many Acts," *Public Opinion*, 7 (Dec.–Jan. 1985): 2.

20. Kleppner, *Who Voted*, especially 24. Core voters voted in both the presidential and the succeeding off-year election; marginals voted in the first but not in the second, and nonvoters participated in neither. Among southerners, the numbers were: 1876–90, core 46.7%, marginal 22.7%, non 30.4%; 1960–78, 30.9%, 17.4%, and 51.5% respectively.

21. Everett C. Ladd, Jr., with Charles D. Hadley, *Transformations of the American Party System: Party Coalitions from the New Deal to the 1970s*, 2d ed. (New York: Norton, 1978); Gerald Pomper, *Voters' Choice: Varieties of American Electoral Behavior* (New York: Dodd, Mead, 1975); Anthony King, "The American Polity in the Late 1970s: Building Coalitions in the Sand," in King, ed., *The New American Political System* (Washington, D.C.: American Enterprise Institute, 1978), 372.

22. Walter Dean Burnham, "American Politics in the 1970's: Beyond Party?," in William N. Chambers and Walter Dean Burnham, *The American Party Systems: Stages of Political Development*, 2d ed. (New York: Oxford Univ. Press, 1975), 336. The contours of presidential elections since the 1960's are covered in Ladd, with Hadley, *Transformation*; Burnham, *Current Crisis*; and successive issues of *Public Opinion*. On the shifting congressional voting universe more generally, one can begin with David Brady, *Critical Elections and Congressional Policy Making* (Stanford, Calif.: Stanford Univ. Press, 1988).

23. Pomper, *Voter's Choice*; Norman Nie, Sidney Verba, and John R. Petrocik, *The Changing American Voter* (Cambridge, Mass.: Harvard Univ. Press, 1976); Walter DeVries and V. Lance Tarrance, *The Ticket Splitter: A New Force*

in American Politics (Grand Rapids, Mich.: Eerdmens, 1972); Jensen, "Last Party System."

24. Robert T. Nakamura, "The Reformed Nominating System: Its Crisis and Uses," *PS*, 16 (Autumn 1983): 672; Robert N. Bellah et al., *Habits of the Heart: Individual and Commitment in American Life* (Berkeley: Univ. of California Press, 1985), 201. House Speaker Jim Wright made the "cannibalism" remark in his resignation speech. *New York Times*, June 1, 1989. On voting behavior in the 1980's, see, among many, Austin Ranney, ed., *The American Elections of 1980* (Washington, D.C.: American Enterprise Institute, 1981); and Gerald Pomper et al., *The Election of 1984: Reports and Interpretations* (New York: Chatham House, 1985). On dealignment, see, also among many, Burnham, *Current Crisis*; Everett C. Ladd, "On Mandates, Realignments, and the 1984 Election," *Political Science Quarterly*, 100 (Spring 1985): 1–25; and Bruce A. Campbell and Richard J. Trilling, *Realignment in American Politics: Toward a Theory* (Austin: Univ. of Texas Press, 1979). There is no better way to trace these changes and feel the texture of the shifting electoral, organizational, and strategic dynamic than to read the successive editions of Nelson Polsby and Aaron Wildavsky, *Presidential Elections: Strategies of American Electoral Politics*, 1st–6th eds. (New York: Scribners, 1964–84).

25. Everett C. Ladd, Jr., "The National Election," *Public Opinion*, 11 (Jan.–Feb. 1989): 60; John Kenneth White and Dwight Morris, "Shattered Images: Political Parties in the 1984 Election," *Public Opinion*, 6 (Dec.–Jan. 1984): 48. In general, see Martin P. Wattenberg, *The Decline of American Political Parties, 1952–1984* (Cambridge, Mass.: Harvard Univ. Press, 1986); and Jeff Fishel, ed., *Parties and Elections in an Anti-Party Age* (Bloomington: Indiana Univ. Press, 1978). Ironically, as the role of parties shrank, they became more disciplined and ideologically taut than they had been for much of the 20th century.

26. *New Republic*, March 19, 1984: 14, 42.

27. *New Statesman*, Dec. 14, 1984.

28. Burnham, "Appearance and Disappearance," 55; *Time*, Aug. 6, 1979: 26; *The Economist*, March 29–April 4, 1986: 14; *New York Times*, Nov. 20, 1989: A14.

29. Ladd, *Where Have All the Voters Gone?*, xxiv; Morris Fiorina, "Collective Responsibility," *Daedalus*, 109 (Summer 1980): 44; David Lebedoff, "Primaries Problem: They Produce Jimmy Carter," *Manchester Guardian Weekly*, Sept. 9, 1979: 17; Aaron Wildavsky, "Oh, Bring Back My Party to Me," *Public Interest*, 57 (Fall 1979): 94–98; William M. Lunch, *The Nationalizing of American Politics* (Berkeley: Univ. of California Press, 1987); Nelson Polsby, *Consequences of Party Reform* (New York: Oxford Univ. Press, 1983).

30. Walter Dean Burnham, "The 1984 Election and the Future of American Politics," in Ellis Sandoz and Cecil V. Crabb, Jr., eds., *Election 84: Landslide Without a Mandate?* (New York: New American Library, 1985), 249.

Bibliographic Material

Contemporary Newspapers
and Journals

The following list contains only the most frequently cited publications. A few are cited in the Notes by abbreviations, as indicated at the head of the Notes section, p. 255.

Advance Guard of Democracy, Nashville, Tenn.
American Review: A Whig Journal, Washington, D.C.
Argus (after early 1856, Atlas and Argus), Albany, N.Y.
Atlas (after early 1856, Atlas and Argus), Albany, N.Y.
The Barnburner, New York
The Battery, Washington, D.C.
The Campaign, Washington, D.C.
The Coon Dissector, Dayton, Ohio
Congressional Globe (later the Congressional Record), Washington, D.C.
Daily Globe, Washington, D.C.
Evening Journal, Albany, N.Y.
Federal Union, Milledgeville, Ga.
Globe, Washington, D.C.
The Grape Shot, New York
Illinois State Register, Springfield
Indiana State Sentinel, Indianapolis
The Log Cabin, New York
Louisville Journal, Louisville, Ky.
Nashville Union, Nashville, Tenn.
The National Intelligencer, Washington, D.C.
New Hampshire Statesman, Concord
New York Globe (later New York Daily Globe)
Ohio State Journal, Columbus
Papers for the People, New York
The Rail Splitter, Cincinnati, Ohio
The Recruit, New York
Register, Raleigh, Va.
Republican Sentinel, Richmond, Va.

Richmond Whig, Richmond, Va.
Rough and Ready, Concord, N.H.
The Signal, Washington, D.C.
Southern Banner, Athens, Ga.
Springfield Republican, Springfield, Mass.
Stars and Stripes, Dayton, Ohio
That Same Old Coon, Dayton, Ohio
Tribune, New York
Union, Washington, D.C.
United States Magazine and Democratic Review, Washington, D.C.
The Yeoman, Harrisburg, Pa.
The Young Guard, New York, then Boston

Bibliographic Note

IN THIS NOTE, I have confined myself largely to discussing the scholarly literature that I have found to be the most useful in writing this book. The pioneering effort that established the alignment–critical realignment dynamic as the basic structuring impulse of American politics after 1789 was William Nisbet Chambers and Walter Dean Burnham, eds., *The American Party Systems* (New York: Oxford University Press, 1967; 2d ed., 1975). The essays in Paul Kleppner et al., *The Evolution of American Electoral Systems* (Westport, Conn.: Greenwood Press, 1981), develop that insight in its fullest flowering. Also important are Walter Dean Burnham, *Critical Elections and the Mainsprings of American Politics* (New York: Norton, 1970); Jerome M. Clubb, William H. Flanigan, and Nancy H. Zingale, *Partisan Realignment: Voters, Parties and Government in American History* (Beverly Hills, Calif.: Sage, 1980, 2nd ed., 1990); and David W. Brady, *Critical Elections and Congressional Policy Making* (Stanford, Calif.: Stanford University Press, 1988).

The notion of the 1838–93 period as a separate era is articulated and developed in Lee Benson, Joel H. Silbey, and Phyllis F. Field, "Toward a Theory of Stability and Change in American Voting Patterns: New York State, 1792–1970," in Joel H. Silbey, Allan G. Bogue, and William H. Flanigan, eds., *The History of American Electoral Behavior* (Princeton, N.J.: Princeton University Press, 1978), 78–105; Lee Benson and Joel H. Silbey, "American Political Eras, 1788–1984: Toward a Normative, Substantive, and Conceptual Framework for the Historical Study of American Political Behavior" (paper presented at the annual meeting of the Social Science History Association, 1978); and Joel H. Silbey, "Beyond Realignment and Realignment Theory: American Political Eras, 1789–1989" in Byron E. Shafer, ed., *The End of Realignment?* (Madison, Wisc.: Univ. of Wisconsin Press, 1991), 3–23. See also Richard L. McCormick, *The Party Period and Public Policy: American Politics from the Age of Jackson to the Progressive Period* (New York: Oxford University Press, 1986).

Understanding the nature and contours of the prepartisan political era and the emergence of a new political imperative begins with Michael Wallace, "Changing Concepts of Party in the United States: New York, 1815–1828," *American Historical Review*, 74 (Dec. 1968): 453–91; Richard Hofstadter, *The*

Idea of the Party System: The Rise of Legitimate Opposition in the United States, 1780–1840 (Berkeley: University of California Press, 1969); Ronald P. Formisano, *The Transformation of Political Culture: Massachusetts Parties, 1790s–1840s* (New York: Oxford University Press, 1983); Richard P. McCormick, *The Second American Party System: Party Formation in the Jacksonian Era* (Chapel Hill: University of North Carolina Press, 1966); Donald B. Cole, *Martin Van Buren and the American Political System* (Princeton, N.J.: Princeton University Press, 1984); Lee Benson, *The Concept of Jacksonian Democracy: New York as a Test Case* (Princeton, N.J.: Princeton University Press, 1967); Richard P. McCormick, *The Presidential Game: The Origins of American Presidential Politics* (New York: Oxford University Press, 1982); Roy F. Nichols, *The Invention of the American Political Parties* (New York: Macmillan, 1967); and Michael F. Holt, "The Election of 1840, Voter Mobilization, and the Emergence of the Second American Party System: A Reappraisal of Jacksonian Voting Behavior," in William J. Cooper, Michael F. Holt, and John McCardell, eds., *A Master's Due: Essays in Honor of David Herbert Donald* (Baton Rouge: Louisiana State University Press, 1985), 16–58.

A number of books and articles are essential for following the new political nation's first phase, through 1860. They include Jean Baker, *Affairs of Party: The Political Culture of Northern Democrats in the Mid-Nineteenth Century* (Ithaca, N.Y.: Cornell University Press, 1983); Daniel Walker Howe, *The Political Culture of the American Whigs* (Chicago: University of Chicago Press, 1979); Joel H. Silbey, *The Partisan Imperative: The Dynamics of American Politics Before the Civil War* (New York: Oxford University Press, 1985); William Gienapp, "Politics Seems to Enter into Everything: Political Culture in the North, 1840–1860," in Stephen Maizlish and John Kushma, eds., *Essays on American Antebellum Politics, 1840–1860* (College Station: Texas A&M University Press, 1982), 15–69; and Michael Holt, *The Political Crisis of the 1850s* (New York: Wiley, 1978), which covers a broader sweep than its title suggests.

Much about what was settling in is best described in studies of the politics of individual states and localities. Among the best of these are Charles G. Sellers, Jr., *James K. Polk, Jacksonian, 1795–1843* (Princeton, N.J.: Princeton University Press, 1957); J. Mills Thornton, *Politics and Power in a Slave Society: Alabama, 1800–1860.* (Baton Rouge: Louisiana State University Press, 1978); Marc Kruman, *Parties and Politics in North Carolina, 1836–1865.* (Baton Rouge: Louisiana State University Press, 1983); Harry L. Watson, *Jacksonian Politics and Community Conflict* (Baton Rouge: Louisiana State University Press, 1981); William G. Shade, "Society and Politics in Antebellum Virginia's Southside," *Journal of Southern History*, 53 (May 1987): 163–93; Shade, *Banks or No Banks: The Money Issue in Western Politics, 1832–1865* (Detroit: Wayne State University Press, 1972); Paul Goodman, "The Politics of Industrialism: Massachusetts, 1830–1870," in Richard Bushman et al., eds., *Uprooted Americans* (Boston: Little, Brown, 1979): 161–207; Ronald P. Formisano, *The Birth of Mass Political Parties: Michigan, 1827–1861* (Princeton, N.J.: Princeton University Press, 1971); and M. Philip Lucas, "The Development of The Second Party System in Mississippi, 1817–1846" (Ph.D. dissertation, Cornell University, 1984).

Studies of popular voting behavior began with Lee Benson's *Concept of Jacksonian Democracy* and are developed in the individual state and local studies referred to, as well as in Paul Kleppner, *The Third Electoral System, 1853–1892* (Chapel Hill: University of North Carolina Press, 1979); Kenneth Winkle, *The Politics of Community: Migration and Politics in Antebellum Ohio* (New York: Cambridge University Press, 1988); John Rozett, "The Social Bases of Party Conflict in the Age of Jackson: Individual Voting Behavior in Greene Country, Illinois, 1838–1845" (Ph.D. dissertation, University of Michigan, 1974); Melvyn Hammarberg, *The Indian Voter: The Historical Dynamics of Party Allegiance During the 1870s* (Chicago: University of Chicago Press, 1977); and Robert Swierenga's and Daniel Walker Howe's papers in Mark A Noll, ed., *Religion and American Politics: From the Colonial Period to the 1980s* (New York: Oxford University Press, 1990). Two other historiographic articles of great value are Peter H. Argersinger and John W. Jeffries, "American Electoral History: Party Systems and Voting Behavior," *Research in Micropolitics*, 1 (1986): 1–34; and William G. Shade, "Parties and Politics in Jacksonian America," *Pennsylvania Magazine of History and Biography*, 110 (Oct. 1986): 483–508.

The best study of the electoral realignment of the 1850's is William Gienapp, *The Origins of the Republican Party, 1852–1856* (New York: Oxford University Press, 1987). See also Daniel Crofts, *Reluctant Confederates: Upper South Unionists in the Secession Crisis* (Chapel Hill: University of North Carolina Press, 1989); and Amy Bridges, *A City in the Republic: Antebellum New York and the Origins of Machine Politics* (New York: Cambridge University Press, 1984).

A number of studies by economic, urban, and labor historians provide insight into the social environment on which the political nation rested. Among the most useful to me were Don H. Doyle, *The Social Order of a Frontier Community: Jacksonville, Illinois, 1825–1870* (Urbana: University of Illinois Press, 1978); Susan Hirsch, *Roots of the American Working Class: The Industrialization of Crafts in Newark, 1815–1860* (Philadelphia: University of Pennsylvania Press, 1978); Michael Feldberg, *The Philadelphia Riots of 1844: A Study of Ethnic Conflict* (Westport, Conn.: Greenwood Press, 1975); Robert C. Kenzer, *Kinship and Neighborhood in a Southern Community: Orange County, North Carolina, 1849–1881* (Knoxville: University of Tennessee Press, 1987); and Kathleen Conzen, *Immigrant Milwaukee, 1836–1860: Accommodation and Community in the Frontier City* (Cambridge, Mass.: Harvard University Press, 1976).

The power, reach, and behavior of government in this political nation are illuminated in Richard L. McCormick's "The Party Period and Public Policy," *Journal of American History*, 66 (Sept. 1979): 279–98; Carter Goodrich, *Government Promotion of American Canals and Railroads, 1800–1890* (New York: Columbia University Press, 1960); Harry N. Scheiber, *Ohio Canal Era: A Case Study of Government and the Economy, 1820–1861* (Athens: Ohio University Press, 1969); J. Willard Hurst, *Law and the Condition of Freedom in the Nineteenth-Century United States* (Madison: University of Wisconsin Press, 1956); Wallace Farnham, "'The Weakened Spring of Government': A Study in Nineteenth-Century American History," *American Historical Review*, 68 (April 1963):

662–90; Harold Hyman and William Wiecek, *Equal Justice Under Law: Constitutional Development, 1835–1875* (New York: Harper & Row, 1982); L. Ray Gunn, *The Decline of Authority: Public Economic Policy and Political Development in New York, 1800–1860* (Ithaca, N.Y.: Cornell University Press, 1988); Peter Wallenstein, *From Slave South to New South: Public Policy in Nineteenth-Century Georgia* (Chapel Hill: University of North Carolina Press, 1987); and Harry Scheiber, "Government and the Economy: Studies of the 'Commonwealth' Policy in Nineteenth-Century America," *Journal of Interdisciplinary History*, 3 (Summer 1972): 135–51.

On the political nation's challengers, dissenters, outsiders, and nonparticipants, see especially Sean Wilentz, *Chants Democratic: New York City and the Rise of the American Working Class, 1788–1850* (New York: Oxford University Press, 1984); Paula Baker, "The Domestication of Politics: Women and American Political Society, 1780–1920," *American Historical Review*, 89 (June 1984): 620–47; Mary P. Ryan, *Women in Public: Between Banners and Ballots, 1825–1880* (Baltimore: Johns Hopkins University Press, 1990); William J. Cooper, *The South and the Politics of Slavery* (Baton Rouge: Louisiana State University Press, 1978); John Niven, *John C. Calhoun* (Baton Rouge: Louisiana State University Press, 1988); James Oakes, "From Republicanism to Liberalism: Ideological Change and the Crisis of the Old South," *American Quarterly*, 37 (Fall 1985): 551–71; Harry L. Watson, "Conflict and Collaboration: Yeomen, Slaveholders and Politics in the Antebellum South," *Social History*, 10 (Oct. 1985): 273–98; William W. Freehling, *The Road to Disunion: Secessionists at Bay, 1776–1854* (New York: Oxford Univ. Press, 1990); and Richard Sewell, *Ballots for Freedom: Antislavery Politics in the United States, 1837–1860* (New York: Oxford University Press, 1976).

The continuation of the political nation in the Civil War and its aftermath is well covered in Allan G. Bogue, *The Congressman's Civil War* (New York: Cambridge University Press, 1989); Ballard C. Campbell, *Representative Democracy: Public Policy and Midwest Legislatures in the Late Nineteenth Century* (Cambridge, Mass.: Harvard University Press, 1980); Morton Keller, *Affairs of State: Public Life in Late Nineteenth-Century America* (Cambridge, Mass.: Harvard University Press, 1977); Margaret Susan Thompson, *The 'Spider Web': Congress and Lobbying in the Age of Grant* (Ithaca, N.Y.: Cornell University Press, 1985); Paula Baker, "The Culture of Politics in the Late Ninteenth Century: Community and Political Behavior in Rural New York," *Journal of Social History*, 18 (Winter 1984): 167–93; Leon Fink, *Workingmen's Democracy: The Knights of Labor and American Politics* (Urbana: University of Illinois Press, 1983); and Richard Oestereicher, "Urban Working-Class Political Behavior and Theories of American Electoral Politics, 1870–1940," *Journal of American History*, 74 (March 1988): 1257–1286.

The end of the political nation is the subject of Richard Jensen, *The Winning of the Midwest: Social and Political Conflict, 1888–1896* (Chicago: University of Chicago Press, 1971); Paul Kleppner, *The Cross of Culture: A Social Analysis of Midwestern Politics, 1850–1900* (New York: Free Press, 1970); Samuel T. McSeveney, *The Politics of Depression: Political Behavior in the Northeast,*

1893–1896 (New York: Oxford University Press, 1972); Richard L. McCormick, *From Realignment to Reform: Political Change in New York State, 1893–1910* (Ithaca, N.Y.: Cornell University Press, 1981); J. Morgan Kousser, *The Shaping of Southern Politics: Suffrage Restriction and the Establishment of the One-Party South, 1880–1920* (New Haven, Conn.: Yale University Press, 1974); John F. Reynolds, *Testing Democracy: Electoral Behavior and Progressive Reform in New Jersey, 1880–1920* (Chapel Hill: University of North Carolina Press, 1988); Stephen Skowronek, *Building a New American State: The Expansion of National Administrative Capacities, 1877–1920* (New York: Cambridge University Press, 1982); and Paula Baker, *The Moral Frameworks of Public Life: Gender, Politics, and the State in Rural New York, 1870–1930* (New York: Oxford University Press, 1991).

An understanding of the twentieth-century political nation can be gleaned, first, from the research of Walter Dean Burnham as summed up in *The Current Crisis in American Politics* (New York: Oxford University Press, 1982). See also Paul Kleppner, *Who Voted: The Dynamics of Electoral Turnout, 1870–1980* (New York: Praeger, 1982); Michael E. McGerr, *The Decline of Popular Politics: The American North, 1865–1928* (New York: Oxford Univ. Press, 1986); David W. Brady et al., "The Decline of Party in the U.S. House of Representatives, 1887–1968," *Legislative Studies Quarterly,* 4 (Aug. 1979): 381–408; Martin Wattenberg, *The Decline of American Political Parties, 1952–1988* (Cambridge, Mass.: Harvard Univ. Press, 1990); Anthony King, ed., *The New American Political System* (Washington, D.C.: American Enterprise Institute, 1978); and Theodore J. Lowi, *The End of Liberalism: Ideology, Policy and the Crisis of Public Authority* (New York: Norton, 1968). A useful statement of where the research on voting behavior now stands in reference to realignment theory is Everett C. Ladd, "The 1988 Elections: Continuation of the Post New Deal System," *Political Science Quarterly,* 104 (Spring 1989): 1–18.

Finally, let me mention three works on the methods and problems involved in the study of political history that significantly contributed to the way I approached this book: Lee Benson, *Toward the Scientific Study of History: Selected Essays* (Philadelphia: Lippincott, 1972); Allan G. Bogue, *Clio and the Bitch Goddess: Quantification in American Political History* (Beverly Hills, Calif.: Sage, 1983); and Samuel P. Hays, *American Political History as Social Analysis: Essays* (Knoxville: University of Tennessee Press, 1980). More recently, J. Morgan Kousser, "Toward 'Total Political History': A Rational Choice Research Program," *Journal of Interdisciplinary History,* 20 (Spring 1990): 521–60, has called on political historians to modify some of their ways and interpretive frameworks in order to bring greater reality and coherence to their arguments.

In addition to the scholarly literature, of course, one can fill up many pages listing the wide array of original source material: the personal manuscripts of politicians, as well as their memoirs; public documents such as the printed records of legislative debates and other government activities; compilations of political and social statistics; and the extensive range of partisan pamphlets, party proceedings, and newspapers that is available to scholars of the American political nation after 1838. The notes to the book indicate how greatly I have relied on these sources not just to develop and texture my argument, but to try to reconstruct the worldviews of the participants, trace their actual political behavior, and describe their reactions to the political processes of which they were a part. Many of these documents are available in microfilm format: the papers of William Henry Seward and the *New York Times* are ready examples. Others have been reproduced in book form, for instance, Herbert Weaver et al., eds., *Correspondence of James K. Polk*, 8 vols. to date (Nashville: Vanderbilt University Press, 1969–); and Frank Freidel, ed., *Union Pamphlets of the Civil War* (Cambridge, Mass.: Harvard University Press, 1967). Other material of this sort is well preserved in the Library of Congress, the New York Public Library, university libraries, and similar archives. Among public documents, the *Congressional Globe* (later the *Congressional Record*), and similar state-level legislative materials, stand out.

Index

Index

In this index an "f" after a number indicates a separate reference on the next page, and an "ff" indicates separate references on the next two pages. A continuous discussion over two or more pages is indicated by a span of page numbers, e.g., "pp. 57–58." *Passim* is used for a cluster of references in close but not continuous sequence.